A Directory of American Fiction Writers

1976 Edition

Names and addresses of more than 800 contemporary fiction writers
whose work has been published in the United States

This Directory has been made possible with support from
the Literature Program of the National Endowment for the Arts.

Published by Poets & Writers, Inc.,
201 West 54 Street, New York, New York 10019, (212) PLaza 7-1766

Distributed by the Publishing Center for Cultural Resources,
27 West 53 Street, New York, New York 10019

Published by Poets & Writers, Inc., a publicly supported, nonprofit,
tax-exempt corporation organized for educational and literary purposes.
Donations to it are charitable contributions under section 170 of the
Internal Revenue Code. Please write or call us for further information.
No permission is needed to reprint from *A Directory of American
Fiction Writers,* but acknowledgment to Poets & Writers, Inc.
will be appreciated.

Copyright © 1976 by Poets & Writers, Inc.

Supported by:
    National Endowment for the Arts
    Leonard Randolph
    Literature Program Director
    Washington, D.C. 20506
    (202) 634-6044

Designed and Produced by:
    Martin Stephen Moskof & Associates, Inc.
    159 West 53 Street
    New York, New York 10019

Distributed by:
    Publishing Center for Cultural Resources, Inc.
    27 West 53 Street
    New York, New York 10019

Staff for Poets & Writers, Inc.:
    Administration
        Galen Williams, *Executive Director*
        Caroline Rand Herron, *Executive Consultant*
        Gil Adler, *Comptroller*
        Helen Georgeou, *Administrative Assistant*
    Coda/Directories
        Cheri Fein, *Publications Director*
        Bobbie Lazar, *Researcher*
        Debby Mayer, *Researcher and Chief Copywriter*
        Nelson Richardson, *Researcher and Copywriter*
        Lisa Merrill, *Business Manager and Copywriter*
        Erin Clermont, *Copywriter*
        Carol Deacon, *Associate and Copywriter*
        Sharon Thomson, *Assistant*
    New York State Readings/Workshops:
        Erin Clermont, *Coordinator*
        Howard Levy, *Assistant*
        Ruth Roth, *Assistant*

Library of Congress Cataloging in Publication Data

Poets & Writers, Inc.
  A Directory of American Fiction Writers

  Includes index.
  1. Authors, American—20th century—Directories.
  2. American fiction—20th century—Bio-bibliography.
  3. Authorship—Handbooks, manuals, etc.   I. Title.
PS129.P6   1976   813'.5'09   75-25710

ISBN 0-913734-04-7
ISBN 0-913734-05-5 pbk.

Price: $10.00 Hardbound/$5.00 Softbound.

Table of Contents

I.   How to Use *A Directory of American Fiction Writers* v

II.   How to Apply for Listing in the Directories vi

III.   Publications Available from Poets & Writers, Inc. vi

IV.   Directory of Fiction Writers (listed alphabetically within each state) 2

V.   Organizations that Sponsor Programs Involving Fiction Writers and Poets 48

VI.   The Service Section 76

       Literary Organizations of Service to Writers 76

       Reference Works: Authors, Publishers, Grants, Other 79

       Fiction Anthologies 82

       Fiction Criticism 86

       Poetry Anthologies 90

       Poetry Criticism 96

       Resources for Creative Writing Teachers 99

       Films 102

       Videotapes 113

       Recordings and Tapes 117

       Book Stores 120

       Acknowledgments 121

VII.   Checklist: How to Organize a Reading or Workshop 122

VIII. Alphabetical Index of Fiction Writers 123

How to Use A Directory of American Fiction Writers

This first edition of *A Directory of American Fiction Writers* contains information about more than 800 living fiction writers whose work has been published in the United States. It includes information on poets only if they also publish fiction. Playwrights, non-fiction writers, journalists, and authors of juvenile fiction are not included in this Directory.

The primary purpose of the Directory is to help groups and individuals locate contemporary writers. It aims to be as complete and accurate as possible, but some information (current as of October 15, 1975) will inevitably be out of date by the time of publication. *The Supplement,* sent free twice a year to all Directory purchasers, updates and augments Directory data. Please send any corrections, changes, or additions to Poets & Writers for publication in *The Supplement.*

For each writer, *A Directory of American Fiction Writers* tries to provide:

Current address. Alternate addresses are included for transient authors.

Telephone number(s)—excepting authors who have not authorized publication of this information.

Work preferences. Interest in teaching and reading is coded by grade levels as follows:

> EL = Elementary school
> JHS = Junior high school
> HS = High school
> COL = College
> Readings
> ALL = interested in all of above
> PITS = Poets-in-the-Schools
> NPS = No preference stated

An asterisk (*) after any of these codes signifies previous teaching experience at that level. Foreign language skills are indicated, as are preferences for working with such special-interest groups as drug addicts, prisoners, migrant workers, ethnic groups, and feminist organizations.

Most recent book—or two periodicals in which the author has published fiction. For fiction writers who also write poetry, the most recent book of poetry or two magazine publications are listed. The aim is to enable prospective sponsors to familiarize themselves with the author's work. Addresses of regional book publishers or periodicals are available from Poets & Writers.

The Directory is organized geographically (by state) so that prospective sponsors can readily locate writers living in their area. Within each state, authors are listed alphabetically. A separate alphabetical index of all fiction writers in the Directory is included.

Fiction writers and poets who are interested in teaching and reading assignments should consult the section called *Organizations that Sponsor Programs Involving Fiction Writers and Poets.* Addresses of the 50 state arts councils are also included there. Where possible, the organization's annual budget for fees and the number of writers hired each year is shown.

The Service Section lists books, films, reference sources, and services of use to both authors and sponsors.

Listing in the Directory does not constitute recommendation by either Poets & Writers, Inc. or the Literature Program of the National Endowment for the Arts, whose support has made this publication possible.

How to Apply for Listing in A Directory of American Fiction Writers or A Directory of American Poets

Any fiction writer or poet who would like to be considered for listing in the Directories should mail the postcard on the order form enclosed in this book to Poets & Writers, Inc. Additional information from each writer will then be requested. Separate application must be made for fiction and poetry.

Although publication credits and/or other professional exposure count heavily, panels of writers meet regularly to review applications and re-evaluate policy. The panels change annually, and names of past and current panelists are available on request.

Information on writers who are accepted for the Directories is first listed in an issue of *The Supplement* pending publication of the next edition of the Directory. Once listed, names will be retained in successive editions unless mail is repeatedly returned as undeliverable and research efforts fail.

Neither Poets & Writers, Inc. nor the Literature Program of the National Endowment for the Arts intend this Directory to be definitive. It is constantly updated and expanded.

Publications Available from Poets & Writers, Inc.

Coda: Poets & Writers Newsletter
News of and for the writing community today.
Size 8½"x11" 28-36 pages $5 a year; $1.25 single issues

"one of the few newsletters that contains news"..."a first class addition to my professional library"..."a definite link to a world I thought I'd have to pass by"... "a good thing to keep us writers from starving"
—from Coda readers

A Directory of American Poets
The revised version of a unique reference work.
Listing 1500 contemporary poets who publish in the
    United States.
Size 8½"x11" 132 pages $6 paperback; $12 hardbound

A Directory of American Fiction Writers
A new and important reference work.
Listing 800 contemporary fiction writers who publish in
    the United States.
Size 8½"x11" 136 pages $5 paperback; $10 hardbound

Both Directories include address(es), telephone number(s), teaching preference and experience, linguistic skills, latest book and publisher.

An important reference section lists anthologies, films, literary organizations, and many other resources.

Supplemental updates are sent free to purchasers of either Directory.

Checks or money orders should be made payable to "Publishing Center" and mailed to Poets & Writers, Inc., 201 W. 54 St., New York, N.Y. 10019. Sales tax is not applicable; postage and handling are included. For your convenience, use the order form enclosed in this book. For further information, call (212) PLaza 7-1766.

A Directory of American Fiction Writers

Directory of Fiction Writers

The Directory is organized geographically, with authors listed alphabetically within the state of primary residence. The New York State listing separates New York City authors from those who live elsewhere in the state. Authors who live outside the United States are listed at the end of this section alphabetically by country.

ALASKA

Leslie Marmon Silko
Box 652, Ketchikan, Alaska 99901
(907) 225-6440
ALL*; has worked for N.Mex. PITS; is American Indian
Poetry: *Laguna Woman* (Greenfield Press, 1973)
Fiction published in *The Man To Send Rain Clouds, Yardbird Reader*

ARIZONA

LaVerne Harrell Clark
4690 N. Campbell Ave., Tucson, Ariz. 85718
alternate address: c/o Mrs. Boyce Harrell, 604 Main St., Smithville, Tex. 78957, (512) 237-2796
ALL*; has worked in Ariz. and N.Mex. PITS; interested in giving slide lectures to Southwestern Indian groups; speaks Spanish
Fiction: *They Sang for Horses* (U. of Arizona Press, 1971)

Robert C.S. Downs
2838 E. Elm St., Tucson, Ariz. 85716
(602) 881-9299
HS*, COL*, readings; speaks French
Novel: *Peoples* (Bobbs-Merrill, 1974)

William Eastlake
1573 Placita Santa Rita, Rio Rico, Ariz. 85621
(602) 281-8339
NPS; has worked for Ariz. PITS; speaks Spanish
Novel: *Dancers in the Scalp House* (Viking, 1975)

Alan Harrington
2831 N. Orlando, Tucson, Ariz. 85712
(602) 326-4559
Unavailable for readings
Novel: *The Secret Swinger* (Alfred A. Knopf, 1966)

Robert W. Houston
226 Old Ina Rd., Tucson, Ariz. 85704
(602) 297-6456
alternate address: Dept. of English, U. of Arizona, Tucson, Ariz. 85721, (602) 884-1836
COL*, readings; is interested in working with Latin American and Spanish groups; speaks Spanish, some Russian, French & Turkish
Novel: *A Drive with Ossie* (St. Martin's Press, 1970)

Anna Lee Walters
Navajo Community College, Tsaile, Ariz. 86503
alternate address: c/o Luther McGlaslin, 101 E. Ohio, Enid, Okla. 73701, (405) 237-5340
JHS*, HS*, COL; is interested in working with American Indians & young people; is American Indian
Poetry: *Voices from the Rainbow* (Viking, 1975)
Fiction published in *Man to Send Rain Clouds*

ARKANSAS

Besmilr Brigham
Rt. 1, Horatio, Arkansas 71842
readings; has worked for Ariz., Tex. PITS; speaks some Spanish, some French
Poetry: *Heaved From The Earth* (Alfred Knopf, 1971)
Fiction published in *The Southern Review, Confrontation*

William Harrison
c/o U. of Arkansas, Fayetteville, Ark. 72701
NPS
Stories: *Roller Ball Murder* (Wm. Morrow, 1974)

James Whitehead
517 E. Lafayette, Fayetteville, Ark. 72707
(501) 575-4301
ALL*
Poetry: *Domains* (Louisiana State U. Press, 1966)
Fiction: *Joiner* (Alfred A. Knopf, 1971)

CALIFORNIA

Keith Abbott
1146 Sutter, Berkeley, Calif. 94707
(415) 527-4192
ALL*; has worked for Calif. PITS
Poetry: *Erase Words* (Cranium Press, 1975)
Fiction: *GUSH, A Novel Starring The Gush Family About The Unemployment Problem in California* (Blue Wind Press, 1975)

Alta
Box 424, San Lorenzo, Calif. 94580
HS*, COL*, readings; is interested in working in mental institutions
Poetry: *I Am Not A Practicing Angel* (Crossing Press, 1975)
Novel: *Pauline & The Mysterious Pervert* (Gotham Books, 1975)

David Antin
201 Pacific Ave., Solana Beach, Calif. 92075
(714) 755-4619
COL*, readings; speaks French, German, Spanish
Poetry: *Talking* (Kulchur Foundation, 1972)
Conceptual Novel: *After the War* (Black Sparrow Press, 1973)

Ron Arias
1629 Jantzen Dr., Colton, Calif. 92324
(714) 925-2999
COL*; is interested in working in prisons, drug rehabilitation centers; speaks Spanish; is Chicano
Fiction: *The Road To Tamazunchale* (West Coast Poetry Review, 1975)

Raymond Barrio
c/o Ventura Press, Box 2268, Sunnyvale, Calif. 94087
COL*; speaks Spanish; is Latino
Novel: *The Plum Plum Pickers* (Ventura Press, 1970)

Peter S. Beagle
311 East Rianda Road, Watsonville, Calif. 95076
(408) 688-2318
readings; speaks French, some Spanish
Novel: *The Last Unicorn* (Viking, 1968; paperback Ballantine Books, 1969)

Robert Bloch
2111 Sunset Crest Dr., Los Angeles, Calif. 90046
(213) 477-1262
alternate address: c/o Molson-Stanton Assoc., Inc., 10889, Wilshire Blvd., Los Angeles, Calif. 90024, (213) 477-1262
COL*
Novel: *American Gothic* (Simon & Schuster, 1974)

Ray Bradbury
10265 Cheviot Dr., Los Angeles, Calif. 90064
alternate address: c/o Harold Matson Co., 22 E. 40th St., New York, N.Y. 10016, (212) 679-4490
NPS
Novel: *The Halloween Tree* (Alfred A. Knopf, 1972; Bantam, 1974)

Richard Brautigan
2546 Geary St., San Francisco, Calif. 94115
NPS
Poetry: *Rommel Drives on Deep into Egypt* (Seymour Lawrence-Delacorte Press, 1971)
Fiction: *The Hawkline Monster: A Gothic Western* (Simon & Schuster, 1974)

Ernest Brawley
841 Union St., San Francisco, Calif. 94133
alternate address: c/o John Hawkins, Literary Agent, 12 E. 41 St., New York, N.Y. 10017, (212) 689-8711
NPS; speaks Spanish, Italian, French
Novel: *The Rap* (Atheneum, 1974; paperback, Dell, 1975)

Hedi Bried (H.W. Blattner)
6 Locksley Ave., Apt. 10M, San Francisco, Calif. 94122
alternate address: c/o John Schaffner, Literary Agent, 425 E. 51 St., New York, N.Y. 10022, (212) MU8-4763
NPS; speaks Spanish, German & French
Fiction published in *50 Best American Short Stories, 12 From The Sixties*

David Bromige
880 1st St., Sebastopol, Calif. 95472
HS*, COL*, readings; speaks Swedish
Poetry: *Tight Corners* (Black Sparrow Press, 1974)
Short Stories: *Out of My Hands* Black Sparrow Press, 1974)

Cecil Brown
Dept. of English, U. of California at Berkeley, Berkeley, Calif. 94720
alternate address: c/o Farrar, Straus & Giroux, 19 Union Sq. W., New York, N.Y. 10003
COL; is Black
Novel: *The Life and Loves of Mr. Jiveass Nigger* (Farrar, Straus & Giroux, 1970; Fawcett World, 1971)

Charles Bukowski
5437 2/5 Carlton Way, Los Angeles, Calif. 90027
(213) 462-0614
NPS
Poetry: *Burning In Water, Drowning In Flame* (Black Sparrow Press, 1974)
Novel: *Factotum* (Black Sparrow Press, 1975)

Jerry Bumpus
4730 College Ave., San Diego, Calif. 92115
(714) 583-7518
readings
Fiction: *Things In Place* (Fiction Collective, 1975)

Raymond Carver
22272 Cupertino Rd., Cupertino, Calif. 95014
(408) 255-4796
COL*, readings
Poetry: *Foreign And Domestic* (Capra Press, 1976)
Short Stories: *Will You Please Be Quiet, Please?* (McGraw-Hill, 1976)

Jeffery Paul Chan
c/o Asian American Studies Dept., San Francisco State U., 1600 Holloway Ave., San Francisco, Calif. 94132
(415) 469-1285
EL*, COL*; has worked for Calif. PITS; is Chinese-American
Fiction published in *Yardbird Reader, Aiiieeeee!*

Frank Chin
373A 4 Ave., San Francisco, Calif. 94118
(415) 668-9653
alternate address: c/o Dorothea Oppenheimer, 866 U.N. Plaza, New York, N.Y. 10017
readings; is Asian-American
Poetry published in *The Young American Writers, Aiiieeeee!*
Fiction published in *Yardbird, Cutting Edges*

Buriel Clay II
P.O. Box 1165, San Francisco, Calif. 94101
(415) 558-2335
EL*, HS*, COL*, readings; has worked for Calif PITS; is Black
Poetry: *Broken Pieces of Clay* (San Francisco Black Writers Workshop, 1974)
Fiction published in *Transfer, Yardbird Reader*

Andrei Codrescu
Box 341, Monte Rio, Calif. 95462
(707) 865-2698
ALL*, readings; has worked for Calif., Nev. PITS; speaks French, Italian, Romanian, Hungarian, Russian
Poetry: *The History Of The Growth Of Heaven* (G. Braziller, 1973)
Fiction: *The Life And Times Of An Involuntary Genius* (G. Braziller, 1975)

Alfred Coppel
270 Tennyson, Palo Alto, Calif. 94301
(415) 326-3003
NPS; speaks Spanish
Novel: *Thirty Four East* (Harcourt Brace Jovanovich, 1974)

Robert Creeley
Box 344, Bolinas Calif. 94924
(415) 868-0147
    alternate address: (Sept.-Dec.) 400 Fargo, Buffalo,
N.Y. 14213, (716) 886-0475
Readings & workshops
Poetry: *A Day Book* (Scribner's, 1973)
Improvisations: *Presences* (Scribner's, 1975)

Art Cuelho, Jr.
20720 S. Fruit Ave., Riverdale, Calif. 93656
    COL, readings; is interested in working in prisons
and with people from rural backgrounds
Poetry published in *North American Poets,
Dacotah Territory*
Fiction published in *Center, Blue Cloud
Quarterly*

Vibiana Chamberlin de Aparicio
1769 Las Lunas St., Pasadena, Calif. 91106
(213) 793-8379
    ALL (COL*); speaks Spanish & German; is Chicana
Poetry published in *An Anthology of Chicano
Literature, Tia Cleta*
Fiction published in *Regeneracion, La Raza*

John Deck
1127 N. Branciforte Ave., Santa Cruz, Calif. 95062
(408) 425-8225
    COL*; speaks Spanish
Short Stories: *Greased Samba and Other Stories*
(Harcourt Brace Jovanovich, 1970)

Philip K. Dick
1405 Cameo La., #4, Fullerton, Calif. 92631
(714) 524-7306
    HS, COL; interested in working in drug
rehabilitation centers; speaks German
Novel: *Flow My Tears, The Policeman Said*
(Doubleday, 1974)

Millicent G. Dillon
4062 Ben Lomond Dr., Palo Alto, Calif. 94306
(415) 493-9392
    COL*, readings
Novel: *The One In The Back Is Medea* (Viking,
1973)

Diane di Prima
P.O. Box 629, Point Reyes, Calif. 94956
(415) 663-8206
    alternate address: c/o Jeanne di Prima, 364 Page St.,
San Francisco, Calif. 94102, (415) 863-6799
ALL*; has worked for Wyo., Mont., Calif., N.Mex.,
Ariz. & Minn. PITS
Poetry: *Loba, Part I* (Capra Press, 1973)
Fiction: *Memoirs of a Beatnik* (Olympia, 1969)

Richard Dokey
4471 W. Kingdon Rd., Lodi, Calif. 95240
(209) 463-8314
    NPS; speaks some Spanish
Fiction published in *The Southwest Review Reader,
Four Elements*

Sam A. Eisenstein
3116 Lake Hollywood Dr., Los Angeles, Calif. 90068
(213) 851-3116
    ALL*; speaks Spanish, French & German
Poetry published in *New York Quarterly, Bachy*
Fiction published in *May My Words Feed Others*

Gary Elder
22 Ardith La., Alamo, Calif. 94507
(415) 837-3831
    HS, COL, readings
Fiction published in *North American Review,
The Far Side of the Storm*

Harlan Ellison
3484 Coy Dr., Sherman Oaks, Calif. 91423
(213) CR1-9636
    Readings only; is interested in working in prisons
Short Stories: *Deathbird Stories* (Harper & Row,
1975)

John Espey
Dept. of English, U. of California at Los Angeles,
405 Hilgard Ave., Los Angeles, Calif. 90024
(213) 825-3319
    NPS; speaks some French
Fiction: *An Observer* (Harcourt Brace Jovanovich,
1965)

Rudy Espinosa
250 Drake St., San Francisco, Calif. 94112
(415) 585-0395
    alternate address: Chicano Studies, Ohlone College,
Freemont, Calif. 94107, (415) 657-2100
COL*, readings; speaks Spanish; is Chicano
Fiction: *El EspejoThe Mirror* (Quinto Sol, 1974)

John L. Figueroa
7910 E. Alpaca St., South San Gabriel, Calif. 91777
(213) 288-3134
    JHS; is interested in working with youth at all levels;
speaks Spanish; is Puerto Rican
Short Stories: *Antonio's World* (Hill & Wang,
1971)

M.F.K. Fisher
Bouverie Ranch, Glen Ellen, Calif. 95442
    NPS; speaks French, Spanish & German
Novel: *Among Friends* (Alfred A. Knopf, 1972)

Daniel Fuchs
430 S. Fuller Ave, #9C, Los Angeles, Calif. 90036
    alternate address: c/o Irving Paul Lazar, 211 S.
Beverly Dr., Beverly Hills, Calif. 90212, (213)
275-6153
NPS
Novel: *West of the Rockies* (Alfred A. Knopf,
1971)

Len Fulton
P.O. Box 1056, Paradise, Calif. 95969
(916) 877-6110
    COL, readings; is interested in working in prisons
Novel: *Dark Other Adam Dreaming* (Dustbooks,
1975)

Ernest J. Gaines
998 Divisadero St., San Francisco, Calif. 94115
    NPS
Novel: *The Autobiography of Miss Jane Pittman*
(Dial, 1971)

Barry Gifford
1213 Peralta Ave., Berkeley, Calif. 94706
(415) 524-8336 or (415) 525-3137
    ALL*; speaks some Spanish & French
    Poetry: *Persimmons: Poems for Paintings* (Shaman Drum Press, 1975)
    Fiction: *A Boy's Novel* (Christopher's Books, 1973)

Sandra M. Gilbert
53 Menlo Pl., Berkeley, Calif. 94707
(415) 527-1260
    alternate address: c/o Cyrilly Abels, Literary Agent, 119 W. 57 St., New York, N.Y. 10019, (212) 247-6438
    HS, COL*, readings; is interested in working with women's groups
    Poetry published in *Poetry, The Nation*
    Fiction published in *Epoch, Tales*

Frank D. Gilroy
c/o H.N. Swanson, Inc., 8523 Sunset Blvd., West Hollywood, Calif. 90069
(213) 652-5385
    NPS
    Novel: *From Noon till Three* (Doubleday, 1973)

Herbert Gold
1051A Broadway, San Francisco, Calif. 94133
(415) 673-1761
    COL*; speaks French & Russian
    Fiction: *Swiftie the Magician* (McGraw-Hill, 1975)

N.V.M. Gonzalez
1337 C St., Hayward, Calif. 94541
    ALL (COL*), readings; is Filipino
    Fiction: *Bamboo Dancers* (Swallow Press, 1973)

Rafael Jesus Gonzalez
Dept. of English, Laney College, 900 Fallon St., Oakland, Calif. 94607
(415) 834-5740
    alternate address: c/o Mr. & Mrs. J.F. Gonzalez, 1114 E. Nevada Ave., El Paso, Tex. 79902, (915) 532-8855
    COL*; speaks Spanish; is Chicano
    Poetry published in *West Coast Review, Mark in Time*
    Fiction published in *El Burro Magazine, Voices of Aztlan*

Robert Gover
226 Ortega Ridge Rd., Santa Barbara, Calif. 93108
(805) 969-0980
    HS, COL*
    Novel: *Tomorrow Now Occurs Again* (Ross-Erikson, 1975)

Susan Griffin
1939 Cedar St., Berkeley, Calif. 94709
(415) 843-5595
    HS*, COL*, readings; has worked for Calif. PITS; is interested in working in prisons, with women, in continuing education
    Poetry: *Letter* (Twowindows Press/Effie's Books, 1974)
    Fiction: *The Sink* (Shameless Hussy Press, 1974)

Albert J. Guerard
635 Gerona Rd., Stanford, Calif. 94305
    alternate address: Dept. of English, Stanford U., Stanford, Calif. 94305, (415) 421-2300
    Readings only; speaks French
    Novel: *The Exiles* (Macmillan, 1963); published in *TriQuarterly, Fiction*

Janet Campbell Hale
5213 Fresno Ave., Richmond, Calif. 94804
    Readings only; is interested in working in prisons; is American Indian
    Novel: *The Owl's Song* (Doubleday, 1974)

James B. Hall
Cardiff House, 1100 High St., Santa Cruz, Calif. 95060
(408) 426-4918
    COL, readings
    Poetry: *The Hunt Within* (Louisiana State U. Press, 1973)
    Novel: *Mayo Sergeant* (New American Library, 1968)

Mark Harris
25571 Via Brava, Valencia, Calif. 91355
    NPS
    Novel: *Killing Everybody* (Dial Press, 1973)

George Hitchcock
325 Ocean View, Santa Cruz, Calif. 95062
(408) 426-0741
    Readings only; has worked for Calif. PITS
    Poetry: *Ship of Bells* (Kayak Press, 1971)
    Stories: *Notes of the Siege Year* (Kayak Press, 1974)

Cecelia Holland
2065 N. Marengo Ave., Pasadena, Calif. 91103
    alternate address: c/o Roberta Pryor, International Creative Management, 40 W. 57 St., New York, N.Y. 10019, (212) 556-5730
    NPS
    Novel: *Great Maria* (Alfred A. Knopf, 1974)

James D. Houston
2-1130 E. Cliff Dr., Santa Cruz, Calif. 95062
(408) 475-2359
    COL*, readings; speaks Spanish & French
    Novel: *A Native Son of the Golden West* (Dial, 1971; Ballantine, 1972)

Christopher Isherwood
145 Adelaide Dr., Santa Monica, Calif. 90402
    alternate address: c/o Candida Donadio, 111 W. 57 St., New York, N.Y. 10019, (212) 757-5076
    Fiction: *Kathleen & Frank* (Simon & Schuster, 1972; Curtis, 1973)

Diane Johnson
46 El Camino Real, Berkeley, Calif. 94705
(415) 841-7925
    COL*, readings
    Novel: *The Shadow Knows* (Alfred A. Knopf, 1974)

Hiroshi Kashiwagi
4314 Pacheco, San Francisco, Calif. 94116
(415) 664-7230
    alternate address: c/o San Francisco Public Library,
    Civic Center, San Francisco, Calif. 94102, (415)
    558-3193, Ext. 3321
    COL*; speaks Japanese; is Asian-American
    Poetry published in *The Affectionate Bear, Synergy*
    Fiction published in *Scop, Crossroads*

George Keithley
1302 Sunset Ave., Chico, Calif. 95926
(916) 343-9161
    COL*, readings; has worked for Tenn., Pa., and Calif.
    PITS
    Poetry: *Song in a Strange Land* (George Braziller,
    1974)
    Fiction published in *North American Review, December*

Calvin Kentfield
Box 224, Stinson Beach, Calif. 94970
    alternate address: c/o Elizabeth McKee, Harold
    Matson Co., 22 E. 40 St., New York, N.Y. 10016,
    (212) 679-4490
    COL*, readings; speaks some French & Spanish
    Fiction: *The Great Green: Memoirs of a Merchant
    Mariner* (Dial, 1974)

Jascha Kessler
218 Sixteenth St., Santa Monica, Calif. 90402
(213) 393-7968
    COL*, readings; speaks Italian, French & German
    Poetry: *After the Armies Have Passed* (New York
    U. Press, 1970)
    Short Stories: *An Egyptian Bondage & Other Stories*
    (Harper & Row, 1967)

Alex Kirack
5361 Central Ave., Bonita, Calif. 92002
    alternate address: c/o Patricia McPherson, 3024
    E St., San Diego, Calif. 92102, (714) 234-2524
    HS, COL*, readings; speaks Spanish; is Chicano
    Poetry: *Space Flutes and Barrio Paths*
    (Fanshen Printing Collective, 1972)
    Fiction: *Street Running Dues* (New
    Foundations, 1972)

Teri Kovak (Shapiro)
1119 Bucknell Dr., Davis, Calif. 95616
(916) 756-2378
    COL*; is interested in working with women's groups
    Fiction published in *Good Housekeeping, Redbook*

Jeremy Larner
916 Kearny, San Francisco, Calif. 94133
(415) 788-6240
    COL*, readings; is interested in working in
    prisons and graduate schools
    Fiction: *Drive, He Said* (Bantam Books, 1971)

Cornel Adam Lengyel
Adam's Acre West, Georgetown, Calif. 95634
(916) 333-4224
    HS, COL*, readings; speaks Hungarian & French
    Poetry: *Four Dozen Songs* (Dragon's Teeth Press,
    1973)
    Fiction published in *A Treasury of Jewish Sea
    Stories, Jewish Currents*

Russell Leong (Wallace Lin)
1020 Stockton, Apt. 405, San Francisco, Calif. 94108
(415) 982-6463
    HS, COL; speaks Chinese (Mandarin & Cantonese
    dialects); is Asian-American
    Poetry published in *Asian-American Authors*
    Fiction published in *AIIIEEEEE!*

John L'Heureux
Dept. of English, Stanford U., Stanford, Calif. 94305
(415) 493-6221 (home) or (415) 497-2637 (office)
    Readings only
    Poetry: *No Place for Hiding* (Doubleday, 1972)
    Stories: *Family Affairs* (Doubleday, 1974)

Leo Litwak
1933 Greenwich, San Francisco, Calif. 94123
(415) 929-8344
    NPS; is interested in working in prisons
    Novel: *Waiting for the News* (Doubleday, 1969)

Susan Lukas
881 Clayton St., San Francisco, Calif. 94117
(415) 665-0870
    COL
    Novel: *Stereopticon* (Stein & Day, 1975)

James G. McClure
115 Russell Ave., Portola Valley, Calif. 94025
(415) 851-7738
    alternate address: c/o Georges Borchardt, 145 E. 52
    St., New York, N.Y. 10022, (212) PL3-5785
    COL
    Novel: *The Hanging of the Angels* (Random House,
    1969)

Michael McClure
264 Downey St., San Francisco, Calif. 94117
    COL*
    Poetry: *September Blackberries* (New Directions,
    1974)
    Novel: *The Adept* (Delacorte Press, 1971)

Oscar Mandel
California Institute of Technology, Pasadena,
Calif. 91109
(213) 795-6811, Ext. 1078
    COL*; speaks French, Spanish, Italian, German & D
    Fables: *The Gobble-Up Stories* (Branden, 1965)

David Meltzer
P.O. Box 9005, Berkeley, Calif. 94709
    HS*, COL*; has worked for Calif. PITS
    Poetry: *Tens: Selected Poems; 1961-1971*
    (McGraw-Hill, 1974)
    Novel: *Star* (Brandon House, 1972)

Leonard Michaels
607 San Miguel Ave., Berkeley, Calif. 94707
    NPS
    Fiction: *I Would Have Saved Them If I Could*
    (Farrar, Straus & Giroux, 1975)

Jack Micheline
229 Ashbury St., San Francisco, Calif. 94117
(415) 668-1094
    EL*, readings
    Poetry: *Kuboya* (Midnight Special Edition, 1973)
    Fiction: *In the Bronx and Other Stories* (Sam
    Hooker Press, 1965)

N. Scott Momaday
Dept. of English, Stanford University, Stanford,
Calif. 94305
(415) 497-2635
  HS, COL
  Fiction: *Names* (Harper & Row, 1973)

Brian Moore
33958 Pacific Coast Hwy., Malibu, Calif. 90265
(213) 457-7940
  COL*
  Novel: *Catholics* (Holt, Rinehart & Winston, 1973)

Toshio Mori
1470 164th Ave., San Leandro, Calif. 94578
(415) 276-4465
  Readings only; is interested in Asian-American studies;
  speaks Japanese; is Asian-American
  Fiction published in *Asian American Heritage,*
  AIIIEEEEE!

William Murray
17 Vicente Terr., Santa Monica, Calif. 90401
  alternate address: c/o Mrs. Natalia D. Murray, 785
  Park Ave., New York, N.Y. 10024, (212) RH4-4009
  ALL, readings; is interested in working in prisons
  and drug rehabilitation centers; speaks French &
  Italian
  Novel: *The Killing Touch* (E.P. Dutton, 1974)

Anais Nin
P.O. Box 26598, Los Angeles, Calif. 90026
  Readings only; speaks Spanish & French
  Collection of 5 Novels: *Cities of the*
  Interior (Swallow, 1975)

Larry Niven
146 N. Gunston Dr., Los Angeles, Calif. 90049
  alternate address: c/o Carl Vogel, 136 El Camino Dr.,
  Beverly Hills, Calif. 90212, (213) CR6-3154
  COL (individual lectures)
  Novel: *The Mote In God's Eye* with Jerry Pournelle
  (Simon & Schuster, 1974)

Marc Norman
28 Latimer Rd., Santa Monica, Calif. 90402
  COL
  Novel: *Oklahoma Crude* (E.P. Dutton, 1973)

Tillie Olsen
1435 Laguna St., #6, San Francisco, Calif. 94115
(415) 346-1137
  readings
  Novel: *Yonnondio (Delacorte, 1974)*

Philip D. Ortego
English Dept., San Jose State University, San Jose,
Calif. 95912
(408) 277-2242
  ALL (HS*, COL*); speaks Spanish & French; is
  Chicano
  Poetry: *Zodiac Square* (Marfel Publications,1974)
  Fiction published in *The New England Review,*
  Arx Magazine

Charlotte Painter
372 63rd St., Oakland, Calif. 94618
  COL*
  Fiction: *Confession From The Malaga Madhouse*
  (Dial, 1971)

Oscar Florentino Penaranda
1336b Guerrero St., San Francisco, Calif. 94110
(415) 824-7622
  alternate address: c/o Francisca Rivero, 119 Crenshaw
  Pacifica, Calif. 94044
  ALL; is interested in working with athletes, especially
  children; has worked in Calif. PITS; speaks Tagalog
  and Visaya; is Filipino
  Poetry published in *American Poetry Review,*
  Variations in Person
  Fiction published in *AIIIEEEEE!, Liwanag*

Victor Perera
P.O. Box 63, Capitola, Calif. 95010
  alternate address: c/o Peter Beagle, 311 E. Rianda,
  Watsonville, Calif. 95076, (408) 688-2318
  COL*; is interested in giving readings in prisons
  & drug rehabilitation centers; speaks Spanish,
  French & Hebrew
  Novel: *The Conversion* (Little, Brown, 1970)

Jerry Pournelle
12051 Laurel Terr., Studio City, Calif. 91604
  HS, COL
  Fiction: *The Mote In God's Eye* with Larry Niven
  (Simon & Schuster, 1974)

John Rechy
4600 Los Feliz, Los Angeles, Calif. 90027
(213) 661-6130
  alternate address: 4101-B La Luz, El Paso, Tex. 79903
  (915) 566-9282
  COL*; speaks Spanish
  Novel: *The Fourth Angel* (Viking, 1973)

Michael Rogers
3003 California St., San Francisco, Calif. 94115
  COL
  Fiction: *Mindfogger* (Alfred A. Knopf, 1973;
  Dell, 1975)

Thomas Robert Sanchez
c/o Zigler-Ross Agency, Suite 1122, 9255 Sunset Blvd.,
Los Angeles, Calif. 90069
(213) 278-0070
  Readings only
  Fiction: *Rabbit Boss* (Alfred A. Knopf, 1973;
  Ballantine Books, 1974)

Mark Schorer
68 Tamalpais Rd., Berkeley, Calif. 94708
(415) 848-8789
  NPS; speaks German, some Italian
  Novel: *The Wars of Love* (McGraw-Hill, 1954)
  and published in *The New Yorker, Esquire*

Hubert Selby, Jr.
635 Westbourne Dr., Hollywood, Calif. 90069
(213) 652-7582
  COL, readings
  Novel: *The Room* (Grove Press, 1971)

Karl Shapiro
Dept. of English, U. of California, Davis, Calif. 95616
  alternate address: 1119 Bucknell Dr., Davis,
  Calif. 95616
  COL
  Poetry: *Selected Poems* (Random House, 1970)
  Fiction: *Edsel* (New American Library, 1972)

Lawrence P. Spingarn
13830 Erwin St., Van Nuys, Calif. 91401
(213) 785-4671
NPS; speaks French, Italian, German, Spanish &
Portuguese
Poetry: *Freeway Problems—And Others* (Perivale
Press, 1970)
Fiction published in *Playgirl, Mississippi Review*

Page Stegner
c/o Crown College, U. of California, Santa Cruz,
Calif. 95060
NPS
Novel: *Hawks and Harriers* (Dial, 1972)

Robert Joe Stout
1502 Citrus Ave., Chico, Calif. 95926
(916) 345-7087
Is interested in working with non-academic adult
or vocational groups; speaks Spanish
Poetry: *Trained Bears on Hoops* (Thorp Springs
Press, 1974)
Novel: *Miss Sally* (Bobbs-Merrill, 1973)

Samuel C. Tagatac
12 N. Alisos, Santa Barbara, Calif. 93103
(805) 962-8351 or (805) 964-6635
COL*, readings; has worked for Calif. PITS;
speaks Ilokano & Tagalog; is Filipino
Poetry published in *AIIIEEEEE!, Asian
American Writers*
Fiction published in *AIIIEEEEE!, AION*

Katharine Topkins
Box 198, Ross, Calif. 94957
(415) 454-5888
COL*
Novel: *Il Boom* with Richard Topkins
(Random House, 1974)

Richard Vasquez
3345 Marengo, Altadena, Calif. 91001
(213) 794-9825
ALL; interested in Chicano Studies; speaks some Spanish
Fiction: *Chicano* (Doubleday, 1971)

Tom Veitch
461 Wilde Ave., San Francisco, Calif. 94134
ALL*
Poetry: *Death College* (Siamese Banana Press,1971)
Fiction: *Eat This* (Angel Hair Books, 1974)

Victor Edmundo Villasenor
1302 Stewart St., Oceanside, Calif. 92054
alternate address: c/o Toni Burbank, Bantam Books,
666 Fifth Ave., New York, N.Y. 10019, (212) 765-6500
JHS*, HS*, COL*; speaks Spanish; is Chicano
Novel: *Macho* (Bantam Books, 1973)

Peter Vincent
1497 Masonic St., San Francisco, Calif. 94117
COL*, readings
Fiction: *Sanglorians Run* (Delacorte, 1971)

Jessamyn West
2480 Third Ave., Napa, Calif. 94558
(707) 226-3264
NPS; is part Indian
Fiction: *Leafy Rivers* (Avon Books, 1974)

Philip Whalen
Zen Center, 300 Page St., San Francisco, Calif. 94102
(415) 626-3697
Readings only
Poetry: *Scenes of Life at the Capital* (Grey Fox
Press, 1971)
Novel: *Imaginary Speeches for a Brazen Head*
(Black Sparrow Press, 1972)

Robin White
Little Lake Rd., Box 691, Mendocino, Calif. 95460
(707) 937-0266
HS, COL; is interested in working in drug rehabilita-
tion centers; speaks Tamil
Fiction: *Be Not Afraid* (Berkley Publishing Corp., 1973)

Herbert Wilner
120 Arguello Blvd., San Francisco, Calif. 94118
HS, COL
Short Stories: *Dovisch in the Wilderness & Other
Stories* (Bobbs-Merrill, 1968)

Janet Lewis Winters
143 W. Portola Ave., Los Altos, Calif. 94022
NPS; speaks French
Poetry: *Poems, 1924-1944* (Swallow Press, 1950)
Fiction published in *McCalls, Saturday Evening Post*

Shawn Hsu Wong
780 Chestnut Street, #3, San Francisco, Calif. 94133
(415) 776-6472
COL*; has worked for Calif. PITS; is Chinese-American
Poetry published in *Greenfield Review, Asian
American Authors*
Fiction published in *Yardbird Reader, AIIIEEEEE!*

Hisaye Yamamoto (DeSoto)
4558 Mont Eagle Pl., Los Angeles, Calif. 90041
NPS; speaks some Japanese, French, Spanish, German &
Latin; is Japanese
Fiction published in *Asian American Heritage,
AIIIEEEEE!*

Al Young
373 Oxford St., Palo Alto, Calif. 94306
(415) 327-5074
Readings only; speaks Spanish & some Russian & Japanese; is Afro-American
Poetry: *Some Recent Fiction* (Holt, Rinehart &
Winston, 1976)
Novel: *Sitting Pretty* (Holt, Rinehart & Winston,
1976)

Curtis Zahn
1352 Miller Dr., Los Angeles, Calif. 90069
(213) 656-4896
alternate address: c/o New Directions Publishing Co.,
333 Sixth Ave., New York, N.Y. 10014
NPS; is interested in working in prisons, for anti-war
& international justice
Poetry published in *New Mexico Quarterly Review,
The New Yorker*
Short Stories: *American Contemporary* (Penguin,
Ltd., 1967)

COLORADO

Seymour Epstein
2924 S. Monroe St., Denver, Colo. 80210
(303) 756-2359
COL*
Fiction: *Looking for Fred Schmidt* (Doubleday, 1973)

Joanne Greenberg
R.D. 3, Box 321, Golden, Colo. 80401
NPS
Novel: *I Never Promised You a Rose Garden* (New American Library, 1973)

James Salter
Box 2738, Aspen, Colo. 81611
(303) 925-3996
NPS; speaks French
Novel: *Light Years* (Random House, 1975)

Ronald Sukenick
2550 Stanford Ave., Boulder, Colo. 80303
Readings only; has worked for Calif. PITS; speaks French, Italian, Spanish
Novel: *98.6* (Fiction Collective, 1975)

John Williams
Director, Creative Writing Program, U. of Denver, Denver, Colo. 80210
alternate address: 1938 S. Madison, Denver, Colo. 80210
COL*
Novel: *Augustus* (Viking, 1972)

James Yaffe
1215 N. Cascade, Colorado Springs, Colo. 80903
(303) 634-0623
COL*
Fiction: *The Voyage of the Franz Joseph* (G.P. Putnam, 1970; Pocket Books, 1971)

CONNECTICUT

C.D.B. Bryan
56 Union St., Guilford, Conn. 06437
alternate address: c/o Carl D. Brandt, Brandt & Brandt, 101 Park Ave., New York, N.Y. 10017, (212) MU3-5890
COL*, readings
Fiction: *The Great Dethriffe* (E.P. Dutton, 1970)

Brian Burland
Book Hill, Essex, Conn. 06426
(202) 767-1629
COL*, readings
Novel: *Surprise* (Harper & Row, 1975)

Henry Carlisle
South St., Washington, Conn. 06793
(203) 868-2545
NPS; speaks French
Novel: *The Land Where The Sun Dies* (G.P. Putnam's Sons, 1975)

Eleanor Clark
2495 Redding Rd., Fairfield, Conn. 06430
NPS; speaks French, Italian
Fiction: *Dr. Heart, A Novella, & Other Stories* (Pantheon, 1974)

Hope Hale Davis
4 Old Orchard Rd., Westport, Conn. 06880
(203) 255-3332
Readings only; speaks some French, Spanish, German
Novella and Short Stories: *The Dark Way to the Plaza* (Doubleday, 1968)

Alexis DeVeaux
26 Tilton St., New Haven, Conn. 06511
(203) 562-9501
alternate address: c/o Marie Brown, Doubleday & Co., 245 Park Ave., New York, N.Y. 10017
ALL*; has worked for Conn. PITS; is Black
Novel: *Spirits in the Street* (Anchor Press, 1973)

Sonya Dorman
Cedar Rd., West Mystic, Conn. 06388
COL
Poetry: *Poems* (Ohio State U. Press, 1970)
Fiction published in *Galaxy, Analog*

Charles Edward Eaton
Merlin Stone, Woodbury, Conn. 06798 (May-Oct.)
(203) 263-2733
alternate address (Nov.-Apr.): 808 Greenwood Rd., Chapel Hill, N.C. 27514, (919) 942-4775
NPS; speaks French, German, Spanish & Portuguese
Poetry: *On the Edge of the Knife* (Abelard-Schuman, 1970)
Novella and Short Stories: *The Girl from Ipanema* (North Country Publishing, 1972)

William Hanley
190 Lounsbury Rd., Ridgefield, Conn. 06877
NPS
Novel: *Mixed Feelings* (Doubleday, 1972)

John Clellon Holmes
Box 75, Shepard St., Old Saybrook, Conn. 06475
COL, readings; is interested in working with beginning writers
Novel: *Get Home Free* (E.P. Dutton, 1964)

Donald Honig
15 Golden Ct., Cromwell, Conn. 06416
Readings only
Novel: *Illusions* (Doubleday, 1974)

Paul Horgan
Box 2600, Wesleyan U., Middletown, Conn. 06457
alternate address: c/o Farrar, Straus & Giroux, 19 Union Sq. W., New York, N.Y. 10003, (212) 741-6900
NPS; speaks French
Novel: *Whitewater* (Farrar, Straus & Giroux, 1970; Paperback Library, 1971)

Maude Hutchins
1046 Pequot Rd., Southport, Conn. 06490
(203) 259-4123
NPS; speaks some Italian & French
Novel: *The Unbelievers Downstairs* (Wm. Morrow, 1967)

Katinka Loeser
170 Cross Hwy., Westport, Conn. 06880
NPS
Fiction: *The Archers at Home* (Atheneum, 1968)

Carole Spearin McCauley
23 Buena Vista Dr., Greenwich, Conn. 06830
(203) JE1-6192
HS, COL*; is interested in working with women's groups; speaks German & French
Poetry published in *Down the Days, Women: Omen*
Novel: *Happenthing in Travel On* (Daughters, Inc. 1975)

Saul Maloff
Painter Hill, Roxbury, Conn. 06783
HS, COL
Fiction: *Heartland* (Scribner's, 1973)

James Merrill
107 Water St., Stonington, Conn. 06378
alternate address: c/o Harry Ford, Atheneum Publishers, 122 E. 42 St., New York, N.Y. 10017, (212) 661-4500
readings; speaks French & Greek
Poetry: *Braving the Elements* (Atheneum, 1972)
Fiction: *The (Diblos) Notebook* (Atheneum, 1965)

Stephen Minot
69 Hickory Hill Rd., Simsbury, Conn. 06070
(203) 658-9293
NPS
Short Stories: *Crossings* (U. of Illinois Press, 1975)

H.L. Mountzoures
292 Pequot Ave., New London, Conn. 06320
NPS
Novel: *The Bridge* (Scribner's, 1972)

Peter Neill
Box 222, Stony Creek, Conn. 06405
(203) 481-2536
HS, COL*
Novel: *Mock Turtle Soup* (Grossman, 1972)

F.D. Reeve
Higganum, Conn. 06441
(203) 345-2194
ALL (HS*, COL*); speaks Russian and French
Poetry: *Nightway* (Farrar, Straus & Giroux, 1975)
Fiction: *White Colors* (Farrar, Straus & Giroux, 1973)

William Styron
R.F.D., Roxbury, Conn. 06783
(203) 354-5939
alternate address: c/o Robert D. Loomis, Random House, 201 E. 50 St., New York, N.Y. 10022, (212) 751-2600
NPS
Novel: *The Confessions of Nat Turner* (Random House, 1967; Modern Library, 1970)

Robert Penn Warren
2495 Redding Rd., Fairfield, Conn. 06430
COL,
Poetry: *Selected Poems* (Random House, 1966)
Fiction: *All the King's Men* (Harcourt, Brace, Jovanovich, 1946)

DISTRICT OF COLUMBIA

Alex Karmel
5024 Klingle St. N.W., Washington, D.C. 20016
(202) 467-5800
COL, readings; speaks French
Historical Novel: *My Revolution* (McGraw-Hill, 1970)

Larry McMurtry
c/o Booked Up Bookstore, 1214 31 St. N.W., Washington, D.C. 20007
(202) 965-3244
NPS
Novel: *All My Friends Are Going To Be Strangers* (Simon & Schuster, 1972)

John Pauker
3006 Porter St. N.W., Washington, D.C. 20008
(202) 244-5974
Readings only; is interested in working in prisons, hospitals, old age homes, mental institutions; has worked in Va. and Md. PITS
Poetry: *A Poetry Of Our Time* (Bilingual, in English and French; Imprimerie Mazarine, 1972)
Fiction published in *The Stone Wall Book of Short Fictions, Voyages*

Ralph Robin
5432 Connecticut Ave. N.W., Apt. 706, Washington, D.C. 20015
(202) 244-6987
HS, COL*; interested in participating in panels and seminars
Poetry: *Cities of Speech* (The Byron Press, 1971)
Fiction published in *Encounter, Accent: An Anthology*

FLORIDA

Rita Mae Brown
1327 N.E. 14th Ct., Ft. Lauderdale, Fla. 33304
alternate address: c/o Charlotte Bunch, Institute for Policy Studies, 1901 Q St., Washington, D.C. 20009, (202) 234-9382
COL*; is interested in working with women & gay people in feminist studies
Poetry: *Songs To A Handsome Woman* (Diana Press, 1973)
Fiction: *Rubyfruit Jungle* (Daughters, 1973)

Erskine Caldwell
Box 820, Dunedin, Fla. 33528
NPS
Novel: *Annette* (New American Library/ Norton, 1974)

Harry Crews
Dept. of English, U. of Florida, Gainesville, Fla. 32601
(904) 392-0777
NPS
Novel: *The Gypsy's Curse* (Alfred A. Knopf, 1974)

James Jones
Writer-in-Residence, Florida State U., Tallahassee,
Fla. 32306
    alternate address: Dell Publishing Co., 1 Dag
    Hammarskjold Plaza, New York, N.Y. 10017, (212)
    832-7300
    COL, readings; is interested in working in veterans'
    hospitals; speaks French
    Novel: *A Touch of Danger* (Doubleday, 1973)

Smith Kirkpatrick
1655 N.W. 10th Ave., Gainesville, Fla. 32605
(904) 372-8222
    COL*; speaks some Spanish
    Novel: *The Sun's Gold* (Houghton Mifflin, 1974)

Jerome Weidman
1390 S. Ocean Blvd., Pompano Beach, Fla. 33062
    alternate address: c/o Brandt & Brandt, 101 Park Ave.,
    New York, N.Y. 10017, (212) MU3-5890
    COL*, readings; speaks some Yiddish
    Novel: *Tiffany Street* (Random House, 1974)

Joy Williams
8128 Midnight Pass Rd., Siesta Key, Fla. 33581
(813) 922-9282 (Nov.-June)
    alternate address: c/o Rust Hills, Box 138, RFD #1,
    Stonington, Conn. 06378, (203) 535-1851 (June-Nov.)
    NPS
    Fiction: *State of Grace* (Doubleday, 1973)

GEORGIA

Marion Montgomery
P.O. Box 115, Crawford, Ga. 30630
(404) 743-5359
    NPS
    Poetry: *The Gull and Other Georgia Scenes* (U. of
    Georgia Press, 1969)
    Novel: *Fugitive* (Harper & Row, 1974)

Michael Mott
1210 Cameron Court N.E., Atlanta, Ga. 30306
(404) 377-4658
    ALL*; has worked for Va. & Ga. PITS; speaks French
    Poetry: *Absence of Unicorns, Presence of Lions*
    (Little, Brown, 1976)
    Novel: *Helmet and Wasps* (Houghton Mifflin, 1966)

HAWAII

John Logan
2520 Rainbow Dr., Honolulu, Hawaii 96822 (til June '76)
(808) 988-7300
    permanent address: 226 Linwood Ave., Buffalo, N.Y.
    14209, (716) 881-2597
    HS*, COL*; has worked for N.Y. PITS
    Poetry: *The Anonymous Lover, Liveright* (W.W.
    Norton, 1973)
    Novella: *The House That Jack Built* (Abbatoir
    Editions, U. of Nebraska Press, 1974)

ILLINOIS

Asa Baber
1108 Austin St., Evanston, Ill. 60202
(312) 492-9319
    HS*, COL*, readings; has worked for Hawaii PITS; is
    interested in working in community centers, prisons;
    speaks French
    Novel: *The Land Of A Million Elephants*
    (Wm. Morrow, 1970)

Warren Beck
c/o Swallow Press, 1139 S. Wabash Ave.,
Chicago, Ill. 60605
(312) 922-8377
    COL, readings; is interested in working with
    adult groups and writers' conferences
    Short Stories: *Rest Is Silence & Other
    Stories* (Swallow, 1963)

Saul Bellow
1126 E. 59th St., Chicago, Ill. 60637
    NPS
    Novel: *Mr. Sammler's Planet* (Viking, 1970;
    Fawcett World, 1974)

George Chambers
908 W. Moss, Peoria, Ill. 61606
(309) 673-6758
    HS*, COL*, readings; is interested in working in
    prisons, drug rehabilitation centers, old age homes
    Poetry published in *Voyages To The Inland Sea IV,
    Trinity Review*
    Novel: *The Bonnyclabber* (December Press, 1972)

Mark Costello
Dept. of English, U. of Illinois, Urbana, Ill. 61801
(217) 333-0426
    NPS
    Short Stories: *The Murphy Stories* (U. of
    Illinois Press, 1973)

Daniel Curley
Dept. of English, U. of Illinois, Urbana, Ill. 61801
(217) 333-2391
    Readings only
    Stories: *In The Hands Of Our Enemies* (U. of
    Illinois Press, 1971)

Ronald Fair
c/o Herbert Fair, 201 W. 92nd, Chicago, Ill. 60620
    alternate address: c/o Frances McCullough, Harper
    & Row, 10 E. 53 St., New York, N.Y. 10022, (212)
    593-7000
    NPS; is Black
    Novel: *We Can't Breathe* (Harper & Row, 1972)

Philip Jose Farmer (Kilgore Trout)
4106 Devon La., Peoria, Ill. 61614
(309) 688-5701
    EL, JHS, HS*, COL*
    Novel: *Venus on the Half-Shell* (Dell, 1975)

Sheldon Frank
2032 N. Kenmore Ave., Chicago, Ill. 60614
(312) 750-1927
    COL
    Fiction published in *Fiction Midwest, Chicago Review*

Paul Friedman
308 W. Illinois St., Urbana, Ill. 61801
(217) 328-3247
    NPS
    Short Stories: *And If Defeated Allege Fraud*
    (U. of Illinois Press, 1971)

Daryl Hine
c/o Poetry Magazine, 1228 N. Dearborn Pkwy., Chicago,
Ill. 60610
(312) 787-1328
    readings; speaks French & some Spanish, Italian &
    German
    Poetry: *Resident Alien* (Atheneum, 1975)
    Verse Novel: *In & Out* (Delta, 1974)

Momoko Iko
751 W. Bittersweet Pl., Chicago, Ill. 60613
(312) 549-2044
    HS*, COL, readings; is Asian-American
    Fiction published in *Roots II, AIIIEEEEE!*

James McCormick
3155 Pine Grove Ave., Chicago, Ill. 60657
(312) 477-2628
    NPS; speaks some German
    Novel: *Bravo* (MacGibbon & Kee, 1965) and in
    Carleton Miscellany

Robie Macauley
1323 N. Sandburg Terr., Chicago, Ill. 60610
    NPS; speaks German
    Short Stories: *The End of Pity* (McDowell,
    Obolensky, 1959) and in *O. Henry Prize Stories,
    Best American Short Stories*

Catherine Petroski
4628 Main St., Downers Grove, Ill. 60515
(312) 852-1066
    alternate address: c/o Mrs. Robert Groom, P.O. Box 465,
    300 Garden Blvd., Belleville, Ill. 62221
    HS*, COL*
    Fiction published in *North American Review,
    Prairie Schooner*

Melinda Popham
1435 N. State Pkwy., Chicago, Ill. 60610
    alternate address: 920 N. Michigan Ave., #806,
    Chicago, Ill. 60611, (312) 751-1977
    COL; speaks French
    Novel: *A Blank Book* (Bobbs-Merrill, 1974)

Richard G. Stern
c/o Dept. of English, Univ. of Chicago, 1050 E.
59th, Chicago, Ill. 60637
(312) 753-3882
    Readings; speaks French, German & Italian
    Novel: *Other Men's Daughters* (E.P. Dutton,
    1973)

John Stewart
512 E. Chalmers, Champaign, Ill. 61820
(217) 333-7781
    Readings only; is Black
    Short Stories & Poems: *Curving Road* (U. of
    Illinois Press, 1975)

Larry Woiwode
430 Oakwood, Woodstock, Ill. 60098
    alternate address: c/o Michael di Capua, Farrar, Straus
    & Giroux, 19 Union Sq. W., New York, N.Y. 10003
    JHS*, HS, COL*; speaks Spanish
    Poetry published in *Sumac, The New Yorker*
    Fiction: *Beyond the Bedroom Wall* (Farrar, Straus
    & Giroux, 1974)

Gene Wolfe
Box 69, Barrington, Ill. 60010
    HS*, COL
    Novel: *Peace* (Harper & Row, 1975)

INDIANA

Philip Appleman
Dept. of English, Indiana U., Bloomington, Ind. 47401
(812) 339-2127
    HS*, COL*; has worked for Ind. and Pa. PITS;
    speaks French
    Poetry: *Summer Love and Surf* (Vanderbilt U.
    Press, 1968)
    Novel: *In the Twelfth Year of the War* (G.P.
    Putnam, 1970)

Donald W. Baker
16 Harry Freedman Place, Crawfordsville, Ind. 47933
    alternate address: Dept. of English, Wabash College,
    Crawfordsville, Ind. 47933, (317) 362-1400
    ALL (HS*, COL*)
    Poetry: *Twelve Hawks* (Sugar Creek Poetry Series,
    1974)
    Fiction published in *New Letters, Carolina Quart-
    erly*

Elaine Gottlieb (Hemley)
1009 N. Niles Ave., South Bend, Ind. 46617
(219) 237-4304
    COL*, readings
    Fiction published in *O. Henry Prize Stories,
    Southern Review*

Joe L. Hensley
2315 Blackmore, Madison, Ind. 47250
(812) 273-1683
    HS*, COL*
    Fiction: *Song of Corpus Juris* (Doubleday, 1974)

Teresinha Alves Pereira
P.O. Box 1105, Bloomington, Ind. 47401
(812) 332-8213
    alternate address: c/o Luis Davila, Woodridge Ave.,
    Box 91, Merlin Hills, Bloomington, Ind. 47401, (812)
    339-5107
    NPS; is interested in working in prisons; speaks
    Portuguese, French, Spanish, Italian; is Brazilian
    Poetry: *Lines of a Broken Alphabet* (Huckster
    Press, 1975)
    Short Stories: *Little Man* (Three Tenses Press, 1975)

Harry Mark Petrakis
80 East Rd.—Dune Acres, Chesterton, Ind. 46304
(219) 787-8283
    COL*; is interested in working in prisons; speaks
    Greek
    Novel: *In The Land Of Morning* (David McKay, 1973)

Samuel Yellen
922 E. University St., Bloomington, Ind. 47401
(812) 336-4594
  NPS
  Poetry: *The Convex Mirror: Collected Poems*
  (Indiana U. Press, 1971)
  Novel: *The Wedding Band* (Atheneum, 1961)

IOWA

Vance Bourjaily
Redbird Farm, Rt. 1, Iowa City, Iowa 52240
(319) 683-2767
  COL*, readings; speaks some Spanish
  Novel: *Brill Among The Ruins* (Dial Press, 1971)

Henry Bromell
Iowa Writer's Workshop, U. of Iowa, Iowa City,
Iowa 52242
(319) 353-3852
  COL*, readings; speaks French
  Short Stories: *The Slightest Distance* (Houghton
  Mifflin, 1974)

Gary Gildner
2915 School St., Des Moines, Iowa 50311
(515) 279-4192
  ALL*; has worked for Kans., Minn., S.Dak., Iowa &
  Mich. PITS
  Poetry: *Nails* (U. of Pittsburgh Press, 1975)
  Fiction published in *Antaeus, New Letters*

John Irving
The Writers' Workshop, U. of Iowa, Iowa City, Iowa
52242
(319) 353-4986
  COL*, readings; interested in giving lectures on
  contemporary and modern fiction; speaks some German
  Novel: *The 158-Pound Marriage* (Random House, 1974)

John Leggett
415 S. Summit St., Iowa City, Iowa 52240
(319) 338-2589 (home) or (319) 353-4986 (office)
  Readings only
  Poetry: *Ross & Tom, Two American Tragedies*
  (Simon & Schuster, 1974)
  Fiction: *Who Took the Gold Away* (Random
  House, 1969)

Julie McDonald
2802 E. Locust, Davenport, Iowa 52803
(319) 355-7246
  ALL*; is interested in working in old age homes; has
  worked for Iowa PITS
  Novel: *Amalie's Story* (Simon & Schuster, 1970;
  Popular Library, 1971)

Robley Wilson, Jr.
Twin Meadows, Route 3, Cedar Falls, Iowa 50613
(319) 266-8487
  HS*, COL*
  Poetry published in *Atlantic, The New Yorker*
  Fiction published in *Esquire, Fiction International*

KANSAS

James Gunn
2215 Orchard La., Lawrence, Kans. 66044
(913) 843-1924
  NPS; is interested in science fiction writing,
  publishing & history
  Fiction: *The Listeners* (New American Library, 1974)

David Ohle
724 Rhode Island St., Lawrence, Kans. 66044
(913) 841-5764
  alternate address: c/o Wayne Propst, Box 591,
  Lawrence, Kans. 66044
  COL
  Novel: *Motorman* (Alfred A. Knopf, 1972)

KENTUCKY

Wendell E. Berry
Port Royal, Ky. 40058
  NPS
  Poetry: *An Eastward Look* (Sand Dollar Press, 1975
  Fiction: *The Memory of Old Jack* (Harcourt,
  Brace, Jovanovich, 1974)

Lillie D. Chaffin
Box 42, Meta Station, Pikeville, Ky. 41501
(606) 432-1972
  readings; is interested in working with summer writing
  workshops, speaking at writing conferences
  Fiction: *Freeman* (Macmillan, 1971)

Guy Davenport
621 Sayre Ave., Lexington, Ky. 40508
(606) 254-1851
  NPS
  Poetry: *Flowers and Leaves* (Jargon Press, 1964)
  Five Stories and Novella: *Tatlin!* (Scribner's, 1974)

Gayl Jones
440 Locust Ave., Lexington, Ky. 40505
(606) 255-6015
  COL; speaks some Spanish; is Black
  Novel: *Corregidora* (Random House, 1975)

Wallace E. Knight
121 Mount Savage Dr., Ashland, Ky. 41101
(606) 324-0867
  COL, readings
  Fiction published in *Best American Short Stories
  of 1973, Atlantic Monthly*

Andrew Lytle
Route 2, Box 216, Sadieville, Ky. 40370
(502) 857-4508
  COL*, readings
  Fiction: *A Novel, Novella, and Four Stories*
  (McDowell-Obolensky, 1958) and in *American
  Literature*

James Still
Box 361, Hindman, Ky. 41822
(606) 785-3389
  alternate address: c/o Lionel Duff, Hindman
  Settlement School, Hindman, Ky. 41822, (606)
  785-5475
  Readings only; is interested in working in
  prisons & old age homes
  Poetry: *Hounds on the Mountain* (Viking, 1937;
  Anvil Press, 1968)
  Fiction: *River of Earth* (Viking, 1940;
  Popular Library, 1971)

LOUISIANA

John William Corrington
1724 Valence St., New Orleans, La. 70115
(504) 899-1474
    NPS
    Poetry: *Lines to the South* (La. State U. Press, 1966)
    Novel: *The Bombardier* (G.P. Putnam, 1970)

Charles East
1455 Knollwood Dr., Baton Rouge, La. 70808
(504) 344-8147
    COL
    Short Stories: *Where the Music Was* (Harcourt,
Brace & World, 1965)

Shirley Ann Grau
1424 N.B.C. Bldg., New Orleans, La. 70112
(504) 525-1613
    HS*, COL*
    Short Stories: *The Wind Shifting West* (Alfred.
A. Knopf, 1973)

David Madden
614 Park Blvd., Baton Rouge, La. 70806
(504) 344-3630
    ALL (HS*, COL*); is interested in working in prisons,
old age homes, orphanages; has worked for La. PITS
    Poetry published in *New Southern Poets, Poem*
    Novel: *Bijou* (Crown Publishers, 1974)

Walker Percy
P.O. Drawer 510, Covington, La. 70433
    HS, COL
    Novel: *Love In The Ruins* (Farrar, Straus
& Giroux, 1971)

MAINE

George Garrett
Box 264, York Harbor, Maine 03911
(207) 363-3232
    ALL*; has worked for Ky. & Ga. PITS; speaks some
Italian, French & German
    Poetry: *For a Bitter Season* (U. of Missouri
Press, 1967)
    Fiction: *The Magic Striptease* (Doubleday, 1973)

Mitchell Goodman
RFD, Temple, Maine 04284
(207) 778-3717
    JHS, HS, COL*; has worked for N.Y. PITS; speaks
French & Spanish
    Poetry: *Light From Under A Bushel* (Perishable
Press, 1969)
    Fiction: *The End of It* (Horizon Press, 1962;
Signet Books, 1963)

Lawrence Sargent Hall
Bay View Rd., Orr's Island, Maine 04066
(207) 833-6628
    COL
    Novel: *Stowaway* (Atlantic-Little, Brown, 1961)

Mary McCarthy
Main St., Castine Maine 04421
    NPS; speaks French & Italian
    Novel: *Birds of America* (Harcourt Brace Jovano-
vich, 1971)

Bern Porter
22 Salmond St., Belfast, Maine 04915
    ALL; is interested in working in drug rehabilitation
centers, prisons & old age homes; speaks French,
Spanish & German; is American Indian
    Poetry: *The Wastemaker* (Abyss Publications, 1973)
    Fiction: *I've Left* (Something Else Press, 1970)

May Sarton
Box 99, York, Maine 03909
(207) 363- 4131
    COL*; speaks French
    Poetry: *Collected Poems* (W.W. Norton, 1974)
    Fiction: *As We Are Now* (W.W. Norton, 1973)

MARYLAND

John Barth
Writing Seminars, John Hopkins U., Baltimore, Md. 2121
(301) 366-3300, Ext. 1453
    NPS
    Novellas: *Chimera* (Random House, 1972)

Charles Deemer
Rt. 5, Box 478, Salisbury, Md. 21801
(301) 546-3860
    HS, COL*; speaks some Russian
    Fiction published in *The Literary Review,
Prism International, Mississippi Review*

Josephine Jacobsen
220 Stony Ford Rd., Baltimore, Md. 21210
(301) 889-0152
    summer address: Whitefield, N.H. 03598, (603) 837-2
    HS, COL, readings; speaks some French
    Poetry: *The Shade-Seller: New & Selected Poems*
(Doubleday, 1974)
    Fiction published in *O. Henry Prize Stories,
Fifty Years of The American Short Story*

Judson Jerome
Downhill Farm, Hancock, Md. 21750
(717) 294-3345
    ALL*; speaks Spanish
    Poetry: *Serenade* (Crown Point Press, 1968)
    Novel: *The Fell of Dark* (Houghton Mifflin, 1966)

Anne Tyler
222 Tunbridge Rd., Baltimore, Md. 21212
    NPS; speaks Persian
    Novel: *Celestial Navigation* (Alfred A.
Knopf, 1974)

Douglass Wallop
Tilghman St., Oxford, Md. 21654
(301) 226-5407
    NPS; is interested in working in old age homes
    Novel: *Howard's Bag* (W.W. Norton, 1973)

MASSACHUSETTS

Raymond H. Abbott
59 School St., Groveland, Mass. 01834
(617) 372-1539
    NPS; speaks Spanish
    Fiction: *Paha Sapa (The Black Hills)* (Akwesasne
Notes, 1975)

Robert H. Abel
159 Summer St., Apt. 44, Amherst, Mass. 01002
(413) 549-6816
  alternate address: c/o Wayne Ude, 15 Hallock St.,
  Amherst, Mass. 01002, (413) 256-6008
  COL*; is interested in fiction organized in non-tra-
  ditional or non-narrative ways
  Fiction published in *Epoch, Kansas Quarterly*

Stephen Becker
Rt. 1, Box 32, Conway, Mass. 01341
(413) 625-6866
  COL*, readings; is interested in 3-day lecture/
  workshop/reading situations; speaks French
  Novel: *The Chinese Bandit* (Random House, 1975)

Anne Bernays
16 Francis Ave., Cambridge, Mass. 02138
(617) 354-2577
  HS*, COL
  Fiction: *Growing Up Rich* (Little, Brown, 1975)

Robert E. Boles
97 Great Western Rd., South Dennis, Mass. 02660
(617) 398-9143
  COL*; is Black & American Indian (Cherokee)
  Fiction: *Curling* (Houghton Mifflin, 1968)

John Jacob Clayton
Taylor Hill Road, Montague, Mass. 01351
(413) 367-9506 or 545-0359
  readings
  Fiction published in *Best American Short Stories,
  O'Henry Award Stories*

George Cuomo
Dept. of English, U. of Massachusetts, Amherst,
Mass. 01002
(413) 545-2030
  COL*; interested in working in prisons
  Poetry: *Geronimo And The Girl Next Door* (BookMark
  Press, 1974)
  Novel: *Pieces From A Small Bomb* (Doubleday, 1976)

Benjamin DeMott
44 Hitchcock Rd., Amherst, Mass. 01002
  NPS
  Novel: *A Married Man* (Harcourt, Brace & World,1968)

J.P. Donleavy
c/o Seymour Lawrence, Inc., 90 Beacon St., Boston,
Mass. 02108
(617) CA7-1719
  NPS
  Novel: *A Fairy Tale of New York* (Seymour
  Lawrence, 1973)

Page Edwards
19 Olive St., Newburyport, Mass. 01950
(617) 462-9916
  ALL*; is interested in working in prisons, drug
  rehabilitation centers, & nursing homes; speaks
  Spanish
  Novel: *Touring* (Viking/Grossman, 1974)

Alan Feldman
48 N. Mill St., Hopkinton, Mass. 01748
(617) 435-4400
  EL*, JHS, HS*, COL*; is interested in working with
  teachers; has worked for N.Y. PITS
  Poetry published in *New American Review, Panache*
  Fiction published in *My Name Aloud, First Issue*

Richard Flanagan
72A Glen St., South Natick, Mass. 01760
(617) 653-0618
  COL*
  Novel: *The Hunting Variety* (G.P. Putnam, 1973)

John Bart Gerald
31 Chilton St., Cambridge, Mass. 02138
(617) 547-2179
  HS, COL*, readings
  Novel: *Conventional Wisdom* (Farrar, Straus &
  Giroux, 1972)

Ivan Gold
96 Bay State Rd., Boston, Mass. 02215
(617) 267-0543
  EL, JHS, HS, COL*; interested in working in old age
  homes
  Novel: *Sick Friends* (E.P. Dutton, 1969)

Hank Heifetz
21 Parkside St., Springfield, Mass. 01104
  Readings only; is interested in working in prisons;
  speaks French, Italian & Spanish
  Fiction: *Where Are the Stars in New York?*
  (Saturday Review Press, 1973)

Don Hendrie, Jr.
57 Ferry St., South Hadley, Mass. 01075
(413) 533-9038
  COL*
  Novel: *Boomkitchwatt* (John Muir Publications,
  1973)

DeWitt Henry
280 Brookline St., #8, Cambridge, Mass. 02139
(617) 868-4174
  COL*
  Fiction published in *Harbinger, Aspect*

George V. Higgins
100 Federal St., Boston, Mass. 02110
  alternate address: c/o Paul R. Reynolds, Inc.,
  12 E. 41 St., New York, N.Y. 10017, (212) 689-8711
  NPS
  Fiction: *A City On A Hill* (Alfred A. Knopf, 1975)

Richard E. Kim
Leverett Rd., Shutesbury, Mass. 01072
(413) 253-9828
  COL*; speaks Korean & Japanese; is Asian-American
  Novel: *Lost Names* (Praeger, 1970)

Maxine Kumin
40 Bradford Rd., Newton, Mass. 02161
(617) 244-4946 or (603) 456-3709
  COL*, readings; speaks French
  Poetry: *House, Bridge, Fountain, Gate* (Viking,1975)
  Fiction: *The Designated Heir* (Viking, 1974)

John P. Marquand, Jr.
c/o Little, Brown & Co., 34 Beacon St., Boston,
Mass. 02106
(617) 227-0730
  NPS
  Fiction: *Sincerely, Willis Wayde* (Little, Brown, 1955)

James A. McPherson
c/o Peter Davison, Atlantic Monthly Press, 8 Arlington
St., Boston, Mass. 02116
(617) 536-9500
    NPS; is Black
    Short Stories: *Hue and Cry* (Atlantic Monthly Press, 1969)

Rose Moss
580 Walnut St., Newtonville, Mass. 02160
(617) 965-2055
    Readings only; speaks Afrikaans & French
    Novel: *The Family Reunion* (Scribner's, 1974)

Jay Neugeboren
252 River Dr., North Hadley, Mass. 01035
(413) 586-3732
    Readings; speaks French
    Novel: *Sam's Legacy* (Holt, Rinehart &
    Winston, 1974)

Paul J.J. Payack
52 South Acton Rd., Stow, Mass. 01775
    COL, readings
    Tales: *Stardust & Broken Glass* (N.Y. Culture
    Review Press, 1975)

Marge Piercy
Box 943, Wellfleet, Mass. 02667
(617) 349-3163
    ALL; is interested in working in women's prisons
    and teaching writing workshops; speaks Spanish, French
    Poetry: *To Be Of Use* (Doubleday, 1973)
    Fiction: *Small Changes* (Doubleday, 1973;
    Fawcett, 1974)

Robert Rushmore
Sage House, Sandisfield, Mass. 01255
(413) 258-4863
    alternate address: c/o Alfreda Rushmore, 1040 Park
    Ave., New York, N.Y. 10028, (212) LE4-1885
    Readings only
    Fiction: *If My Love Leaves Me* (Bobbs-Merrill, 1975)

Jessie Schell
302 Walnut St., Brookline, Mass. 02146
(617) 734-5277
    ALL (COL*); is interested in working in old age homes
    Novel: *Sudina* (E.P. Dutton, 1967) and fiction
    published in *Prize Stories 1975: The O. Henry Awards*

R.D. Skillings
28 Cottage St., Provincetown, Mass. 02657
(617) 487-9960
    NPS
    Short Stories: *Alternative Lives* (Ithaca House, 1974)

David R. Slavitt
Box 325, Harwich, Mass. 02645
(617) 432-1680
    ALL*; speaks French
    Poetry: *Vital Signs* (Doubleday, 1975)
    Fiction: *The Killing of the King* (Doubleday, 1974)

Barry Spacks
16 Abbott St., Wellesley, Mass. 02181
(617) 237-9733
    COL*, readings; speaks French
    Poetry: *Teaching The Penguins To Fly* (Godine, 1975)
    Novel: *Orphans* (Harper's Magazine Press, 1972)

Robert Steiner
11 Hatfield, Northampton, Mass. 01060
(413) 584-6580
    COL*
    Novel: *Quill* (Harper & Row, 1973)

Robert Stone
c/o Houghton Mifflin Co., 2 Park St., Boston, Mass.
02107
(617) 725-5000
    COL*, readings
    Novel: *Dog Soldiers* (Houghton Mifflin, 1974)

Jonathan Strong
c/o Dept. of English, East Hall, Tufts U., Medford,
Mass. 02155
(617) 628-5000
    Unavailable for readings & workshops
    Novel: *Ourselves* (Atlantic, Little-Brown, 1971;
    paperback, Ballantine Books, 1972)

Alexander Louis Theroux
Adams House (C-12), Harvard U., Cambridge, Mass. 02138
(617) 498-2066
    COL*, readings; is interested in working in prisons;
    speaks French & Italian
    Fiction: *The Schinocephalic Waif* (Godine, 1975)

Robert Ullian
32 Shepard St., Apt. 33, Cambridge, Mass. 02138
(617) 876-8490
    alternate address: c/o Janet Ullian, 21 W. Loines Ave
    Merrick, N.Y. 11566, (516) FR9-9744
    EL, JHS, HS, COL*; is interested in working with
    elderly writers & small children; speaks Spanish &
    French
    Fiction published in *The Secret Life of Our Times,
    Esquire*

John Updike
50 Labor in Vain Rd., Ipswich, Mass. 01938
    NPS
    Fiction: *Picked-Up Pieces* (Alfred A. Knopf,
    1975)

Arturo Vivante
Main St., Wellfleet, Mass. 02667
(617) 349-6619
    ALL (COL*, HS*); speaks Italian & French.
    Novel: *Doctor Giovanni* (Little, Brown, 1969)

Dan Wakefield
84 Revere St., Boston, Mass. 02114
    Readings only; is interested in presenting informal
    lectures and discussions
    Novel: *Starting Over* (Seymour Lawrence-Delacorte
    Press, 1973)

Richard Wilbur
Dodwells Rd., Cummington, Mass. 01026
    alternate address: Box KK, Wesleyan Station,
    Middletown, Conn. 06457
    NPS
    Poetry: *Opposites* (Harcourt, Brace, Jovanovich,
    1973)
    Fiction published in *New Yorker Anthology*

MICHIGAN

Carol Berge
c/o Dept. of English, Thomas Jefferson College, Allendale, Michigan 49401 (until June, 1976)
  alternate address: c/o Charles Neighbors, 240 Waverly Place, New York, N.Y. 10014, (212) 924-8296
  COL*; has worked for Conn. PITS; is interested in working in drug rehabilitation centers; speaks Spanish, some French
  Poetry: *From A Soft Angle: Poems About Women* (Bobbs-Merrill, 1971)
  Novel: *Acts Of Love* (Bobbs-Merrill, 1973; paperback PocketBooks Inc., 1974)

Albert Dee Drake
1790 Grand River Ave., Okemos, Mich. 48864
(517) 349-0552
  HS*, COL*, readings; speaks some French
  Poetry: *Returning to Oregon* (Cider Press, 1975)
  Fiction: *The Hem of Harvest* (Peaceweed Press, 1975)

Barbara Drake
1790 Grand River Rd., Okemos, Mich. 48864
(517) 349-0552
  ALL*; has worked for Mich. PITS
  Poetry published in *Fifth Assembling, Three Rivers Poetry Journal*
  Fiction published in *North American Review, Moving Out*

Stuart Dybek
320 Monroe, Kalamazoo, Mich. 49007
  ALL*; has worked for Mich. PITS; is interested in working in drug rehabilitation centers & mental hospitals & in conducting workshops in science fiction; speaks some French
  Poetry published in *Pebble, The Sou'wester*
  Fiction published in *The Iowa Review, The Sou'wester*

Hugh B. Fox
526 Forest, East Lansing, Mich. 48823
  Readings only; is interested in working with Chicanos and American Indians; speaks Spanish, Italian, French, Japanese, Arabic, Polish; is Chicano
  Poetry: *Huaca* (Ghost Dance Press, 1975)
  Short Stories: *Peeple* (Dustbooks, 1973)

Lucia A. Fox
1049 Cresenwood Rd., East Lansing, Mich. 48823
(517) 332-5622 or (517) 353-0769
  COL, readings; is interested in working with Chicano & bilingual groups; speaks Spanish & some French; is Peruvian
  Poetry: *Monstruos Aereos y Submarinos* (Superspace, 1974)
  Fiction published in *El rostro de la patria, La tapada*

Dan Gerber
2905 S. Ramshorn Dr., Fremont, Mich. 49412
(616) 924-3464
  HS*, COL*, readings; has worked for Minn., Ariz., Ind. & Mich. PITS
  Poetry: *Departure* (Sumac Press, 1973)
  Novel: *Out of Control* (Prentice-Hall, 1974; Warner, 1975)

Donald Hall
1715 S. University, Ann Arbor, Mich. 48104
(313) 761-8785
  ALL*; has worked for N.Y., Conn., Minn. & Mich. PITS
  Poetry: *The Yellow Room* (Harper & Row, 1971)
  Fiction published in *Transatlantic Review, Iowa Review*

Jim Harrison
R.R. 1, Lake Leelanau, Mich. 49653
(616) 256-9693
  JHS*, HS*, COL*, readings; has worked for N.Y., Ariz., Mich., & Minn. PITS; is interested in working in old age homes, prisons, & drug rehabilitation centers
  Poetry: *Letters to Yesenin* (Sumac Press, 1974)
  Fiction: *Farmer* (Viking, 1976)

James W. Thompson
P.O. Box 07243, Detroit, Mich. 48207
(313) 571-2309
  alternate address: c/o Charline Thompson, 16142 Wisconsin Ave., Detroit, Mich., (313) 342-9361
  EL, HS, COL*; is Afro-American
  Poetry: *First Fire* (Paul Breman Ltd., 1970)
  Fiction published in *Transatlantic Review, Black Short Stories*

James Tipton
7547 N. Osborn Rd., Elwell, Mich. 48832
(517) 463-5731
  ALL*; has worked for Mich. PITS
  Poetry: *Bittersweet* (Cold Mountain Press, 1974)
  Fiction published in *Cimarron Review, Carolina Quarterly*

MINNESOTA

William D. Elliott
3308 Cedar La., Bemidji, Minn. 56601
(218) 751-1041
  ALL (COL*); is interested in working in prisons and old age homes; speaks some French
  Poetry published in *Nimrod, The Carleton Miscellany*
  Fiction published in *Ann Arbor Review, New Orleans Review*

Alvin Greenberg
456 Summit Ave., St. Paul, Minn. 55102
(612) 225-8723
  COL*, readings; has worked for Minn. PITS
  Poetry: *Metaform* (U. of Massachusetts Press, 1975)
  Novel: *Going Nowhere* (Simon & Schuster, 1971; Avon, 1973)

Frederick Manfred
R.R. 3, Luverne, Minn. 56156
(507) 283-4664
  Readings only; is interested in working with young writers; speaks Dutch
  Poetry: *Winter Count* (Thorp Springs Press, 1975; reprint)
  Novel: *The Manly-Hearted Woman* (Crown Publishers, 1975)

Ellen Douglas
410 Wetherbee St., Greenville, Miss. 38701
  HS*, COL*, readings
  Novel: *Apostles of Light* (Houghton Mifflin, 1973)

Margaret Walker
Director of Black Studies, Jackson State College,
Jackson, Miss. 39203
COL; is Black
Fiction: *Jubilee* (Houghton Mifflin, 1966;
Bantam, 1967)

Gordon Weaver
Rt. 3, Box 240, Purvis, Miss. 39475
(601) 544-2627
HS*, COL*, readings; has worked for Miss. & La.
PITS; speaks German, French & Spanish
Poetry published in *DeKalb Literary Arts
Journal, Three Rivers Poetry Journal*
Novel: *Give Him A Stone* (Crown Publishers, 1975)

Eudora Welty
1119 Pinehurst St., Jackson, Miss. 39202
Unavailable for readings
Fiction: *The Optimist's Daughter* (Random House,
1972; Fawcett World, 1973)

MISSOURI

Stanley Elkin
225 Westgate, University City, Mo. 63130
(314) 727-4312
COL*, readings
Novellas: *Searches and Seizures* (Random House,
1973)

William Gass
Dept. of Philosophy, Washington U., St. Louis, Mo.
63130
(314) 863-0100
alternate address: 6304 Westminster Pl., St. Louis,
Mo. 63130, (314) 725-0317
Readings only
Novella: *Willie Masters' Lonesome Wife* (Alfred
A. Knopf, 1971)

Thomas McAfee
Dept. of English, U. of Missouri, Columbia, Mo. 65201
(314) 882-6066
ALL (JHS*, HS*, COL*); is interested in working in
prisons & drug rehabilitation centers; has worked
for Ill. PITS
Poetry: *I'll Be Home Late Tonight* (U. of Missouri
Press, 1967)
Novel: *Rover Youngblood* (Richard Baron, 1969)

Howard Nemerov
6970 Cornell.Ave., St. Louis, Mo. 63130
alternate address: c/o Dept. of English, Washington
U., St. Louis, Mo. 63130, (314) 863-0100
COL
Poetry: *Gnomes & Occasions* (U. of Chicago
Press, 1973)
Fiction: *Stories, Fables & Other Diversions*
(Godine, 1971)

William Peden
408 Thilly Ave., Columbia, Mo. 65201
(314) 442-1228
NPS; speaks French and Spanish
Novel: *Twilight at Monticello* (Houghton Mifflin, 1973)

David Ray
5517 Crestwood Dr., Kansas City, Mo. 64110
(816) 523-2766 or (816) 276-1168
COL*, readings; interested in working in orphanages,
homes for deprived and dependent children; has work
in Mich., Pa., Kans., and Mo. PITS
Poetry: *Gathering Firewood: New Poems and Select*
(Wesleyan U. Press, 1974)
Fiction published in *Epoch, Ohio Review*

Shirley W. Schoonover
456 Julian Pl., Kirkwood, Mo. 63122
(314) 821-1488
COL*, readings
Novel: *Sam's Song* (Coward, McCann & Geoghegan
1969)

Howard Schwartz
920 Bermuda, St. Louis, Mo. 63121
alternate address: Dept. of English, U. of Missouri,
8001 Natural Bridge Rd., St. Louis, Mo. 63121, (314)
453-5541
COL*, readings
Poetry published in *Chicago Review, Minnesota
Review*
Stories: *Lilith's Cave* (Isthmus Press, 1975)

Dave Smith
302 West Arch, Nevada, Mo. 64772
ALL (JHS*, HS*, COL*); has worked for Mich.
PITS; speaks French
Poetry: *The Fisherman's Whore* (Ohio U.
Press, 1974)
Fiction published in *Sou'wester, Miscellany*

Robert S. Thompson
4310-A Stevendale Dr., Columbia, Mo. 65201
HS, COL*
Fiction published in *Harper's, A Short
Anthology of Insanity*

Constance Urdang
6943 Columbia Pl., St. Louis, Mo. 63130
Prefers not to give readings
Poetry: *The Picnic in the Cemetery* (George
Braziller, 1975)
Novel: *Natural History* (Harper & Row, 1969)

MONTANA

Madeline DeFrees
135 E. Central Ave., Missoula, Mont. 59801
(406) 549-5951
HS*, COL*; has worked for Mont. PITS
Poetry published in *Modern Poetry of Western
America, Northwest Review*
Fiction published in *Mundus Artium, Minnesota
Review*

William Kittredge
306 S. Third W., Missoula, Mont. 59801
alternate address: Dept. of English, U. of Montana,
Missoula, Mont. 59801, (406) 549-6605
HS, COL*
Fiction published in *Atlantic, TriQuarterly*

Ken McCullough
c/o English Dept., Montana State U., Bozeman,
Mont. 59715
(406) 587-7857
  ALL*; has worked for Mont. PITS; is interested in
  working in prisons; speaks French
  Poetry: *Migrations* (Stone-Marrow Press, 1972)
  Fiction published in *The North Stone Review*
  & *Again, Dangerous Visions*

Dean Phelps
2303 12th Ave. N., Billings, Mont. 59101
(406) 252-2343
  HS*, COL*
  Poetry: *Shoshoni River Witching Hour* (Holmgangers
  Press, 1975)
  Fiction published in *Virginia Quarterly Review, Wind*

NEBRASKA

Wright Morris
c/o University of Nebraska Press, 901 N. 17 St.,
Lincoln, Nebr. 68508
(402) 472-3581
  NPS
  Novel: *The Deep Sleep* (Univ. of Nebraska
  Press, 1975)

NEVADA

Randall Reid
14605 Geronimo Trail, Reno, Nev. 89502
  COL*
  Novel: *Lost and Found* (Simon & Schuster, 1975)

NEW HAMPSHIRE

Russell Banks
RFD #1, Northwood Narrows, N.H. 03261
(603) 942-7751
  HS*, COL*, readings; speaks Spanish, some French
  Poetry: *Snow* (Granite Press, 1975)
  Fiction: *Family Life* (Avon, 1975)

Rosellen Brown
Sand Hill Rd., R.F.D. 1, Peterborough, N.H. 03458
(603) 924-7039
  EL*, HS, COL*; has worked for Vt. and N.H. PITS; is
  interested in working in prisons, drug rehabilitation
  centers, old age homes; speaks some French
  Poetry: *Some Deaths In The Delta* (U. of Mass.
  Press, 1970)
  Short Stories: *Street Games* (Doubleday, 1974)

Alan Lelchuk
RFD 2, Canaan, N.H. 03741
  alternate address: c/o Georges Borchardt, 145 E. 52
  St., New York, N.Y. 10022, (212) PL3-5785
  Readings only
  Fiction: *Miriam at Thirty-four* (Farrar, Straus
  & Giroux, 1974)

John Morressy
East Sullivan, N.H. 03445
(603) 847-3203
  COL*
  Fiction: *Under A Calculating Star* (Doubleday, 1975)

Norval Rindfleisch
17 Spring St., Exeter, N.H. 03833
(603) 772-6877
  HS*, COL*; is interested in working in adult education
  Short Stories: *In Loveless Clarity* (Ithaca
  House, 1972)

Mark Smith
Old Mountain Rd., Northwood, N.H. 03261
(603) 942-8159
  COL*
  Novel: *The Death of the Detective* (Alfred A.
  Knopf, 1974)

Thomas Williams
13 Orchard Dr., Durham, N.H. 03824
(603) 868-7378 or (603) 744-3592 (summer)
  COL*, readings; has worked for N.Y. PITS; speaks
  Japanese & French
  Poetry published in *New American Review, Harper's*
  Fiction: *The Hair of Harold Roux* (Random
  House, 1974)

John A. Yount
29 Woodridge Rd., Durham, N.H. 03824
(603) 868-7348
  alternate address: c/o John L. Yount, 1005 Fleming St.,
  Columbia, Tenn. 38401, (615) 388-4/
  COL*, readings
  Novel: *The Trapper's Last Shot* (Random House,1973)

NEW JERSEY

Nelson Algren
38 Quinn St., Patterson, N.J. 17501
  NPS
  Short Stories: *The Last Carousel*
  (G.P. Putnam, 1973)

Brock Brower
154 Balcort Drive, Princeton, N.J. 08540
(609) 924-0621
  COL*; is interested in working in the United Nations
  Novel: *The Late, Great Creature* (Atheneum, 1972)

Walter Cummins
30 Wetmore Ave., Morristown, N.J. 07960
(201) 267-2589
  HS*, COL*; has worked in N.J. PITS
  Novel: *Into Temptation* (Caravelle Books, 1968)

Welch D. Everman
2852 Yorkship Rd., Fairview-Camden, N.J. 08104
  ALL (JHS*, COL*); is interested in working in prisons,
  halfway houses, drug rehabilitation centers
  Novel: *Orion* (Ithaca House, 1975)

Paul Griffith
34 Witherspoon St., Princeton, N.J. 08540
(609) 924-2125
  COL*; is interested in working with alcoholic rehabilitation
  Novel: *My Stillness* (Vanguard Press, 1972)

Kristin Hunter
366 Fountain Ave., Camden, N.J. 08105
(609) 423-0275; ask for Freida Davis
  COL*, readings; speaks some French; is Black
  Novel: *The Survivors* (Scribner's, 1975)

Edmund Keeley
140 Littlebrook Rd., Princeton, N.J. 08540
(609) 921-9290
  COL*; is interested in reading translations and
  lecturing to Greek-American groups; speaks Modern
  Greek, French & German
  Poetry published in *The New Yorker, The Nation*
  Novel: *Voyage to a Dark Island* (Curtis
  Books, 1972)

Frederik Pohl
386 W. Front St., Red Bank, N.J. 07701
(201) 741-5917
  COL*; speaks some Italian
  Short Stories: *The Best of Frederik Pohl* (Doubleday, 1975; Ballantine Books)

Sharon Spencer
72 Watchung Ave., Upper Montclair, N.J. 07043
  COL*; speaks Italian
  Novel: *The Space Between* (Harper & Row, 1974)

John A. Williams
693 Forest Avenue, Teaneck, N.J. 07666
  Readings only; is Black
  Novel: *Mothers'" and the Foxes* (Doubleday,
  1975)

NEW MEXICO

Rudolfo Anaya
7118 Edwin Ct. N.E., Albuquerque, N.Mex. 87110
(505) 298-2432
  COL*; interested in working with Chicanos;
  speaks Spanish; is Chicano
  Novel: *Bless Me, Ultima* (Quinto Sol, 1971)

Charles G. Bell
1260 Canyon Rd., Santa Fe, N.Mex. 87501
(505) 982-0124
  Readings only; speaks German, Italian, French, Spanish
  Poetry: *Delta Return* (reprint from Indiana U.
  Press by Norman Berg, 1969)
  Novel: *The Half Gods* (Houghton Mifflin, 1968)

Stanley Berne
Dept. of English, Eastern New Mexico U., Portales,
N.Mex. 88130
(505) 562-2332
  COL*, readings; speaks French
  Poetry: *The New Rubaiyat Of Stanley Berne, Vol. I*
  (American-Canadian, 1974)
  Fiction: *The Unconscious Victorious and Other
  Stories* (Horizon, 1973)

John Brandi
Box 356, Guadalupita, N.Mex. 87722
  ALL (EL*, JHS*, COL*), readings; has worked for
  N.Mex. PITS; is interested in working in prisons,
  drug rehabilitation centers & old age homes;
  speaks Spanish
  Poetry: *In A December Storm* (Tribal Press, 1975)
  Novella: *Narrow Gauge To Riobamba*
  (Christophers Press, 1975)

Mary Cable
206 McKenzie St., Santa Fe, N.Mex. 87501
(505) 982-1617
  ALL
  Fiction published in *The New Yorker*

Grey Cohoe
P.O. Box 852, Shiprock, N.Mex. 87420
  NPS; speaks Navajo; is American Indian
  Poetry published in *The Whispering Wind, Nimrod*
  Fiction published in *South Dakota Review;
  Culture, Encounters & Contrasts*

Stanley Crawford
P.O. Box 56, Dixon, N.Mex. 87527
(505) 579-4288
  COL*; speaks French
  Fiction: *Log of the S.S. The Mrs. Unguentine*
  (Alfred A. Knopf, 1972)

Cecil Dawkins
Box 2114, Taos, N.Mex. 87571
(505) 776-2672
  alternate address: Writer-in-Residence, Stephens
  College, Columbia, Mo. 65201, (314) 442-2211
  HS*, COL*; interested in working in prisons, drug
  rehabilitation centers, old age homes, with women's
  studies programs
  Novel: *The Live Goat* (Harper & Row, 1971)

Stanley Noyes
634 E. Garcia, Santa Fe, N.Mex. 87501
(505) 982-4067
  ALL (JHS*, HS*, COL*); has worked for N.Mex. PITS;
  speaks French
  Poetry: *Faces and Spirits* (The Sunstone
  Press, 1974)
  Novel: *Shadowbox* (Macmillan, 1970)

Bill Rane
310 Mt. Carmel, Socorro, N.Mex. 87801
(505) 835-1386
  NPS; speaks some Spanish
  Poetry & Prose: *Talfulano* (The Smith, 1975)

Frank Waters
Box 1127, Taos, N.Mex. 87571
(505) 776-2356
  NPS
  Novel: *Pike's Peak* (Swallow Press, 1971)

Arlene Zekowski
Dept. of English, Eastern New Mexico U., Portales,
N.Mex. 88130
(505) 562-2232
  COL*, readings; speaks French & Spanish, some Italian
  Poetry: *The Age of Iron* (American-Canadian, 1973)
  Novel: *Seasons of the Mind* (Horizon Press, 1973)

NEW YORK (OUTSIDE NEW YORK CITY)

Harry Barba
47 Hyde Blvd., Ballston Spa, N.Y. 12020
(518) 885-7397
  ALL (JHS*, HS*, COL*); speaks French, German
  & Armenian
  Novel: *For the Grape Season* (Macmillan, 1960)

Helen Barolini
33 Ellis Place, Ossining, New York 10652
  COL; speaks Italian, French, some Spanish
  Fiction published in *Cosmopolitan, Arizona Quarterly*

John Batki
208 Locksley Road, Syracuse, N.Y. 13224
(315) 446-6451
ALL (EL*, COL*), readings; has worked for N.Y. PITS
Poetry: *The Mad Shoemaker* (Toothpaste Press, 1973)
Fiction published in *Droll And Murderous Visions,
O. Henry Awards Anthology*

Joe David Bellamy
St. Lawrence U., Canton, N.Y. 13617
(315) 379-6191, 386-2866
ALL*, readings
Poetry published in *Paris Review, Iowa Review*
Fiction published in *Quartet, Center*

Audrey F. Borenstein
4 Henry Ct., New Paltz, N.Y. 12561
(914) 255-7333
readings; is interested in reading for older women's
groups and in working with groups exploring dreaming,
middle age, aging
Fiction published in *Ascent, Kansas Quarterly*

Joseph Bruchac, III
Greenfield Center, N.Y. 12833
(518) 584-1728
ALL*, readings; has worked for N.Y., Vt. PITS; is in-
terested in working in prisons, on Indian reserva-
tions; speaks German
Poetry: *Flow* (Cold Mountain Press, 1975)
Novel: *Road To Black Mountain* (Thorp Springs
Press, 1975)

Frederick Busch
Box 63, Poolville, N.Y. 13432
(315) 824-4262
COL*, readings; speaks French
Novel: *Manual Labor* (New Directions, 1974)

Hortense Calisher
Yaddo, Saratoga Springs, N.Y. 12866
(518) 584-0196, Ext. 0746 (winter) or Ext. 5491 (summer)
alternate address: 205 W. 57th St., New York,
N.Y. 10019, (212) PL7-9235
COL; is interested in working in prisons and drug
rehabilitation centers; speaks French and some German
Novel: *Herself* (Arbor House, 1972; Dell, 1973)

Kelly Cherry
c/o Mike Cherry, 64 Kensington Rd., Bronxville,
N.Y. 10708
COL*
Poetry published in *Carolina Quarterly,
Southern Poetry Review*
Novel: *Sick And Full of Burning* (Viking, 1974)

Gerald Cohen
80 Prospect Terr., East Rutherford, N.Y. 07073
(201) 933-8677, (201) 933-9239 or (212) 262-3584
JHS*, HS*, COL*, readings; has worked for N.J.
PITS; is interested in working in prisons, drug
rehabilitation centers, old age homes, with the
deaf & blind, & at teachers', librarians', &
writers' conferences; speaks French & some
Spanish & Hebrew
Fiction published in *The Small Pond Review,
Manhattan Mind*

Arthur Coleman
104 Searington Rd., Searingtown, N.Y. 11507
(516) 484-2391
COL*
Fiction: *A Case in Point* (Watermill, 1975)

Jack Dann
Box 555, Johnson City, N.Y. 13790
NPS
Fiction published in *New Worlds #5, Strange
Bedfellows*

George Davis
40 E. Sidney Ave., Mt. Vernon, N.Y. 10550
ALL; interested in working in prisons; is Black
Novel: *Coming Home* (Random House, 1972)

Nicholas Delbanco
RD 2, Spraguetown Rd., Greenwich, N.Y. 12834
(518) 692-7878
HS, COL*, readings; speaks French
Novel: *Small Rain* (Wm. Morrow, 1975)

Sigrid de Lima
408A Storms Rd., Valley Cottage, N.Y. 10989
(212) 358-6775
alternate address: c/o Russell & Volkening, Inc.,
551 Fifth Ave., New York, N.Y. 10017, (212) MU2-5340
NPS
Novel: *Oriane* (Harcourt Brace Jovanovich, 1968)

E.L. Doctorow
170 Broadview Ave., New Rochelle, N.Y. 10804
NPS
Novel: *Ragtime* (Random House, 1975)

M.D. Elevitch
Washington Spring Rd., Palisades, N.Y. 10964
(914) 359-2995
COL*, readings; speaks Italian & French
Novel: *Grips or, Efforts to Revive the Host*
(Grossman, 1972)

George P. Elliott
113 Dorset Rd., Syracuse, N.Y. 13210
(315) 475-6782
COL*, readings; has worked for N.Y. PITS
Poetry: *From the Berkeley Hills* (Harper & Row, 1969)
Novel: *Muriel* (E.P. Dutton, 1972)

Israel Emiot (Goldwasser)
c/o Pat Janus, 952 Whalen Rd., Penfield, N.Y. 14526
NPS; has worked for N.Y. PITS; speaks Yiddish, German,
Polish, Russian, Hebrew & Slavonic languages
Poetry published in *The Golden Chain, Treasury of
Jewish Poetry*
Short Stories: *My Yesterdays* (JCC of Greater
Rochester, 1973)

Carol Emshwiller
43 Red Maple Dr., Wantagh, N.Y. 11793
(516) 735-6688
HS, COL, readings; speaks some French
Short Stories: *Joy in Our Cause* (Harper & Row,
1974)

Raymond Federman
227 Depew Ave., Buffalo, N.Y. 14214
(716) 835-9611
COL*, readings; is bilingual writer (French & English)
Poetry: *Among the Beasts* (Millas-Martin, 1967)
and in *Westcoast Review, Evergreen Review*
Novel: *Double or Nothing* (Swallow Press, 1972)

Leslie A. Fiedler
154 Morris Ave., Buffalo, N.Y. 14214
(716) 838-4105
NPS; speaks Italian, French
Novel: *The Messengers Will Come No More* (Stein & Day, 1974)

Gregory Fitz Gerald
11 Dresser Rd., Box 784, Adams Basin, N.Y. 14410
(716) 352-4305
HS*, COL*; speaks German, French & Spanish
Fiction published in *Fiction International, Quest*

Joan Carole Hand
RR 3, Box 147-A, Rocky Point, N.Y. 11778
(516) 744-6160
alternate address: c/o Writers Unlimited, 113 Prince St., New York, N.Y. 10013, (212) 475-6810
ALL*; has worked for N.Y. & Pa. PITS
Poetry published in *Karamu, Three Rivers Quarterly*
Novella: *Your Witch* (Despa Press, 1973)

Edward Hannibal
118 Pantigo Rd., East Hampton, N.Y. 11937
(516) 324-9653
HS, COL
Fiction: *Dancing Man* (Simon & Schuster, 1973)

Carol Hebald
1400 Genesee St., Utica, N.Y. 13502
(315) 797-7749
alternate address: c/o June Halpern, 1423 W. 15th Ave., Hollywood, Fla. 33020
COL*, readings; speaks French and knows Latin
Poetry published in *Antioch Review, Massachusetts Review*
Fiction published in *North American Review*

Rose Graubart Ignatow
17th St. & Gardiner Ave., East Hampton, N.Y. 11937
(516) 324-4875
ALL (EL*)
Fiction published in *Best Short Stories of 1974, Confrontation*

Charles Johnson
65 Hagerman Landing, Rocky Point, N.Y. 11778
COL, readings; is Black
Novel: *Faith and the Good Thing* (Viking, 1974)

Robert Kelly
Bard College, Annandale-on-Hudson, N.Y. 12504
(914) 758-6549
COL*, readings
Poetry: *The Loom* (Black Sparrow Press, 1975)
Fiction: *Cities* (Frontier Press, 1972)

Konstantinos Lardas
68 Wakefield Ave., Yonkers, N.Y. 10704
(914) 237-1462
COL*, readings; speaks Modern Greek; is Greek
Poetry: *And In Him, Too; In Us* (U. of Michigan Generation Press, 1964)
Short Story: *A Tree of Man* (Hunter Press, 1968); also published in *The Best American Short Stories of 1973, South Dakota Review*

Clayton W. Lewis
24 Oak St., Geneseo, N.Y. 14454
(716) 243-0536
JHS, HS*, COL*; has worked for N.Y. PITS
Fiction published in *Transatlantic, Carolina Quarterly*

Herbert Lieberman
2 Apple Tree Close, Chappaqua, N.Y. 10514
Unavailable for readings; speaks German & Spanish
Fiction: *Brilliant Kids* (Macmillan, 1975)

David Lunde
1179 Central Ave., Dunkirk, N.Y. 14048
(716) 366-4771
ALL (JHS*, HS*, COL*); has worked for N.Y. PITS; speaks French
Poetry: *Sludge Gulper 1* (Basilisk Press, 1971)
Fiction published in *Galaxy, Whispers*

Alison Lurie
Dept. of English, Cornell University, Ithaca, N.Y. 14850
(607) 256-3492
COL*
Fiction: *The War Between the Tates* (Random House, 1974)

James McConkey
R.D. 1, Trumansburg, N.Y. 14886
(607) 387-9830
COL*, readings
Novel: *A Journey to Sahalin* (Coward, McCann & Geoghegan, 1971)

D. Keith Mano
Box 152, Cherry Hill Rd., Blooming Grove, N.Y. 10914
(914) 496-3186
HS, COL*, readings
Novel: *The Bridge* (Doubleday, 1973)

Eugene Mirabelli
29 Bennett Terr., Delmar, N.Y. 12054
COL*; speaks Italian
Novel: *No Resting Place* (Viking, 1972)

Willie Morris
Box 702, Bridgehampton, N.Y. 11932
NPS; speaks Spanish
Novel: *The Last of the Southern Girls* (Alfred A. Knopf, 1973)

Cynthia Ozick
34 Soundview St., New Rochelle, N.Y. 10805
readings
Fiction: *The Pagan Rabbi and Other Stories* (Alfred A. Knopf, 1971)

Kathrin Perutz
16 Avalon Rd., Great Neck, N.Y. 11021
(516) 482-3681
    COL; interested in working in prisons; speaks French,
German
    Fiction: *Mother is a Country* (Harcourt Brace
Jovanovich, 1970)

Robert Phillips
Cross River Rd., Katonah, N.Y. 10536
(914) 232-9209
    HS*, COL*, readings; speaks some German
    Poetry published in *The Paris Review, New York
Quarterly*
    Short Stories: *The Land of Lost Content*
(Vanguard, 1970)

Charles Plymell
Box 64, Cherry Valley, N.Y. 13320
(607) 264-3204
    ALL*; has worked for N.Y. PITS
    Poetry: *The Trashing of America* (Kulchur
Foundation, 1975)
    Fiction: *The Last of the Moccasins* (City
Lights, 1971)

Carlene Hatcher Polite
Dept. of English, SUNY at Buffalo, N.Y. 14209
    COL*; is Black
    Fiction: *Sister X and The Victims of Foul Play*
(Farrar, Straus & Giroux, 1975)

Susan Quist
Box 335, Cherry Valley, N.Y. 13320
    ALL*; has worked in Pa. PITS
    Poetry published in *Telephone, Penumbra*
    Novel: *Indecent Exposure* (Walker & Co., 1974;
New American Library, 1975)

Ishmael Reed
c/o Alan S. Walker, Program Corporation of America,
234 N. Central Ave., Hartsdale, N.Y. 10530
(914) 428-5840
    NPS
    Poetry: *A Secretary to the Spirits* (Nok
Publishers, 1975)
    Fiction: *The Last Days of Louisiana Red* (Random
House, 1974)

Joe Ribar
24 Allen St., Hudson, N.Y. 12534
(518) 828-4195
    ALL (HS*, COL*); has worked for N.Y. PITS
    Poetry: *The Book of the Buffalo* (Figtree, 1971)
    Fiction published in *The Carolina Quarterly,
Toothpaste*

Norma Rosen
11 Mereland Rd., New Rochelle, N.Y. 10804
(914) 576-3057
    COL*; speaks French
    Novel: *Touching Evil* (Harcourt Brace, 1969;
Popular Library, 1972)

Arthur J. Roth
Box A/D, Amagansett, N.Y. 11930
(516) 324-9683
    COL*; speaks some Spanish & French
    Novel: *A Terrible Beauty* (Farrar, Straus
& Giroux, 1958; Popular Library, 1973)

Henry H. Roth
288 Piermont Ave., S. Nyack, N.Y. 10960
(914) 358-2399
    COL, readings
    Fiction published in *Making A Break, Story
Quarterly*

Berton Roueche
Stony Hill Rd., Amagansett, N.Y. 11930
(516) 267-3822
    HS, COL*
    Novel: *Feral* (Harper & Row, 1974)

Ed Sanders
Box 24, Lake Hill, N.Y. 12448
    alternate address: c/o Brandt & Brandt, 101 Park
Ave., New York, N.Y. 10017, (212) 683-5890
    readings
    Poetry: *Egyptian Hieroglyphics* (Institute of
Further Studies, 1973)
    Fiction: *Shards of God* (Grove Press, 1970)

Pamela Sargent
Box 586, Johnson City, N.Y. 13790
    NPS; speaks some French
    Novel: *Cloned Lives* (Fawcett-Gold Medal, 1975)

Wilfrid Sheed
Rysam and High Sts., Sag Harbor, N.Y. 11963
    NPS
    Novel: *The Cure* (Farrar, Straus & Giroux, 1973)

Louis Simpson
P.O. Box 91, Port Jefferson, N.Y. 11777
    readings; speaks French & Italian
    Poetry: *Adventures of the Letter I* (Harper &
Row, 1971)
    Fiction: *Riverside Drive* (Atheneum, 1962)

Muriel Spanier
7 Ridge Dr. E., Great Neck, N.Y. 11021
(516) 487-6429
    COL*, readings; speaks French
    Fiction published in *Colorado Quarterly,
Saturday Evening Post*

Jean Stafford
929 Fireplace Rd., East Hampton, N.Y. 11937
    Readings only
    Short Stories: *The Collected Stories of Jean
Stafford* (Farrar, Straus & Giroux, 1969)

Barry Targan
46 Burgoyne St., Schuylerville, N.Y. 12871
(518) 695-3586
    ALL*; has worked for N.Y. & Vt. PITS
    Poetry: *Thoreau Stalks the Land Disguised as a
Father* (Greenfield Review Press, 1975)
    Short Stories: *Harry Belten and the Mendelssohn
Violin Concerto* (U. of Iowa Press, 1975)

Robert M. Ward
Box 102, Hobart College, Geneva, N.Y. 14456
(315) 789-0530
    ALL; is interested in working in prisons, drug rehabi-
litation centers, old age homes
    Fiction: *Shedding Skin* (Harper & Row, 1972)

David Warren
514 Edgewood Pl., Ithaca, N.Y. 14850
(607) 273-1283
    NPS
    Novel: *The World According to Two-Feathers*
    (Ithaca House, 1973)

Hilma Wolitzer
11 Ann Dr., Syosset, N.Y. 11791
(516) 921-1328
    ALL (JHS*, HS*, COL*); is interested in working in
    prisons, drug rehabilitation centers and old age
    homes
    Novel: *Ending* (Wm. Morrow, 1974; Bantam, 1975)

George Zebrowski
Box 586, Johnson City, N.Y. 13790
(607) 797-9211
    HS*, COL*; speaks Polish
    Fiction: *Star Web* (Harlequin, 1975)

NEW YORK CITY

Edward Abbey
c/o Don Congdon, Harold Matson Co., 22 E. 40th St.,
New York, N.Y. 10016
(212) 679-4490
    COL*; has worked in Ariz.-N.Mex. Indian schools;
    speaks Spanish
    Novel: *The Monkey Wrench Gang* (Lippincott, 1975)

Walter Abish
5 E. 3 St., New York, N.Y. 10003
(212) 982-3074
    HS*, COL*, readings; is interested in working in
    prisons, libraries, community centers; speaks German
    Poetry: *Duel Site* Tibor de Nagy Editions, 1970)
    Novella & Short Stories: *Minds Meet* (New
    Directions, 1975)

Renata Adler
c/o The New Yorker Magazine, 25 W. 43 St., New York,
N.Y. 10036
(212) OX5-1414
    NPS; speaks German, French, Italian
    Fiction published in *The New Yorker, The O'Henry
    Prize Collection*

Mimi Ariel Albert
Box 389 Cooper Station, New York, N.Y. 10003
(212) 473-5468
    COL*, readings; is interested in working in prisons,
    drug rehabilitation centers, old age homes, and in
    working with women; speaks French & Italian
    Stories & Poetry: *The Small Singer* (Shameless
    Hussy Press, 1975)

Bill Amidon
532 E. 5 St., New York, N.Y. 10009
(212) OR3-2169
    alternate address: c/o George Blecher, 125 E. 93 St.,
    New York, N.Y. 10028, (212) 427-4620
    ALL; is interested in working in prisons and
    drug rehabilitation centers
    Novel: *Charge..!* (Bobbs-Merrill, 1971)

Roger Angell
1261 Madison Ave., New York, N.Y. 10028
(212) LE4-0715
    NPS
    Stories: *The Stone Arbor* (Viking, 1962)

Charles Angoff
140 W. 86 St., Apt. 14B, New York, N.Y. 10024
(212) TR4-3605
    COL*; is interested in working in old age homes;
    speaks Yiddish
    Poetry: *Prayers At Midnight* (Manyland Books,
    1971)
    Novel: *Mid-Century* (A.S. Barnes & Co., 1974)

Frieda Arkin
c/o Fox Chase Agency, 419 E. 57 St., New York, N.Y.
10022
    HS, COL
    Fiction: *The Dorp* (Dial Press, 1969)

Sheila Ascher (AscherStraus)
176B 123rd St., Rockaway Park, N.Y. 11694
(212) 474-6547
    ALL; is interested in working with experimental
    groups & women & in mounting "environmental"
    fictions in galleries, museums, universities
    All work is in collaboration with Dennis Straus
    Fiction published in *Aphra, The Paris Review*

Isaac Asimov
10 W. 66 St., Apt. 33-A, New York, N.Y. 10023
(212) 362-1564
    readings (high fee)
    Short Stories: *Tales Of The Black Widowers*
    (Doubleday, 1974)

Louis Auchincloss
1111 Park Ave., New York, N.Y. 10028
(212) FI8-3723
    NPS
    Novel: *The Partners* (G.K. Hall, 1974; Paperback
    Library, 1975)

Kofi Awoonor
c/o Loretta Barrett, Doubleday & Co., 277 Park Ave.,
New York, N.Y. 10017, (212) 953-4561
    HS, COL; speaks Ewe, French; is Black
    Fiction: *Night Of My Blood* (Doubleday, 1971)

James Baldwin
137 W. 71 St., New York, N.Y. 10023
    NPS; is Black
    Novel: *If Beal Street Could Talk* (Dell, 1973)

Lefty Barretto
c/o Aquarius, 273 E. 10 St., New York, N.Y. 10009
(212) 777-0248
    HS*, COL*, readings; is interested in working in
    prisons; speaks Spanish; is Puerto Rican
    Novel: *Jibaro, A Puerto Rican Story* (New America
    Library, 1974)

Donald Barthelme
113 W. 11 St., New York, N.Y. 10014
    COL
    Fiction: *The Dead Father* (Farrar, Straus &
    Giroux, 1975)

Jonathan Baumbach
307 Sterling Place, Brooklyn, N.Y. 11238
(212) 638-7328
    readings
    Novel: *Reruns* (Fiction Collective, 1974)

Michael Benedikt
315 W. 98 St., New York, N.Y. 10025
(212) MO6-8878
  COL*, readings; speaks some French
  Poetry: *Sky* (Wesleyan U. Press, 1969)
  Prose Poems & Fictions: *Mole Notes* (Wesleyan U.
  Press, 1971)

Hal Bennett
c/o Owen Caster, William Morris Agency, 1350 Ave. of
the Americas, New York, N.Y. 10019
(212) JU6-5100
  alternate address: 170 S. Park St., #1, Hackensack,
  N.J. 07601
  NPS
  Fiction: *Lord of Dark Places* (Bantam, 1971)

Thomas Berger
c/o Harold Matson Co., 22 E. 40 St., New York, N.Y.
10016, (212) 679-4490
  readings
  Fiction: *Sneaky People* (Simon & Schuster, 1975)

Deirdre Levinson Bergson
220 W. 93 St., Apt. 12AB, New York, N.Y. 10025
(212) 799-6254
  COL*; is interested in working in prisons
  Novel: *Five Years (Andre Deutsch, 1966)*

Eleanor Bergstein
425 Riverside Dr., New York, N.Y. 10025
(212) 866-0923
  HS, COL; is interested in working in prisons and
  with women's groups; speaks Italian, some French
  Novel: *Advancing Paul Newman* (Viking, 1974)

Kenneth Bernard
788 Riverside Dr., New York, N.Y. 10032
(212) WA6-6579
  readings
  Short Fiction Collection: *Two Stories* (The
  Perishable Press, 1973)

Lebert Bethune
110 W. 96 St., Apt. 16C, New York, N.Y. 10025
(212) 866-8059
  ALL (COL*); speaks French; is Black
  Poetry: *Kites & Other Flyers* (U. of West Indies
  Press, 1975)
  Fiction published in *Best Short Stories by Negro
  Writers*

Ann Birstein
440 West End Ave., Apt. 16B, New York, N.Y. 10024
(212) 873-2160
  HS*, COL*; has worked for N.Y. PITS; speaks French,
  some Yiddish
  Novel: *Dickie's List (Coward McCann & Geoghegan,
  1973)*

George Blecher
125 E. 93 St., New York, N.Y. 10028
(212) 427-4620
  ALL (COL*), readings; speaks French, Danish, Swedish,
  Norwegian
  Fiction published in *Survival Prose, New American
  Review*

Florence Bonime
37 Washington Sq. W., New York, N.Y. 10011
(212) 477-3703
  COL*; speaks some French, some Spanish
  Fiction: *A Thousand Imitations* (Harcourt, Brace,
  Jovanovich, 1967)

John Bowers
200 Waverly Pl., New York, N.Y. 10014
  alternate address: c/o Georges Borchardt, Inc.,
  145 E. 52nd St., New York, N.Y. 10022,
  (212) PL3-5785
  HS, COL; interested in working in prisons and
  old age homes
  Novel: *No More Reunions* (E.P. Dutton, 1973)

Kay Boyle
c/o A. Watkins Agency, 77 Park Ave., New York,
N.Y. 10016
(212) 532-0080
  NPS; speaks French & German
  Poetry: *Testament for My Students* (Doubleday,1970)
  Fiction: *The Underground Woman* (Doubleday, 1974)

Millen Brand
242 E. 77 St., New York, N.Y. 10021
(212) TR9-0034
  readings; speaks French, Spanish
  Poetry: *Local Lives* (Clarkson Potter, 1975)
  Fiction: *Savage Sleep* (Crown Publishers, 1968)

Maeve Brennan
c/o Russell & Volkening, Inc., 555 Fifth Ave.,
New York, N.Y. 10017
(212) 682-5340
  NPS
  Short Stories: *Christmas Eve* (Scribner's, 1974)

Richard P. Brickner
245 E. 72 St., New York, N.Y. 10021
(212) RE4-1675
  readings
  Fiction: *Bringing Down The House* (Scribners,
  1972)

Harold Brodkey
255 W. 88 St., New York, N.Y. 10024
  COL, readings
  Short Stories: *First Love & Other Sorrows*
  (Dial Press, 1958)
  Fiction published in *The New Yorker, Esquire*

Claude Brown
c/o New American Library, 1301 Ave. of the Americas,
New York, N.Y. 10019, (212) 956-3800
  COL; is Black
  Novel: *Manchild In The Promised Land* (Macmillan,
  1965; New American Library, 1971)

Kenneth H. Brown
150 74 St., Brooklyn, N.Y. 11209
(212) TE6-1116
  COL*; speaks French
  Novel *The Narrows* (Dial Press, 1970)

Wesley Brown
538 W. 148th St., #1B, New York, N.Y. 10031
(212) 234-9269
  ALL*; interested in working in prisons, drug rehabili-
  tation centers and old age homes; is Black
  Poetry published in *Black Creation, Broadway Boogie*
  Fiction published in *Black Creation, We Be
  Word Sorcerers*

Michael Brownstein
33 St. Mark's Pl., New York, N.Y. 10003
(212) 477-1232
  HS*, COL*; has worked for N.Y., W.Va. PITS; speaks
  French
  Prose Poems: *Brainstorms* (Bobbs-Merrill, 1971)
  Novel: *Country Cousins* (G. Braziller, 1974)

Cynthia Buchanan
1160 Third Ave., #8A, New York, N.Y. 10021
(212) 744-3517
  HS, COL, readings; is interested in doing creative
  dramatics in prisons, mental health institutions and
  with children; speaks Spanish
  Novel: *Maiden* (Wm. Morrow, 1972)

Frederick Buechner
c/o Atheneum, 122 E. 42 St., New York, N.Y. 10017
(212) 661-4500
  readings; speaks French, some Russian, some German
  Novel: *Love Feast* (Atheneum, 1974)

William S. Burroughs
77 Franklin St., or Box 842, Canal St. Station, New
York, N.Y. 10013
(212) 431-4153
  alternate address: c/o James Grauerholz, 306 E. 6 St.,
  Apt. 3, New York, N.Y. 10003, (212) 674-7384
  readings; speaks Spanish, French
  Filmscript As Fiction: *The Last Words Of Dutch
  Schultz* (Viking Press, 1975)

William S. Burroughs, Jr.
c/o E.P. Dutton, 201 Park Ave. S., New York, N.Y. 10003
(212) OR4-5900
  NPS
  Novel: *Kentucky Ham* (E.P. Dutton, 1973)

Steve Cannon
285 E. 3 St., New York, N.Y. 10009
(212) 674-2426
  COL*, readings; has worked for Pa. PITS; speaks
  German
  Fiction: *Groove, Bang & Jive Around* (Olympia
  Press, 1969)

Truman Capote
870 United Nations Plaza, New York, N.Y. 10017
  NPS
  Novel: *The Dogs Bark: Private Places & Public
  People* (Random House, 1973)

Don Carpenter
c/o E.P. Dutton & Co., 201 Park Ave. S., New York,
N.Y. 10003, (212) OR4-5900
  NPS
  Novel: *Getting Off* (E.P. Dutton, 1971; Pocket
  Books, 1972)

Rafael E. Catala
164-10 84th Ave., Jamaica, N.Y. 11432
  COL, readings; interested in working in prisons;
  speaks Spanish; is Cuban
  Poetry: *Circulo Cuadrado* (Anaya-Las Americas,
  1974)
  Fiction published in *Romanica, Aqui*

Diana Chang
190 E. 72 St., New York, N.Y. 10021
  NPS; is Asian-American
  Poetry published in *Asian American Heritage, New
  York Quarterly*
  Fiction: *Eye to Eye* (Harper & Row, 1974)

Jerome Charyn
39 W. 67th St., #802, New York, N.Y. 10023
(212) 595-8479
  alternate address: c/o Martin Smith, 428 W. 89th St.,
  New York, N.Y. 10028, (212) 348-3120
  COL*
  Novel: *Blue Eyes* (Simon & Schuster, 1975)

Robert Chatain
345 Riverside Dr., New York, N.Y. 10025
(212) 865-3236
  alternate address: c/o Lynn Nesbit, International
  Creative Management, 40 W. 57 St., New York,
  N.Y. 10019, (212) 556-5600
  NPS
  Poetry published in *Poetry, New American Review,
  Chicago Review*
  Fiction published in *Playboy, New American Review*

John Cheever
c/o Alfred A. Knopf, Inc., 201 E. 50 St., New York,
N.Y. 10022
(212) 751-2600
  NPS
  Fiction: *World of Apples* (Alfred A. Knopf, 1973)

Dan Cheifetz
865 West End Ave., New York, N.Y. 10025
  ALL; speaks some French and Spanish
  Fiction: *Theatre In My Head* (Little,
  Brown, 1972)

Merle Molofsky-Chianese
12 Crown St., Brooklyn, N.Y. 11225
  COL*
  Fiction: *Grail Green,* anthologized in
  Storefront (Aware Press, 1972)

Arthur A(llen) Cohen
160 E. 70 St., New York, N.Y. 10021
(212) 249-2618
  NPS; speaks French, Hebrew
  Fiction: *In The Days Of Simon Stern* (Random
  House, 1973)

Marvin Cohen
513 E. 13 St., Apt. 8, New York, N.Y. 10009
(212) 533-2362
  HS*, COL*, readings; has worked for N.Y. PITS
  Prose Poems: *The Monday Rhetoric of the Love
  Club & Other Parables* (New Directions, 1973)

Evan S. Connell
c/o Elizabeth McKee, Harold Matson Co., 22 E. 40 St.,
New York, N.Y. 10016, (212) 679-4490
    NPS
    Novel: *The Connoisseur* (Alfred A. Knopf, 1974)

Kent Cooper
118 Ridge St., New York, N.Y. 10002
(212) 228-5632
    NPS
    Fiction published in *Saturday Evening Post,
    Red Clay Reader*

Robert Coover
c/o E.P. Dutton & Co., 201 Park Ave. S., New York,
N.Y. 10003
(212) 674-5900
    alternate address: c/o Georges Borchardt, 145 E.
    52nd St., New York, N.Y. 10022, (212) PL3-5785
    Readings only; speaks Spanish, some French and German
    Stories: *Pricksongs & Descants* (E.P. Dutton,
    1969; New American Library, 1970)

James Gould Cozzens
c/o Harcourt Brace Jovanovich, 757 Third Ave.,
New York, N.Y. 10017
(212) 754-3100
    NPS
    Novel: *Morning, Noon & Night* (Harcourt
    Brace Jovanovich, 1968)

Gwen Cravens
33 W. 95 St., New York, N.Y. 10025
(212) 865-1282
    HS, COL; is interested in working in drug rehabilita-
    tion centers; speaks German, French & Spanish
    Fiction published in *In Youth, The New Yorker*

Max Crawford
c/o Curtis Brown, Ltd., 60 E. 56 St., New York,
N.Y. 10022, (212) PL5-4200
    NPS
    Novel: *The Backslider* (Farrar, Straus & Giroux,
    1976)

Thomas Curley
429 E. 80 St., New York, N.Y. 10021
    COL, readings
    Fiction: *Nowhere Man* (Holt, Rinehart & Winston,
    1967)

Edward Dahlberg
c/o Nicholas Ellison, Thomas Y. Crowell Publishers,
666 Fifth Ave., New York, N.Y. 10019
(212) 489-3433
    NPS
    Novel: *The Olive of Minerva* (Thomas Y. Crowell,
    1976)

L.J. Davis
138A Dean St., Brooklyn, N.Y. 11217
(212) 625-3365
    HS*, COL*, readings; has worked for N.Y. PITS
    Novel: *Walking Small* (George Braziller, 1974)

Fielding Dawson
49 E. 19 St., New York, N.Y. 10003
(212) 254-4076
    HS, COL*
    Short Stories: *The Man Who Changed Overnight*
    (Black Sparrow Press, 1975)

Samuel R. Delany
c/o Henry Morrison, Inc., 58 W. 10 St., New York,
N.Y. 10011
(212) 260-7600
    NPS
    Novel: *Dhalgren* (Bantam Books, 1975)

Don Delillo
145 E. 37 St., New York, N.Y. 10016
    Not available for readings
    Novel: *Great Jones Street* (Houghton Mifflin,
    1973)

Peter DeVries
c/o A. Watkins Agency, 77 Park Ave., New York,
N.Y. 10016
(212) LE2-0080
    NPS
    Novel: *The Glory of the Hummingbird* (Little,
    Brown 1974)

Joan Didion
c/o Farrar, Straus & Giroux, 19 Union Sq. W., New York,
N.Y. 10003
(212) 741-6900
    NPS
    Novel: *Play It As It Lays* (Farrar, Straus &
    Giroux, 1970; Bantam Books, 1971)

May Dikeman
70 Irving Pl., New York, N.Y. 10003
(212) GR5-4533
    NPS
    Novel: *The Devil We Know* (Atlantic Monthly
    Press, 1973)

Stephen Dixon
5 W. 75 St., New York, N.Y. 10023
(212) SC4-9039
    COL*
    Fiction published in *Story Quarterly, Making A Break*

Owen Dodson
350 West 51 St., No. 17B, New York, N.Y. 10019
    ALL; is interested in working in prisons & drug
    rehabilitation centers; is Black
    Poetry: *Confession Stone* (Paul Breman Ltd., 1971)
    Fiction: *Boy at the Window* (Farrar, Straus &
    Giroux, 1951)

Roslyn Drexler
131 Greene St., New York, N.Y. 10012
    COL
    Novel: *That Cosmopolitan Girl* (M. Evans
    & Co., 1975)

Helen Duberstein
463 West St., #904D, New York, N.Y. 10014
    EL*, COL*, readings; is interested in working in
    prisons, drug rehabilitation centers, old age homes,
    with disturbed children
    Poetry: *The Human Dimension* (Gnosis, 1971)
    Fiction published in *Ingenue, Confrontation*

Marilyn Durham
c/o Ann Elmo, 52 Vanderbilt Ave., New York, N.Y. 10017
(212) 686-9282
    NPS
    Novel: *Dutch Uncle* (Harcourt Brace Jovanovich,
    1974)

Martin S. Dworkin
129 E. 17 St., New York, N.Y. 10003
(212) 254-2960
  HS, COL*; speaks French
  Poetry published in *Pocket Poetry, Transatlantic Review*
  Fiction published in *Transatlantic Review, Event*

Helene Dworzan
463 West St., New York, N.Y. 10014
(212) 242-8077
  ALL; speaks French, German & Yiddish
  Novel: *Le Temps de la Chrysalide* (Rene Julliard, 1957)

John Ehle
c/o Candida Donadio & Associates, 111 W. 57 St., New York, N.Y. 10019
(212) 757-5076
  NPS
  Novel: *The Changing of the Guard* (Random House, 1975)

Ralph Ellison
c/o Owen Laster, Wm. Morris Agency, 1350 Ave. of the Americas, New York, N.Y. 10019
(212) 586-5100
  NPS
  Fiction: *Invisible Man* (Modern Library, 1963)

Richard Elman
419 W. 115 St., New York, N.Y. 10025
(212) 662-8771
  COL*, readings; speaks French & Spanish
  Fiction: *Crossing Over & Other Stories* (Scribner's, 1973)

Kenward Elmslie
104 Greenwich Ave., New York, N.Y. 10011
(212) WA9-5777
  JHS, HS, readings; speaks French
  Poetry: *Circus Nerves* (Black Sparrow Press, 1972)
  Novel: *The Orchid Stories* (Doubleday, 1973)

Leslie Epstein
221 W. 82 St., New York, N.Y. 10024
(212) 799-9275
  COL*; is interested in working in prisons
  Novel: *P.D. Kimerakov* (Little, Brown, 1975)

F.M. Esfandiary
Box 61, Village Station, New York, N.Y. 10014
(212) 989-2827
  NPS; is interested in working in prisons; speaks French, Persian, Arabic
  Novel: *Identity Card* (Grove Press, 1966)

David Evanier
Box 705, Grand Central Station, New York, N.Y. 10017
(212) 677-9650, Ext. 306
  alternate address: c/o Seymour Evanier, 34-15 74th St., Jackson Heights, N.Y. 10072
  HS, COL*, readings; is interested in working in old age homes
  Novel: *The Swinging Headhunter* (November House, 1973)

Frederick Exley
c/o Lynn Nesbit, International Creative Management, 40 W. 57 St., New York, N.Y. 10019
(212) 556-5600
  NPS
  Novel: *Pages From A Cold Island* (Random House, 1975)

James T. Farrell
308 E. 79 St., New York, N.Y. 10021
  NPS
  Poetry: *Collected Poems* (Fleet, 1965)
  Fiction: *Judith and Other Stories* (Doubleday, 1973)

Irvin Faust
417 Riverside Dr., New York, N.Y. 10025
  HS, COL
  Novel: *A Star in the Family* (Doubleday, 1975)

Ross Feld
570 Westminster Rd., Brooklyn, N.Y. 11230
(212) 287-5201
  COL*
  Poetry: *Plum Poems* (Jargon Society, 1972)
  Fiction: *Years Out* (Alfred A. Knopf, 1973)

Harold Flender
37 Riverside Dr., New York, N.Y. 10023
(212) 787-1425
  NPS; speaks French
  Novel: *To Be* (Manor Books, 1973)

Shelby Foote
c/o Dial Press, 1 Dag Hammarskjold Plaza, 245 E. 47 St., New York, N.Y. 10017
(212) 832-7300
  NPS
  Fiction: *Three Novels* (Dial, 1964)

Paula Fox
306 Clinton St., Brooklyn, N.Y. 11201
  NPS; speaks Spanish
  Fiction: *The Slave Dancer* (Bradbury Press, 1973)

B.H. Friedman
435 E. 52 St., New York, N.Y. 10022
  COL*, readings; speaks some French
  Novel: *Almost a Life* (Viking, 1975)

Bruce Jay Friedman
20 E. 63 St., New York, N.Y. 10021
  alternate address: c/o Candida Donadio, 111 W. 57 St., New York, N.Y. 10019, (212) 757-5076
  COL
  Novel: *Stern* (Pocket Books, 1970)

Sanford Friedman
37 W. 12 St., New York, N.Y. 10011
(212) 929-4184
  COL
  Novellas: *Still Life* (Saturday Review Press Dutton, 1975)

William Gaddis
c/o Candida Donadio & Associates, 111 W. 57 St., New York, N.Y. 10019
(212) 757-5076
  NPS
  Novel: *J R* (Alfred A. Knopf, 1975)

Kenneth Gangemi
211 E. 5 St., New York, N.Y. 10003
(212) 777-4795
NPS
Poetry: *Lydia* (Black Sparrow Press, 1970)
Novel: *Olt* (Grossman, 1969)

Leonard Gardner
c/o Robert Lescher, 155 E. 71 St., New York, N.Y. 10021
(212) 249-7600
NPS
Novel: *Fat City* (Farrar, Straus & Giroux, 1969;
Dell, 1972)

Martha Gellhorn
c/o Cyrilly Abels, 119 W. 57 St., New York, N.Y. 10019
(212) 247-6438
NPS
Novel: *The Lowest Trees Have Tops* (Dodd, Mead,
1969)

Brendan Gill
c/o The New Yorker, 25 W. 43 St., New York, N.Y. 10036
(212) OX5-1414
NPS
Short Stories: *Ways of Loving* (Harcourt
Brace Jovanovich, 1974)

Penelope Gilliat
c/o The New Yorker, 25 W. 43 St., New York, N.Y. 10036
(212) OX5-1414
NPS
Novel: *Unholy Fools* (Viking, 1973)

Daniela Gioseffi
276 Henry St., Brooklyn, N.Y. 11201
(212) 624-3348
alternate address: c/o Richard J. Kearney, 3413
Avenue H, Brooklyn, N.Y. 11210
ALL*; has worked for N.Y. PITS; is interested in
working in prisons, drug rehabilitation centers, old
age homes; is a multi-media & visual writer
Poetry published in *Rising Tides* & *Woman:
The New Voice*
Fiction published in *MS.* & *Fiction International*

Len Giovannitti
c/o Robert Lescher, 155 E. 71 St., New York, N.Y. 10021
(212) 249-7600
NPS
Novel: *The Man Who Won the Medal of Honor*
(Random House, 1973)

Joanna Glass
c/o Lucy Kroll, 390 West End Ave., New York, N.Y. 10023
(212) TR7-0627
NPS
Novel: *Reflections on a Mountain Summer* (Alfred
A. Knopf, 1974)

Julian Gloag
784 Columbus Ave., #16E, New York, N.Y. 10025
alternate address: 4 Place du 18 Juin, 1940, Paris,
France 75006
COL*; speaks French
Novel: *A Woman of Character* (Random House, 1973)

Gail Godwin
c/o Paul R. Reynolds Inc., 12 E. 41 St., New York,
N.Y. 10017, (212) 689-8711
COL*
Novel: *The Odd Woman* (Alfred A. Knopf, 1974)

Gerald Jay Goldberg
c/o Georges Borchardt, Inc., 145 E. 52 St., New York,
N.Y. 10022
(212) PL3-5785
COL*, readings; speaks French & Spanish
Short Stories: *126 Days of Continuous Sunshine*
(Dial, 1972)

Alan Goldfein
c/o James Landis, Wm. Morrow & Co., 105 Madison Ave.,
New York, N.Y. 10016
(212) 889-3050
NPS
Fiction: *Heads: A Metafictional History of Western
Civilization* (Wm. Morrow, 1973)

William Goldman
c/o Harcourt Brace Jovanovich, 757 Third Ave., New
York, N.Y. 10017
(212) 754-3100
NPS
Fiction: *Wigger* (Harcourt Brace Jovanovich, 1974)

Lois Gould
144 East End Ave., New York, N.Y. 10028
alternate address: c/o Lynn Nesbit, International
Creative Management, 40 W. 57 St., New York, N.Y.
10019, (212) 556-5600
HS, COL, readings
Novel: *Final Analysis* (Random House, 1974;
Avon, 1975)

William Goyen
277 West End Ave., New York, N.Y. 10023
(212) 877-9397
COL*; speaks French & Spanish
Fiction: *The Collected Stories Of William Goyen*
(Doubleday, 1975)

Robert Granat
c/o Simon & Schuster, 630 Fifth Ave., New York,
N.Y. 10020, (212) CI5-6400
NPS
Fiction: *Regensis* (Simon & Schuster, 1973)

Hannah Green
52 Barrow St., New York, N.Y. 10014
(212) CH3-3070
Readings only; is interested in giving short-term
college workshops
Novel: *The Dead of the House* (Doubleday, 1972)

Antoni Gronowicz
132 E. 82 St., New York, N.Y. 10028
(212) 288-6479
COL*; speaks French & Polish
Poetry published in *The Nation, Cambridge Review*
Novel: *The Hookmen* (Dodd, Mead, 1973)

Vertamae Grosvenor
311 W. 97 St., Apt. 2W, New York, N.Y. 10025
(212) 749-2824
alternate address: c/o Ron Hobbs, Agent, 211 W.
58 St., New York, N.Y. 10017, (212) 687-1417
EL*, HS*, COL*; has worked for N.Y. PITS; is
interested in working in prisons & old age homes;
speaks French & Gullah; is Afro-American
Poetry: *Plain Brown Rapper* (Doubleday, 1975)
Fiction published in *Essence, Redbook*

A.B. Guthrie, Jr.
c/o Brandt & Brandt, 101 Park Ave., New York,
N.Y. 10017
(212) MU3-5890
NPS
Fiction: *The Last Valley* (Houghton Mifflin, 1975)

Joan Haggerty
22 E. 89 St., New York, N.Y. 10028
(212) 831-9224
HS, COL, readings; is interested in psychodrama
for children & adults & in working with women
Fiction: *Daughters of the Moon* (Bobbs-
Merrill, 1971)

Isidore Haiblum
160 W. 77 St., New York, N.Y. 10024
(212) 595-1538
COL; speaks Yiddish
Novel: *The Wilk Are Among Us* (Doubleday,
1975)

Nancy Hallinan
276 Riverside Dr., New York, N.Y. 10025
(212) 222-6936
ALL (JHS*)
Novel: *A Voice From the Wings* (Alfred A.
Knopf, 1965)

Peter Handke
c/o Kurt Bernheim, 575 Madison Ave., New York,
N.Y. 10022
(212) 753-5320
NPS
Novel: *Short Letter, Long Farewell* (Farrar,
Straus & Giroux, 1974)

Curtis Harnack
205 W. 57 St., New York, N.Y. 10019
Readings only
Memoir-Novel: *We Have All Gone Away* (Doubleday,
1973)

Julie Hayden
78 W. 11 St., New York, N.Y. 10011
NPS
Fiction published in *The New Yorker*

Shirley Hazzard
200 E. 66 St., New York, N.Y. 10021
NPS; is interested in reform of international
organizations; speaks Italian & French
Fiction: *The Bay of Noon* (Atlantic-Little, Brown, 1970)

Robert Heinlein
c/o Lurton Blassingame, 60 E. 42 St., New York,
N.Y. 10017
(212) 682-3020
NPS
Novel: *Time Enough For Love* (G.P. Putnam,
1973; paperback, Berkley Publishers, 1974)

Joseph Heller
390 West End Ave., New York, N.Y. 10024
NPS
Novel: *Something Happened* (Alfred A. Knopf,
1974)

James Leo Herlihy
c/o Jay Garon, Apt. 17D, 415 Central Park W.,
New York, N.Y. 10025
NPS
Novel: *Season of the Witch* (Simon & Schuster,
1971)

John Hersey
c/o Alfred A. Knopf, Inc., 201 E. 50 St., New York,
N.Y. 10022
(212) 751-2600
NPS
Fiction: *The President* (Alfred A. Knopf, 1975)

Carol Hill
52 W. 9 St., New York, N.Y. 10011
HS, COL
Fiction: *Let's Fall in Love* (Random House,
1974; paperback, Ballantine Books, 1975)

Chester Himes
c/o Roslyn Targ Agency, 325 E. 57 St., New York,
N.Y. 10022
(212) 753-9810
NPS
Novel: *The Real Cool Killers* (New American
Library, 1975)

Edward Hoagland
463 West St., New York, N.Y. 10014
(212) 691-6177
COL*
Essays: *Walking the Dead Diamond River*
(Random House, 1973)

Sandra Hochman
180 E. 79 St., New York, N.Y. 10021
(212) 988-7825
ALL; is interested in working with women's groups;
speaks French & Spanish
Poetry: *Futures* (Viking, 1974)
Fiction: *Walking Papers* (Viking, 1970)

Stanley Hoffman
c/o Sterling Lord, 660 Madison Ave., New York,
N.Y. 10021
(212) 751-2533
NPS
Novel: *Solomon's Temple* (Viking, 1974)

Spencer Holst
463 West St., Apt. 313C, New York, N.Y. 10014
(212) 929-5770
Readings only
Prose Poems published in *America, A Prophecy*
& *Red Crow*
Fiction: *Language of Cats & Other Stories*
(McCall Publishing, 1971; Avon, 1973)

Israel Horovitz
7 W. 84 St., New York, N.Y. 10024
alternate address: c/o Sabier Agency, Inc. 667
Madison Ave., New York, N.Y. 10021, (212) 838-484
COL*, readings; speaks French
Poetry: *Spider Poems & Other Writings* (Harper
& Row, 1974)
Novel: *Cappella* (Harper & Row, 1973)

William Humphrey
c/o William Koshland, Editorial Dept., Alfred A. Knopf,
201 E. 50 St., New York, N.Y. 10022
(212) 751-2600
   NPS
   Novel: *Proud Flesh* (Alfred A. Knopf, 1973)

Evan Hunter
c/o Scott Meredith, 580 Fifth Ave., New York,
N.Y. 10036
(212) 245-5500
   NPS
   Novel: *Streets of Gold* (Harper & Row, 1975)

Robert Hutchinson
87 Barrow St., Apt. 2F, New York, N.Y. 10014
(212) 924-1437
   COL*
   Poetry: *Standing Still While Traffic Moved About
   Me* (Eakins Press, 1971)
   Fiction published in *Harper's, Southwest Review*

Charles Israel
c/o Simon & Schuster, 630 Fifth Ave., New York,
N.Y. 10020
(212) CI5-6400
   NPS
   Fiction: *Hostages* (Simon & Schuster, 1966)

Peter Israel
c/o Georges Borchardt, Inc., 145 E. 52 St., New York,
N.Y. 10022
(212) 753-5785
   NPS
   Novel: *Hush Money* (Thomas Y. Crowell, 1974)

Elizabeth Janeway
15 E. 80 St., New York, N.Y. 10021
   alternate address: c/o Lordly & Dame (Lecture Agent),
   51 Church St., Boston, Mass. 02116, (617) 482-3593
   NPS; is interested in speaking to women's groups
   Novel: *Accident* (Harper & Row, 1964)

Joe Johnson
215 W. 92 St., New York, N.Y. 10025
(212) 877-7619
   Readings only; is Afro-American
   Poetry: *Codes/Heat* (Emerson-Hall, 1975)
   Fiction published in *Yardbird Reader,
   Black Creation*

Erica Jong
c/o Sterling Lord, Sterling Lord Agency, 660 Madison
Ave., New York, N.Y. 10021, (212) 751-2533
   COL*, readings; speaks Italian, French, German
   Poetry: *Loveroot* (Holt, Rinehart & Winston, 1975)
   Novel: *Fear of Flying* (Holt, Rinehart & Winston,
   1973; New American Library (Signet) 1975)

June M. Jordan
c/o Wendy Weil, Literary Agent, 3 E. 48 St., New York,
N.Y. 10017
(212) PL3-2605
   JHS*, HS*, COL*, readings; is Black
   Poetry published in *For Chile, For Neruda &
   Keeping the Faith*
   Novel: *His Own Where* (Thomas Y. Crowell, 1972)

Stephen M. Joseph
270 First Ave., New York, N.Y. 10009
   ALL*; is interested in working in prisons, drug
   rehabilitation centers, old age homes; has worked
   for Minn., Wyo., N.Y. and N.J. PITS; speaks Spanish
   Novel: *The Shark Bites Back* (McGraw-Hill, 1970)

John Jurkowski
c/o Robert Lescher Literary Agency, 155 E. 71 St.,
New York, N.Y. 10021
(212) 249-7600
   COL
   Fiction published in *The New Yorker, The North
   American Review*

Johanna Kaplan
411 West End Ave., Apt. 11E, New York, N.Y. 10024
(212) 362-9032
   COL, readings; speaks some Hebrew
   Novella & short stories: *Other People's Lives*
   (Alfred A. Knopf, 1975)

Arno Karlen
350 Bleecker St., New York, N.Y. 10014
(212) 691-2893
   COL*; speaks French
   Poetry published in *Saturday Review, Harper's*
   Novella and short stories: *White Apples*
   (Lippincott, 1961); published in *New American
   Review, Transatlantic Review*

Lila Karp
114 Spring St., New York, N.Y. 10012
(212) 925-0272
   COL*; is interested in teaching writing to women;
   speaks some Spanish & French
   Novel: *The Queen Is In the Garbage* (Vanguard
   Press, 1969)

Elia Katz
229 E. Kingsbridge Rd., Bronx, N.Y. 10458
   alternate address: c/o Bantam Books, 666 Fifth Ave.,
   New York, N.Y. 10019, (212) 765-6500
   NPS
   Novel: *Armed Love* (Bantam Books, 1972)

Steve Katz
37 Crosby St., New York, N.Y. 10013
(212) 431-6972
   alternate address: c/o Georges Borchardt, Inc.,
   145 E. 52 St., New York, N.Y. 10022, (212) 753-5785
   COL*, readings; is interested in working in prisons,
   drug rehabilitation centers, with community groups;
   speaks Italian & French
   Poetry: *Cheyenne River Wild Track* (Ithaca
   House, 1974)
   Novel: *SAW* (Alfred A. Knopf, 1973)

Bel Kaufman
1020 Park Ave., New York, N.Y. 10028
(212) BU8-8783
   HS*, COL*; speaks Russian & French
   Fiction: *Up the Down Staircase* (Prentice-Hall,
   1965; Avon, 1966)

Sue Kaufman
544 E. 86 St., New York, N.Y. 10028
(212) LE5-1227
   NPS; speaks French
   Novel: *Falling Bodies* (Doubleday, 1974)

William Melvin Kelley
c/o Doubleday & Co., 277 Park Ave. S., New York,
N.Y. 10017
(212) 953-4561
   NPS
   Novel: *A Different Drummer* (Doubleday, 1973)

John Oliver Killens
1392 Union St., Brooklyn, N.Y. 11213
   COL; is Black
   Fiction: *Cotillion* (Trident, 1971; Pocket
   Books, 1972)

Galway Kinnell
161 E. 81 St., New York, N.Y. 10028
(212) 249-2023
   alternate address: Sheffield, Vt. 05866
   COL; has worked for Mich. PITS; speaks French
   Poetry: *Book of Nightmares* (Houghton
   Mifflin, 1971)
   Fiction: *Black Light* (Houghton Mifflin, 1966)

Norma Klein
27 W. 96 St., New York, N.Y. 10025
(212) 866-0192
   alternate address: c/o Dr. & Mrs. E. Klein, 47 E. 88
   St., New York, N.Y. 10028
   Readings only; is interested in working with feminist
   groups
   Novel: *Coming to Life* (Simon & Schuster, 1974)

John Knowles
c/o Random House, 201 E. 50 St., New York, N.Y. 10022
(212) PL1-2600
   NPS
   Novel: *Paragon* (Random House, 1971; Bantam
   Books, 1972)

Kenneth Koch
29 Bank St., New York, N.Y. 10014
(212) 243-7307 or (212) 280-2465
   ALL*; has worked for N.C., R.I. & Okla. PITS; is
   interested in working in old age homes; speaks
   French & Italian
   Poetry: *The Art of Love* (Random House, 1975)
   Novel: *The Red Robins* (Random House-Vintage,
   1975)

Jerzy Kosinski
c/o S.F.I, 60 W. 57 St., New York, N.Y. 10019
(212) 246-0128
   HS*, COL*; interested in teaching English Prose and
   Criticism; speaks Russian, Polish & French
   Novel: *Cockpit* (Houghton Mifflin, 1975)

Richard Kostelanetz
P.O. Box 73, Canal St. Station, New York, N.Y. 10013
(212) 564-3250 (service)
   COL*; is a visual and sound poet and fictioneer
   Poetry: *Portraits from Memory* (Ardis, 1975)
   Fiction: *Openings & Closings* (Editions 99, 1975)

(Mary) Zane Kotker
490 West End Ave., New York, N.Y. 10024
(212) 787-5648
   HS, COL
   Fiction: *Bodies in Motion* (Alfred A. Knopf, 1972)

Norman Kotker
490 West End Ave., New York, N.Y. 10024
(212) 787-5648
   COL; speaks French
   Novel: *Herzl the King* (Scribner's, 1972)

Robert Kotlowitz
54 Riverside Dr., New York, N.Y. 10024
   COL
   Novel: *Somewhere Else* (Charterhouse, 1972)

Vaughn Koumjian
320 Wadsworth Ave., New York, N.Y. 10040
(212) WA3-0699
   COL; is interested in working in prisons, drug rehabilitation centers, old age homes
   Fiction published in *Minnesota Review, Ararat*

Jose Kozer
123-35 82 Rd., Apt. 2G, Kew Gardens, N.Y. 11415
(212) 544-9097
   COL*, readings; is interested in working in prisons;
   speaks Spanish, Portuguese & some French; is Cuban
   Poetry: *Este Judio de Numeros y Letras* (Imprenta
   Editora Catolica, 1975)
   Fiction published in *Exilio, El Cuento*

Elaine Kraf
116 W. 72 St., New York, N.Y. 10023
(212) 724-5811
   ALL; is interested in working with disturbed adoles-
   cents in New York City; speaks some French
   Novel: *The House of Madelaine* (Doubleday, 1971)

David Kranes
c/o Elizabeth McKee, Matson Agency, 22 E. 40 St.,
New York, N.Y. 10016
(212) 679-4490
   NPS
   Novel: *Margins* (Alfred A. Knopf, 1972)

John Lahr
418 E. 88 St., New York, N.Y. 10028
(212) 289-3533
   Readings only; is interested in working in prisons
   Fiction: *Hot to Trot* (Alfred A. Knopf, 1974)

Kenneth Lamott
c/o Elizabeth McKee, Harold Matson Co. Inc., 22 E. 40
St., New York, N.Y. 10016
(212) 679-4490
   NPS
   Novel: *The Bestial Day Parade* (David McKay, 1967)

Ring Lardner, Jr.
c/o Russell & Volkening, 551 Fifth Ave., New York,
N.Y. 10017
(212) MU2-5340
   NPS
   Novel: *The Ecstasy of Owen Muir* (New American
   Library, 1972)

Harper Lee
c/o J.B. Lippincott Co., 521 Fifth Ave., New York,
N.Y. 10017, (212) MU7-3980
   NPS
   Novel: *To Kill a Mockingbird* (Lippincott, 1960;
   Popular Library, 1972)

Fritz Leiber
c/o Robert P. Mills, Ltd., 156 E. 52 St., New York,
N.Y. 10022
(212) PL2-6132
  NPS
  Fiction: *The Best of Fritz Leiber* (Ballantine
  Books, 1973)

John Leonard
c/o Marilyn Marlow, 60 E. 56 St., New York, N.Y. 10022
(212) PL5-4200
  NPS
  Novel: *Black Conceit* (Doubleday, 1973)

Doris Lessing
c/o John Cushman Associates, 25 W. 43 St., New York,
N.Y. 10036
(212) MU5-2052
  NPS
  Novel: *Memoirs of a Survivor* (Alfred A. Knopf,
  1975)

Phillip Lopate
50 W. 71 St., New York, N.Y. 10023
(212) 873-6699
  ALL*; has worked for N.J. & Conn. PITS
  Poetry: *The Eyes Don't Always Want to Stay Open*
  (Sun Press, 1973)
  Prose Memoirs: *Being With Children* (Doubleday,
  1975)

Bruce Lowery
c/o Georges Borchardt, Inc., 145 E. 52 St., New York,
N.Y. 10022, (212) PL3-5785
  NPS
  Novel: *Werewolf* (Vanguard, 1969)

Dan McCall
c/o Joan Daves, 515 Madison Ave., New York, N.Y.
10022, (212) PL9-6250
  NPS
  Novel: *Jack, the Bear* (Doubleday, 1974)

Cormac McCarthy
c/o Candida Donadio & Associates, 111 W. 57 St.,
New York, N.Y. 10019
(212) 757-5076
  NPS
  Novel: *Child of God* (Random House, 1974)

Joseph McElroy
121 Madison Ave., New York, N.Y. 10016
  COL*, readings; is interested in working in prison;
  speaks French & Spanish
  Novel: *Lookout Cartridge* (Alfred A. Knopf, 1974)

Thomas McGuane
c/o Farrar, Straus & Giroux, 19 Union Sq. W., New York,
N.Y. 10003
(212) 741-6900
  NPS
  Novel: *Ninety-Two in the Shade* (Farrar, Straus
  & Giroux, 1973)

Tom McHale
c/o Paul Reynolds, 12 E. 41 St., New York, N.Y. 10017
(212) 689-8711
  NPS
  Novel: *Alinsky's Diamond* (Lippincott, 1974)

Georgia McKinley
435 W. 57 St., New York, N.Y. 10019
(212) JU2-4923
  HS; is interested in working in drug rehabilitation
  centers and old age homes; speaks French
  Novel: *Follow the Running Grass* (Houghton
  Mifflin, 1969)

Norman Mailer
c/o Scott Meredith Agency, 580 Fifth Ave., New
York, N.Y. 10036
(212) 245-5500
  NPS
  Fiction: *Why Are We In Vietnam* (G.P.
  Putnam, 1967)

Clarence Major
c/o Marcia Higgins, William Morris Agency, 1350 Avenue
of the Americas, New York, N.Y. 10019
(212) 586-5100
  ALL*; has worked for Conn. & N.Y. PITS; speaks some
  Spanish; is Black
  Poetry: *The Syncopated Cakewalk* (Barlenmir
  House, 1974)
  Fiction: *Reflex and Bone Structure* (Fiction
  Collective, 1975)

John Malone
c/o Georges Borchardt Literary Agency, 145 E. 52 St.,
New York, N.Y. 10022
(212) 753-5785
  NPS
  Novel: *The Corruption of Harold Hoskins* (Charterhouse, 1973)

Marya Mannes
169 E. 78 St., New York, N.Y. 10021
(212) 744-1576
  NPS; speaks French, German & Italian
  Novel: *They* (Doubleday, 1968)

Wallace Markfield
c/o Alfred A. Knopf, 201 E. 50 St., New York,
N.Y. 10022
(212) 751-2600
  NPS
  Novel: *Teitelbaum's Window* (Alfred A. Knopf, 1970)

Paule Marshall
407 Central Park W., New York, N.Y. 10025
(212) 749-1699
  COL*; speaks French; is Black
  Fiction: *The Chosen Place, the Timeless People*
  (Harcourt Brace Jovanovich, 1969)

Sharon Bell Mathis
c/o The Viking Press, 625 Madison Ave., New York,
N.Y. 10022
(212) PL5-4330
  NPS; is interested in working in prisons, drug rehabi
  litation centers, old age homes; is Black
  Poetry published in *Negro History Bulletin,
  Night Comes Softly*
  Fiction published in *Essence, Black World*

Peter Matthiessen
c/o Candida Donadio & Associates, 111 W. 57 St., Ne
York, N.Y. 10019
(212) 757-5076
  NPS
  Novel: *Far Tortuga* (Random House, 1975)

William Maxwell
544 E. 86 St., New York, N.Y. 10028
(212) RE7-1461
  NPS
  Fiction: *The Old Man at the Railroad Crossing*
  (Alfred A. Knopf, 1966) and in *O. Henry Prize
  Stories 1975*

Julian Mazor
c/o Robert Lescher, 155 E. 71 St., New York, N.Y. 10021
(212) 249-7600
  NPS
  Short Stories: *Washington and Baltimore* (Alfred
  A. Knopf, 1968)

Larry Melford
464 Quincy St., Brooklyn, N.Y. 11216
  COL, readings; is interested in working in old age
  homes; is Afro-American
  Fiction published in *Black Creation, Aries*

Louise Meriwether
1691 E. 174 St., #7D, Bronx, N.Y. 10472
(212) 542-6968
  COL; is interested in working in prisons, drug
  rehabilitation centers; is Black
  Novel: *Daddy Was a Number Runner* (Prentice-Hall,
  1970)

W.S. Merwin
c/o Harry Ford, Atheneum Publishers, 122 E. 42 St.,
New York, N.Y. 10017
(212) 661-4500
  COL
  Poetry: *Writings to an Unfinished Accompaniment*
  (Atheneum, 1973)
  Prose: *The Miners Pale Children* (Atheneum, 1970)

Barton Midwood
317 W. 87 St., #3B, New York, N.Y. 10024
(212) 580-0695
  JHS*, HS*, COL*,readings; speaks Spanish & German
  Stories: *Phantoms* (E.P. Dutton, 1970)

Arthur Miller
c/o Phyllis Jackson, International Creative Management,
40 W. 57 St., New York, N.Y. 10019, (212) 556-5600
  NPS
  Novel: *The Creation of the World and Other Business*
  (Viking, 1973)

Henry Miller
c/o Scott Meredith, Scott Meredith Literary Agency,
580 Fifth Ave., New York, N.Y. 10036
(212) 245-5500
  NPS
  Novel: *On Turning Eighty* (Capra Press, 1974)

Alison Mills
c/o Ornette Coleman, 131 Prince St., Apt. 3, New York,
N.Y. 10012
  alternate address: c/o Theodore Mills, 940 Westchester Pl., Los Angeles, Calif. 90019
  HS, COL*; is interested in working in prisons & drug
  rehabilitation centers; is Black
  Novel: *Francisco* (Reed, Cannon & Johnson, 1974)

Mark Mirsky
194 First Ave., New York, N.Y. 10009
(212) OR4-2135
  alternate address: c/o Mrs. Piper, Dept. of English,
  City College of N.Y., New York, N.Y. 10031
  NPS
  Novellas: *The Secret Table* (George Braziller,
  1975)

Ursule Molinaro
816 Broadway, New York, N.Y. 10003
(212) 673-1439
  HS, COL*, readings; speaks French, Italian, Germa
  Portuguese & Spanish
  Novel: *The Borrower* (Harper & Row, 1971)

Toni Morrison
c/o Random House, 201 E. 50 St., New York, N.Y.1C
(212) 572-2165
  NPS; is Black
  Novel: *Sula* (Alfred A. Knopf, 1974)

Leslie Newman
c/o Georges Borchardt, Inc., 145 E. 52 St.,
New York, N.Y. 10022
(212) 753-5785
  NPS
  Novel: *Gathering Force* (Simon & Schuster, 1974)

Hugh Nissenson
411 West End Ave., New York, N.Y. 10024
(212) 873-5193
  COL, readings
  Short Stories: *In the Reign of Peace* (Farrar,
  Straus & Giroux, 1972)

Craig Nova
4 Milligan Pl., New York, N.Y. 10011
(212) 691-8997
  COL*; readings; is interested in working in
  veterans' hospitals
  Fiction: *The Geek* (Harper & Row, 1975)

Sidney Offit
23 E. 69 St., New York, N.Y. 10021
  JHS, HS; is interested in working in drug rehabilitation
  Novel: *Only A Girl Like You* (Coward McCann, 197

William O'Rourke
115 Charles St., New York, N.Y. 10014
(212) 675-6740
  COL*
  Novel: *The Meekness Of Isaac* (Thomas Y. Crowe
  1974)

Manuel Ramos Otero
129 Perry St., #5C, New York, N.Y. 10014
(212) 989-1731
  COL*; speaks Spanish and some French; is Puert
  Rican
  Short Stories: *Orgasmos Prohibidos y Otros Ritos*
  (Editorial Puerto, 1974)

Iris Owens
c/o Arlene Donovan, International Creative Manage
40 W. 57 St., New York, N.Y. 10019
(212) 586-0440
  NPS
  Novel: *After Claude* (Farrar, Straus & Giroux, 1973

Ron Padgett
342 E. 13 St., New York, N.Y. 10003
(212) 477-4472
ALL*, readings; has worked for N.Y., Conn., W. Va.,
Del., Okla., Va., N.J., & Minn. PITS; speaks French,
some Italian & Spanish
Poetry: *Crazy Compositions* (Big Sky Books, 1975)
Novel: *Antlers In The Treetops* with Tom Veitch
(Coach House Press, 1973)

Grace Paley
126 W. 11 St., New York, N.Y. 10011
(212) WA9-4905
NPS
Short Stories: *Enormous Changes At The Last Minute*
(Farrar, Straus & Giroux, 1975)

Joseph Papaleo
3902 Manhattan College Pkwy., New York, N.Y. 10471
(212) 543-5863
is interested in working in old age homes; speaks
Italian; is Italian-American
Novel: *Out Of Place* (Little Brown, 1970)

Richard Peck
17 Grace Court Alley, Brooklyn, N.Y. 11201
(212) 852-0348
JHS*, HS*, COL*, readings; does demonstration
teaching and creative writing workshops, particularly
with junior-high students and teacher-training groups
Poetry published in *Saturday Review, Eternity*
Novel: *The Ghost Belonged To Me* (Viking, 1975)

Richard Perry
260 Audubon Ave., New York, N.Y. 10033
(212) 795-6476
COL*; has worked in N.Y. PITS; is Black
Novel: *Changes* (Bobbs-Merrill, 1974)

Edward Pomerantz
365 W. 28th St., New York, N.Y. 10001
(212) 255-6277
HS*, COL*; is interested in working in prisons, drug
rehabilitation centers, old age homes; has worked for
N.Y. PITS
Novel: *Into It* (Dial, 1972)

Katherine Anne Porter
c/o Cyrilly Abels, Literary Agent, Suite 1410,
119 W. 57 St., New York, N.Y. 10019
(212) 247-6438
COL
Fiction: *A Christmas Story* (Delacorte, 1967)

Chaim Potok
c/o Alfred A. Knopf, Inc., 201 E. 50 St., New York,
N.Y. 10022
(212) 751-2600
NPS
Fiction: *In The Beginning* (Alfred A. Knopf,
1975)

J.F. Powers
c/o Thomas Collins Associates, 225 E. 57 St.,
New York, N.Y. 10022
NPS
Short Stories: *Look How The Fish Live* (Alfred
A. Knopf, 1975)

Nancy Price
c/o Mrs. H.J. Thompson, Little, Brown & Co.,
747 Third Ave., New York, N.Y. 10017
(212) 688-8380
alternate address: c/o Marcia Higgins, Wm. Morris
Agency, 1350 Avenue of the Americas, New York,
N.Y. 10019, (212) 586-5100
NPS
Fiction: *A Natural Death* (Little, Brown, 1973)

Richard Price
365 West End Ave., Apt. 10F, New York, N.Y. 10024
(212) 580-0743
alternate address: c/o Ellen Joseph (Editor), Houghto
Mifflin, 551 Fifth Ave., New York, N.Y. 10017, (212)
877-8050
COL*, readings
Novel: *Bloodbrothers* (Houghton Mifflin, 1976)

Carmen Puigdollers
165 West End Ave., Apt. 27B, New York, N.Y. 10023
alternate address: c/o Irma Garcia, 446 E. 88 St.,
New York, N.Y. 10028, (212) 369-5084
ALL (JHS*, HS*, COL*); speaks Spanish; is
Puerto Rican
Poetry: *Dominio Entre Alas* (Las Americas
Publishing, 1955)
Fiction published in *El Mundo Newspaper,
Orfeo Literary Review*

James Purdy
236 Henry St., Brooklyn, N.Y. 11201
(212) 858-0015
COL*, readings; is interested in working in prisons
and drug rehabilitation centers; speaks Spanish
Poetry: *Sunshine Is An Only Child* (Aloe Editions,
1973)
Novel: *The House of the Solitary Maggot* (Doubleday, 1973)

Mario Puzo
c/o William Targ, G.P. Putnam's Sons, 200 Madison Ave
New York, N.Y. 10016
(212) 883-5500
NPS
Novel: *The Godfather Papers And Other Confessions*
(G.P. Putnam, 1972; Fawcett World, 1973)

Thomas Pynchon
c/o Candida Donadio, 111 W. 57th St., New York,
N.Y. 10019
(212) PL7-5076
NPS
Novel: *Gravity's Rainbow* (Viking, 1973; Bantam,
1974)

Peter Rand
26 Leroy St., #19, New York, N.Y. 10014
(212) 255-5632
COL*; readings; is interested in working in old
age homes & prisons & with veterans; speaks French
Novel: *Firestorm* (Doubleday, 1969)

Phyllis Raphael
390 West End Ave., New York, N.Y. 10024
(212) 595-5286
NPS
Fiction: *They Got What They Wanted* (W.W. Norton,
1972; Popular Library, 1973)

Edward Rivera
321 W. 100th St., New York, N.Y. 10025
  HS, COL; speaks Spanish
  Fiction published in *Growing Up In America*

Gilbert Rogin
c/o Sports Illustrated, Time Life Bldg., New York,
N.Y. 10020
(212) 556-3123
  NPS
  Novel: *What Happens Next?* (Random House, 1971)

Anne Roiphe
130 E. 95th St., New York, N.Y. 10028
  NPS
  Fiction: *Long Division* (Simon & Schuster, 1972)

Leo Rosen
36 Sutton Place S., New York, N.Y. 10022
  NPS; speaks Yiddish
  Fiction: *Dear "Herm"* (McGraw-Hill, 1975)

Judith Rossner
575 West End Ave., New York, N.Y. 10024
  alternate address: c/o Julian Bach Agency, 3 E. 48th
  St., New York, N.Y. 10017, (212) 753-2605
  NPS
  Novel: *Looking for Mr. Goodbar* (Simon & Schuster,
  1975)

Norman Rosten
84 Remsen St., Brooklyn, N.Y. 11201
  COL*
  Poetry: *Thrive Upon The Rock* (Trident, 1965)
  Novel: *Over and Out* (George Braziller, 1972)

Philip Roth
c/o Farrar, Straus & Giroux, 19 Union Sq. W., New
York, N.Y. 10003
  Unavailable for readings
  Fiction: *My Life as a Man* (Holt, Rinehart &
  Winston, 1974)

Earl Rovit
8 E. 96th St., New York, N.Y. 10028
(212) 876-1409
  COL*
  Novel: *Crossings* (Harcourt Brace Jovanovich,
  1973)

Michael Rumaker
c/o Harold Ober Associates, 40 E. 49 St., New York,
N.Y. 10017
(914) 358-1176
  COL*
  Poetry published in *From the Belly of the Shark,
  The Nation*
  Fiction: *Gringos & Other Short Stories* (Grove
  Press, 1967)

Charles L. Russell
626 Riverside Dr., Apt. 15-O, New York, N.Y. 10031
(212) 283-4695
  HS, COL; is Black
  Novella: *A Birthday Present for Katheryn Kenyatta*
  (McGraw-Hill, 1970)

J.R. Salamanca
c/o Alfred A. Knopf, Inc., 201 E. 50 St., New York,
N.Y. 10022
(212) 751-2600
  NPS
  Fiction: *An Embarkation* (Alfred A. Knopf, 1973)

J.D. Salinger
c/o Harold Ober Assoc., Inc., 40 E. 49 St.,
New York, N.Y. 10017
(212) 759-8600
  Not available for readings
  Fiction: *Raise High the Roof Beam Carpenters
  & Seymour* (paper; Bantam, 1971)

William Saroyan
c/o Contracts Dept., Doubleday & Co., 245 Park Ave.,
New York, N.Y. 10017
(212) 953-4561
  NPS
  Fiction: *The Tooth and My Father* (Doubleday,
  1974)

Susan Fromberg Schaeffer
783 E. 21st St., Brooklyn, N.Y. 11210
  Readings only; speaks Spanish
  Poetry: *Granite Lady* (Macmillan, 1974)
  Novel: *Ania* (Macmillan, 1974)

Budd Schulberg
c/o Ad Schulberg, 300 E. 57 St., New York, N.Y. 10022
(212) PL9-1341
  NPS
  Novel: *Sanctuary Five* (New American Library,
  1969)

Lore Segal
280 Riverside Dr., New York, N.Y. 10025
(212) MO3-1524
  HS, COL*, readings; interested in working in old age
  homes; speaks German, some Spanish
  Fiction: *The Juniper Tree and other Tales from
  Grimm* (Farrar, Straus & Giroux, 1974)

Judith Johnson Sherwin
271 Central Park W., New York, N.Y. 10024
(212) 787-2306
  HS*, COL*, readings; is interested in working in
  prisons, drug rehabilitation centers, with women's
  groups, dramatic groups, multimedia, & with horror
  story & science fiction fans; has worked for N.Y.
  PITS; speaks French
  Poetry: *Impossible Buildings* (Doubleday, 1973)
  Short Stories: *The Life of Riot* (Atheneum, 1970)

David Shetzline
c/o Lynn Nesbit, International Creative Management,
40 W. 57 St., New York, N.Y. 10019
(212) 556-5726
  NPS
  Fiction: *Heckletooth III* (Random House, 1969)

Alix Kates Shulman
c/o Curtis Brown, Ltd., 60 E. 56th St., New York,
N.Y. 10022
(212) 755-4200
  NPS
  Novel: *Memoirs of an Ex-Prom Queen* (Alfred A.
  Knopf, 1972)

Clancy Sigal
c/o Avon Books, The Hearst Corporation, 959 Eighth
Ave., New York, N.Y. 10019
    NPS
    Fiction: *Weekend in Dinlock* (Avon, 1970)

Layle Silbert
505 LaGuardia Pl., New York, N.Y. 10012
(212) 677-0947
    HS, COL, readings; speaks French
    Fiction published in *South Dakota Review,*
The Literary Review

Charles Simmons
c/o New York Times Book Review, 229 W. 43 St.,
New York, N.Y. 10036
(212) 556-7443
    NPS
    Novel: *An Old Fashioned Darling* (Coward,
McCann, 1971; paperback, New American Library,
1972)

I.B. Singer
209 W. 86 St., New York, N.Y. 10024
    COL
    Fiction: *Passions* (Farrar, Straus & Giroux, 1975)

Sabire Soledad
c/o Barretto, 271 E. 10 St., #1, New York,
N.Y. 10009
(212) 254-1454
    alternate address: c/o Elaine Markson, 44 Greenwich
Ave., New York, N.Y. 10011, (212) 243-8480
    NPS; speaks Spanish & German; is Puerto Rican
    Novel: *Jibaro* with Manuel Barretto (New American
Library, 1974)

Barbara Probst Solomon
271 Central Pk. West, New York, N.Y. 10024
(212) 874-3842
    COL*, readings; speaks French & Spanish
    Novel: *In Need* (Harper & Row, 1975)

Theodore Solotaroff
210 W. 78 St., New York, N.Y. 10024
    COL
    Fiction: *The Red Hot Vacuum* (Atheneum, 1970)

Susan Sontag
c/o Roger W. Straus, Farrar, Straus & Giroux, 19
Union Sq. W., New York, N.Y. 10003
(212) 741-6900
    NPS; is interested in working in women's prisons;
speaks French
    Novel: *Death Kit* (Farrar, Straus & Giroux, 1967)
and in *Atlantic Monthly, Playboy*

Gilbert Sorrentino
c/o Karen Hitzig, Wm. Morris Agency, 1350 Ave. of the
Americas, New York, N.Y. 10019
(212) 586-5100
    NPS
    Poetry: *Corrosive Sublimate* (Black Sparrow
Press, 1971)
    Novelette: *Splendide-Hotel* (New Directions, 1973)

Peter Sourian
30 E. 70 St., New York, N.Y. 10021
(212) 879-6299
    NPS; speaks French, Spanish & some German
    Fiction: *The Gate* (Harcourt, Brace, Jovanovich,
1965) and in *Ararat*

Terry Southern
c/o Arlene Donovan, 40 W. 57 St., New York,
N.Y. 10019
    NPS
    Novel: *Blue Movie* (New American Library, 1971)

Peter Spielberg
321 W. 24 St., New York, N.Y. 10011
(212) 989-4298
    alternate address: c/o Dept. of English, Brooklyn
College, Brooklyn, N.Y. 11210, (212) 780-5195
    Readings only; speaks German
    Novel: *Twiddledum Twaddledum* (George Braziller,
1974)

Paul Spike
c/o R. Newman, 287 Park Ave. S., New York, N.Y. 10010
    NPS; speaks Spanish
    Novel: *Photographs of My Father* Alfred A.
Knopf, 1973)

Norman Spinrad
26 Grove St., New York, N.Y. 10014
    HS, COL, readings
    Novel: *Passing Through the Flame* (Berkeley/
Putnam, 1975)

Wallace Stegner
c/o Brandt & Brandt, 101 Park Ave., New York,
N.Y. 10017
(212) 683-5890
    NPS
    Novel: *Angle of Repose* (Doubleday, 1971)

Michael Gregory Stephens
520 W. 110 St., Apt. 4-A, New York, N.Y. 10025
(212) 222-7537
    COL*; speaks French & Spanish
    Poetry: *Alcohol Poems* (Loose Change Press, 1973)
    Fiction: *Season at Coole* (E.P. Dutton, 1972)

Daniel Stern
1230 Park Ave., New York, N.Y. 10028
    COL*, readings
    Novel: *Final Cut* (Viking, 1975)

Shane Stevens
c/o Lynn Nesbit, International Creative Management,
40 W. 57 St., New York, N.Y. 10019
(212) 556-5600
    COL*, readings
    Novel: *Dead City* (Holt, Rinehart & Winston, 1974)

Alma Stone
523 W. 112 St., New York, N.Y. 10025
    NPS
    Novel: *The Banishment* (Doubleday, 1973)

Theodore Sturgeon
c/o Ballantine Books, Inc., 201 E. 50 St., New York,
N.Y. 10022
(212) 751-2600
    NPS
    Fiction: *More Than Human* (Ballantine, 1975)

Piri Thomas
347 W. 21 St., New York, N.Y. 10011
(212) 989-3414
ALL*; speaks Spanish; is Puerto Rican
Poetry published in *The Rican Journal, From
the Belly of the Shark*
Fiction: *The Man Who Spins the Web*
(Praeger, 1975)

John A. Thompson
418 Central Park W., New York, N.Y. 10025
(212) 749-1256
Readings
Poetry: *The Talking Girl & Other Poems*
(Pym-Randall Press, 1968)
Fiction published in *Commentary, Harper's*

Dalton Trevisian
c/o William Koshland, Knopf Publishers, 201 E. 50 St.,
New York, N.Y. 10022
(212) 751-2600
NPS
Short Stories: *The Vampire of Curitiba & Other
Stories* (Alfred A. Knopf, 1972)

Calvin Trillin
12 Grove St., New York, N.Y. 10011
HS, COL
Fiction: *Barnett Frummer Is An Unbloomed Flower*
(Viking, 1969; paperback, E.P. Dutton, 1971)

Niccolo Tucci
25 E. 67 St., New York, N.Y. 10021
NPS
Fiction: *Before My Time* (Simon & Schuster, 1962)

Frederic Tuten
317 E. 10 St., New York, N.Y. 10009
NPS; speaks Italian & Spanish
Fiction: *The Adventures of Mao on the Long March*
(Citadel Press, 1971)

Henry Van Dyke
40 Waterside Plaza, New York, N.Y. 10010
alternate address: c/o Perry Knowlton, Curtis Brown
Agency, 60 E. 56 St., New York, N.Y. 10022, (212)
755-4200
COL*; is interested in working with prison inmates
who write fiction; speaks German
Novel: *Dead Piano* (Farrar, Straus & Giroux,
1971)

Gore Vidal
c/o L. Arnold Weissberger, 120 E. 56th St., New York,
N.Y. 10022, (212) PL8-0800
NPS
Novel: *Myron* (Random House, 1975)

Kurt Vonnegut, Jr.
c/o Donald Farber, 800 Third Ave., New York, N.Y.
10017
No public appearances
Fiction: *Breakfast of Champions* (Seymour
Lawrence, 1973)

Alice Walker
55 Midwood, Brooklyn, N.Y. 11225
alternate address: c/o Wendy Weil, Julian Bach Liter-
ary Agency, 3 E. 48 St., New York, N.Y. 10017, (212)
753-2605
Readings only
Poetry: *Revolutionary Petunias* (Harcourt Brace
Jovanovich, 1973)
Short Stories: *In Love & Trouble* (Harcourt Brace
Jovanovich, 1973)

Gerald Walker
58 W. 68 St., New York, N.Y. 10028, (212) 595-6987
COL*
Novel: *Cruising* (Stein & Day, 1970; Fawcett, 1971)

Karl Wang
102-40 62nd Ave., Apt. 6C, Forest Hills, N.Y. 11375
(212) 592-7155
Readings only; speaks Chinese (Mandarin); is Chinese
Poetry published in *The Greenfield Review, Poetry
Newsletter*
Fiction published in *Riverrun, The Greenfield Review*

Ron Welburn
P.O. Box 244, Vanderveer Station, Brooklyn, N.Y. 11210
Readings only; is interested in working in prisons;
is Afro-American
Poetry: *Peripheries: Selected Poems 1966-1968*
(Greenfield Review Press, 1972)
Fiction published in *Neworld, Essence*

Elie Wiesel
c/o Georges Borchardt, Inc., 145 E. 52 St., New York,
N.Y. 10022
(212) PL3-5785
NPS
Novel: *The Oath* (Random House, 1973; Avon, 1974)

Edward G. Williams
801 West End Ave., Apt. 5BB, New York, N.Y. 10025
(212) 222-5214
HS, COL; is interested in working in drug rehabilitation centers; is Black
Fiction: *Not Like Niggers* (St. Martin's Press, 1969)

Tennessee Williams
c/o Bill Barnes, International Creative Management,
40 W. 57 St., New York, N.Y. 10019, (212) 556-5600
NPS
Novel: *Moise & the World of Reason* (Simon &
Schuster, 1975)

Calder Willingham
c/o Robert L. Rosen, 39 W. 55 St., New York,
N.Y. 10019
(212) 541-8641
NPS
Novel: *The Big Nickel* (Dial, 1975)

Meredith Sue Willis
236 Clinton St., Brooklyn, N.Y. 11201
(212) 522-0794
ALL (EL*, JHS*, HS*); is interested in working in
old age homes, hospitals & other institutional
settings; speaks Spanish, some French
Fiction published in *Epoch, Minnesota Review*

Charles Wright
c/o Farrar, Straus & Giroux, 19 Union Sq. W.,
New York, N.Y. 10003
(212) 741-6900
 NPS; is interested in working in prisons, drug
 rehabilitation centers & old age homes; speaks
 French, German & Portuguese; is Black
 Fiction published in *Yardbird Journal,*
 Black Short Stories

Sarah E. Wright
780 West End Ave., New York, N.Y. 10025
 COL; is Black
 Poetry: *Give Me A Child* with Lucy Smith (Kraft,
 1955)
 Novel: *This Child's Gonna Live* (Delacorte Press,
 1969)

Rudolph Wurlitzer
234 E. 23 St., New York, N.Y. 10010
(212) 889-2032
 COL, readings; speaks French
 Fiction: *Quake* (E.P. Dutton, 1972)

Richard Yates
28 W. 26 St., Apt. 7A, New York, N.Y. 10010
(212) 924-3087
 HS, COL*; is interested in working in prisons
 Novel: *Disturbing the Peace* (Seymour Lawrence-
 Delacorte Press, 1975)

Marguerite Young
375 Bleecker St., New York, N.Y. 10014
(212) AL5-6018
 COL*, readings
 Poetry published in *Partisan Review, Saturday Review*
 Fiction: *Miss MacIntosh, My Darling*
 (Scribner's, 1965)

Sol Yurick
220 Garfield Pl., Brooklyn, N.Y. 11215
(212) 788-0458
 HS, COL; is interested in working in prisons, drug
 rehabilitation centers & old age homes
 Novel: *An Island Death* (Harper & Row, 1975)

Roger Zelazny
c/o Henry Morrison, Inc., 58 W. 10 St., New York,
N.Y. 10011
 COL*
 Novel: *Doorways in the Sand* (Harper & Row, 1975)

Louis Zukofsky
c/o Grossman Publishers, 625 Madison Ave., New York,
N.Y. 10022
 NPS; speaks French, German & Yiddish
 Poetry: *"A"22 & "A"23* (Grossman, 1975)
 Novel: *Little* (Grossman, 1970)

NORTH CAROLINA

Daphne Athas
Box 224, Chapel Hill, N.C. 27514
(919) 929-1526
 COL*; is interested in working in prisons
 Poetry published in *Transatlantic Review, Southern*
 Review
 Novel: *Entering Ephesus* (Viking, 1971)

Doris Betts
Box 142, Sanford, N.C. 27330
(919) 933-2481
 HS, COL
 Short Stories: *Beasts Of The Southern Wild*
 (Harper & Row, 1973)

Christopher Brookhouse
Box 653, Chapel Hill, N.C. 27514
(919) 542-2387
 NPS
 Poetry: *Scattered Light* (U. of North Carolina
 Press, 1970)
 Stories: *If Lost, Return* (Loom Press, 1973)

Fred Chappell
305 Kensington Rd., Greensboro, N.C. 27403
(919) 275-7510
 HS*, COL*, readings; is interested in working in
 prisons, drug rehabilitation centers, old age homes;
 speaks some French & Italian
 Poetry: *River* (Louisiana State U. Press, 1975)
 Novel: *The Gaudy Place* (Harcourt Brace
 Jovanovich, 1974)

Lance Jeffers
1008 Ancroft St., Durham, N.C. 27707
(919) 596-5848
 alternate address: c/o Theodore Hudson, 1816
 Varnum St. N.E., Washington, D.C. 20018
 HS*, COL*, readings; is Black
 Poetry: *When I Know the Power of My Black*
 Hand (Broadside Press, 1974)
 Fiction published in *A Galaxy of Black*
 Writing, Confrontation

Norman Macleod
P.O. Box 756, Pembroke, N.C. 28372
(919) 521-4214, Ext. 246
 COL*, readings
 Poetry: *Pure as Nowhere* (Golden Goose Press,
 1952)
 Fiction: *The Bitter Roots* (Smith & Durrell, 1941)
 and in *Pembroke Magazine*

Heather Ross Miller
40 Elm St., Badin, N.C. 28009
(704) 422-5066
 COL*; has worked for N.C. PITS
 Poetry: *Horse Horse, Tyger Tyger* (Red Clay Books,
 1973)
 Fiction: *A Spiritual Divorce and Other Stories*
 (John F. Blair Co., 1974)

Ruth Moose
Rt. 2, Stony Mountain, Albemarle, N.C. 28001
(704) 983-1032
 JHS, COL*, readings; is interested in working in old
 age homes
 Fiction published in *Ohio Review, Southern Calif.*
 Review

Guy Owen
107 Montgomery St., Raleigh, N.C. 27607
(919) 833-9913
 JHS*, HS*, COL*; has worked for N.C. & S.C. PITS
 Poetry: *The White Stallion and Other Poems*
 (John Blair, 1969)
 Fiction: *Journey for Joedel* (Crown, 1970)

Reynolds Price
4813 Duke Station, Durham, N.C. 27706
  Readings only; speaks French and Italian
  Novel: *The Surface of Earth* (Atheneum, 1975)

Elizabeth Sewell
3913 Dogwood Dr., Greensboro, N.C. 27410
(919) 299-9312
  NPS; speaks French, some German
  Poetry: *Signs and Cities* (U. of North Carolina
  Press, 1968)
  Novel: *Now Bless Thyself* (Doubleday, 1963)

Lee Smith
306 Burlage Cir., Chapel Hill, N.C. 27514
(919) 967-3808
  HS*, COL, readings
  Novel: *Fancy Strut* (Harper & Row, 1973)

Max Steele
c/o Dept. of English, U. of North Carolina,
Chapel Hill, N.C. 27514
(919) 929-3286
  HS, COL
  Short Stories: *Where She Brushed Her Hair*
  (Harper & Row, 1967)

Robert Watson
527 Highland Ave., Greensboro, N.C. 27403
(919) 274-9962
  COL*
  Poetry: *Selected Poems* (Atheneum, 1974)
  Novel: *Three Sides of the Mirror* (G.P. Putnam's,
  1966)

John Foster West
Rt. 4, Box 379-C, Boone, N.C. 28607
(704) 295-7704
  COL*; has worked for N.C. PITS
  Poetry: *This Proud Land* (McNally & Loftin, 1974)
  Novel: *Appalachian Dawn* (Moore Publishing, 1972)

Sylvia Wilkinson
109 Williams St., Chapel Hill, N.C. 27514
(919) 929-3235
  ALL*; has worked for Va., N.C. & Md. PITS
  Fiction: *Cale* (Avon Books, 1973)

NORTH DAKOTA

William Borden
307 Princeton St., Grand Forks, N.Dak. 58201
(701) 775-5224
  COL*, readings; speaks some French & Greek
  Novel: *Superstoe* (Harper & Row, 1968)

OHIO

Robert Canzoneri
195 Cornell Ct., Westerville, Ohio 43081
(614) 890-1009
  HS*, COL*; has worked in Ohio PITS
  Poetry: *Watch Us Pass* (Ohio State U. Press, 1968)
  Short Stories: *Barbed Wire and Other Stories*
  (Dial, 1970)

B. Felton
17102 Ridgeton Dr., Cleveland, Ohio 44128
(216) 991-9245 (between 4 & 5 p.m. or after 10 p.m.)
  HS, COL*, readings; has worked for Ohio PITS; is
  Black
  Poetry: *Conclusions* (Monarch Publishing, 1971)
  Fiction published in *Sattvas Review, Broadside*
  Authors & Artists

Robert Flanagan
181 N. Liberty St., Delaware, Ohio 43015
(614) 369-4820
  JHS*, HS*, COL*; is interested in working in prisons,
  old age homes, military camps; has worked for Ohio
  PITS
  Poetry: *On My Own Two Feet* (Fiddlehead Books,
  1973)
  Novel: *Maggot* (Warner Paperback Library, 1971)

Galen Green
1214 E. Whittier, #C, Columbus, Ohio 43206
(614) 253-0324
  ALL*; is interested in working in prisons, drug reha-
  bilitation centers, old age homes; speaks some Spanish
  Poetry: *Apple Grunt* (Hamburger Press, 1971)
  Fiction published in *West Coast Review,*
  Confrontation

Calvin Hernton
171 W. College St., Oberlin, Ohio 44074
(216) 774-6357
  HS, COL*; speaks French, Spanish & Swedish; is Black
  Poetry published in *The Poetry of Black America,*
  Yardbird Reader
  Novel: *Scarecrow* (Doubleday, 1974)

Josephine Johnson
4907 Klatte Rd., Cincinnati, Ohio 45244
  alternate address: c/o Simon & Schuster, 630 Fifth
  Ave., New York, N.Y. 10020, (212) CI5-6400
  NPS
  Fiction: *Seven Houses* (Simon & Schuster, 1973)

Bernard Kaplan
2566 Kemper Rd., #201, Shaker Heights, Ohio 44120
(216) 791-7732
  ALL (HS*, COL*); is interested in working in old age
  homes; has worked for R.I. PITS; speaks French
  Stories: *Prisoners of This World* (Grossman, 1970)

Robert Lowry
3747 Hutton St., Cincinnati, Ohio 45226
(513) 321-6245
  ALL (COL*); speaks French, some Italian
  Fiction: *Party of Dreamers* (Fleet, 1962)

Howard McCord
Dept. of English, Bowling Green University, Bowling
Green, Ohio 43403
(419) 372-0370
  NPS; has worked for Wash. PITS; speaks Spanish
  Poetry: *Selected Poems* (Crossing Press, 1975)
  Novella: *The Arctic Desert* (Stooge Editions, 1975)

Jack Matthews
24 Briarwood Dr., Athens, Ohio 45701
(614) 593-8915
  NPS; has worked for Ohio and Kans. PITS
  Novel: *Pictures of the Journey Back* (Harcourt
  Brace, Jovanovich, 1973)

David Nemec
c/o Ann Fueger, 285 Saddler Rd., Bay Village,
Ohio 44140
(216) 871-2310
    HS, COL, readings; is interested in working in prisons,
    drug rehabilitation centers, mental hospitals; speaks
    some French
    Stories: *Survival Prose* (Bobbs-Merrill, 1971)

Philip F. O'Connor
221 Curtis Ave., Bowling Green, Ohio 43402
(419) 352-1698
    alternate address: c/o Chairman, Dept. of English,
    Bowling Green U., Bowling Green, Ohio 43402, (419)
    372-2576
    Readings only
    Novella & Stories: *A Season for Unnatural
    Causes* (U. of Illinois Press, 1975)

Ira Sadoff
219 W. Whiteman St., Yellow Springs, Ohio 45387
    alternate address: c/o Literature Dept., Antioch
    College, Yellow Springs, Ohio 45387, (513) 767-7331
    COL*; speaks some French
    Poetry: *Settling Down* (Houghton Mifflin, 1975)
    Fiction published in *Transatlantic Review,
    Paris Review*

Hollis Summers
181 N. Congress, Athens, Ohio 45701
(614) 492-4156
    Readings; has worked for Ohio PITS
    Poetry: *Start from Home* (Rutgers U. Press, 1972)
    Short Stories: *How They Chose the Dead*
    (Louisiana State U. Press, 1973)

Diane Vreuls
172 Elm St., Oberlin, Ohio 44074
(216) 774-1737
    Readings only
    Novel: *Are We There Yet?* (Simon & Schuster, 1975)

Austin M. Wright
3454 Lyleburn Pl., Cincinnati, Ohio 45220
(513) 751-2328
    COL*
    Fiction: *First Persons* (Harper & Row, 1973)

OREGON

M.F. Beal
Rt. 2, Box 97, Seal Rock, Oreg. 97376
    HS, COL; interested in working with women
    Fiction: *Amazon One* (Little, Brown, 1975)

Thomas Doulis
2236 N.E. Regents Dr., Portland, Oreg. 97212
(503) 287-3484
    COL*, readings; speaks Greek
    Novel: *The Quarries of Sicily* (Crown, 1969)

Lawson Fusao Inada
1447 E. Main, Ashland, Oreg. 97520
(503) 482-8655
    ALL*; has worked for Ariz. PITS; speaks Japanese;
    is Asian-American
    Poetry: *Before the War* (Wm. Morrow, 1971)
    Fiction published in *Yardbird III, Roots II*

Ken Kesey
Route 8, Box 477, Pleasant Hill, Oreg. 97401
(503) 747-5796
    COL
    Screenplay & collected short pieces: *Garage Sale*
    (Viking, 1972)

Ursula K. LeGuin
3321 N.W. Thurman St., Portland, Oreg. 97210
    alternate address: c/o Virginia Kidd, Box 278,
    Milford, Pa. 18337, (717) 296-6205
    COL; is interested in giving workshops; speaks
    French & Italian
    Fiction: *The Wind's Twelve Quarters* (Harper
    & Row, 1975)

Richard Lyons
574 W. 13th Ave., Eugene, Oreg. 97401
(503) 345-6700
    alternate address: Dept. of English, U. of Oregon,
    Eugene, Oreg. 97403, (503) 686-3911
    COL*, readings; speaks some Spanish
    Fiction published in *The Phoenix, Northwest Review*

Anthony Ostroff
4647 S.W. Dosch Rd., Portland, Oregon 97201
(503) 244-9020
    readings; speaks French
    Poetry published in *American Review, Harper's
    Magazine*
    Fiction published in *Texas Quarterly, Quarterly
    Review Of Literature*

PENNSYLVANIA

Christopher Davis
6436 Overbrook Ave., Philadelphia, Pa. 19151
(215) 878-1096
    summer address: Lake Luzerne, N.Y. 12846
    COL*, readings; speaks Italian, some French & Spanish
    Novel: *The Sun in Mid-Career* (Harper & Row, 1975)

Stephen Goodwin
Bryn Mawr College, Bryn Mawr, Pa. 19010
(215) LA5-1000
    HS, readings; speaks French & German
    Novel: *Kin* (Harper & Row, 1975)

Kim Yong Ik
1103 La Clair Ave., Pittsburgh, Pa. 15218
    HS, COL; is Asian-American
    Stories: *Love in Winter* (Doubleday, 1968)

Arthur Winfield Knight
P.O. Box 439, California, Pa. 15419
(412) 938-8956
    COL*, readings; has worked for Pa. PITS
    Poetry: *What You Do With Your Aloneness* (N.Y.
    Culture Review, 1975)
    Novella: *All Together, Shift* (The SmithHorizon
    Press, 1972)

Carl Larsen
84 Susquehanna Ave., Lock Haven, Pa. 17745
(717) 748-9443
    EL*, COL*, readings; has worked for N.Y. PITS
    Poetry published in *Fine Frenzy, Live Poetry*
    Novel: *The Book of Eric Hammerscoffer*
    (Tarot Press, 1964)

Audrey Lee
c/o Eko Publications, P.O. Box 5492, Philadelphia,
Pa. 19143
　　Readings only
　　Fiction published in *Essence, Playgirl*

Jerre Mangione
1901 Walnut St., Philadelphia, Pa. 19103
(215) 567-0254
　　Readings only; is interested in ethnicity and in
　　lecturing on the Federal Writer's Project of the
　　30's; speaks Italian
　　Novel: *Mount Allegro* (Crown Publishers, 1972)

Ezekiel Mphahlele
c/o Dept. of English, University of Pennsylvania,
Philadelphia, Pa. 19174
(215) 243-6380
　　COL*; is Black
　　Novel: *The Wanderers* (Macmillan, 1972)

Joseph Nicholson
1313 W. Fourth St., Flemington, Pa. 17745
(717) 748-3745
　　COL*, readings
　　Poetry published in *Three Rivers Poetry Journal,
　　Wormwood Review*
　　Short Fiction & Prose Poems: *Odds Without End*
　　(Lock Haven State College Chapbook Series, 1971)

Natalie L.M. Petesch
6320 Crombie St., Pittsburgh, Pa. 15217
(412) 521-2802
　　alternate address: c/o Rachel Maines, 5660 Beacon,
　　Pittsburgh, Pa. 15217, (412) 521-3461
　　HS, COL*, readings; speaks French
　　Fiction: *After The First Death There Is No Other*
　　(U. of Iowa Press, 1974)

Paul West
117 Borrowes Bldg., University Park, Pa. 16802
(814) 865-3548 or (814) 865-6381
　　COL*, readings; speaks French
　　Novel: *Bela Lugosi's White Christmas* (Harper &
　　Row, 1973)

RHODE ISLAND

R.V. Cassill
22 Boylston Ave., Providence, R.I. 02906
(401) 751-4949
　　readings
　　Fiction: *The Goss Women* (Doubleday, 1974)

John Hawkes
18 Everett Ave., Providence, R.I. 02906
(415) 274-7222
　　HS, COL*, readings
　　Novel: *Death, Sleep & the Traveler* (New
　　Directions, 1974)

James S. Reinbold
22 Keene St., Providence, R.I. 02906
　　COL*; has worked in R.I. PITS
　　Fiction published in *Esquire, Greensboro Review*

Franklin Zawacki
689 Hope St., Providence, R.I. 02906
(401) 351-7219
　　alternate address: c/o Edwin Honig, 32 Fort Ave.,
　　Cranston, R.I. 02910
　　ALL; is interested in working in prisons; speaks
　　Spanish & French
　　Fiction published in *Hellcoal Annual, Cowhunting*

SOUTH CAROLINA

Franklin Ashley
207 Watermark Pl., Columbia, S.C. 29210
(803) 779-6528
　　HS*, COL*; has worked for S.C. and Ind. PITS; is
　　interested in working in drug rehabilitation cen-
　　ters; speaks French
　　Fiction: *Hard Shadows* (Peaceweed Press, 1975)

James Dickey
4620 Lelia's Ct., Columbia, S.C. 29206
(803) 787-9962
　　COL*; speaks French, Spanish, German & Italian
　　Poetry: *The Eye-Beaters, Blood, Victory, Madness,
　　Buckhead, and Mercy* (Doubleday, 1970)
　　Fiction: *Deliverance* (Houghton Mifflin, 1970)

Barry Hannah
207 Holly Ave., Clemson, S.C. 29631
　　NPS
　　Novel: *Nightwatchmen* (Viking, 1973)

Robert T. Sorrells
P.O. Box 1573, Clemson, S.C. 29631
(803) 654-5438
　　COL*, readings
　　Fiction published in *American Review, Penthouse*

SOUTH DAKOTA

John R. Milton
630 Thomas, Vermillion, S.Dak. 57069
(605) 624-2133
　　NPS
　　Poetry: *The Blue Belly of the World* (Spirit
　　Mound Press, 1974)
　　Fiction published in *Stories Southwest, The Smith*

TENNESSEE

Isabel J. Glaser
5383 Mason Rd., Memphis, Tenn. 38117
(901) 682-8501
　　ALL (EL*, JHS*, HS*); is interested in working in
　　drug rehabilitation centers, old age homes, detention
　　centers for young females
　　Fiction published in *Mississippi Review, Wind*

Dorothy Stanfill
1 Mimosa Dr., Jackson, Tenn. 38301
(901) 422-2860
　　alternate address: c/o Mrs. Ted Cunliffe, 16 Mimosa
　　Dr., Jackson, Tenn. 38301
　　HS*, COL*, readings; is interested in working with
　　teenagers, the elderly & families with problems
　　Fiction published in *Mississippi Review, New
　　Writers*

Rosemary Stephens
64 N. Yates Rd., Memphis, Tenn. 38117
(901) 682-0485
Readings; speaks French
Poetry: *Eve's Navel* (South and West, 1975)
Fiction published in *Universe Ahead, Today's Stories from Seventeen*

Allen Tate
Running Knob Hollow Rd., Sewanee, Tenn. 37375
COL*; speaks French & Italian
Poetry: *The Swimmers and Other Selected Poems* (Scribner's, 1971)
Fiction: *The Fathers* (G.P. Putnam, 1938; Swallow Press, 1960)

TEXAS

Max Apple
Dept. of English, Rice U., Houston, Tex. 77001
(713) 528-4141
alternate address: c/o Chairman, Dept. of English, Rice U., Houston, Tex. 77001
COL*; speaks Yiddish
Fiction published in *American Review 22, Ohio Review*

L.D. Clark
604 Main St., Smithville, Tex. 78957
(512) 237-2796
ALL (COL*), readings; speaks French, Spanish
Novel: *The Dove Tree* (Doubleday, 1961)
Fiction published in *Stories Southwest*

James Crumley
6303 Shoal Creek Blvd., Austin, Tex. 78757
(512) 451-2721
alternate address: c/o A.R. Crumley, P.O. Box 505, Vanderbilt, Tex. 77991, (512) 284-3338 or (512) 547-2555
COL*
Novel: *The Wrong Case* (Random House, 1975)

Nephtali De Leon
2907 Second St., Lubbock, Tex. 79415
(806) 763-3729
alternate address: c/o Priscilla Salazar, 4036 Morrison Rd., Denver, Colo. 80219, (303) 237-4036
HS*, COL*; interested in working with children & youth; speaks Spanish & French; is Chicano
Poetry: *Coca Cola Dream & Other Poems* (Trucha, 1974)
Fiction published in *We Are Chicanos, Floricanto*

Robert Lopez Flynn
101 Cliffside Dr., San Antonio, Tex. 78231
(512) 492-1127
HS*, COL*
Novel: *The Sounds of Rescue, The Signs of Hope* (Alfred A. Knopf, 1970)

Zulfikar Ghose
1602 The High Rd., Austin, Tex. 78746
(512) 327-0639
COL*, readings; is Asian
Poetry: *The Violent West* (Macmillan, 1972)
Fiction: *The Incredible Brazilian* (Holt, Rinehart & Winston, 1972)

Caroline Gordon
1730 E. Northgate Dr., Apt. 1061, Irving, Tex. 75602
alternate address: c/o Mrs. Percy Wood, Jr., 54 Hodge Rd., Princeton, N.J. 08540, (609) 924-3355
NPS; speaks some Italian, some French
Novel: *The Glory of Hera* (Doubleday, 1972)

Rolando Hinojosa
1220 W. Henrietta, Kingsville, Tex. 78363
(512) 592-8645
COL, readings; has worked for Tex. PITS; speaks Portuguese & Spanish; is Chicano
Novel: *Estampas del Valle y Otras Obras* (Quinto Sol, 1974)

Walter R. McDonald
3804 52nd St., Lubbock Tex. 79413
(806) 792-8554
COL*, readings
Poetry: *Caliban in Blue* (Texas Tech Press, 1974)
Fiction published in *The Bicentennial Collection of Texas Short Stories, South Dakota Review*

Carlos Morton
7931 Parral Dr., El Paso, Tex. 79915
(915) 591-2552
alternate address: c/o Gini Kopecky, 333 W. 22 St., Apt. 3-D, New York, N.Y. 10011, (212) 989-2746
HS, COL*, readings; speaks Spanish; is Chicano
Poetry: *White Heroin Winter* (One Eye Press, 1971)
Fiction published in *El Grito, La Luz*

Estela Portillo
131 Clairemont, El Paso, Tex. 79912
(915) 584-8841
alternate address: c/o A. Armendariz, 6252 Arapaho, El Paso, Tex. 79908, (915) 772-7943
HS*, COL*, readings; speaks Spanish; is Chicano
Poetry: *Impressions of a Chicana* (Quinto Sol, 1974)
Short Stories: *Rain of Scorpions* (Quinto Sol, 1974)

Tomas Rivera
5912 Trone Trail, San Antonio, Tex. 78238
(512) 684-5372
JHS*, HS*, COL*; has worked for Tex. PITS; speaks Spanish & French; is Chicano
Poetry: *Always and Other Poems* (Sisterdale Press, 1973)
Novel & Short Stories: *The Earth Did Not Part* (Quinto Sol, 1971)

Ricardo Sanchez
7845 Lilac Way, #103, El Paso, Tex. 79915
(915) 592-3827
alternate address: c/o Estela Silva, 3014 Rivera Ave., El Paso, Tex. 79905, (915) 533-0222
JHS*, HS*, COL*, readings; has worked for Tex. PITS; is interested in working with inmates; speaks Spanish; is Chicano
Poetry: *Canto y Grito Mi Liberacion—The Liberation of a Chicano Mind* (bilingual; Doubleday Anchor Books, 1973)
Fiction published in *Obras, Los Cuatro*

43

Les Standiford
778 Camino Real, El Paso, Tex. 79922
(505) 589-4592
  alternate address: c/o Dept. of English, U. of Texas,
El Paso, Tex. 79968
JHS*, HS*, COL*, readings; is interested in working
in prisons
Fiction published in *Bicentennial Collection of
Texas Short Stories, New and Experimental Fiction
From Texas*

R.G. Vliet
247 N. Houston St., New Braunfels, Tex. 78130
  Readings only; speaks Spanish
Poetry: *The Man With The Black Mouth* (Kayak
Books, 1970)
Fiction: *Rockspring: A Novel* (Viking, 1974)

James P. White
3503 Monclair, Odessa, Tex. 79762
(915) 366-9796
  NPS; speaks French
Poetry published in *Texas Quarterly, Kansas
Quarterly*
Fiction published in *Bicentennial Collection of
Texas Short Stories, Descant*

Jon Manchip White
Dept. of English, U. of Texas at El Paso, El Paso,
Tex. 79902
(915) 544-6499
  COL*, readings; speaks French, Spanish & Welsh
Poetry: *The Mountain Lion* (Wesleyan Press, 1971)
Novel: *The Garden Game* (Bobbs-Merrill, 1974)

VERMONT

Ben Birnbaum
Cedarhaven, Shelburne, Vt. 05401
(802) 985-3855
  JHS, HS, COL; speaks Hebrew and Yiddish
Fiction published in *Penthouse*

T. Alan Broughton
68 N. Union St., Burlington, Vt. 05401
(802) 864-4250
  COL*; has worked for Vt. PITS; speaks some Italian
Poetry: *In The Face Of Descent* (Carnegie-Mellon U.
Press, 1975)
Short Stories & Narrative Poems: *The Man On The
Moon* (Barlenmir House, 1975)

Margaret Edwards
68 N. Willard St., Burlington, Vt. 05401
(802) 862-4468
  COL*, readings; speaks French
Poetry published in *The Arizona Quarterly,
Stonecloud*
Fiction published in *Redbook, The Greensboro
Review*

John Gardner
c/o English Dept., Bennington College, N. Bennington,
Vt. 05257
(802) 442-8582
  HS, COL
Stories & Tales: *The King's Indian* (Knopf, 1974)

Jan Herman
Box 21, West Glover, Vt. 05875
(802) 525-3580
  COL*; speaks some French
Anti-Novel: *Cut Up or Shut Up* (Editions
Agentzia, Paris, 1972)

Dick Higgins
Box 26, West Glover, Vt. 05875
(802) 525-4468
  COL, readings; speaks German, French & Swedish
Poetry: *Modular Poems* (Unpublished
Editions, 1975)
Fiction: *A Book About Love & War & Death*
(Something Else Press, 1972)

David Huddle
Dept. of English, U. of Vermont, Burlington, Vt. 05451
(802) 879-7540
  JHS*, HS*, COL*, readings; has worked for Vt. PITS
Poetry published in *Esquire, The Georgia Review*
Short Stories: *A Dream With No Stump Roots In It*
(U. of Missouri Press, 1975)

Ward Just
Roxbury Rd., Warren, Vt. 05674
  NPS
Fiction: *Nicholson At Large* (Little, Brown, 1975)

Bernard Malamud
Dept. of English, Bennington College, Bennington,
Vt. 05201
  NPS
Short Stories: *Rembrandt's Hat* (Farrar, Straus
& Giroux, 1973; Pocket Books, 1974)

Geoffrey Wolff
Prickly Mountain, Warren, Vt. 05674
(802) 496-2643
  HS, COL*, readings; is interested in working in
prisons, drug rehabilitation centers, and old age
homes; speaks Spanish & French
Novel: *The Sightseer* (Random House, 1974)

VIRGINIA

Dick Dabney
2806 Key Blvd., Arlington, Va. 22201
(703) 243-9148
  NPS; interested in working in prisons
Fiction: *Old Man Jim's Book of Knowledge* (Randon
House, 1973)

R.H.W. Dillard
Box 9671, Hollins College, Va. 24020
(703) 366-8460
  COL*, readings
Poetry: *After Borges* (La. State U. Press, 1972)
Novel: *The Book of Changes* (Doubleday, 1974)

Nancy Hale
Box 467, Rt. 8, Charlottesville, Va. 22901
  NPS; is interested in writers' conferences
Fiction: *Secrets* (Coward-McCann & Geoghegan,
1971)

Joseph Maiolo
RR 1, Box 158, Ashburn, Va. 22011
(703) 777-7909
  COL*, readings; is interested in working in prisons;
speaks some Italian
Novella: *Elverno* (Blairwood Publishers, 1972)

Eleanor Ross Taylor
1101 Rugby Rd., Charlottesville, Va. 22903
  NPS
  Poetry: *Welcome Eumenides* (Braziller, 1972)
  Fiction published in *Sewanee Review* & *Prize Stories 1971: The O. Henry Awards*

Peter Taylor
1101 Rugby Rd., Charlottesville, Va. 22903
  NPS
  Short Stories: *Collected Stories of Peter Taylor* (Farrar, Straus & Giroux, 1969; paperback, Farrar, Straus & Giroux, 1971)

WASHINGTON

Floyce Alexander
Rt. 1, Box 220, Granger, Wash. 98932
(509) 854-1644
  ALL (COL*); is interested in working in prisons and with young minority groups, especially Native Americans; speaks Spanish
  Poetry: *Machete* (Lillabulero Press, 1972)
  Fiction published in *Journeybook, Spectrum*

Mary Barnard
7100 Evergreen Hwy., Vancouver, Wash. 98664
(206) 693-1342
  COL
  Poetry published in *The New Yorker Book of Poems*
  Fiction published in *Kenyon Review, Yale Review*

Jack Cady
933 Tyler St., Port Townsend, Wash. 98368
  ALL (EL*, HS*, COL*), readings
  Short Stories: *The Burning* (U. of Iowa Press, 1972)

Charles Henley
Rt. 3, Box 70, Davenport, Wash. 99122
  alternate address: c/o Anne or Chester Henley, 2857 Greenview Dr., Jackson, Miss. 39212, (601) 372-5993
  ALL*; has worked for S.C. PITS; is interested in working in prisons, drug rehabilitation centers, old age homes, homes for disturbed children & in conducting workshops for groups attempting to start or improve their publications
  Short Stories: *The Samaritan* (Crane Press, 1975)

Colleen McElroy
2200 N.E. 75th Street, Seattle, Wash. 98115
(206) LA4-9676
  ALL*; has worked for Wash. PITS; is interested in working in prisons; speaks French, German & Swahili;
  Poetry: *Music From Home* (Southern Illinois U. Press, 1975)
  Fiction published in *Sojourner Collective, Dark Waters*

David Wagoner
1075 Summit Ave. E., Seattle, Wash. 98102
(206) 329-0921
  COL*, readings; is interested in working in prisons; has worked for Idaho, Wash. & Hawaii PITS
  Poetry: *Sleeping in the Woods* (Indiana U. Press, 1974)
  Novel: *Tracker* (Atlantic-Little, Brown, 1975)

Douglas Woolf
P.O. Box 215, Tacoma, Wash. 98401
  NPS
  Novel: *Spring of the Lamb* (Jargon Books, 1972)

WISCONSIN

Thomas Bontly
9077 N. Meadowlark Lane, Bayside, Wis. 53217
  COL*
  Novel: *The Adventures Of A Young Outlaw* (G.P. Putnam, 1974)

Ray Puechner
Ray Peekner Literary Agency, 2625 N. 36th St., Milwaukee, Wis. 53210
(414) 442-5539
  COL, readings
  Novel: *A Grand Slam* (Warner Paperback Library, 1973)

R.E. Sebenthal
104 Thompson St., Mt. Horeb, Wis. 53572
(608) 437-3547
  NPS
  Poetry: *Acquainted with a Chance of Bobcats* (Rutgers U. Press, 1970)
  Fiction: *The Cold Ones* under pseudonym of Paul Kruger (Simon & Schuster, 1972)

WYOMING

Peggy Simson Curry
3125 Garden Creek Rd., Casper, Wyo. 82601
(307) 235-6918
  ALL*; has worked in Wyo. & S.Dak. PITS
  Fiction: *Fictional Biography I* (Houghton Mifflin, 1973)

CANADA

Margaret Atwood
Box 1401, Alliston, Ont. Canada LOM 1AO
(705) 435-4175
  readings
  Poetry: *Power Politics* (Harper & Row, 1973)
  Fiction: *Surfacing* (Simon & Schuster, 1973)

John Ditsky
English Dept., University of Windsor, Windsor, Ontario, Canada
  alternate address: 18235 Oak Dr., Detroit, Mich. 48221, (313) 863-0967
  COL*, readings; speaks French & some German
  Poetry published in *Western Humanities Review, The New York Times*
  Fiction published in *First Encounter, South Florida Review*

William Kuhns
R.R.1, Alcove, Quebec, Canada
(819) 459-2523
  ALL
  Novel: *The Reunion* (Wm. Morrow, 1973; New American Library, 1974)

Eugene McNamara
166 Randolph Pl., Windsor, Ontario, Canada
(519) 254-0797
  HS*, COL*, readings; has worked for Mich. PITS
  Poetry: *Passages* (Sono Nis Press, 1972)
  Fiction published in *Denver Quarterly, Malahat Review*

Joyce Carol Oates
c/o English Dept., U. of Windsor, Windsor, Ontario, Canada
  NPS
  Poetry: *Angel Fire* (La. State U. Press, 1973)
  Short Stories: *The Goddess and Other Women* (Vanguard, 1974)

Joanna Ostrow
RR2, North Gower, Ontario K0A 2T0, Canada
  NPS
  Novel: *In The Highlands Since Time Immemorial* (Alfred A. Knopf, 1970)

Leon Rooke
Literature & American Language Dept., Southwest Minnesota State College, Marshall, Minn. 56258
  ALL (COL*)
  Novella: *Vault* (Lillabulero Press, 1974)

Elizabeth Spencer
2300 St. Matthew, Apt. 610, Montreal, Quebec H3H 2J8, Canada
(514) 935-2072
  COL; speaks Italian & some French
  Novel: *The Snare* (McGraw-Hill, 1972)

Robert Sward (Vasudeva)
1050 Saint David St., Victoria, British Columbia, Canada V8S 4Y8
(604) 598-2173
  ALL*; has worked for Wash. & British Columbia PITS
  Poetry: *Poems: New & Selected (1957-1975)* (Coach House Press, 1976)
  Novella: *The Jurassic Shales* (Coach House Press, 1975)

Audrey Thomas
3305 W. 11th Ave., Vancouver, British Columbia, Canada
  Readings; is interested in working in mental hospitals & with blind children; speaks some French
  Novel: *Blown Figures* (Talonbooks, 1975; Alfred A. Knopf, 1976)

ENGLAND

Elliott Baker
52 Park Close, London W14 8NH, England
  alternate address: c/o Morton L. Leavy, 437 Madison Ave., New York, N.Y. 10022
  NPS
  Short Stories: *Unrequited Loves* (G.P. Putnam, 1974)

J.G. Ballard
c/o John Wolfers, 3 Regent Sq., Bloomsbury, London, W.C.1, England
  NPS
  Novel: *Concrete Island* (Farrar, Straus & Giroux, 1974)

George Barker
Bintry House, Itteringham, Aylsham, Norfolk, England
phone: Saxthorpe 240
  alternate address: c/o William Coakley, 120 W. 71 St., Apt. 2R, New York, N.Y. 10023, (212) 873-6884
  HS*, COL*, readings
  Poetry: *In Memory of David Archer* (Faber & Faber, 1973)
  Fiction: *The Dead Seagull* (George Lehman, 1950)

Roald Dahl
Gipsy House, Great Missenden, Bucks, England
Telephone: 2757
  COL; speaks Norwegian
  Short Stories: *Switch Bitch* (Alfred A. Knopf, 1974)

Hans Koning (Koningsberger)
c/o Anthony Sheil Ltd., 52 Floral St., London WC 2, England
Telephone: 836.8376
  alternate address: c/o Lois Wallace, Wallace, Aitken & Sheil, 118 E. 61 St., New York, N.Y. 10021, (212) 751-1944
  HS*, COL*, readings; has presented writing seminars in ghetto high schools; speaks French, Dutch & German
  Novel: *The Petersburg-Cannes Express* (Harcourt Brace Jovanovich, 1975)

George Lamming
14A Highbury Place, London N5, England
  alternate address: c/o Holt, Rinehart & Winston, 383 Madison Ave., New York, N.Y. 10017, (212) MU8-9100
  COL; is Black
  Novel: *Water with Berries* (Holt, Rinehart & Winston, 1972)

Hugh J. Parry (James Cross)
Alexander Pl., London, S.W.7, England
  alternate address: Social Research Group, George Washington University, 2401 Virginia Ave. N.W., Washington, D.C. 20037, (202) 331-8706
  NPS
  Novel: *To Hell for Half a Crown* (Random House, 1967)

Frederic Michael Raphael
The Wick, Langham, Colchester, Essex, England
Telephone: Colchester 322108
  COL*, readings; interested in working in prisons; speaks French, some Italian, Greek & Spanish
  Novel: *Richard's Things* (Bobbs-Merrill, 1975)

Paul Theroux
19 Pattenden Rd., London S.E. 6, England
  alternate address: c/o Blanche Gregory, Inc., 2 Tudor City Pl., New York, N.Y. 10017, (212) OX7-0828
  COL*, readings; is interested in working in prisons; speaks French & Italian
  Novel: *The Black House* (Houghton Mifflin, 1975)

FRANCE

Samuel Astrachan
84220, Gordes, France (April-December)
72-00-66
  January-March: Writer-in-residence, Wayne State U. Detroit, Mich. 48202
  NPS; speaks French
  Novel: *Rejoice* (Dial, 1970)

Chandler Brossard
15 Rue de la Huerette, Paris 5e, France
  alternate address: c/o Iris Brossard, 217 E. 22nd St., Apt. 16, New York, N.Y. 10010, (212) 689-4864
  NPS; speaks some Italian
  Novel: *Did Christ Make Love* (Bobbs-Merrill, 1973)

Mavis Gallant
14, Rue Jean Ferraudi, Paris, XIIIe, France
   alternate address: c/o Georges Borchardt, Inc.,
145 E. 52nd St., New York, N.Y. 10022, (212) PL3-5785
NPS
   A Novella & Short Stories: *The Pegnitz Junction*
(Random House, 1973)

Harry Mathews
35, Rue de Varenne, Paris, France 75007
(01) 222-01-67
   alternate address: c/o Maxine Groffsky, 104 Greenwich
Ave., New York, N.Y. 10014, (212) 924-2615
COL*, readings; speaks French & Italian
Poetry: *The Planisphere* (Burning Deck, 1974)
Fiction: *The Sinking of the Odradek Stadium and
Other Novels* (Harper & Row, 1975)

Frederic Prokosch
'Ma Trouvaille,' Plan de Grasse, Alpes Maritimes,
France
   alternate address: c/o Robert Giroux, Farrar, Straus
& Giroux, Inc., 19 Union Sq. W., New York, N.Y. 10003,
(212) 741-6900
NPS
   Novel: *America, My Wilderness* (Farrar, Straus
& Giroux, 1972)

ITALY

Anthony Burgess
Piazza S. Cecilia, #16/A, Rome, Italy
   NPS
   Novel: *The Clockwork Testament or Enderby's
End* (Alfred A. Knopf, 1975)

David Ely
Costa San Giorgio 47, Florence, Italy
   alternate address: c/o Roberta Pryor, International
Creative Management, 40 W. 57 St., New York, N.Y.
10019, (212) 556-5600
COL
Novel: *Mr. Nicholas* (G.P. Putnam, 1974)

MEXICO

Paul Alexander Bartlett
Calle Benito Juarez 103, Comala, Colima, Mexico
   readings; speaks Spanish
   Fiction: *When The Owl Cries* (Macmillan, 1970)

Leonard Wallace Robinson
Apdo. 462, San Miguel Allende, Guanajuato, Mexico 20452
Telephone: 21452
   COL*
   Novel: *The Listening Room* (New American Library, 1976)

MOROCCO

Paul Bowles
2117 Tanger Socco, Tangier, Morocco
   readings; speaks French, Spanish, Moghrebi
   Poetry: *The Thicket Of Spring* (Black Sparrow,
1972)
   Short Stories: *The Time Of Friendship* (Holt,
Rinehart & Winston, 1967)

SPAIN

Harris Dulany
Calle de San Jose 13, Altea (Alicante), Spain
   alternate address: c/o Betty Anne Clark, International
Creative Management, 40 W. 57 St., New York,
N.Y. 10019, (212) 556-5600
ALL; is interested in working in prisons, drug reha-
bilitation centers, old age homes; speaks Spanish
Novel: *Perfect Summer* (Redbook, 1974)

SWITZERLAND

Vladimir Nabokov
The Palace Hotel, Montreux, Switzerland
   NPS
   Novel: *Bend Sinister* (McGraw-Hill, 1975)

Irwin Shaw
Klosters, Switzerland
   alternate address: c/o Irving P. Lazar, 211 S. Beverly
Dr., Beverly Hills, Calif. 90212, (213) CR5-6153
Not available for readings; speaks French
Novel: *Nightwork* (Delacorte, 1975)

"LOST" WRITERS

Correspondence to the following writers has been returned.
Current information would be most appreciated.

Iowa
E. Lagomarsino

Pennsylvania
John Wideman

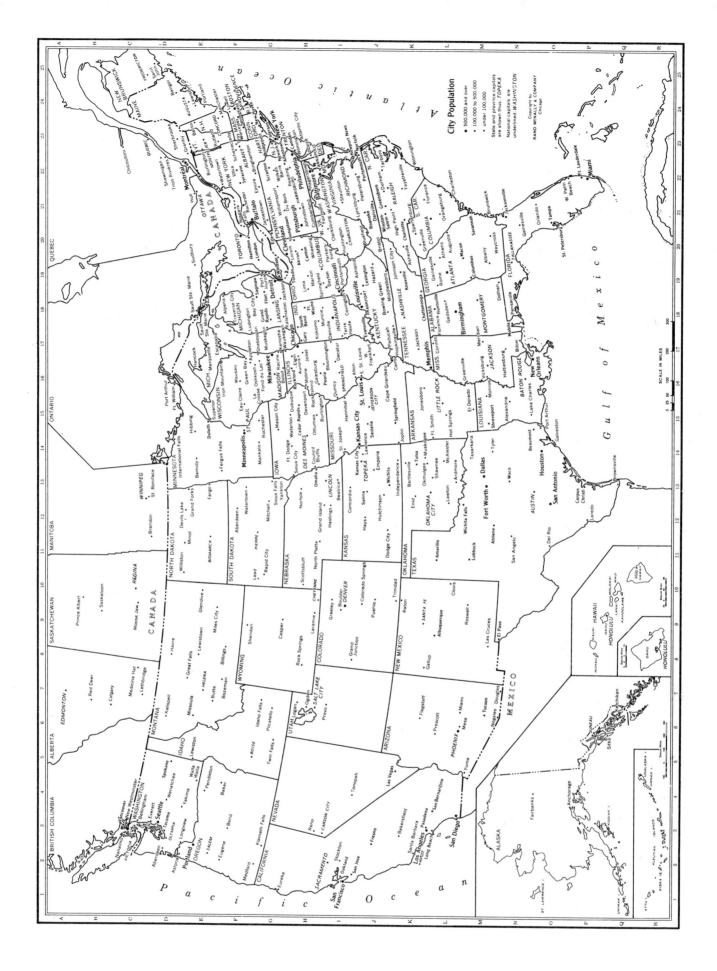

City Population

• 500,000 and over
• 100,000 to 500,000
• under 100,000

State and province capitals
are shown thus: TOPEKA
National capitals are
underlined WASHINGTON

Copyright by
RAND McNALLY & COMPANY
Chicago

The Sponsors

Organizations that Sponsor Programs Involving Fiction Writers and Poets

The purpose of this listing is to facilitate contact between authors—especially those planning to tour—and interested sponsors throughout the United States.

In order to provide accurate current information in this Directory, Poets & Writers, Inc. sent questionnaires to over 500 organizations that sponsor poetry and fiction programs. Because replies were incomplete and inconsistent, the listing that follows is irregular. Addresses, telephone numbers, and names of administrators are usually included, and budget information and extent of annual sponsorship (e.g. "5 writers" or "10 writers") is provided whenever figures were supplied.

The section is organized geographically, with sponsors listed alphabetically within each state. The New York State listing separates New York City sponsors from those located elsewhere in the state.

Authors interested in reading assignments should bear in mind that while most of the state arts councils have instituted Poets-in-the-Schools programs, few sponsor regular readings. Letters of inquiry to colleges might be sent to the chairman of student activities as well as to the administrator indicated in the listing, since their programming schedules and budgets are often separate.

ALABAMA

Alabama State Council on the Arts and Humanities
Marlo Bussman, Editor
322 Alabama St., Montgomery, Ala. 36104
(205) 832-6758
Budget: $12,000 for visiting writers; $7,000 for Poets-in-the-Schools
14 writers

Seminar Literary Arts Committee & Creative Writing Roundtable
Jack H. Mooney, Chairman & Coordinator
2659 Oxford Dr., Montgomery, Ala. 36111
(205) 293-7641 (office) or (205) 288-5837 (home)
Budget: no set amount
Three writers

University of Alabama Visiting Writers Series
Thomas Rabbitt, Director of Creative Writing
Dept. of English
University, Ala. 35486
(205) 348-5065
Budget: Over $2,500 per year
4-6 writers

ALASKA

Alaska State Council on the Arts
Roy Helms, Executive Director
360 K St., Rm. 240, Anchorage, Alaska 99501
(907) 279-3824
Budget: $10,000 per year for writers-in-residence (in state only); $5,000 per year for Poets-in-the-Schools
Eight writers

ARIZONA

Arizona Commission on the Arts and Humanities
Nancy Pierce, Director
Literature Program
6330 N. Seventh St., Phoenix, Ariz. 85014
(602) 271-5884
Budget: $18,000 per year for Poets-in-the-Schools
20 writers

Arizona State University
Jerry Keeran, Chairman
Cultural Affairs Board
Memorial Union, Complex 208, Tempe, Ariz. 85281
(602) 965-5658
Budget: $2,500 per year
Six writers

South West Poets Conference
Randall Ackley, Director
Navajo Community College at Tsaile (Ariz.), via Navajo, N.Mex. 87328
(602) 724-3311
Budget: $2,000-$3,000 per year
12 writers

University of Arizona
Lois Shelton, Creative Writing Program
Dept. of English
Tucson, Ariz. 85712
(602) 884-2462
Ten writers

University of Arizona Poetry Center
Lois Shelton, Director
1086 N. Highland, Tucson, Ariz. 85719
(602) 884-2462
Budget: indefinite
Eight writers

ARKANSAS

Office of Arkansas State Arts and Humanities
Sandra Perry, Executive Director
404 Train Station Sq., Little Rock, Ark. 72201
(501) 371-2539
Budget: $5,000 per year for Poets-in-the-Schools
15 writers

Office of Arkansas State Arts and Humanities
Carol Gaddy, Artists-in-Schools Coordinator
400 Train Station Sq., Little Rock, Ark. 72201
(501) 371-2539
Budget: $2,000 per year
Two full-time resident poets
Ten part-time poets
Seven visiting writers

University of Arkansas
James Whitehead, Miller Williams, Program in Creative Writing
Dept. of English
Fayetteville, Ark. 72701
(501) 575-4301
Eight writers

CALIFORNIA

American River College
Chairman, Committee on Speakers and Programs
Dept. of English
4700 College Oak Dr., Sacramento, Calif. 95814
(916) 484-8102
Three writers

Cabrillo College
Morton Marcus
English Division
6500 Soquel Dr., Aptos, Calif. 95003
(408) 475-6000
Budget: $500 per year
Ten writers

California Arts Commission
Leslie Olmstead, Public Information Manager
808 'O' St., Sacramento, Calif. 95814
(916) 445-1530
Acts as referral organization only

California Institute of the Arts
Chairperson, Complementary Education
24700 McBean Pkwy., Valencia, Calif. 91355
(805) 255-1050
Eight writers

California Institute of Technology
Director of Creative Writing
Dept. of English
Pasadena, Calif. 91109

California State University at Chico
Clark Brown
Dept. of English
First and Normal Sts., Chico, Calif. 95929
(916) 895-6151
Seven writers

California State University at Fresno
Director of Creative Writing
Dept. of English
Shaw & Cedar Ave., Fresno, Calif. 93710
(209) 487-9011

California State University at Hayward
Director of Creative Writing
Dept. of English
25800 Hillary St., Hayward, Calif. 94542
(415) 884-3000

California State University at Long Beach
Elliot Fried, Creative Writing Coordinator
Dept. of English
6101 E. 7th St., Long Beach, Calif. 90840
(213) 498-4244
Six writers

California State University at Los Angeles
Chairman
Dept. of English
5151 State University Ave., Los Angeles, Calif. 90032
(213) 224-2576
2-3 writers

California State University at Sacramento
Director of Creative Writing
Dept. of English
6000 J St., Sacramento, Calif. 95819
(916) 454-6011

California State University at Sacramento
Geri Lidgard
Cultural Programs Committee
6000 J St., Sacramento, Calif. 95819
(916) 454-6329
Six writers

California State University at San Jose
Director of Creative Writing
Dept. of English
125 S. Seventh St., San Jose, Calif. 95114
(408) 277-2000

California State College at Sonoma
Director of Creative Writing
Dept. of English
1801 E. Cotati Ave., Rohnert Park, Calif. 94928
(707) 795-2011

California Writers Guild
Collette Burns, President
7055 Shoup Ave., Canoga Park, Calif. 91307
(213) 340-2303

Cody's Bookstore
Alan Soldofsky, Jon Ford, Jana Harris, Rick Foster
Poetry at Cody's
2450 Telegraph (at Haste), Berkeley, Calif. 94704
(415) 845-7852
75 writers

College of Marin
Director of Creative Writing
Dept. of English
Kentfield, Calif. 94904

College of Marin
Director
Writer's Conference
Kentfield, Calif. 94904

De Anza College
Frank Berry, Director
The De Anza Poetry Series
21250 Stevens Creek Blvd., Cupertino, Calif. 95014
(408) 257-5550, Ext. 249 or Ext. 466
    Budget: $50-100 per reading
    Eight writers

Foothill College
Director of Creative Writing
Dept. of English
12345 El Monte Rd., Los Altos Hills, Calif. 94022
(415) 948-8590

Humboldt State University
Richard C. Day
Dept. of English
Arcata, Calif. 95521
(707) 826-3759
    Two writers

Intersection Center for Religion and Art
Barbara Gravelle, Program Director
756 Union St., San Francisco, Calif. 94133
(415) 397-6061
    Budget: $40 per writer
    Seven writers per week

Lone Mountain College
Director of Creative Writing
Dept. of English
2800 Turk Blvd., San Francisco, Calif. 94118
(415) 752-7000

Moorpark College
Director of Creative Writing
Dept. of English
7075 Campus Rd., Moorpark, Calif. 94321

Otis Art Institute of Los Angeles County
M. McCloud, Director of Creative Language
Dept. of Humanities, 2401 Wilshire Blvd., Los Angeles,
Calif. 90057
(213) 387-5288
    $50-$100 per writer
    Four-ten writers

The Poetry Center
Lewis MacAdams, Jr.
San Francisco State University
1600 Holloway Ave., San Francisco, Calif. 94132
(415) 469-2227
    50 writers per year

Poets Essayists Novelists (P.E.N.) American Center
Gwen Bristow, President
Box 144, Encino, Calif. 91316

Poets-in-the-Schools for California
Floyd Salas & Carolee Sanchez, Co-Directors
San Francisco State U., 1600 Holloway Ave.,
San Francisco, Calif. 94132
(415) 469-1433 or (415) 469-2227
    102 writers (in-state writers only)

Pomona College
R.G. Barnes
Dept. of English
Claremont, Calif. 91711
(714) 626-8511, Ext. 2212
    Nine writers

St. Mary's College
Director
Committee on Lectures
Moraga, Calif. 94575
(415) 376-4411

St. Mary's College
Director of Creative Writing
Dept. of English
Moraga, Calif. 94575
(415) 376-4411

San Diego State University
Fred Moramarco, Director
School of Literature
San Diego, Calif. 92182
(714) 286-5443
    Budget: varies
    Four writers

San Francisco Art Institute
Director of Creative Writing
Dept. of English
800 Chestnut, San Francisco, Calif. 94133
(415) 771-7020

Stanford University
Richard Scowcroft, Director
Creative Writing Center
Dept. of English
Stanford, Calif. 94305
(415) 947-2637
    Five writers

Squaw Valley Community of Writers
Blaire Fuller and Oakley Hall, Directors
P.O. Box 2352, Olympic Valley, Calif. 95730
(415) 433-4619
    20 writers

University of California at Berkeley
Director of Creative Writing
Dept. of English
Berkeley, Calif. 94720
(415) 845-6000

University of California at Davis
Jack Hicks
Speakers & Lecturers Committee
Dept. of English
809 Sproul Hall, Davis, Calif. 95616
(916) 752-1658 or (916) 758-1875
    Budget: $1,500-2,000 per year
    12 writers

University of California at Irvine
James McMichael, Director
California Poetry Reading Circuit
Dept. of English, Irvine, Calif. 92664
(714) 833-6712
  Budget: $600 per year
  Three writers

University of California at Los Angeles
Frederick Burwick, Acting Chairman
Dept. of English
405 Hilgard, Los Angeles, Calif. 90024
  Budget: $400-800 per year
  4-5 writers

University of California at Los Angeles
Director
Office of Cultural and Recreational Affairs
405 Hilgard, Los Angeles, Calif. 90024
(213) 825-3671

University of California at Northridge
R.H. Deutsch
Dept. of English
18111 Nordhoff St., Northridge, Calif. 91324
(213) 885-1200
  Six writers

University of California at Santa Barbara
Director of Creative Writing
Dept. of English
Santa Barbara, Calif. 93107

University of California at Santa Cruz
Director of Creative Writing
Dept. of English
Santa Cruz, Calif. 95060

University of the Pacific
Charles Clerc
Dept. of English
Stockton, Calif. 95204
(209) 946-2122
  Two writers

COLORADO

Colorado College
Director of Creative Writing
Dept. of English
Colorado Springs, Colo. 80903

Colorado Council on the Arts and Humanities
Judith Wray, Director
Artists-in-the-Schools
1550 Lincoln St., Rm. 205, Denver, Colo. 80203
(303) 892-2617
  Eight writers (Poets-in-the-Schools only; in-state
  writers only)

Colorado State University
Mary Crow
Fine Arts Series
Dept. of English, Fort Collins, Colo. 80523
(303) 491-6843 or (303) 482-9923
  Budget: varies
  12 writers

University of Colorado at Boulder
Director
Creative Writing Program
Dept. of English, Boulder, Colo. 80302
(303) 492-7922
  Six-seven writers

University of Denver
Director of Creative Writing
Dept. of English
Denver, Colo. 80210

CONNECTICUT

Connecticut College
Chairman
Dept. of English
New London, Conn. 06320

Connecticut Commission on the Arts
Leanna Loomer, Program Assistant or
Jed Schlosberg, Program Associate
340 Capitol Ave., Hartford, Conn. 06106
(203) 566-4770

Connecticut Poetry Circuit
Jean Maynard, Director
The Honors College, Wesleyan U., Middletown,
Conn. 06457
(203) 347-9411
  12 writers

Enfield Central Library
Director of Poetry Readings
10 Middle Rd., Enfield, Conn. 06082

Housatonic Valley Regional High School
Donald Kobler, Coordinator
Visiting Artists Program
Falls Village, Conn. 06031
(203) 824-5123
  Budget: $50 per day to $500 per week
  12 writers

Quinnipiac College
Director of Creative Writing
Dept. of English
Mt. Carmel Ave., Hamden, Conn. 06518

Salisbury School
S. Grant Rudnicki, Chairman
English Department
Salisbury, Conn. 06068
(203) 435-2931
  Budget: $500 per year
  One writer

University of Bridgeport
Director of Creative Writing
Dept. of English
Bridgeport, Conn. 06602

Yale University
Director of Creative Writing
Dept. of English
108 Linsly-Chittenden, New Haven, Conn. 06518
(203) 436-8856

Ziesing Bros.' Book Emporium
Michael Ziesing
Box 562, Willimantic, Conn. 06226
(203) 423-5836
  Ten writers

DELAWARE

Delaware State Arts Council
Sophie Consagra, Executive Director
803 Wilmington Tower, S-803, 1105 Market St.,
Wilmington, Del. 19801
(302) 571-3540
  Budget: $5,000 per year
  Eight writers

Jewish Community Center
Director of Poetry Readings
101 Garden of Eden Rd., Wilmington, Del. 19803
(302) 478-5660

DISTRICT OF COLUMBIA

The American University
Kermit Mayer, Colloquium Director or Tom Cannon
Dept. of Literature
Massachusetts & Nebraska Aves. N.W., Washington,
D.C. 20016
(202) 686-2450 (Mayer) or (202) 686-0361 (Cannon)

Ascension Poetry Theâtre
E. Ethelbert Miller, Coordinator
P.O. Box 441, Howard University, Washington, D.C.
20059
(202) 232-3066 or (202) 636-7242
  25 writers

D.C. Black Writers Workshop
Annie Crittenden, Director
615 Kensington Pl., N.E., Washington, D.C. 20011
(202) 832-8932

District of Columbia Public Library
Octave S. Stevenson, Chief
Language and Literature Division
901 G St., N.W., Washington, D.C. 20001
(202) 727-1264
  42 writers

Folger Shakespeare Library
Leni Spencer, Advisor
Poetry Office
201 East Capitol St., S.E., Washington, D.C. 20003
(202) 547-2461 or (202) 546-4800, Ext. 27
  35-50 writers

Jewish Community Center of Greater Washington
Mrs. Tommy Feldman, Director of Literary Arts
Kass Judaic Library
6125 Montrose Rd., Rockville, Md. 20852
(301) 881-0100
  20 writers (programs must have Judaic content)

Library of Congress
John C. Broderick, Chief
Manuscript Division
Washington, D.C. 20540
(202) 426-5383
  16 writers

National Endowment for the Arts
Leonard Randolph, Director
Literature Programs
1425 K St. N.W., Washington, D.C. 20506
(202) 382-6186

Textile Museum
Director
Poetry & Literature Series
2320 S St. N.W., Washington, D.C. 20008
(202) 667-0441
  12 writers

Washington Poetry Center
Roderick Jellema, Director
c/o Dept. of English, U. of Maryland, College Park,
Md. 20742
(301) 587-9205

FLORIDA

Rollins College
Director of Creative Writing
Dept. of English
Winter Park, Fla. 32789

Apalachee Poetry Center
Van K. Brock, Director
418 Williams Bldg., Florida State U., Tallahassee,
Fla. 32306
(904) 644-6047

Eckerd College Writing Workshop
Peter Meinke, Director
St. Petersburg, Fla. 33733
(813) 867-1166
  Budget: varies
  Four writers

Fine Arts Council of Florida
S. Leonard Pas, Jr., Director
Department of State, The Capitol, Tallahasee, Fla. 32304
(904) 488-4343

Florida State University
Van K. Brock, Faculty Advisor
Poetry Arts Coop
418 Williams Bldg., Tallahassee, Fla. 32306
(904) 644-6047
  Budget: $1,000 per quarter
  Six writers

Florida State University
David K. Kirby, Director
Writing Programs
Dept. of English, Tallahassee, Fla. 32306
(904) 644-5819
  One writer

Santa Fe Community College
Barbara Kirkpatrick
Spring Arts Festival
P.O. Box 1530, 3000 N.W. 83 St., Gainesville,
Fla. 32602
(904) 377-5161
  Budget: $500-$2,000 per year
  Six writers

University of Florida
Smith Kirkpatrick, Writing Program Director
Florida Writers' Conference and Visiting Poets Program
Dept. of English, Gainesville, Fla. 32601
(904) 392-0777
   Budget: $40,000
   Nine writers

GEORGIA

Agnes Scott College
Margret G. Trotter
Creative Writing
English Dept., Decatur, Ga. 30030
(404) 373-2571
   Three writers

Albany State College
Director of Creative Writing
Dept. of English
Albany, Ga. 31705

Atlanta University Center
Director of Creative Writing
55 Walnut St. N.W., Atlanta, Ga. 30314

Augusta College
Charles L. Willig
Dept. of English
2500 Walton Way, Augusta, Ga. 30904
(404) 828-3706
   Three writers

Emory University
Michael Mott, Writer-in-Residence
Dept. of English
Atlanta, Ga. 30322
(404) 377-2411, Ext. 7535
   Budget: $1,500 per year
   Four writers

Georgia Council for the Arts
Jane Ferriss, Program Director
Suite 706, 225 Peachtree St., N.E., Atlanta, Ga. 30303
(404) 656-3990
   Budget: $12,500 per year for Poets-in-the-Schools
   Seven writers

Georgia State University
Director of Creative Writing
Dept. of English
Athens, Ga. 30601

Mercer University
Thomas B. Young
Dept. of English
Box 46, Mercer U., Macon, Ga. 31207
(912) 743-1511, Ext. 211 or 226
   Eight-ten writers

Poetry at Callanwolde
Robert Holland, Chairman
980 Briarcliff Rd., N.E., Atlanta, Ga. 30030
(404) 872-5338
   25 writers

HAWAII

Hawaii Council of Teachers of English
Director
Dept. of English as a Second Language
U. of Hawaii, 1890 East-West Rd., Honolulu, Hawaii
96822
(808) 948-8610

Hawaii Literary Arts Council
John Unterecker, President
c/o Dept. of English, U. of Hawaii
1733 Donaghho Rd., Honolulu, Hawaii 96822
(808) 947-8727
   Five writers

Hawaii State Foundation on Culture and the Arts
Alfred Preis, Executive Director
250 S. King St., Rm. 310, Honolulu, Hawaii 96813
(808) 548-4145

University of Hawaii
Ian MacMillan, Chairman of Creative Writing
Dept. of English
1733 Donaghho Rd., Honolulu, Hawaii 96822
(808) 948-7619

IDAHO

Idaho State Commission on the Arts and Humanities
Suzanne Taylor, Executive Director
State House, Boise, Idaho 83720
(208) 384-2119

Idaho Poets-in-the-Schools
M.K. Browning, Director
c/o Dept. of English, Lewis and Clark State College,
Lewiston, Idaho 83501
(208) 746-2341
   Six writers

University of Idaho
Director of Creative Writing
Dept. of English
Moscow, Idaho 83843

ILLINOIS

Central Illinois Cultural Affairs Consortium
Norma Murphy, Executive Director
1501 W. Bradley Ave., Peoria, Ill. 61606
(309) 674-7355

Illinois Arts Council
Jane Turczyn, Special Projects Coordinator—Literature
111 N. Wabash Ave., Rm. 1610, Chicago, Ill. 60602
(312) 793-3520
   Budget: $17,500 per year
   55 writers

Northwestern University
Elliott Anderson, Director
Writing Program
101 University Hall, Evanston, Ill. 60201
(312) 492-3490
   12 writers

The Poetry Forum
Suzanne Brabant, Poetry Forum Representative
1420 North Ave., Bannockburn, Ill. 60015
(312) 945-0382

Shimer College
Robert Schuler
Humanities Area
Mt. Carroll, Ill. 61053
(815) 244-6575
    Budget: indefinite
    Three writers

Southern Illinois University
Director of Creative Writing
Dept. of English
Carbondale, Ill. 62901
(618) 453-2121

University of Chicago at Chicago Circle
Director of Creative Writing
Dept. of English
Box 4348, Chicago, Ill. 60680

University of Illinois
Director of Creative Writing
Dept. of English
Urbana, Illinois 61801

University of Illinois at Chicago Circle
Chairman
Program for Writers
University Hall, 601 S. Morgan, Chicago, Ill. 60680
(312) 996-2285

INDIANA

Indiana Arts Commission
Cindy Gehrig, Education Program Director
155 E. Market, Suite 614, Indianapolis, Ind. 46204
(317) 633-5649
    10-15 writers

Indiana Council of Teachers of English
Edward B. Jenkinson, President
English Curriculum Study Center, 1125 Atwater,
Bloomington, Ind. 47401
(812) 337-3311
    Two writers

Indiana University
Kenneth R.R. Gros Louis, Chairperson
Dept. of English
Ballantine Hall, Bloomington, Ind. 47401
(812) 337-8224
    4 writers

Saint Mary's College
Director of Creative Writing
Dept. of English
Notre Dame, Ind. 46556
(219) 284-4516

University of Notre Dame
Director of Creative Writing
Dept. of English
Notre Dame, Indiana 46556

IOWA

Cornell College
Robert Dana, Chairman
Dept. of English
Mt. Vernon, Iowa 52314
(319) 895-8311
    Budget: $100-$150
    4 writers

Iowa State Arts Council
Nancy Stillians, Educational Development Director
State Capitol Bldg., Des Moines, Iowa 50319
(515) 281-5297
    Budget: $9,000 per year
    8-12 writers

Iowa Writers' Workshop
Director
c/o English-Philosophy Bldg., U. of Iowa,
Iowa City, Iowa 52242
(319) 353-4986
    Ten writers

University of Iowa
Paul Engle, Director
International Writing Program
Iowa City, Iowa 52242

University of Northern Iowa
Director of Creative Writing
Dept. of English
Cedar Falls, Iowa 50613
(319) 273-2821

KANSAS

Kansas Arts Commission
Mary Lee Johns, Special Projects Consultant
Suite 100, 117 W. 10th St., Topeka, Kans. 66612
(913) 296-3335
    Budget: $6,000 per year to be matched
    by Poets-in-the-Schools sponsor
    17 writers

Kansas Poetry Circuit
S.J. Sackett, Director
Box 386, Hays, Kans. 67601
(913) 625-9248

Kansas State University
Ben M. Nyberg, Creative Writing Director
Dept. of English
Denison Hall, Manhattan, Kans. 66506
(913) 532-6716
    Four writers

University of Kansas
Director of Creative Writing
Dept. of English
Lawrence, Kans. 66044
(913) 864-2700

Wichita Office of Community Arts
Director
225 W. Douglas, Wichita, Kans. 67202
(316) 262-0611

Wichita State University
Coordinator
Creative Writing Program
Dept. of English, Wichita, Kans. 67208
(316) 689-3130
    Five writers

Wichita State University
Director
New Writers Group
Dept. of English, Wichita, Kans. 67208
(316) 689-3456

KENTUCKY

Brescia College
S.M. Gehres, Chairman
Dept. of Humanities
120 W. 7th St., Owensboro, Ky. 43201
(502) 685-3131
    Budget: $400 per year
    One writer

Kentucky Arts Commission
Nash Cox, Executive Director
100 W. Main St., Frankfort, Ky. 40601
(502) 564-3757
    Four writers

University of Kentucky
Director of Creative Writing
Dept. of English
Limestone & Euclid, Lexington, Ky. 40506

LOUISIANA

Louisiana Council for Music & Performing Arts, Inc.
Literature Program Associate
7524 St. Charles Ave., New Orleans, La. 70118
(504) 527-5070

Louisiana State University
Warren Eyster, Creative Writing Program Director
Dept. of English
Allen Hall, Baton Rouge, La. 70803
(504) 388-2236
    Budget: $4,000 per year
    Eight writers

New Orleans Poetry Forum
Lee Grue, Director
828 Lesseps St., New Orleans, La. 70117
(504) 947-6007
    Five writers

Tulane University
Director of Creative Writing
Dept. of English
6823 St. Charles Ave., New Orleans, La. 70118

University of Southwest Louisiana
Herbert V. Fackler; Director of Creative Writing
Dept. of English
Lafayette, La. 70501
(318) 233-3850

University of Southwest Louisiana
Director
Sigma Tau Delta
USL Drawer 4691, Lafayette, La. 70501
(318) 233-3850

MAINE

Bowdoin College
Herbert R. Coursen
Dept. of English
Brunswick, Maine 04011
(207) 725-8731, ext. 552
    Budget: varies
    5-6 writers

Maine State Commission on the Arts and Humanities
Gigi Ledkovsky
State House, Augusta, Maine 04330
(207) 289-2724
    Budget: $16,100 for Poets-in-the-Schools;
    $2,000 for literature/writers
    Five writers

University of Maine at Orono
Gerard Dullea
Dept. of English
Stevens Hall, Orono, Maine 04473
(207) 866-7307
    Budget: $750 per year
    Three writers

MARYLAND

Goucher College
Brooke Peirce, Chairman
Dept. of English
Towson, Baltimore, Md. 21204
(301) 825-3300
    Budget: varies
    Five writers

Maryland Arts Council
Linda Vlasak, Project Director
15 W. Mulberry St., Baltimore, Md. 21201
(301) 685-7470
    Budget: $50,000 per year for Poets-in-the-Schools;
    $6,000 per year in other grants
    16 writers (in-state only)

Maryland Writers Council
Kathleen Owens, Project Coordinator
P.O. Box 1330, Johns Hopkins University, Baltimore,
Md. 21218
(30l) 727-6350, ext. 345
    95 writers

University of Maryland at Baltimore
Director of Creative Writing
Dept. of English
5401 Wilkins Ave., Baltimore, Md. 21228

University of Maryland at College Park
Roderick Jellema, Director
Creative Writing Program
Dept. of English, College Park, Md. 20742
(301) 454-4162
    Budget: $1,200 per year
    Seven writers

MASSACHUSETTS

Blacksmith House Poetry Coffeeshop
Gail Mazur, Director
5 Walnut Ave., Cambridge, Mass. 02140
(617) 868-5753 (home)
    Budget: By contribution
    30 writers

Boston University
Director of Creative Writing
Dept. of English
Boston, Mass. 02215

Brandeis University
Head, Lectures and Colloquia Committee
Dept. of English
Waltham, Mass. 02154
(617) 647-2625
   Budget: $400 per year
   Three writers

Commonwealth of Massachusetts
Council on the Arts & Humanities
Nancy Brimhall, Coordinator
Artists-in-Schools Poetry Component
14 Beacon St., Rm. 606, Boston, Mass. 02108
(617) 723-3851
   Budget: $69,000 per year for Poets-in-the-Schools
   Three residencies: $1,000 per month per writer
   20 writers

Emerson College
James Randall
Dept. of English
130 Beacon St., Boston, Mass. 02116
(617) 262-2010, ext. 255
   Five writers

Fine Arts Work Center in Provincetown
Writing Chairman
24 Pearl St., Provincetown, Mass. 02657
(617) 487-9960
   12 writers

Harvard University
Chairman, Creative Writing Program
Dept. of English
Cambridge, Mass. 02138

Massachusetts Institute of Technology
Patricia Cumming, Writing Program
77 Massachusetts Ave., Rm. 14E-310, Cambridge,
Mass. 02139
(617) 253-7894
   Seven writers

Mount Holyoke College
Don Hendrie or Richard Johnson
Dept. of English
South Hadley, Mass. 01075
(413) 538-2146
   6-8 writers

Simon's Rock
Robert Hahn, Chairman
English Program
Great Barrington, Mass. 01230
(413) 528-0771 (school) or (413) 528-2988 (home)
   Budget: $500 per year
   Two writers

Smith College
Director of Creative Writing
Dept. of English
Northampton, Mass. 01060

Stone Soup Poetry
Jack Powers, Executive Editor
313 Cambridge St., Boston, Mass. 02114
(617) 523-9481
   200-300 writers

Tufts University
Chairman
Dept. of English
Medford, Mass. 01730
(617) 628-5000
   Invitation only

University of Massachusetts
Director
Distinguished Visitors Program
c/o Campus Center, Amherst, Mass. 01002
(413) 545-0111

University of Massachusetts
Dorothy Krass, Artists Resources Coordinator
Arts Extension Service
Hills House N., Amherst, Mass. 01002
(413) 545-2013
   Provides booking service to local community
   groups and school districts

University of Massachusetts
Manager
Fine Arts Council
Herter Hall, Amherst, Mass. 01002
(413) 545-0202

University of Massachusetts
Donald Junkins, Director
Master of Fine Arts Program in English
458 Bartlett Hall, Amherst, Mass. 01002
(413) 545-2409

Wellesley College
Rose Moss or Marcia Stubbs
Dept. of Creative Writing
Wellesley, Mass. 02181
(617) 235-0320
   Budget: varies
   20 writers

Williams College
Chairman
Dept. of English
Williamstown, Mass. 01267
(413) 597-2276
   Budget: $1,500 per year
   Six writers

MICHIGAN

Detroit Metropolitan Black Arts Association
Director
350 Madison Ave., Suite 305, Detroit, Mich. 48226
(313) 862-4572

Grand Valley State Colleges
Ronald Dwelle, Director of Creative Writing
Dept. of English, 492 Mackinac Hall
Allendale, Mich. 49401
(616) 895-6611
   Five writers

Kalamazoo College
Harold J. Harris, Dept. of English
Kalamazoo, Mich. 49001
(616) 383-8485
   Ten writers

Michigan Council for the Arts
Steve Heck, Literature Activities Coordinator
1200 Sixth Ave., Executive Plaza, Rm. 160,
Detroit, Mich. 48226
(313) 256-3731
    Budget: $21,000 per year
    40 writers (in-state writers only)

Michigan State University
Linda Wagner or Albert Drake, Lecture Committee
Dept. of English
East Lansing, Mich. 48824
(517) 353-8897
    Budget: $500 per year
    3-5 writers

Miles Modern Poetry Committee
Faye Kicknosway, Chairman
c/o Dept. of English, Wayne State U., State Hall,
4866 Third, Rm. 314, Detroit, Mich. 48202
    Budget: $200 per writer
    Five writers

Northern Michigan University Poetry Union
Jim Livingston, Dept. of English
Marquette, Mich. 49855
(906) 227-2750
    Budget: $2,500 per year
    Four writers

Oakland University
Dorothy Owen, Director
Conference Dept.
Rochester, Mich. 48063
(313) 377-3272
    Budget: $1,500-$2,000 per year

Thomas Jefferson College—National Poetry Festival
Jeff Brown, Director of Programming
Campus Activities
Dept. of English, Allendale, Mich. 49401
(616) 895-6611, ext. 242
    Budget: varies
    Five Writers

Wayne State University
Director of Creative Writing
Dept. of English
Detroit, Mich. 48202

Western Michigan University
Martin Grossman, Programs Committee
c/o English Dept., Kalamazoo, Mich. 49001
(616) 383-0945
    Budget: $200-$300 per writer
    Eight writers

MINNESOTA

Carleton College
Keith Hainson, Director
Arts Program
Northfield, Minn. 55057
(507) 645-4431
    Budget: $600 per year
    Three writers

COMPAS
(Community Programs in the Arts and Sciences)
Molly LaBerge, Director
Old Federal Courts Bldg., 75 W. 5th St., St. Paul,
Minn. 55102
(612) 227-8241
    Three writers

Hamline University
George F. Appel, Director
Poetry Under the Arch
St. Paul, Minn. 55104
(612) 641-2457
    Budget: $2,000 per year
    Four writers

Macalester College
Peter Murray, Chairman
Dept. of English
1600 Grand Ave., St. Paul, Minn. 55105
(612) 647-6387
    Budget: $250 per year
    Three writers

Minneapolis College of Art and Design
Richard Shaw, Chairman
Division of Liberal Arts
113 E. 25th St., Minneapolis, Minn. 55404
(612) 874-0300
    Budget: $300-$500 per year
    Seven writers

Minnesota State Arts Council
Director of Literature
314 Clifton Ave., Minneapolis, Minn. 55403
(612) 874-1335

St. Cloud State College
Catherine Scholer or Liz Moore
Atwood Board of Governors
Atwood Center, St. Cloud, Minn. 56301
(612) 255-3712
    Budget: $2,000 per year
    8-12 writers

St. Olaf College
Lowell E. Johnson, Chairman
Dept. of English
Northfield, Minn. 55057
(507) 663-3200
    Five writers

St. Paul Council of Arts & Sciences
Molly LaBerge, Poets-in-the-Schools Director
Old Federal Courts Bldg., 75 W. 5th St., St. Paul,
Minn. 55102
(612) 227-8241

Southwest Minnesota State College
Philip Dacey, Coordinator of Creative Writing
Marshall, Minn. 56258
(507) 537-7158
    Eight writers

University of Minnesota
Director
Dept. of Creative Writing
Minneapolis, Minn. 55455
(612) 373-0107

University of Minnesota
Director
Poetry Series
Morris, Minn. 56267

University of Minnesota at Morris
Richard T. Johnson
Morris Campus Union Board
Student Activities Office, Morris, Minn. 56267
(612) 589-2222
   Eight writers

MISSISSIPPI

Mississippi Arts Commission
Terry Hummer, Director
Artists-in-the-Schools
Box 1341, Jackson, Miss. 39205
(601) 354-7336
   Budget: $5,000 per year for Poets-in-the-Schools
   12 writers

Tougaloo College
N.J. Townsend, Academic Dean
Tougaloo, Miss. 39174
(601) 956-4941, ext. 22
   Budget: varies
   Six writers

University of Southern Mississippi
Director, Center for Writers
Southern Station, Box 37, Hattiesburg, Miss. 39401
(601) 266-7180

MISSOURI

Jewish Community Center
Gloria Goodfriend, Poetry Director
American Poets Series
8201 Holmes, Kansas City, Mo. 64131
(816) 361-5200, ext. 69
   Five writers

The Lindenwood Colleges
Howard A. Barnett, Chairman
Dept. of English, St. Charles, Mo. 63301
(314) 723-7152
   One writer

Missouri State Council on the Arts
Emily Rice, Executive Director or Sharon
Elder Zehntner, Artists-in-Schools Coordinator
Suite 410, 111 S. Bemiston, St. Louis, Mo. 63105
(314) 721-1672
   Fifteen writers

Northeast Missouri State University
Andrew Grossbardt
Dept. of Language and Literature
Kirksville, Mo. 63501
(816) 665-5121
   Three writers

St. Louis Poetry Center
Charles Guenther, President
2935 Russell Blvd., St. Louis, Mo. 63104

St. Louis University
Director of Creative Writing
Dept. of English
St. Louis, Mo. 63103

Stephens College
Cecil Dawkins, Director of Bachelor of Fine
Arts Program in Creative Writing
Dept. of English, Columbia, Mo. 65201
(314) 442-2211
   Six writers

University of Missouri
Dan Jaffe, Writers Series
Dept. of English
5315 Holmes, Kansas City, Mo. 64110
(816) 276-1305
   Budget: $1,000 per year
   Seven writers

University of Missouri at Columbia
William Peden, Writing Program Director or
John R. Roberts, Chairman
Dept. of English
231 Arts and Sciences Bldg., Columbia, Mo. 65201
(314) 882-6421
   Ten writers

Washington University
Director of Creative Writing
Dept. of English
St. Louis, Mo. 63130

MONTANA

Montana Arts Council
Patricia K. Simmons, Program Director
Artists in Schools
235 E. Pine St., Missoula, Mont. 59801
(406) 543-8286
   Two writers

University of Montana
Director of Creative Writing
Dept. of English
Missoula, Mont. 59801

NEBRASKA

Nebraska Arts Council
Gloria Bartek, Program Coordinator
Oak Park, 7367 Pacific St., Omaha, Nebr. 68114
(402) 554-2122
   Nine writers

University of Nebraska
Donald Gregory
Dept. of English
140 Andrews Hall, Lincoln, Nebr. 68508
(402) 472-3191
   Budget: $400 per year
   One writer

NEVADA

Nevada State Council on the Arts
James D. Deere, Executive Director
560 Mill St., Reno, Nev. 89502
(702) 784-6231
   Budget: $4,000 per year for Poets-in-the-Schools

NEW HAMPSHIRE

Dartmouth College
Director of Creative Writing
Dept. of English
Hanover, N.H. 03755
(603) 646-2316

Hawthorne College
Secretary
Cultural Programs Committee
Antrim, N.H. 03340
(603) 588-6341
   Budget: $150 per writer
   Six writers

New Hampshire Commission on the Arts
Marie Harris, Coordinator
Artists-in-the-Schools
Phenix Hall, 40 N. Main St., Concord, N.H. 03301
(603) 271-2789
   15 writers

University of New Hampshire
Director of Creative Writing
Dept. of English
Durham, N.H. 03824
(603) 862-2717
   Six writers

NEW JERSEY

Catalysts for Creativity
Debra Stein, Director
4 Grace Way, Morristown, N.J. 07960
(201) 539-7176
   Budget: varies
   Six writers

New Jersey State Council on the Arts
Linda Constant Buki, Program Director
Artists-in-Schools
27 W. State St., Trenton, N.J. 08625
(609) 292-6130
   Budget: $20,000 per year
   20-30 writers

Poets & Writers of New Jersey
Wm. J. Higginson
The Old School House, Cranbury, N.J. 08512
Send correspondence to: Box 2702, Paterson, N.J.
07509
(201) 345-4239
   Does not sponsor readings; is a service organization
   for New Jersey writers and organizations interested
   in writers

Princeton University
Theodore Weiss, Director, Reading Series
Creative Writing Program
185 Nassau St., Princeton, N.J. 08540
(609) 452-4712
   Seven writers

Rutgers University
Director of Creative Writing
Dept. of English
New Brunswick, N.J. 08903

Rutgers University
Frank McQuilkin
Rutgers-Camden Poetry Series
Camden, N.J. 08102
(609) 964-1766
   Budget: varies
   Three writers

Trenton State College English Club
Faculty Advisor
Trenton, N.J. 08625
(609) 771-2297 or (609) 771-2298
   Five writers

William Carlos Williams Poetry Center
Joan Stahl, Poetry Coordinator
Paterson Free Public Library, 250 Broadway,
Paterson, N.J. 07501
(201) 279-4200
   Three writers

NEW MEXICO

New Mexico Arts Commission
Stanley Noyes, Director
Santa Fe Poets-in-the-Schools Program
Lew Wallace Bldg., State Capitol, Santa Fe, N.Mex.
87501
(505) 827-2061
   12 writers per year (in-state writers only)

New Mexico State University
Director
El Grito del Sur
Chicano Studies Dept., Las Cruces, N.Mex. 88001

New Mexico State University
Keith Wilson, Poet-in-Residence
The Writing Center
Dept. of English, Box 3E, Las Cruces, N.Mex 88003
(505) 646-3931
   Budget: varies
   Five or six writers

University of New Mexico
Gene Frumkin, Director of Creative Writing
Dept. of English, Humanities Bldg. 217
Albuquerque, N.Mex 87131
(505) 277-6347
   Ten writers

NEW YORK CITY

Academy of American Poets
Elizabeth Kray, Executive Director
1078 Madison Ave., New York, N.Y. 10028
(212) 988-6783
   Budget: varies
   60 writers

Academy of American Poets
Coordinator
Poet in New York Series
1078 Madison Ave., New York, N.Y. 10028
(212) 988-6783

Academy of American Poets
Coordinator
Ten Poets Series
1078 Madison Ave., New York, N.Y. 10028
(212) 988-6783

**Board of Education of the City
of New York - District Office 22**
Ruth D. Abramowitz, Curriculum Supervisor
3109 Newkirk Ave., Brooklyn, N.Y. 11226
(212) 856-8333 or (212) 856-5879
  Four writers

Brooklyn College
James Merritt
Poetry & Wine Series
English Dept., Bedford & Avenue H, Brooklyn, N.Y. 11210
(212) 780-5195
  Budget: $2,500 per year
  Ten writers

**Brooklyn Museum - Brooklyn Arts
& Culture Association**
Vinnie-Marie D'Ambrosio, Coordinator
200 Eastern Pkwy., Brooklyn, N.Y. 11238
(212) 783-4077
  20 writers

Calliope Salon
Ree Dragonette, Director
D306, Westbeth, 463 West St., New York, N.Y. 10014
(212) 243-2989
  Budget: $25 per writer
  Four writers

CAPS (Creative Artists Public Service Program)
250 W. 57 St., New York, N.Y. 10019
(212) 247-7701
  Annual grants for individual writers

City College of New York
Barry Wallenstein
Dept. of English
133 St. & Convent Ave., New York, N.Y. 10031
(212) 621-2177
  Ten writers

City College of New York
Director
Graduate Program of Creative Writing
137 St. & Convent Ave., New York, N.Y. 10031
(212) 621-2381

Columbia University
Michael Andre
c/o Unmuzzled Ox, Box 374, Planetarium Station,
New York, N.Y. 10024
(212) 431-8829
  25 writers

Columbia University School of the Arts
Frank MacShane, Chairman or
William Jay Smith, Co-Chairman
Writing Division
404 Dodge, New York, N.Y. 10027
(212) 280-4391
  Budget: $3,000 per year
  20 writers

Cooper Union
Brian Swann, Director
Poetry Series for Humanities Division
Cooper Square, New York, N.Y. 10003
(212) 254-6300, Ext. 265
  Five-ten writers

Katherine Engel Center for Senior Citizens
Charles Elvey
23 W. 73 St., New York, N.Y. 10023
(212) 874-3945

Exchange for the Arts
Bliem Kern, Director
463 West St., New York, N.Y. 10014
(212) 850-7015
  25 writers

Focus II Coffeehouse
Shaun Farragher, Director
Poets in Focus
163 W. 74 St., New York, N.Y. 10023
(212) 787-9628
  24 writers

Gay Academics Union at CUNY Graduate Center
Patrick Cullen, Director
Contemporary Gay Writers
300 W. 108 St., 8D, New York, N.Y. 10025
(212) 866-8960
  Budget: $300 per year
  Three writers

Greenwich House Day Center for Senior Citizens
Susan Axelrod, Group Worker
27 Barrow St., New York, N.Y. 10014
(212) 675-3435

Herbert H. Lehman College
Guillermo Ramirez, Chairman
Dept. of Puerto Rican Studies
Bedford Park Blvd. W., Bronx, N.Y. 10468
(212) 960-8281
  Budget: $100 per lecturer
  One writer

Manhattan Theatre Club
Janet Sternburg, Poetry Series Director
514 West End Ave., Apt. 2B, New York, N.Y. 10024
(212) 877-1002
  Budget: $1,450 per year
  22 writers

The Museum of Modern Art
Barbara Jakobson or Gini Alhadeff
The Junior Council
21 W. 53 St., New York, N.Y. 10019
(212) 956-6112
  Budget: $100 per reading
  Nine writers

New American Art Gallery
William B. Kern, Jr., Director
230 Riverside Dr., New York, N.Y. 10025
(212) 850-7015
  10-25 writers

The New School
Daniel Halpern
66 W. 12 St., New York, N.Y. 10011
(212) 736-2599
  Budget: $2,000 per year
  20 writers (by invitation)

The New Wilderness Foundation, Inc.
Charles Morrow
365 West End Ave., New York, N.Y. 10024
(212) 799-0636
    Budget: $750 per year
    12 writers

New York Kantorei
Gomer Rees
325 Riverside Dr., New York, N.Y. 10027
(212) 865-7035

New York Poets Cooperative
Robert Kramer
240 E. 240 St., Bronx, N.Y. 10470
(212) 549-2962 (office) or (212) 994-4249 (home)
    Budget: $200 per year
    Two writers per week

New York State Council on the Arts
June Fortess, Director
Literature Program
250 W. 57 St., New York, N.Y. 10019
(212) 397-1752
    Does not sponsor readings or workshops; is
    interested in learning about activities

New York University
Loeb Poetry Committee
Program Office, Loeb Program Board, 566 LaGuardia Pl.,
New York, N.Y. 10012
(212) 598-2027
    Budget: $50-$200 per writer
    Seven writers

Poetry Center of the 92nd Street YM-YWHA
Grace Schulman, Director or Marianne
Clay, Assistant to the Director
1395 Lexington Ave., New York, N.Y. 10028
(212) 427-6000, Ext. 711 or 712
    45 writers

Poetry Series at the West End
Diane Stevenson, Director
610 W. 113 St., Apt. 6C, New York, N.Y. 10026
(212) 864-0451
    Budget: $15-$20 per writer
    40 writers

The Poetry Society of America
Charles Wagner, Executive Secretary
15 Gramercy Pk., New York, N.Y. 10003
(212) 254-9628 or (212) 254-9683
    Several dozen writers

Poets and Writers, Inc.
Galen Williams, Executive Director
201 W. 54 St., New York, N.Y. 10019
(212) PL7-1766
    Information on availability of poets
    Partial fee supplementation for readings/
    workshops in New York State

Poets at the Book Gallery
Sonia Pilcer or Victoria Sullivan
c/o Book Gallery, 240 W. 72nd St., New York, N.Y.
10023
(212) 873-0670
    20 writers

Queens College
Frederick Buell
Dept. of English
Flushing, N.Y. 11367
    Four writers

Richmond College of CUNY
Herbert Leibowitz
Language, Literature and Philosophy Dept.
130 Stuyvesant Pl., Staten Island, N.Y. 10301
(212) 720-3074
    Budget: $1,000 per year
    Six writers

St. Mark's in the Bowery
Maureen Owen or Larry Fagin
Poetry Project
10 St. & Second Ave., New York, N.Y. 10003

Shelley Society of New York
Annette B. Feldmann, President
144-20 41st Ave., Apt. 322, Flushing, N.Y. 11355
(212) 460-1384 or (212) 359-0425 (home)
    Five writers

Teachers & Writers Collaborative
Steven Schrader, Director
186 W. 4 St., New York, N.Y. 10014
(212) 691-6590
    Hires writers only on regular weekly basis for
    entire school year

Theatre of Latin America, Inc.
Joanne Pottlitzer, Director
344 W. 36 St., New York, N.Y. 10018
(212) 947-4615
    12 writers

Town Hall
Candance Leeds, Assistant Director
123 W. 43 St., New York, N.Y. 10036
(212) 582-2424
    Budget: varies
    Six writers

Village Poetry Workshop
Shirley R. Powell
24 Jane St., #3A, New York, N.Y. 10014
(212) 924-0228
    Six writers

Westbeth Feminist Collective
Dolores Walker & Gwendolyn Gunn, Coadministrators
463 West St., New York, N.Y. 10014
(212) 691-0015 or (212) 691-1727
    Budget: $20 per writer
    8-10 writers

York College
Director of Creative Writing
Dept. of English
150 St. & Jamaica Ave., Flushing, N.Y. 11351
(212) 969-4131

NEW YORK (OUTSIDE NEW YORK CITY)

Albany Public Library
Bill O'Connor, Assistant to the Director
19 Dove St., Albany, N.Y. 12210
(518) 465-1463
    Two writers

Auburn Community College
Howard Nelson
Dept. of English
Franklin St., Auburn, N.Y. 13021
(315) 253-7345
  Budget: $350 per year
  Two writers

Bard College
Alison Dale, Chairman
Bard Literature Club
Annandale-on-Hudson, N.Y. 12504
(914) 758-8522
  Eight writers

Bay Shore-Brightwaters Public Library
John E. Clark, Library Director
One So. Country Rd., Brightwaters, N.Y. 11718
(516) 665-4350
  Budget: $350 per speaker
  Three writers

Board of Cooperative Educational Services
Ava M. Favara
Rosemary Kennedy-Cultural Arts Center
2850 N. Jerusalem Rd., Wantagh, N.Y. 11793
(516) 781-4044, ext. 83 or 84
  12 writers

Bryant Library
Elizabeth Teitler
Program and Public Relations Office
Paper Mill Rd., Roslyn, N.Y. 11050
(516) 767-6046
  Three writers

Canisius College
Kenneth M. Sroka
Dept. of English
2001 Main St., Buffalo, N.Y. 14208
(716) 883-7000, Ext. 808
  Budget: $600 per year
  Two writers

Cazenovia College
Norma E. Bentley, Chairman
Dept. of English
Cazenovia, N.Y. 13035
(315) 655-3466

Colgate University
Bruce Berlind
Dept. of English
Hamilton, N.Y. 13346
(315) 824-4290
  Six writers

The College of White Plains
Carol Gartner, Chairman
Division of Arts and Letters
N. Broadway, White Plains, N.Y. 10603
(914) 949-9494
  Three writers

Cornell University
Baxter Hathaway, Chairman
Committee on Creative Writing
245 Goldwin Smith Hall, Ithaca, N.Y. 14853
(607) 256-4740
  Eight writers

Council on the Arts for Cortland, N.Y., Inc.
Janet B. Steck, Executive Director
Box 683, Cortland, N.Y. 13045
(607) 753-0722

Dowling College
Sandy Haft, Assistant Dean of Students or
E. Knuth, Coordinator of Student Activities
Idlehour Blvd., Oakdale, N.Y. 11769
(516) 589-6100
  Budget: $500 per year
  Six writers

Emelin Theater for the Performing Arts
Norman Kline, Managing Director
Library La., Mamaroneck, N.Y. 10543
(914) 698-3045
  Four writers

Empire State College
Jan Rosenberg, Coordinator
The Learning Center
SUNY at Old Westbury, Box 130, Old Westbury, N.Y. 11568
(516) 997-4700

Everson Museum of Art
Barbara J. Beckos
Education Dept.
401 Harrison St., Syracuse, N.Y. 13202
(315) 474-6064
  Budget: varies
  Four writers

Friends of the East Islip Public Library
Jill Hayden, President
381 E. Main St., East Islip, N.Y. 11730
(516) 581-9200
  One writer

Friends Of The John C. Hart Memorial Library
Hilda White, Director
Poets & Writers Series
Box 62, Shrub Oak, N.Y. 10588
(914) 528-9092
  Budget: $300 per year
  Three writers

Friends World College
Diane Levy, Advisor
Dept. of English
Plover La., Lloyd's Harbor, Huntington, N.Y. 11743
(516) 549-4110

Greater Middletown Arts Council, Inc.
Marian Feman, Executive Director
120 North St., Middletown, N.Y. 10940
(914) 342-2133
  Five writers

Great Neck Library
Joseph Covino, Director
Bayview Ave., Great Neck, N.Y. 11024
(516) 466-8055
  Ten writers

Guild Hall of East Hampton, Inc.
Enez Whipple, Director
158 Main St., East Hampton, N.Y. 11937
(516) 324-0806
  Six writers

Harborfields Public Library
Jay R. Peyser, Programming & Publicity
Taylor Ave., Greenlawn, N.Y. 11740
(516) 757-7675
    Four writers

Hartwick College
Beverly Tanenhaus
Dept. of English
Oneonta, N.Y. 13820
(607) 432-4200, Ext 293
    Seven writers

Hewlett-Woodmere Public Library
Diane Dobsovits
1125 Broadway, Hewlett, N.Y. 11557
(516) 374-1967

Hofstra University
Arthur Gregor, Director
Creative Writing Program
Dept. of English, Hempstead, N.Y. 11550
(516) 560-3882
    Six writers

Hofstra University
Rowena Smith, Associate Director
Upward Bound
Hempstead, N.Y. 11550
(516) 560-3279
    Three writers

Houghton College
John Leax, Coordinator of Creative Writing
Houghton, N.Y. 14744
(716) 567-2614, ext. 149
    Budget: $200-$300 per year
    Two writers

The Hudson River Museum
Barbara Eager, Assistant Curator of Education
511 Warburton Ave., Yonkers, N.Y. 10701
(914) 963-9441
    Budget: $100 per writer
    One writer

Huntington Public Library
Director of Poetry Readings
338 Main St., Huntington, N.Y. 11743
(516) 427-5165

International Center of New York, Inc.
Stanley Barkan, Director
Cross-Cultural Communications Poetry Series
P.O. Box 383, Merrick, N.Y. 11566
(516) 868-5635
    Budget: $25 per writer
    30 writers

Jewish Community Center of Utica
Frances Savett, Director
Cultural Arts
2310 Oneida St., Utica, N.Y. 13501
(315) 733-2343
    Budget: $500-$800 per year
    Four-seven writers

Jewish Community Center of Greater Rochester
Lillian Silver, Arts Assistant
1200 Edgewood Ave., Rochester, N.Y. 14618
(716) 473-4000
    Eight writers

Katonah Village Library
Robert Phillips, Director of Cultural Events
Bedford Rd., Katonah, N.Y. 10536
(914) 232-9209
    Four writers

Kirkland College
Katharine Dewart, Chairman
Arts Division
Clinton, N.Y. 13323
(315) 859-4257
    Budget: varies
    Four writers

Long Beach Public Library
Carol Donner, Program Coordinator
111 W. Park Ave., Long Beach, N.Y. 11561
(516) 432-7201
    Budget: $100-$250 per writer
    Three writers

Emily Lowe Art Gallery,
Robert Littman, Director
1000 Fulton St., Uniondale, N.Y. 11553
(516) 560-3275 or (516) 560-3276

Marist College
Ursula Freer, Director of Student Activities
North Rd., Poughkeepsie, N.Y. 12601
(914) 471-3240
    Budget: $150-$200 per year
    One or two writers

Marymount College
Ruth Anyon
Lecture Committee
Tarrytown, N.Y. 10591
(914) 631-3200
    Two writers

Mercy College
Iris Wittko, Director of Student Activities
Concert and Lecture Bureau
555 Broadway, Dobbs Ferry, N.Y. 10522
(914) 693-4500
    Three writers

Mid-Hudson School Study Council
George Simpson, Executive Secretary
Bldg. C.H.F. 102, SUNY at New Paltz, New Paltz,
N.Y. 12561
(914) 257-2195

Mineola Public Schools
Joseph D. La Rosa, Director
Mineola Arts Program
Mineola High School, Armstrong Rd., Garden City Park
N.Y. 11040
(516) 747-6700, Ext. 744
    Budget: $3,000 per year
    Seven writers

Mount Vernon YM-YWHA
Ed Korn, Educational Cultural Director
30 Oakley Ave., Mt. Vernon, N.Y. 10550
    send correspondence to 234 Mountaindale Rd.,
    Yonkers, N.Y. 10710 (212-731-6006, days;
    914-664-0500, evenings)

Nassau Library System
Julia G. Russell
Age Level Services
Roosevelt Field, Garden City, N.Y. 11530
(516) 741-0060

New York State Poets-in-the-Schools, Inc.
Myra Klahr, Director
125 King St., Chappaqua, N.Y. 10514
(914) 238-4481
    111 writers

North Shore Community Arts Center
Norma Reiner or Bernice Olenick
236 Middle Neck Rd., Great Neck, N.Y. 11021
(516) 466-3636
    Budget: $200 per writer
    Three writers

Orange County Community College
Bigelow R. Green, Coordinator of Cultural Affairs
South St., Middletown, N.Y. 10940
(914) 343-1121
    Budget: $2,000-$3,000 per year
    Four writers

Oswego Writing Arts Festivals
Roger Dickinson-Brown, Director
SUNY at Oswego, Dept. of English, Oswego, N.Y.13126
(315) 341-2362 or (315) 341-2150
    Budget: $500-$1,000 per year
    Six writers

Port Washington Public Library
Virginia E. Parker, Assistant Director
245 Main St., Port Washington, N.Y. 11050
(516) 883-4400
    18 writers

C.W. Post College
Director of Creative Writing
Dept. of English
Greenvale, N.Y. 11548
(516) 299-2391

The James Prendergast Library Association
Catherine Way, Program Coordinator
509 Cherry St., Jamestown, N.Y. 14701
(716) 484-7135
    Three writers

Putnam Arts Council
Harriet Anhalt Horowitz, Director
Creative Writing Workshops and Readings
Box 156, Mahopac, N.Y. 10541
(914) 628-3664
    Two writers

Rensselaer Polytechnic Institute
Charles H. Saile, Director
Rensselaer Newman Foundation Chapel & Cultural
Center
2125 Burdett Ave., Troy, N.Y. 12181
(518) 274-7793
    Three writers

Roberson Center for the Arts and Sciences
Philip Carey, Coordinator
Educational Services
30 Front St., Binghamton, N.Y. 13905
(607) 772-0660
    Budget: $100 per day
    Two writers

Rochester Poetry Central
Jim Havelin, Director
256 Whipple La., Rochester, N.Y. 14622
(716) 266-4889

Rochester Poetry Society
Pat Janus
952 Whalen Rd., Penfield, N.Y. 14526
(716) 381-8356

Rockland Community College
Dan Masterson, Chairman
Writers Series
145 College Rd., Suffern, N.Y. 10901
(914) 356-4650
    Six writers

Rosary Hill College
Peter A. Siedlecki, Director
Dept. of English
4380 Main St., Buffalo, N.Y. 14226
(716) 839-3600, Ext. 304
    Budget: $500 per year
    Two writers

Roslyn Public Schools
Nicholas Wandmacher, Cultural Arts Coordinator
Box 367, Roslyn, N.Y. 11576
(516) 621-4900, Ext. 210
    One writer

St. Lawrence University
Joe David Bellamy
fiction international
Canton, N.Y. 13617
(315) 379-6191
    Budget: varies
    12 writers

St. Thomas Aquinas College
Patricia Rock
New Directions/New Dimensions
Rt. 340, Sparkill, N.Y. 10976
(914) 359-6400, Ext. 285
    Two writers

Sarah Lawrence College
Joseph Papaleo, Fiction or Jane Cooper, Poetry
Writing Faculty
Bronxville, N.Y. 10708
(914) 337-0700
    Eight writers

Schenectady County Community College
Grayce Susan Burian, Assistant Professor
Dept. of General Education
Washington Ave., Schenectady, N.Y. 12305
(518) 346-6211
    Budget: $300 per year

School of Cultural Arts
Mary Wood
Box 1606, Westhampton Beach, N.Y. 11977
(516) 288-2222

Elizabeth Seton College
Director of Creative Writing
Dept. of English
1061 N. Broadway, Yonkers, N.Y. 10701
(914) 969-4000

Skidmore College
Robert Foulke, Chairman
Dept. of English
Saratoga Springs, N.Y. 12866
(518) 584-5000
 Ten writers

Southampton College
R.B. Weber
Dept. of English
Southampton, N.Y. 11968
(516) 283-4000, Ext. 242
 Six writers

South Huntington Public Library
Director of Poetry Readings
2 Melville Rd., Huntington Station, N.Y. 11746
(516) 549-4411

State University College at Brockport
Al Poulin, Jr., Director
The Writer's Forum
Brockport, N.Y. 14420
(716) 395-2503 or (716) 637-3844
 20-30 writers

State University College at Cortland
Director of Creative Writing
Dept. of English
Cortland, N.Y. 13045
(607) 753-4307

State University College at New Paltz
Joanna Kraus or Maurice Recchia, Chairman
Dept. of Elementary Education
New Paltz, N.Y. 12603
(914) 257-2324

Street Press
Dan Murray
1 Somerset Ave., Mastic, N.Y. 11950
(516) 281-1893
 Budget: $300 per year
 11 writers

SUNY at Albany
Chairman
Dept. of English
1400 Washington Ave., Albany, N.Y. 12222
(518) 457-8434
 Budget: $300 (maximum) per writer
 Two writers

SUNY at Binghamton
Chairman, Convocations Committee
Dept. of English
Binghamton, N.Y. 13901
(607) 798-2168
 Budget: $750 per year
 Six writers

SUNY at Buffalo
Chairman
Poetry Committee
c/o Dept. of English, Buffalo, N.Y. 14214
(716) 831-4927 or (716) 835-0909
 Budget: $700 per year
 Five writers

SUNY at Buffalo
Leslie A. Fiedler, Chairman
Dept. of English
Annex B-9, Buffalo, N.Y. 14214
(716) 831-2211
 8 writers (by invitation only)

SUNY at Buffalo
Bonnie Gutnick
University Union Activities Board
Literary Arts Committee
Rm. 261, Norton Hall, Main St., Buffalo, N.Y. 14214
(716) 831-5112 or 5113
 Budget: $200-$300 per writer
 15 writers

SUNY at Cobleskill
Chariman
Humanities Dept. or CAFAC
Cobleskill, N.Y. 12043
(518) 234-5011
 Two writers

SUNY at Cortland
David Toor
Transition Workshop
Dept. of English, Cortland, N.Y. 13045
(607) 753-4307
 15 writers

SUNY at Geneseo
Thomas E. Matthews or Maureen A. O'Neill
College Activities Center
Geneseo, N.Y. 14454
(716) 245-5855
 Budget: $1,000 per year

SUNY at New Paltz
Associate Coordinator
College Activities Office
Student Union Bldg., Rm. 203, New Paltz, N.Y. 12561
(914) 257-2193
 Five writers

SUNY at Plattsburgh
Bruce Butterfield
Dept. of English
Champlain Valley Hall, Plattsburgh, N.Y. 12901
(518) 564-2138
 One writer

SUNY at Purchase
Michael H. Baird, Director
Division of Continuing Education
Purchase, N.Y. 10577
(914) 253-5077
 One writer

SUNY at Stony Brook
Tom Gatten
Dept. of English
Stony Brook, N.Y. 11794
(516) 246-5080
 Ten writers

Suffolk Cooperative Library System
Kathleen Sheehan
627 N. Sunrise Service Rd., Bellport, N.Y. 11713
(516) 286-1600

Suffolk County Community College
David B. Axelrod, Advisor
Apprecult, Visiting Writers Program
533 College Rd., Selden, N.Y. 11784
(516) 233-5241
    Budget: $100-$200 per writer
    18 writers

Syosset High School
Director of Poetry Readings
Southwoods Rd., Syosset, N.Y. 11791
(516) 921-5500

Syosset Public Library
Sheila Stein, Head of Adult Services
225 S. Oyster Bay Rd., Syosset, N.Y. 11791
(516) 921-7191
    Four writers

Syracuse University
Coordinator of the Writing Programs
Visiting Writers' Series
Dept. of English, Syracuse, N.Y. 13210
(315) 423-2171 or 2173
    Five writers

Thrall Public Library
Mattie B. Gaines, Library Director
22 Orchard St., Middletown, N.Y. 10940
(914) 342-5877
    Budget: $50-$125 per writer
    Five writers

Tompkins County Community College
Murray Cohen
Humanities Dept.
North St., Dryden, N.Y. 13053
(607) 844-8211, Ext. 269

Union College
Barbara LaBarba
Library
Schenectady, N.Y. 12308
(518) 370-6000

University of Rochester
Chairman
Plutzik Poetry Series
Dept. of English, Rochester, N.Y. 14627
(716) 275-4091
    Six writers

Upstate New York Poetry Circuit
Robert G. Koch, Director
Harkness Hall, U. of Rochester, Rochester, N.Y. 14627
(716) 275-2340
    Four writers

Vassar College
Chairman
Lecture Committee
Dept. of English, Poughkeepsie, N.Y. 12601
(914) 452-7000
    Six writers

Wappingers Central School
Dennis J. Hannan, English Dept. Head
Roy C. Ketcham Sr. High School
Myers Corners Rd., Wappingers Falls, N.Y. 12590
(914) 297-3727
    Budget: $500 per year
    Four writers

Wells College
Bruce Bennett, Director
Creative Writing
Dept. of English, Aurora, N.Y. 13026
(315) 364-3316
    Budget: $500 per year
    Five writers

Westchester Community College
Judith Glazer, Dean of Community Services
75 Grasslands Rd., Valhalla, N.Y. 10595
(914) 946-1616

Woodstock Poetry Festival
Marguerite Harris, Director
Jones Quarry Rd., Woodstock, N.Y. 12498
(914) 679-2971
    Budget: $300 per year
    Ten writers

YM-YWHA of Mid-Westchester
Barry Shrage
999 Wilmot Rd., Scarsdale, N.Y. 10583
(914) 472-3300
    Budget: $300 per year
    Four writers

Yonkers Public Library
Mrs. David Schoenfeld, Coordinator
Community Services
Will Library, 1500 Central Park Ave., Yonkers,
N.Y. 10710
(914) 337-1500
    Seven writers

NORTH CAROLINA

Duke University
Director of Creative Writing
Dept. of English
Durham, N.C. 27708

North Carolina Arts Council
Halsey M. North, Executive Director
Dept. of Cultural Resources
Raleigh, N.C. 27611
(919) 829-7897
    Budget: $10,000 per year for Poets-in-the-Schools;
    $7,000 per year for readings (in-state writers only);
    $20,000 per year for literary magazines
    84 writers

North Carolina Poetry Circuit
William Harmon, Director
Dept. of English
St. Andrews College, Laurinburg, N.C. 28352

Pembroke State College
Director of Creative Writing
Dept. of English
Pembroke, N.C. 28372

University of North Carolina
Director of Creative Writing
Dept. of English
Chapel Hill, N.C. 27514

University of North Carolina at Greensboro
Tom Kirby-Smith
Dept. of Creative Writing
Greensboro, N.C. 27412
Six writers

University of North Carolina at Wilmington
Director of Creative Writing
Dept. of English
Wilmington, N.C. 28401

NORTH DAKOTA

North Dakota Council on the Arts and Humanities
Glenn Scott, Program Director
Minard Hall, Rm. 320, North Dakota State U.,
Fargo, N.Dak. 58102
(701) 237-7143
Budget: $7,000 per year for Poets-in-the-Schools;
$2,000-8,000 per year in grants (in-state writers only)
Two writers

North Dakota State University
Director of Creative Writing
Dept. of English
Fargo, N.Dak. 58102

University of North Dakota
John Little, Chairperson
Lectures Committee
Dept. of English, Grand Forks, N.Dak. 58201
(701) 777-3321
Budget: $8,000 per year
Ten writers

OHIO

Antioch College
Dianne F. Sadoff, Chairperson
Dept. of Literature
Yellow Springs, Ohio 45387
(513) 767-7331, ext. 338
Three or four writers

Ashland College
Director of Creative Writing
Dept. of English
Ashland, Ohio 44805
(419) 289-4142

Bowling Green University
Howard McCord, Director
Creative Writing Program
Bowling Green, Ohio 43403
(419) 372-0370
20 writers

Case Western Reserve University
Director of Creative Writing
Dept. of English
10900 Euclid Ave., Cleveland, Ohio 44106

Cleveland Institute of Art
Helen Weinberg, Chairman
Visiting Artists Committee
11141 East Blvd., Cleveland, Ohio 44106
(216) 421-4322
Four writers

Cleveland State University
Alberta T. Turner, Director
C.S.U. Poetry Center
Euclid at 24th St., Cleveland, Ohio 44115
(216) 687-3986
Budget: $1,500 per year
Five writers

Hiram College
M.L. Vincent, Chairman
Dept. of English
Hiram, Ohio 44234
(216) 569-3211
Budget: $1,000 per year
Five writers

Jewish Community Center
Director of Poetry Readings
3505 Mayfield Rd., Cleveland, Ohio 44118

Oberlin College
Stuart Friebert, Director
Creative Writing Program
Rice Hall, Oberlin, Ohio 44074
(216) 774-1221, Ext. 4173.
Eight writers

Ohio Arts Council
Richard Jones, Coordinator
Poets-in-the-Schools Program
50 W. Broad St., Columbus, Ohio 43215
(614) 466-2613
Budget: $30,000 per year for Poets-in-the-Schools
30 writers (5-20 day residencies only)

Ohio Poets' Association
Richard Snyder & Robert McGovern, Co-Directors
RD 4, Box 131, Ashland, Ohio 44805
(419) 323-4435

Ohio State University
Robert Canzoneri, Creative Writing Director
Dept. of English
164 W. 17th Ave., Columbus, Ohio 43210
(614) 422-0270
Seven writers

Ohio University
Director of Creative Writing
Dept. of English
Athens, Ohio 45701
Seven writers

Poetry Circuit of Ohio
Robert W. Daniel, Director
Box 247, Gambier, Ohio 43022
(614) 427-2244, ext. 254

University of Cincinnati
John McCall, Chairman
Dept. of English
Cincinnati, Ohio 45221
(513) 475-2480
 Budget: varies
 10-15 writers

OKLAHOMA

Oklahoma Arts & Humanities Council
Marlynn Likens, Asst. Arts Program Director
Jim Thorpe Bldg., P.O. Box 53553, Oklahoma City,
Okla. 73105
(405) 521-2931
 One writer (in-state writers only)

OREGON

Linn Benton Community College
Robert Miller, Director of Student Activities
6500 S.W. Pacific Blvd., Albany, Oreg. 97231
(503) 928-2361, ext. 71
 Budget: varies
 Two writers

Eastern Oregon State College
George A. Venn, Creative Writing Director
Ars Poetica
Humanities Division, La Grande, Oreg. 97850
(503) 963-2171
 Budget: varies
 Three writers

Lewis and Clark College
Diane Meisenheimer
Dept. of English
0615 S.W. Palatine Hill Rd., Portland, Oreg. 97219
(503) 244-6161
 Six writers

Mt. Hood Community College
Kathryn Terrill, Creative Writing Coordinator
Literature and Composition
26000 S.E. Stark St., Gresham, Oreg. 97222
(503) 666-1561
 30 writers

Oregon Arts Commission
Gary M. Young, Program Director
316 Oregon Bldg., 494 State St., Rm. 328, Salem,
Oreg. 97301
(503) 378-3625
 Budget: $25,000 per year for Poets-in-the-Schools
 Nine writers

Oregon State University
Roger Weaver
Dept. of English
228 N.W. 28th St., Corvallis, Oreg. 97330
(503) 753-5211
 Budget: $600 per year
 Six writers

Portland Poetry Festival, Inc.
c/o Marty Cohen, Mindy Aloff, Festival Coordinators
5926 N. Princeton, Portland, Oreg. 97203
(503) 285-4451
 Budget: varies
 37 writers

Portland State University
Primus St. John, Advisor
Poetry Committee
Dept. of English, Box 751, Portland, Oreg. 97207
(503) 229-3521
 Budget: varies
 Seven writers

Reed College
Director of Creative Writing
Dept. of English
Portland, Oreg. 97202
(503) 771-1112

University of Oregon
Richard Lyons, Director
Creative Writing Program
English Dept., Eugene, Oreg. 97403
(503) 686-3961
 Budget: $125 per writer
 Four writers

University of Portland
Mary-Margaret Dundore
Student Cultural Arts Board
161 Buckley Center, Portland, Oreg. 97203
(503) 283-7205
 Budget: varies
 Four writers

PENNSYLVANIA

Bryn Mawr College
Director of Creative Writing
Dept. of English
Bryn Mawr, Pa. 19010

California State College
Arthur Winfield Knight, Director
Creative Writing Program
3rd & College, California, Pa. 15419
(412) 938-8956
 Budget: varies
 Two writers

Carnegie-Mellon University
Gerald Costanzo
Creative Writing Program
Dept. of English, Baker Hall, Pittsburgh, Pa. 15213
(412) 621-2600
 16-20 writers

Dickinson College
Steven Edersheim, Chairman
The Belles Lettres Society and The Student
Senate Cultural Affairs Committee
H.U. Box 337, Carlisle, Pa. 17013
(717) 249-7319 (after 5:00 p.m.)
 Budget: $2,500 per year
 Eight writers

Dickinson College Poetry Series
Mary Watson Carson
Office of Student Services
Carlisle, Pa. 17013
(717) 243-5121, Ext. 555
 Six writers

International Poetry Forum
Samuel Hazo, Director
4400 Forbes Ave., Pittsburgh, Pa. 15213
(412) 621-9893
  20 writers

Lincoln University
C. James Trotman, English Dept. Chairman
Melvin B. Tolson Society
Lincoln University, Pa. 19352
(215) 932-8300, ext. 295
  Budget: $200 per writer
  Four writers

Mansfield State College
T.E. Porter
Dept. of English
Mansfield, Pa. 16933
(717) 662-2114, Ext. 394
  Budget: $600 per year
  Four writers

Middle Earth Books
Samuel D. Amico
1134 Pine St., Philadelphia, Pa. 19107
(215) 922-6824
  Six writers

Pennsylvania Council on the Arts
Peter Carnahan, Literature Director or
John D. Hesselbein, Poetry Coordinator
503 N. Front St., Harrisburg, Pa. 17101
(717) 787-6883
  Budget: $47,000 per year
  26 writers

Pennsylvania State University
Director of Creative Writing
Dept. of English
University Park, Pa. 16802

Slippery Rock College
Director of Creative Writing
Dept. of English
Slippery Rock, Pa. 16057

Stephen Crane Society
Mindy Stern
Lafayette College
200 High St., Easton, Pa. 18042
(215) 252-9565
  Ten writers

Swarthmore College
Creative Writing Director
English Department
Swarthmore, Pa. 19081
(215) 544-7900, Ext. 258
  Four writers

Temple University
Eugene Chesnick
Dept. of English
Philadelphia, Pa. 19122
(215) 787-7000
  Four writers

University of Pennsylvania
Daniel Hoffman or Jerre Mangione
Writing Program
Dept. of English, 34th & Spruce, Philadelphia, Pa. 19104
(215) 243-7345
  Six writers

University of Pittsburgh
M.M. Culver, Director
Writing Program
Dept. of English, Pittsburgh, Pa. 15260
(412) 624-6514
  Ten writers

YM-YWHA Poetry Center
Henry Braun, Coordinator or Betty Waskow, Director
of Adult Education
401 S. Broad St., Philadelphia, Pa. 19147
(215) 545-4400
  27 writers

RHODE ISLAND

Brown University
Michael Harper, Director
Creative Writing Program
Box 1852, Brown U., Providence, R.I. 02912
(401) 863-2393
  Four writers

Providence College
Director of Creative Writing
Fine Arts Council
Dept. of English, Providence, R.I. 02918
(401) 865-2292

Rhode Island College
Director of Creative Writing
Dept. of English
Providence, R.I. 02881

Rhode Island School of Design
C. Fenno Hoffman, Chairman
Liberal Arts Division
Providence, R.I. 02903
(401) 331-3507
  Budget: $1,600 per year
  Four writers

Rhode Island State Council on the Arts
Ann Vermel, Executive Director
4365 Post Rd., East Greenwich, R.I. 02818
(401) 884-6410
  Budget: $78,000 per year for Arts-in-Education
  One writer-in-residence

SOUTH CAROLINA

Columbia College
Director of Creative Writing
Dept. of English
Columbia, S.C. 29203

South Carolina Arts Commission
Scott Sanders, Director
Arts in Education Division
829 Richland St., Columbia, S.C. 29201
(803) 758-3442
  30 writers

University of South Carolina
Daniel B. Marin, Chairman
Lectures Committee
Dept. of English, Columbia, S.C. 29208
(803) 777-2272
  Budget: $1,200 per year for speakers
  One writer

SOUTH DAKOTA

Black Hills Writer's Group
Irene Kverne, Workshop Chairman
926 College Ave., Rapid City, S.Dak. 57701
(605) 343-8509
  Budget: $100 per writer
  One writer

Huron College
Director of Creative Writing
Dept. of English
Huron, S.Dak. 57350

South Dakota Arts Council
Dennis Holub, Program Director
Writers-in-the-Schools Program
108 W. 11th St., Sioux Falls, S.Dak. 57102
(605) 339-6646
  Nine writers

South Dakota State University
Director of Creative Writing
Dept. of English
Brookings, S.Dak. 57006

University of South Dakota
Patrick Gross
Coyote Student Center
Programs Office, Vermillion, S.Dak. 57069
(605) 677-5334

TENNESSEE

Fisk College
Director of Creative Writing
Dept. of English
Nashville, Tenn. 37203

Friends of Memphis and Shelby County Libraries
Helen D. Lockhart, Coordinator
Community Relations & Adult Programs
1850 Peabody, Memphis, Tenn. 38104
(901) 534-9661

LeMoyne-Owen College
Director of Creative Writing
Dept. of English
Memphis, Tenn. 38126

Memphis Arts Council
Director of Poetry Readings
P.O. Box 4682, Memphis, Tenn. 38104
(901) 278-2950

Poetry Society of Tennessee
Bee Bacherig Long, President
103 Eastland Dr., Memphis, Tenn. 38111
(901) 323-1571
  Three writers

Tennessee Arts Commission
Gordon Holl, Arts Program Director
222 Capitol Hill Bldg., Nashville, Tenn. 37219
(615) 741-1701
  Budget: $19,000-20,000
  Four writers plus residential poets

Tennessee Poetry Circuit
Paul Ramsey or Reed Sanderlin
c/o U. of Tennessee, Chattanooga, Tenn. 37401
(615) 755-4238
  Budget: $100-250 per writer
  12 writers

Vanderbilt University
Vereen M. Bell, Chairman
Visiting Writers Program
Dept. of English, Box 1620, Sta. B, Nashville,
Tenn. 37235
  Budget: $6,000 per year
  Six writers

TEXAS

Altruistic Enterprises
Charles B. Taylor
5303 Ravensdale, Austin, Tex. 78723
(512) 476-1915
  40 writers

Amarillo Art Center Association
Thomas Matthews
P.O. Box 447, Amarillo, Tex. 79105

Rice University
Walter Isle, Chairman
Dept. of English
Main St., Houston, Tex. 77001
(713) 528-4141
  Three writers

Southern Methodist University
Charles Oliver, Faculty Advisor
Espejo
Dept. of English, Dallas, Tex. 75205
(214) 692-2957
  Four writers

Sul Ross State University
Paul A. Lister, Director
Creative Writing Program
Alpine, Tex. 79830
  Two writers

Texas Commission on the Arts
Bill Jamison, Education & Humanities Programs Officer
Education Programs
P.O. Box 13406, Capitol Station, Austin, Tex. 78711
(512) 475-6593
  Budget: $19,000 per year for Poets-in-the-Schools
  Ten writers

Texas Southern University
Director of Creative Writing
Dept. of English
Houston, Tex. 77004

University of Houston
Sylvan Karchmer, Director of Creative Writing
Dept. of English
Houston, Tex. 77004
(713) 729-2720
  Three writers

University of St. Thomas
Director of Creative Writing
Dept. of English
Houston, Tex. 77006

University of Texas at Austin
Roger Abrahams, Chairman
Dept. of English
Austin, Tex. 78712
(512) 471-2291
  Budget: varies
  Ten writers

UTAH

Southern Utah State College
David Lee, Chairman
Dept. of English
Cedar City, Utah 84720
(801) 586-4411
  Two writers

University of Utah
Robert Mezey
Dept. of English
Salt Lake City, Utah 84112
(801) 581-7392 or 581-6168
  Budget: $1,500 per year
  Seven writers

Utah State Institute of Fine Arts
Literature Program Associate
609 E. South Temple St., Salt Lake City, Utah 84102

VERMONT

Bennington College
Alan Cheuse
Literature & Languages Division
Bennington, Vt. 05201
(802) 442-5401, Ext. 227
  Six writers

Castleton State College
Fine Arts Chairman
Artists-in-Residence Program
Castleton, Vt. 05735

Crossroads Arts Council
Mrs. Joseph Teta, Artist-in-Residence
1 Belmont Ave., Rutland, Vt. 05701
(802) 775-1154
  Budget: varies
  Two writers

Goddard College
Director of Creative Writing
Dept. of English
Plainfield, Vt. 05667

Middlebury College
Robert Pack, Director of Creative Writing
Dept. of English
Middlebury, Vt. 05753

University of Vermont
T. Alan Broughton, Director
Writers Workshop
Dept. of English, 315 Old Mill, Burlington, Vt. 05401
(802) 656-3056
  Three writers

Vermont Council on the Arts
Ellen McCulloch-Lovell, Program Director
136 State St., Montpelier, Vt. 05602
(802) 828-3291
  Budget: $6,000 per year for Writers-in-the-Schools;
  personal grants also available for in-state writers
  Ten writers (primarily from Northern New England)

VIRGINIA

Hollins College
R.H.W. Dillard, Chairman
Creative Writing Program
Dept. of English, Box 9671, Hollins College, Va. 24020
(703) 362-6316
  Budget: $7,000 per year
  Eight writers

Institute of Southern Culture
Quentin Vest
Longwood College, Farmville, Va. 23901
(804) 392-9356, Ext. 33
  Budget: $500 per year

Longwood College
Literary Advisor
Gyre
Dept. of English, Farmville, Va. 23901
(804) 392-9356

University of Virginia
Writing Program Director
Dept. of English
115 Wilson Hall, Charlottesville, Va. 22903
  Six or seven writers

Virginia Commission of the Arts and Humanities
Frank R. Dunham, Executive Director
1215 State Office Bldg., Richmond, Va. 23219
(804) 770-4492
  Budget: $10,000 per year for Poets-in-the-Schools
  15 writers

Virginia Polytechnic Institute and State University
William M. White or Robert Hazel
Dept. of English
Blacksburg, Va. 24061
(703) 957-6917
  Budget: varies
  Two writers

Washington and Lee University
S.P.C. Duvall
Glasgow Endowment Committee
Dept. of English, Lexington, Va. 24450
(703) 463-9111, Ext. 244
  Two writers

WASHINGTON

The Evergreen State College
Director of Creative Writing
Dept. of English
Olympia, Wash. 98505
(206) 866-6385

Eye-5
Adrienne H. Alexander, Executive Director
217 E. 17th Ave., Olympia, Wash. 98501
(206) 352-0245
Budget: $100 per day
Two writers

Tacoma Public Schools
Jack Motler, Director of Cultural Projects
P.O. Box 1357, Tacoma, Wash. 98401
(206) 383-1811

University of Washington
Robert D. Stevick, Chairman
Dept. of English, GN-30
Seattle, Wash. 98195
(206) 543-2690
Nine writers

Washington State Arts Commission
Marilyn C. Hoyt, Administrative Assistant
1151 Black Lake Blvd., Olympia, Wash. 98504
(206) 753-3860
17 writers

Washington State University
G.S. Sharat Chandra, Coordinator for Poetry or
Donald H. Ross, Director of Creative Writing
Dept. of English, Avery Hall, Pullman, Wash. 99163
(509) 335-4832
Two writers

Western Washington State College
Eugene Garber
Dept. of English
Bellingham, Wash. 98225
(206) 676-3209
Three writers

WEST VIRGINIA

West Virginia Arts and Humanities Council
Jim Andrews, Associate Director
Rm. B-531, State Office Building No. 6, 1900 Washington
St., E., Charleston, W.Va. 25305
(304) 348-3711
Eight writers

WISCONSIN

Beloit College
Marion K. Stocking, Chairman
Poetry Committee
Beloit, Wis. 53511
(608) 365-3391
Budget: $150 per writer
Eight writers

University of Wisconsin at Eau Claire
Bruce Edward Taylor, Director of Creative Writing
Dept. of English
Eau Claire, Wis. 54701
(715) 836-2639
Budget: $200 per writer
Four writers

University of Wisconsin at Green Bay
Tom Churchill or Peter Cooley
College of Creative Communication
Green Bay, Wis. 54301
(414) 465-2469 or 465-2491
Budget: $1,200 per year
Four writers

University of Wisconsin at Madison
Phillip Harth, Chairman
Dept. of English
7187 White Hall, 600 N. Park St., Madison, Wis. 53706
(608) 263-3800
One writer

University of Wisconsin at Milwaukee
Director of Creative Writing
Dept. of English
Milwaukee, Wis. 53211

University of Wisconsin at Stevens Point
David Engel, Director of Creative Writing
University Writers Program
Nelson Hall, Stevens Point, Wis. 54481
(715) 346-0123
Budget: $1,000 per year
Six writers

Wisconsin Arts Board
Paul Reichel, Program Coordinator
123 W. Washington Ave., Madison, Wis. 53702
(608) 266-6959
Budget: $9,000 per year for Poets-in-the-Schools
15 writers (preference given to in-state writers)

WYOMING

University of Wyoming
Director
Poets on Campus Program
Dept. of English, Hoyt Hall, Laramie, Wyo. 82070
(307) 766-2204

Wyoming Council on the Arts
Charles Levendosky, Director
Poetry Programs of Wyoming
P.O. Box 3033, Casper, Wyo. 82601
(307) 265-5434
15 writers

Wyoming Writers
Vandi Moore, President
Jelm, Wyo. 82063
(307) 745-9581
Budget: varies
Ten writers

CANADA

Canada Council on the Arts
John G. Prentice, Chairman
151 Sparks St., Ottawa, Ontario K1P 5V8, Canada
(613) 237-3400

Concordia University—Loyola Campus
Judith S. Herz, Chairman
Dept. of English
7141 Sherbrooke St. W., Montreal, Quebec H4B 1R6,
Canada
(514) 482-0320
   Budget: $100 per writer
   Eight writers

University of Victoria
Charles Lillard, Lecturer
Dept. of Creative Writing
Victoria, British Columbia V8W 2Y2, Canada
(403) 477-6911, local 850
   12 writers (Canadian only)

University of Windsor
Director
Creative Writing Program
Windsor, Ontario, Canada
(519) 253-4232

IRELAND & ENGLAND

An Chomharlie Ealaion (Arts Council for Ireland)
Director
70 Merrion Sq., Dublin 2, Ireland
(01) 646-85

Arts Council of Great Britain
105 Picadilly, London W1V OAV, England
629-9495

The Service Section

Literary Organizations of Service to Writers

The following national and regional organizations provide services for the writing community. A separate list of their newsletters and bulletins appears under *Reference Works* in The Service Section of this directory.

The Academy of American Poets is a nonprofit organization whose purpose is to "encourage, stimulate, and foster the production of American poetry."

Each year, the Academy sponsors a number of awards to both published and unpublished poets. These awards include the $10,000 Fellowship; the Copernicus Award of $10,000; the Edgar Allan Poe Award of $5,000; the Walt Whitman Award of $1,000 and publication of a first book of poetry; the Lamont Poetry Selection, now awarded for publication of a poet's second book; and prizes of $100 each given to student poets at some 80 colleges and universities throughout the United States. The Harold Morton Landon Translation Award of $1,000 is given biennially.

In New York City, the Academy presents readings in parks and libraries and literary walking tours through New York neighborhoods.

They also serve as a clearinghouse for information about poets and poetry. An informal monthly bulletin, *Poetry Pilot*, is sent to all friends of the Academy who contribute at least $5 a year. For further information, write The Academy of American Poets, 1078 Madison Ave., New York, N.Y. 10028, (212) 988-6783.

Advocates for the Arts, a program of ACA, represents all sectors of the arts community on legal and economic issues such as censorship, postage, tax, and copyright. Membership in ACA is available for a $15 contribution and includes receipt of *Arts Advocate*, the quarterly publication of Advocates for the Arts.

For further information regarding ACA and Advocates for the Arts, contact Michael Newton, President, ACA, Room 820, 1564 Broadway, New York, N.Y. 10036, (212) 586-3731.

Associated Councils of the Arts is a national service organization for state and community arts councils. Membership, currently over 800, includes universities, libraries, museums, arts professionals and volunteers. ACA's main function has been to improve the professional capabilities of state and community arts councils. This is accomplished through exchange of information in the form of bulletins, newsletters, and professional publications, and through a program of seminars held throughout the year in various parts of the country.

Another of ACA's primary functions is to help increase public money for the arts at the national, state, and local levels. A third function is documenting the arts industry through research and publication of data.

A directory listing 532 arts agencies in the U.S. is published by ACA under the title *Guide to Community Arts Agencies*. The most recent edition was updated in late fall of 1974 and costs $6.50. It may be ordered directly from ACA.

Associated Writing Program, operating with a grant from the National Endowment for the Arts, is a national non-profit organization with a membership of 50 individual writers and 70 college writing programs.

AWP acts as a general clearinghouse for information on 180 writing programs, generally on the graduate level, and gives information to institutions wishing to establish these programs. It has also established a placement service for writers who wish either permanent or temporary jobs.

A *Newsletter*, published seven times a year, is sent free to members; it includes information on scholarships, awards, conferences, writing programs, and new publications. To provide publishing outlets for young writers, AWP edits *Intro*, a yearly anthology of student work selected from member writing programs all over the country. A catalogue of U.S. graduate and undergraduate writing programs is now available at no cost to members and institutions interested in establishing writing programs. Membership dues are $200 a year for writing programs; $10 a year for individuals; and $5 a year for students and unemployed writers. Write to Associated Writing Program, Kathy Walton, Executive Secretary, Washington College, Chesterton, Md. 21620, (301) 778-2800.

The Authors Guild, Inc. is an organization of 4,200 authors; **The Dramatists Guild, Inc.** has 2,300 members. Together, the Guilds form *The Authors League of America*.

Both Guilds protect and promote the professional interests of their members, acting jointly through the League on issues such as copyright protection, taxation, and freedom of expression. The Authors Guild publishes a bimonthly *Bulletin* with news and professional advice for authors. It is free to members.

The Authors Guild has prepared an excellent recommended Trade Book Contract and Guide which is free to members and provides them with information on contract practices and terms. The Guilds and League support the Copyright Revision Bill; legislation recommending a study on library royalties for authors; and legislation to restore a tax deduction for charitable donations of manuscripts, as well as modifications of IRS rulings which adversely affect authors. In freedom of speech and copyright cases, they often file briefs in the Supreme Court and Appellate Courts, and they participate as amicus curiae in major contract and copyright cases. The Guild has also supported legislation to protect literary magazines endangered by ruinous postal rate increases.

Membership dues are $35 a year. Write to The Authors Guild, Inc., 234 W. 44 St., New York, N.Y. 10036, (212) OX 5-4145.

Beyond Baroque Foundation runs a small press library, a referral service for readings and workshops, and a press which publishes literary magazines and books. The Beyond Baroque Library houses a collection of 3,000-4,000 university and small press publications of the 1970's which have been catalogued for use in the library's reading room. (They may not be removed on loan.) The "Poets

Bureau," a telephone referral service for arranging readings in Los Angeles and the surrounding area, is free; the number is (213) 392-5763. Poets from outside the area who are planning a visit are urged to call or write well in advance for possible placement.

For reading and workshop sponsors in the Los Angeles area, Beyond Baroque offers planning assistance and contacts with writers. Sponsors outside the area may telephone for suggestions and advice.

The Foundation's free literary publications, *Newsletters* and *Beyond Baroque 751 Newforms*, contain news of the West Coast literature community, as well as poetry, fiction, and graphics.

Beyond Baroque is supported by the National Endowment for the Arts, the Coordinating Council of Literary Magazines, public donations, and a volunteer staff. For further information contact Beyond Baroque Foundation, 1639 West Washington Blvd., Venice, Calif. 90291, (213) 392-5763.

Carnegie Fund for Authors was founded in the 1890's when Andrew Carnegie gave the Author's Club a New York City Water Bond. Later he gave them another water bond, and at his death bequeathed them $200,000. This fund is now used to provide emergency grants, usually of $500, to professional writers with emergency financial troubles. Applicants must have had at least one commercially published book; applications should be made to Carnegie Fund for Authors, W.L. Rothenberg, 330 Sunrise Highway, Rockville Centre, N.Y. 11570.

COSMEP (Committee of Small Magazine Editors and Publishers) is a membership association of 700 literary magazine and small press editors, about 80% literary. Their publications are sent free to members and include a monthly newsletter; lists of bookstores and libraries in the U.S that are particularly interested in small press material; and various pamphlets on distribution, production, etc. One national and several regional conferences are held each year.

They are interested in enlarging their mailing list and welcome inquiries from individuals and organizations about the small press scene. Membership is $20 a year. Write to COSMEP, Richard Morris, Coordinator, P.O. Box 703, San Francisco, Calif. 94101, (415) 776-1943.

CCLM (The Coordinating Council of Literary Magazines) is a national nonprofit organization which gives grants to non-commercial literary magazines. Though it does not directly support individual writers, CCL. does give magazine grants earmarked for authors' payments. News about grants and the little magazine community will be sent upon request and at no charge to any interested individual or group.

CCLM membership, currently about 400, is open to non-commercial literary magazines which have published for at least a year and have printed at least three issues. Members may participate directly in the election of Grants Committees. There is no membership fee. For further information, contact CCLM, 80 Eighth Ave., New York, N.Y. 10011, (212) 675-8605.

The Copyright Office of the Library of Congress disseminates free information, instructions, and forms for the registration of all types of written, performed, or recorded material which are eligible for copyright registration. Of particular value to writers is a series of free circulars defining copyright limits and procedures. This series includes: *General Information on Copyright* (Circular 1), *Selected Bibliography for Writers* (Circular 2C), *The Copyright Notice* (Circular 3), *Copyright Fees* (Circular 4), *Renewal of Copyright* (Circular 15), *How To Investigate the Copyright Status of A Work* (Circular 22), *Copyright Information About Pictorial, Graphic, and Sculptural Works* (Circulars 70, 70A, and Chart 70), and *Copyright for Sound Recordings* (Circular 56). For a complete list of publications, write for *Publications of the Copyright Office*, which is available free from the Register of Copyrights, Library of Congress, Washington, D.C. 20559, (703) 557-8700.

Note: The Copyright Office cannot give legal advice. If you need information or guidance on publishing your work, obtaining royalty payments, or prosecuting possible copyright infringers, it may be necessary to consult an attorney. In cases of copyright infringement, apply to Volunteer Lawyers for the Arts for possible legal assistance (see their listing below).

National Endowment for the Arts is an independent federal agency created by Act of Congress in 1964 in order to channel federal money into the arts.

The Literature Program of the National Endowment for the Arts assists writers through individual fellowships—totalling $770,000 to 154 writers in fiscal year 1974-75; indirect grants to literary magazines and matching grants to small presses; aid to service organizations providing information and technical guidance to the writing community; and funds for the placement of professional writers in elementary and secondary school classrooms in small developing colleges and in communities.

For applications and more information about grants, write to the National Endowment for the Arts, Leonard Randolph, Literature Program Director, Washington, D.C. 20506, (202) 634-6044.

New England Small Press Association (NESPA) is a membership organization of writers, literary magazine editors, small press publishers, librarians, teachers, and readers who live both in and outside of the New England area.

They exhibit members' publications at college, university, and public libraries; publish a brochure listing all member magazines and presses; and publish a list of NESPA members wishing to read or lecture which is sent to all college English departments, libraries, and book stores in New England. They also maintain a permanent NESPA library in Amherst, Massachusetts, and operate the New England Distribution Service out of Logos Bookstore in Amherst. They are interested in the distribution of literary magazines and small press books and work closely with COSMEP.

For membership and other information, contact Diane Kruchkow, 53 Lime St., Newburyport, Mass. 01950 or Ritchie Darling, 45 Hillcrest Pl., Amherst, Mass. 01002.

Poetry Society of America, founded in 1910, aims "to foster a deeper awareness of poetry in the United States and to help support and encourage the work of worthy poets."

They award monthly and annual prizes totalling around $10,000 and sponsor poetry readings and regular poetry workshops. In most cases, only the 700 members are eligible for the prizes, though a few significant exceptions are made.

Annual dues are $18 and Society open meetings are held monthly, with an annual April banquet. Applications for membership and detailed information on all prizes may be obtained by writing The Poetry Society of America, Charles Wagner, Executive Secretary, 15 Gramercy Park, New York, N.Y. 10003, (212) 254-9628.

Poets & Writers, Inc. serves as a national nonprofit information center for contemporary writers.

With support from The Literature Program of the National Endowment for the Arts, they have published a second edition (1975) of *A Directory of American Poets* and *A Directory of American Fiction Writers* (1976 edition), both of which are updated twice a year with free supplements. They also publish *Coda*, a 28-36 page newsletter which prints news of interest to the writing community. For *Coda* subscription information, call or write.

With funds from the New York State Council on the Arts, Poets & Writers, Inc. provides fee money to writers for readings and workshops given in New York State. Many other state Arts Councils help fund similar projects; for information, please write your state Arts Council which is listed in the *Administrators Listing* of this directory.

For advice and information, write to Poets & Writers, Inc., Galen Williams, Executive Director, 201 W. 54 St., New York, N.Y. 10019, (212) PLaza 7-1766.

Poets-in-the-Schools. Most state Arts Councils have poetry projects, including Poets-in-the-Schools (PITS). For information, write to your state Arts Council; addresses are in the *Administrators Listing* of this directory.

In some cases, community Arts Councils are interested in poetry programs. For a listing of 532 community arts councils published by the Associated Councils of the Arts, send $6.50 to A.C.A., Room 820, 1564 Broadway, New York, N.Y. 10036, (212) 586-3731.

P.E.N. (Poets, Playwrights, Essayists, Editors, and Novelists) **American Center** is a 54-year-old international nonprofit organization with centers in some 60 countries and a membership of about 1,600 in America.

They sponsor a competition for prisoners interested in writing and conduct a correspondence course and a pen-pal matching service for interested prisoners. They give grants to established writers who have financial emergencies (maximum $500) and fight against legal and political repression of writers and censorship throughout the world. They also sponsor and arrange touring book exhibits and an exhibit featuring translation.

In cooperation with Columbia School of the Arts, they were instrumental in setting up The Translation Center (see list-ing below). The P.E.N. Translation Committee continues its work in sponsoring conferences, gives grants to translators, and works to give due recognition to translators, both credit and adequate remuneration. The P.E.N. Translation Prize of $1,000 is given annually, as is the Goethe House-P.E.N. Translation Prize of $500 for translations from the German.

P.E.N. administers the $3,000 Ernest Hemingway Foundation Award for the best first novel. "P.E.N. Portraits," a series of interviews with authors, is broadcast over WNYC-AM under P.E.N. sponsorship. Major medical and income protection insurance are available to members.

Among its publications are the *P.E.N. Newsletter*, published approximately eight times a year, and a quarterly, *The American Pen*. They also publish an annually updated poster, *Writers In Prison!*, listing imprisoned writers around the world. Other annual publications include *Grants and Awards Available to American Writers*, which gives information on domestic and foreign grants for American writers. A companion volume for foreign writers is also available. The price for either book is $1 for P.E.N. members, $2 for non-members. P.E.N. also counsels writers who want to apply for grants but don't know where to begin.

For further information on any program, contact P.E.N. American Center, Kirsten Michalski, Executive Secretary, 156 Fifth Ave., New York, N.Y. 10010, (212) 255-1977.

Science Fiction Writers of America is a world-wide organization of over 450 science-fiction writers writing in English. Membership is open to any science-fiction writer who has published a book or whose work has appeared in a major science-fiction magazine in the U.S. United States citizenship is not required. Annual dues are $12.50

The organization provides members with legal advice and represents the members on legal and political issues such as the Copyright Revision Bill. A free publication, *The Forum*, featuring reports on science-fiction publishers and markets, is sent to members 10 times a year. Members are also sent a free copy of the membership directory and five issues per year of the *Bulletin*, which contains articles on all aspects of the science-fiction field. Nonmembers may receive the *Bulletin* for $10 per year. The membership directory costs $2 for nonmembers.

Each year SFWA presents the Nebula Awards, a group of five honorary awards for best published novel, novella, novelette, short story, and drama—including film, TV, or stage drama.

For additional information, contact Charles Grant, Executive Secretary, Science Fiction Writers of America, 44 Center Grove Rd., Apt. H-21, Dover, N.J 07801, (201) 361-3089.

The Translation Center is a clearinghouse and unpaid agent for translators and publishers. Sponsored by Columbia University School of the Arts and a board of nationally known translators, the Center keeps on file the names of translators and editors particularly interested in translation.

They publish an annual journal, *Translation*, which costs $4 a year and is supplemented by an informational *News-*

letter. The *Newsletter* is sent free to subscribers and includes listings of forthcoming books in translation and books that the Center feels need to be translated.

Awards of $10,000 each are given to several young writers interested in perfecting their skill in a foreign language, especially one of the lesser-known languages of Asia or Africa. The Center has helped young translators by referring them to editors who need a reading, evaluation, or sample translation of a particular book.

Funding for the Center is provided by the National Endowment for the Arts and the New York State Council on the Arts.

For further information contact The Translation Center, Constance Hirsch, Coordinator, 307A Mathematics Hall, Columbia University, New York, N.Y. 10027, (212) 280-2305.

Volunteer Lawyers for the Arts handles art-related legal problems for writers and other artists and art groups who cannot afford counsel. The more than 250 lawyers on the volunteer rolls regularly deal with problems which include: incorporation as a not-for-profit group, securing tax exemptions, negotiating and drafting contracts, copyright, tax, labor and immigration. In fiscal 1974 an estimated $500,000 worth of legal services were donated through the program. Prospective clients are welcome to write to VLA to inquire about eligibility.

VLA also publishes a newspaper, *Art & the Law*, which addresses issues of art and law of importance to both visual and performing artists. Regular news includes developments in copyright and tax law, recent publications, and a report on legislation of significance to artists. Although subscriptions are free from VLA, contributions are welcome. VLA also publishes a helpful and clearly-written pamphlet, *Not-For-Profit Corporations & Unincorporated Associations: A Guide for Arts Groups*, for which a dollar contribution is requested.

Branch offices in New York State have been—or are in the process of being—established in Albany, Buffalo, Glens Falls, Huntington, Oneonta, Potsdam, Poughkeepsie, and Utica. VLA-type groups, modelled after the New York office, have set up shop in Berkeley, Boston, Chicago, Dallas, Los Angeles, Portland, Trenton, and Washington, D.C. For the addresses of these offices andór more information, contact the main office of VLA at 36 W. 44 St., Suite 1110, New York, N.Y. 10036, (212) 575-1150.

Reference Works

This section contains 44 reference works grouped under three headings: 1. Authors; 2. Publications; 3. Grants and Publishing: Where and How. A list of newsletters on writing and publishing is also included.

Only works containing information on contemporary American authors have been included.

These listings are not complete, and suggestions for additional titles are welcome.

Reference Works: Authors

This sections lists 13 publications which contain biographical information on contemporary American poets and fiction writers. They appear in alphabetical order by title. Prices are not given, except for particularly inexpensive volumes. Most titles can be found in libraries and book stores or ordered directly from the publisher. Publishers' addresses are listed in *Books In Print*, which is available in libraries and book stores.

Many of the reference works listed in the following section "Reference Works: Publications," are also indexed by author and supplement the works listed here.

A Bibliographical Checklist of 75 Postwar American Authors (tentative title). Serendipity Books, 1975. Distributed by Serendipity Books, 1790 Shattuck Ave., Berkeley, Calif. 94709. All publications by each author, including broadsides, chapbooks, and translations, are described. It does not include work published in magazines and anthologies.

Biography Index. H.W. Wilson. Hardcover only: nine volumes from 1946-1973. A cumulative index of biographical material on important persons in all fields. It is arranged alphabetically by names and indexed by professions and occupations.

Contemporary American Poetry: A Checklist. By Lloyd Davis and Robert Irwin. Scarecrow Press, 1975. Hardcover only: $7. This checklist serves as a selective bibliographical guide to contemporary American poetry published in collections through 1973. While primarily designed to provide information about poets whose reputations have been established since 1950, it also contains listings for poets born after 1900 who were actively publishing into the fifties and sixties. More than 3,200 poetry books by nearly 110 poets are listed in alphabetical arrangement by author. Publication information is included for each book title entry. The checklist can be used in conjunction with Zulauf and Weiser's *Index of American Periodical Verse*.

Contemporary Authors. Edited by Clare D. Kinsman and Mary Ann Tennenhouse. Gale Research Co., 1962-1973 (new volumes published semi-annually). This series of volumes contains information on 28,000 comtemporary writers of the world listed alphabetically. Alternate volumes contain a cumulative index of all previous volumes.

Contemporary Novelists of the English Language. Edited by James Vinson. St. Martin's Press, 1972. Hardcover only. This volume provides biographies, bibliographies, critical comments, the authors' own remarks on their work, and lists critical studies recommended by the authors. More than 600 contemporary novelists are covered.

Contemporary Poets of the English Language. Edited by Rosalie Murphyand James Vinson. Second Edition. St. Martin's Press, 1974. Hardcover only. Biography, bibliography, and critical comments (including in some cases the poets' own comments on their work) are provided on more than 1,100 contemporary English language poets. Poets are listed alphabetically by geographical area.

A Directory of American Fiction Writers. Poets & Writers, Inc., 1976. Hardcover: $10. Paperback: $5. Distributed by Publishing Center for Cultural Resources, 27 W. 53 St., New York, N.Y. 10019. This volume provides addresses, brief notes on teaching experience and preferences, and the most recent publications for over 800 American fiction writers. Also listed are 500 sponsors of readings and workshops. A Service Section lists anthologies, critical works, films, videotapes, records and tapes, teaching materials, reference works, and organizations in the fields of contemporary American poetry and fiction. Supplemental updates, published to times a year, are sent free to purchasers.

A Directory of American Poets. Poets & Writers, Inc., 1975. Hardcover: $12. Paperback: $6. Distributed by Publishing Center for Cultural Resources, 27 W. 53 St., New York, N.Y. 10019. This volume provides addresses, brief notes on teaching experience and preferences, and the most recent publications for over 1,500 American poets. Also listed are 450 sponsors of readings and workshops. A Service Section lists anthologies, critical works, films, videotapes, records and tapes, teaching materials, reference works, and organizationsin the fields of contemporary American poetry and fiction. Supplemental updates, published two times a year, are sent free to purchasers.

Handbook of Contemporary American Poetry. By Karl Malkoff. Crowell, 1973. Out of print. This work shows the development of modern American poetry written and published since 1940. It contains essays on 70 individual poets with a biographical sketch and discussion of each poet's principal themes and development. It also includes articles on groups and movements.

Living Black American Authors: A Biographical Directory. Edited by Ann Allen Schockley and Sue P. Chandler. R.R. Bowker, 1973. Hardcover only: $12.95. This volume is a good source on contemporary Black novelists and poets. Biographical information is provided for 450 authors. An appendix includes an index of titles mentioned and a list of 20 Black publishers with their addresses.

Modern Black Poets: A Collection of Critical Essays. Edited by Donald B. Gibson. Prentice-Hall, 1973. Hardcover: $7.95. Paperback: $1.95. Sixty essays cover Black poetry from the twenties to the present, including individual pieces on Hughes, Cullen, Tolson, Hayden, Baraka, Lee, Sanchez, and Giovanni. There is no index, but the selected bibliography is useful. This work is not a reference work but may be used for reference.

Twentieth Century Authors: A Biographical Dictionary of Modern Literature. Edited by Stanley J. Kunitz and Howard Haycraft. H.W. Wilson Co., 1942. First Supplement, 1955. Hardcover only. This is an alphabetical listing of 2,550 world authors with biographical and autobiographical sketches, bibliographies, and pictures of the authors.

The Writers Directory 1973-75. St. Martin's Press, 1973. Hardcover only. This is a good comprehensive directory, not limited to poetry and fiction.

Reference Works: Publications

This section lists 15 publications alphabetically by title, which contain indices of poems, stories, and books by contemporary American poets and fiction writers. Prices have been omitted except for particularly inexpensive volumes. Most titles can be found in libraries and book stores or ordered directly from the publisher. Publishers' addresses are listed in *Books In Print*, which is available at libraries and book stores.

Many of the reference works listed in the preceding section, "Reference Works: Authors," are also indexed by publication and supplement the works listed here.

Black American Fiction Since 1952: A Preliminary Checklist. By Frank Deodene and William P. French. Chatham Booksellers, 1970. Paperback only: $2.50. Distributed by Chatham Booksellers, 38 Maple St., Chatham, N.J. 07928. This volume lists books with publisher and date. It is of limited reference value (only 44 pages in all) but could be useful.

Black American Poetry Since 1944: A Preliminary Checklist. By Frank Deodene and William P. French. Chatham Booksellers, 1971. Distributed by Chatham Booksellers, 38 Maple St., Chatham, N.J. 07928. Paperback only: $3.50. This volume lists separately published works by Black poets from 1944 through Spring 1971. It is limited in reference value because of its small size (only 41 pages) but could be useful.

Chicorel Index to Poetry in Anthologies and Collections in Print. Volumes 4, 5, 6. Edited by Marietta Chicorel. Chicorel Library, 1974. Hardcover only: $49.50 each volume. This work indexes world poetry published in anthologies and on records and tapes by title of poem, first line, collection title and editor, and translator. It is particularly complete on more recent anthologies but is not annotated.

Fiction Catalog. 8th Edition. Wilson, 1971. The *Fiction Catalog* covers English language fiction of all periods, including contemporary. 4,315 works are indexed by author, title, and subject, with an annotation of each work. A special section lists publishers and distributors of books listed. This is one of the standard reference works on fiction. It is updated annually with supplements.

Granger's Index to Poetry. 6th Edition. Edited by William J. Smith. Columbia University Press, 1973. Hardcover only: $80. Anthologies of poetry in English published through the end of 1970 are indexed by author, title, subject (5,000 subject categories are employed), and first lines of poems. The total number of anthologies indexed is 514, including older works but also 121 newer anthologies with much contemporary and avant-garde poetry of the past decade. The author index lists some 12,000 poets. It is not annotated.

Index of American Periodical Verse 1972. By Sander Zulauf and Irwin Weiser. Scarecrow, 1974. Hardcover only: $15. This work indexes all poetry published in magazines during 1972 by author, title, and translator. Magazines are listed with addresses. A previous volume covers the year 1971. These works are excellent sources for contemporary poems not indexed elsewhere.

Index to Black Poetry. By Dorothy Chapman. G.K. Hall, 1974. Hardcover only. 94 books by individual poets and 33 anthologies are indexed by title, first line, author, and subject of poem.

Index to Little Magazines. Johnson Reprints (1940-42). Swallow (1966-69). Other volumes out of print (ten volumes in all). Hardcover only. Indexed by author and periodical, this is a good source for contemporary poets and fiction writers through 1969.

Margins: A Review of Little Magazines and Small Press Books. Edited by Tom Montag. Published monthly at $6 a year by Margins, 2912 North Hackett, Milwaukee, Wis. 53211. This magazine is an ongoing source for criticism of new poetry and fiction. It publishes no poetry, only reviews.

Parnassus: Poetry in Review. Published twice a year since 1972 by Parnassus, 205 W. 89 St., New York, N.Y. 10024. $8 a year, $15 for two years. Parnassus publishes no poetry, only reviews of poetry. It is a standard source for criticism on current work. An index of poets and reviewers is printed in every fourth issue.

Poetry Information. Edited by Peter Hodgkiss, c/o The National Poetry Centre, 21 Earls Court Square, London SW5, England. Published twice a year. $5 for four issues; single issues $1.50. This magazine publishes reviews only. Although edited in London, a good half of it is devoted to reviews of current American poetry. An appendix includes bibliographies of articles and book reviews on contemporary poets.

The Reader's Advisor. Vol. I: A Guide to the Best in American and British Literature Except Drama. Edited by Sarah L. Prakken. R.R. Bowker, 1974. Hardcover only. This volume provides annotated lists of reference books, modern American poetry and fiction collections, and criticism.

Science Fiction Story Index, 1950-1968. Edited by Frederick Siemon. American Library Association, 1971. Paperback: $3.95. This volume indexes over 3,400 stories by author, title, anthology title and anthology editor.

Short Story Index. Edited by Dorothy E. Cook and Isabel S. Monro. Wilson, 1953. Supplements: 1950-68. This work together with its supplements indexes 96,336 stories in 6,620 collections. English language stories in anthologies and collections can be located by author, title, title and editor of collection, and subject. The collections indexed are listed in a separate section. Each supplement also includes a list of publishers and distributors with their addresses.

Ulrich's International Periodicals Directory. Edited by Merle Rohinsky. 16th Edition. R.R. Bowker, 1973 (published biennially). Hardcover only. Published in two volumes, this directory lists some 55,000 periodicals from all countries by title under 249 subject headings.

Grants and Publishing: Where and How

This section lists a selection of books and periodicals on the business aspects of writing and publishing. Ordering information is provided for each listing.

A list of newsletters published by organizations which serve the literature community appears at the end of this section.

Books In Print 1975. R.R. Bowker Co. (annual). Library edition only: $75. This multi-volume work lists 440,000 books published in the U.S. in 1975 and indexes them by author, title, and subject, with full ordering information (publisher, price, and ISBN number). An appendix includes the names and addresses of all major U.S. commercial and university presses and many small presses. It is distributed by R.R. Bowker Co., 1180 Avenue of the Americas, New York, N.Y. 10036, (212) 764-5100.

Checklist for Organizers of Poetry Readings and Workshops. 2 pp. Available free from Poets & Writers, Inc., 201 W. 54 St., New York, N.Y. 10019, (212) PLaza 7-1766.

Coda: Poets & Writers Newsletter. Published five times a year. Subscriptions: $5; single issues: $1.25. *Coda*, a 28-36 page newsletter, prints articles and information of interest to poets, fiction writers, editors, publishers, and others concerned with contemporary literature in America. Back issues include in-depth articles on writers' colonies, copyright protection, postage, book fairs, and taxes and the writer. Available from Poets & Writers, Inc., 201 W. 54 St., New York, N.Y. 10019, (212) PLaza 7-1766.

COSMEP Technical Pamphlet Series: Production Design, Promotion, Distribution, Library and Bookstore Sales, The Poet as Printer. These 30-60 page pamphlets are available free to members of COSMEP and to all small presses in New York State. COSMEP membership is available to all U.S. small presses. Write to COSMEP, Richard Morris, Coordinator, P.O. Box 703, San Francisco, Calif. 94101, (415) 776-1934. For further information on COSMEP, see that listing under *Literary Organizations* in the Service Section of this directory.

Directory of Small Magazine/Press Editors and Publishers. See *International Directory of Little Magazines and Small Presses*.

Grants and Awards Available to American Writers. 7th Edition. P.E.N. American Center, 1975. Paperback only: $1 to members, $2 to nonmembers. This volume is an annual listing of foreign and domestic grants over $500 which are offered to American writers. To order, contact P.E.N. American Center, 156 Fifth Ave., New York, N.Y. 10010, (212) 255-1977. For further details on membership in P.E.N., see that listing under *Literary Organizations* in the Service Section of this directory.

Grants and Awards Available to Foreign Writers. P.E.N. American Center, 1975. Paperback only: $1 to members, $2 to nonmembers. This volume is a comprehensive list of grants over $500 assisting travel by foreign writers to the U.S. It is compiled from research done in the fall of 1974. To order, contact P.E.N. American Center, 156 Fifth Ave., New York, N.Y. 10010, (212) 255-1977. For further details on membership in P.E.N., see that listing under *Literary Organizations* in the Service Section of this directory.

The Grants Register. St. Martin's Press, 1975. Hardcover only: $19.50. This is a directory of graduate level awards, prizes, scholarships, and research grants in the arts, sciences, and professions. It is published every two years. Countries covered include the U.S., Canada, Britain, Ireland, Australia, New Zealand, South Africa, and the developing nations. A list of other reference works on grants is appended. Order it from St. Martin's Press, 175 Fifth Ave., New York, N.Y. 10010, (212) 674-5151.

International Directory of Little Magazines and Small Presses. 11th Edition 1975-76. (Annual.) Hardcover: $8.95. Paperback: $5.95. Distributed by Dustbooks, P.O. Box 1056, Paradise, Calif. 95969, (916) 877-6110. This directory provides the names of the editors, editorial policy, fees paid to contributors, and addresses for hundreds of little magazines and small presses. It is intended as a guide for writers interested in submitting their work for publication. Magazines and presses are listed alphabetically but are also indexed by region and major field of interest.

A companion volume is published annually under the title **Directory of Small Magazine/Press Editors and Publishers.** The 6th edition (1975-76) is available in paperback for $3.50 from Dustbooks (at the address above). Editors and publishers of small magazines, presses, and papers are listed alphabetically by name with the name and address of the publication.

Addresses in both the *International Directory of Little Magazines and Small Presses* and the *Directory of Small Magazine/Press Editors and Publishers* are updated monthly in **Small Press Review.** In addition to new addresses and names, *Small Press Review* prints reviews, news, and features on small press publishing. It is available from Dustbooks for $6 a year to individuals or $10 a year to institutions. Books published by small presses are listed annually in **Small Press Record of Books,** which is available from Dustbooks in paperback only for $4.50. The 4th edition was published in 1975. Previous editions list books published 1966-68 (1st edition, $2), 1969-71 (2nd edition, $2.50), and 1972-73 (3rd edition, $3.50).

Literary Market Place. R.R. Bowker Co. (annual). Paperback only: $21.50. This is a complete directory, listing names, addresses, and phone numbers of practically every individual and group of importance in the publishing field, especially in commercial publishing: agents, book clubs, awards, publishers, reviewers, radio and TV stations, printers, writers' associations, etc. It is published annually by R.R. Bowker Co., 1180 Avenue of the Americas, New York, N.Y. 10036, (212) 764-5100.

Magazines for Libraries. R.R. Bowker Co., 1972. Paperback only: $24.50. This is a guide to magazine selection for public school and college libraries. It describes the content of about 4,500 magazines. A supplement, compiled in 1974 and available for $16.50, includes annotations for another 1,800 titles. Order from R.R. Bowker Co., 1180 Avenue of the Americas, New York, N.Y. 10036, (212) 764-5100.

The Publish-It-Yourself Handbook: Literary Tradition & How-To. Pushcart Press, 1974. Paperback only: $4.50. This is a guide to self-publishing and includes legal information, publicity tips, lists of directories and presses, and essays on the great tradition of self-publishing by authors who have pioneered. It is distributed by Pushcart Press, P.O. Box 845, Yonkers, N.Y. 10701, (914) 963-3454.

Small Press Record of Books. See *International Directory of Little Magazines and Small Presses.*

Small Press Review. See *International Directory of Little Magazines and Small Presses.*

The Whole COSMEP Catalog. Dustbooks, 1973. Paperback only: $4.95. This is a catalog of small press advertisements published in 1973. It is intended as a visual supplement to the *International Directory of Little Magazines and Small Presses,* listed in this section. *The Whole COSMEP Catalog* may be ordered from Dustbooks, P.O. Box 1056, Paradise, Calif. 95969, (916) 877-6110.

Writers Market. (Annual.) Edited by Jane Koester and Rose Adkins. Paperback only: $12.50. This is a good annotated listing of magazine and book publishers with their addresses, names of editors, and editorial policies. It may be ordered from Writers Market, 9933 Alliance Rd., Cincinnati, Ohio 45242, (513) 984-0710.

Newsletters on Writing and Publishing

The following is a list of newsletters that serve the writing community. For information about availability, see the corresponding entry in this directory under *Literary Organizations.*

ACA Bulletin (Associated Councils of the Arts)
Art & the Law (Volunteer Lawyers for the Arts)
Arts Advocate (Advocates for the Arts)
AWP Newsletter (Associated Writing Programs)
Authors Guild Bulletin (The Authors Guild, Inc.)
Coda: Poets & Writers Newsletter (Poets & Writers, Inc.)
COSMEP Newsletter (Committee of Small Magazine Editors and Publishers)
CCLM Newsletter (Coordinating Council of Literary Magazines)
P.E.N. Newsletter (P.E.N. American Center)
Poetry Pilot (The Academy of American Poets)
SFWA Bulletin (Science Fiction Writers of America)
The Translation Center Newsletter (The Translation Center)

Fiction Anthologies

Only anthologies of contemporary American fiction are included. If the major part of an anthology consists of British fiction or fiction written before the Second World War, the book has not been included.

There are a total of 127 anthologies listed alphabetically by title under three headings: General (69), Ethnic (35), and Science Fiction (23). Titles can be ordered through book stores or directly from publishers. Publishers' addresses can be found in *Books In Print,* which is available at book stores and libraries.

General

ABOUT WOMEN: AN ANTHOLOGY OF CONTEMPORARY FICTION, POETRY, AND ESSAYS. Edited by Stephen Berg and S.J. Marks. Fawcett World Library, 1974. Paperback only.

ACCENT: AN ANTHOLOGY 1940-1960. Edited by Daniel Curley et al. University of Illinois Press, 1973. Hardcover only.

ALABAMA PRIZE STORIES, NINETEEN SEVENTY. Edited by O.B. Emerson. The Strode Publishers, 1970. Hardcover only.

THE AMERICAN LANDSCAPE: A CRITICAL ANTHOLOGY OF PROSE & POETRY. Edited by John Conron. Oxford University Press, 1974. Paperback textbook edition only.

AMERICAN LITERARY ANTHOLOGY 3: THE THIRD ANNUAL COLLECTION OF THE BEST FROM THE LITERARY MAGAZINES. Edited by George Plimpton and Peter Ardery. Viking Press, 1970. Paperback only.

AMERICAN LITERARY ANTHOLOGY, VOLUME II. Edited by George Plimpton and Peter Ardery. Random House, 1968. Hardcover and paperback.

AMERICAN UTOPIAS: SELECTED SHORT FICTION. Edited by Arthur O. Lewis. Arno Press, 1971. Hardcover only.

ANTHOLOGY OF HOLOCAUST LITERATURE. Edited by Glatstein et al. Jewish Publication Society of America, 1969: hardcover edition. Atheneum, 1972: paperback textbook edition.

THE BEAT GENERATION & THE ANGRY YOUNG MAN. Essays, stories, and excerpts from larger works. Edited by Gene Feldman and Max Gartenberg. Books for Libraries Press, 1958. Hardcover only.

THE BEAT SCENE. Edited by Elias Wilentz. Corinth Books, 1952. Paperback only. Distributed by RPM Distributors, P.O. Box 1785, Rockville, Md. 20850.

THE BEST AMERICAN SHORT STORIES. Edited by Martha Foley. Selected and published annually. Houghton Mifflin. Hardcover only.

BEST LITTLE MAGAZINE FICTION, 1970. Edited by Curt W. Johnson and Alvin Greenberg. New York University Press, 1971. Hardcover and paperback.

BITCHES AND SAD LADIES: AN ANTHOLOGY OF SHORT FICTION BY AND ABOUT WOMEN. Edited by Pat Rotter. Harper's Magazine Press, 1974. Hardcover only.

BREAKTHROUGH FICTIONEERS. Edited by Richard Kostelanetz. Fiction using unusual techniques. Something Else Press, 1973. Distributed by Serendipity Books, 1790 Shattuck Ave., Berkeley, Calif. 94709.

CLIFTON FADIMAN'S FIRESIDE READER. Edited by Clifton Fadiman. Simon & Schuster, 1961. Hardcover only.

CRAFT & VISION: THE BEST FICTION FROM THE SEWANEE REVIEW. Edited by Andrew Lytle. Delacorte, 1971. Hardcover only.

CUTTING EDGES. Edited by J. Hicks. Holt, Rinehart & Winston, 1973. Paperback text edition only.

DUES: AN ANNUAL OF NEW EARTH WRITING, NUMBERS 1 & 2. Edited by Ron Welburn. Emerson Hall Publishers, 1973. Hardcover only.

DUTTON REVIEW. VOL. 1, NO. 1. Edited by Hal Scharlatt et al. E.P. Dutton, 1971. Paperback only.

EXPLOITED EDEN: LITERATURE ON THE AMERICAN ENVIRONMENT. Edited by R.J. Gangewere. Harper & Row, 1972. Paperback textbook edition only.

EXTREME UNCTIONS AND OTHER LAST RITES. Edited by Robert Bonazzi. Latitudes Press, 1974. Hardcover and paperback. Distributed by Serendipity Books Distribution, 1790 Shattuck Ave., Berkeley, Calif. 94709.

THE FAR SIDE OF THE STORM: NEW RANGES OF WESTERN FICTION. Edited by Gary Elder. Dustbooks, 1975. Distributed by Dustbooks, P.O. Box 1056, Paradise, Calif. 95969.

FICTION ONE HUNDRED: AN ANTHOLOGY OF SHORT STORIES. Edited by J. Pickering. Macmillan, 1974. Paperback only.

THE FIFTIES: FICTION, POETRY, DRAMA. Edited by Warren French. Everett-Edwards, Inc., 1971. Hardcover only.

THE FIRST MS. READER. Edited by Ms. Editors. Paperback Library, 1973. Paperback only.

HOW WE LIVE. CONTEMPORARY LIFE IN CONTEMPORARY FICTION. Edited by Penny C. Hills and L. Rust Hills. Macmillan, 1971. Paperback only.

INTRO FIVE. Edited by Walton Beacham and George Garrett. University Press of Virginia, 1974. Paperback only.

INTRODUCTION TO FICTION. Edited by Paul J. Dolan and Joseph T. Bennett. John Wiley & Sons, 1974. Paperback textbook edition only.

LITERATURE FOR OUR TIME. Edited by Benjamin P. Atkinson and Harlow O. Waite. Books for Libraries Press, 1958. Hardcover only.

LITERATURE IN AMERICA: THE MODERN AGE. Edited by C. Kaplan. Free Press, 1971. Paperback only.

LITTLE REVIEW ANTHOLOGY, 1970. Edited by Margaret Anderson. Horizon Press, 1970. Hardcover and paperback.

LIVING AMERICAN LITERATURE. Edited by W. Tasker Witham. Frederick Ungar Publishing Co., 1947. Hardcover only.

MAKING A BREAK: VOLUME TWO OF NEW DEPARTURES IN FICTION. Edited by Robert Bonazzi. Hardcover and paperback. Distributed by Serendipity Books, 1790 Shattuck Ave., Berkeley, Calif. 94709.

MODERN AGE: LITERATURE. Edited by Leonard Lief and James F. Light. Holt, Rinehart & Winston, 1972. Hardcover textbook edition only.

MODERN AMERICAN CLASSICS: AN ANTHOLOGY OF SHORT FICTION. Edited by David R. Weimer. Random House, 1970. Paperback textbook edition only.

MODERN OCCASIONS: NEW FICTION, POETRY, DRAMA AND CRITICISM BY TWENTY-ONE WRITERS. Edited by Philip Rahv. Farrar, Straus & Giroux, 1966. Hardcover and paperback.

MODERN OCCASIONS TWO: NEW FICTION, CRITICISM, POETRY. Edited by Philip Rahv. Kennikat Press, 1974. Hardcover only.

THE NEW CONSCIOUSNESS: AN ANTHOLOGY OF THE NEW LITERATURE. Edited by Albert LaValley. Winthrop Publishers, 1972. Paperback textbook edition only.

NEW DIRECTIONS. Semiannual collections edited by James Laughlin et al. New Directions. Hardcover and paperback.

NEW VOICES 4: AMERICAN WRITING TODAY. Edited by Charles I. Glicksberg. Hendricks House, 1960. Hardcover only.

ORBIT. A series of anthologies published annually. Edited by Damon Knight. Publishers vary. Hardcover and paperback.

PRIZE STORIES 1975: THE O. HENRY AWARDS. Edited by William Abrahams. Doubleday. Selected and published annually. Hardcover only.

THE PROCESS OF FICTION: CONTEMPORARY STORIES AND CRITICISM, 2nd EDITION. Edited by Barbara McKenzie. Harcourt Brace Jovanovich, 1974. Paperback textbook edition only.

THE PUSHCART PRIZE, 1976: BEST OF THE SMALL PRESSES. Edited by Bill Henderson et al. Pushcart Press, 1976. Hardcover and paperback. Distributed by Pushcart Press, P.O. Box 845, Yonkers, N.Y. 10701.

QUARTERLY REVIEW OF LITERATURE'S 30th ANNIVERSARY RETROSPECTIVE (VOLUME XIX). Edited by T. Weiss and R. Weiss. Quarterly Review of Literature, 1975, 16 Haslet Ave., Princeton, N.J. 08540. Hardcover and paperback.

QUARTET-STORIES. Edited by Harold P. Simonson. Harper & Row, 1973. Paperback textbook edition only (instructor's manual free).

READING FOR UNDERSTANDING: FICTION, DRAMA, POETRY. Edited by Caroline Schrodes et al. Macmillan, 1968. Paperback textbook edition only.

RITES. Edited by John Cofferata. McGraw-Hill, 1974. Hardcover only.

SCENES FROM AMERICAN LIFE: CONTEMPORARY SHORT FICTION - 1972. Edited by Joyce C. Oates. Random House, 1972. Paperback textbook edition only.

SEARCHING FOR AMERICA. Edited by Ernece B. Kelly. National Council of Teachers of English, 1972. Paperback textbook edition only.

THE SECRET LIFE OF OUR TIMES: NEW FICTION FROM ESQUIRE. Edited by Gordon Lish. Doubleday, 1973. Hardcover only.

SHADOW WITHIN. Edited by Richard L. Cherry et al. Houghton Mifflin, 1973. Paperback textbook edition only (instructor's manual available).

THE SINGLE VOICE: AN ANTHOLOGY OF CONTEMPORARY FICTION. Edited by Jerome Charyn. Macmillan, 1969. Paperback only.

THE SMITH/FICTION (No. 14). Edited by Harry Smith. The Smith, 1972. Paperback only. Distributed by Horizon Press, 156 Fifth Ave., New York, N.Y. 10010.

SOUTHERN WRITING IN THE SIXTIES: FICTION. Edited by John W. Corrington and Miller Williams. Louisiana State University Press, 1966. Hardcover only.

STATEMENTS: NEW FICTION FROM THE FICTION COLLECTIVE. Edited by Israel Horowitz et al. Braziller, 1975. Hardcover and paperback.

STORIES FROM THE SIXTIES. Edited by Stanley Elkin. Doubleday, 1971. Paperback only.

SURFICTION: FICTION NOW AND TOMORROW. Edited by Raymond Federman. Swallow Press, 1975. Hardcover only.

SURVIVAL PROSE: AN ANTHOLOGY OF NEW WRITING. Edited by George Becker and John B. Gerald. Bobbs-Merrill, 1971. Hardcover only.

THREE: 1971. Edited by Arthur Gould et al. Random House, 1971. Hardcover only.

TWELFTH ANNIVERSARY PLAYBOY READER. Edited by Hugh M. Hefner. Trident. Hardcover only.

12 FROM THE SIXTIES. Edited by Richard Kostelanetz. Dell, 1967. Paperback only.

UNDERGROUND ANTHOLOGY. Edited by G. Keen. St. Martin's Press, 1973. Paperback only.

UNDERSTANDING AMERICAN POLITICS THROUGH FICTION. Edited by Myles L. Clowers and Lorin Letendre. McGraw-Hill, 1973. Paperback textbook edition only (instructor's manual available).

UNDER 30: FICTION, POETRY & CRITICISM OF THE NEW AMERICAN WRITERS. Edited by Charles Newman and William A. Henkin, Jr. Indiana University Press, 1970. Hardcover only.

VOICES OF BROOKLYN. Edited by Sol Yurick. American Library Association, 1973. Hardcover only.

WINTER'S TALES. Semiannual collections edited by C. Hobhouse and A.D. Maclean. St. Martin's Press. Hardcover only.

WRITER'S CHOICE: TWENTY AMERICAN AUTHORS INTRODUCE THEIR OWN BEST STORY. Edited by L. Rust Hills. David McKay, 1974. Hardcover only.

WRITER'S VOICE. Edited by K. Symes. Holt, Rinehart & Winston, 1973. Paperback textbook edition only.

Ethnic

AFFIRMATION: A BILINGUAL ANTHOLOGY 1919-1966. Edited by Jorge Guillen (translated by Julian Palley). University of Oklahoma Press, 1971. Hardcover and paperback. Spanish-speaking authors.

AIIIEEEEE! AN ANTHOLOGY OF ASIAN-AMERICAN WRITERS. Edited by Jeffrey Chan et al. Howard University Press, 1974. Hardcover only.

AZTLAN: AN ANTHOLOGY OF MEXICAN-AMERICAN LITERATURE. Edited by Stan Steiner and Luis Valdez. Random House, 1972. Paperback only.

BALTIMORE AFRO-AMERICAN: BEST SHORT STORIES BY AFRO-AMERICAN WRITERS, 1925-50. Edited by H.L. Faggett and Nick A. Ford. Kraus Reprints, 1950. Hardcover only.

BLACK FIRE: AN ANTHOLOGY OF AFRO-AMERICAN WRITING. Edited by LeRoi Jones and Roy Neal. William Morrow, 1968. Hardcover and paperback.

BLACK AMERICAN WRITER, VOLUME I FICTION. Edited by C.W. Bigsby. Penguin Books, Inc., 1971. Paperback only.

THE BLACK EXPERIENCE: AN ANTHOLOGY OF AMERICAN LITERATURE FOR THE 1970'S. Edited by Francis E. Kearns. Viking Press, 1970. Paperback only.

BLACK FIRE: AN ANTHOLOGY OF AFRO-AMERICAN WRITING. Edited by LeRoi Jones and Roy Neal. William Morrow, 1968. Hardcover and paperback.

BLACK IDENTITY: A THEMATIC READER. Edited by Francis E. Kearns. Holt, Rinehart & Winston, 1970. Paperback textbook edition and teacher's edition.

BLACK SHORT STORY ANTHOLOGY. Edited by Woodie King. Columbia University Press, 1972. Hardcover textbook edition. New American Library, 1972. Paperback edition.

BLACK WRITERS OF AMERICA: A COMPREHENSIVE ANTHOLOGY. Edited by Richard Barksdale and Kenneth Kinnamon. Macmillan, 1972. Hardcover textbook edition only.

THE BROADSIDE ANNUAL. Edited by Jill W. Boyer. Broadside Series. Paperback only. Black writers.

THE CHICANOS: MEXICAN AMERICAN VOICES. Edited by Ed Ludwig and James Santibanez. Penguin Books, 1971. Paperback only.

DARK SYMPHONY: NEGRO LITERATURE IN AMERICA. Edited by James A. Emanuel and Theodore L. Gross. The Free Press, 1968. Hardcover and paperback.

FROM THE BARRIO: A CHICANO ANTHOLOGY. Edited by Luis O. Salinas and Lillian Faderman. Canfield Press (Harper & Row), 1973. Paperback textbook edition only.

FROM THE ROOTS: SHORT STORIES BY BLACK AMERICANS. Edited by Charles L. James. Dodd, Mead & Co., 1970. Paperback textbook edition only (instructor's manual free).

GALAXY OF BLACK WRITING. Edited by R. Baird Shuman. Moore Publishing Co., 1970. Hardcover only.

GHETTO SIXTY EIGHT. Edited by Sol Battle. Panther House, 1970. Paperback and library binding.

JEWISH-AMERICAN LITERATURE: AN ANTHOLOGY. Edited by Abraham Chapman. New American Library, 1974. Paperback only.

LITERATURE OF AMERICAN JEWS. Edited by Theodore L. Gross. Free Press, 1973. Hardcover only.

THE MAN TO SEND RAIN CLOUDS: CONTEMPORARY STORIES BY AMERICAN INDIANS. Edited by Kenneth Rosen. Viking Press, 1974. Hardcover and paperback.

MAY MY WORDS FEED OTHERS: AN ANTHOLOGY OF VERSE AND FICTION FROM THE RECONSTRUCTIONIST MAGAZINE. Edited by Chayym Zeldis. A.S. Barnes, 1973. Hardcover only. Jewish writers.

NEW BLACK VOICES: AN ANTHOLOGY OF CONTEMPORARY AFRO-AMERICAN LITERATURE. Edited and with an introduction and biographical notes by Abraham Chapman. New American Library, 1972. Paperback only.

NOMMO: AN ANTHOLOGY OF MODERN BLACK AFRICAN AND BLACK AMERICAN LITERATURE. Edited by William R. Robinson. Macmillan, 1972. Paperback textbook edition only.

OUT OF OUR LIVES: A SELECTION OF CONTEMPORARY BLACK FICTION. Edited by Quandra P. Stadler. Howard University Press, 1974. Hardcover only.

RIGHT ON: AN ANTHOLOGY OF BLACK LITERATURE. Edited by Bradford Chambers and Rebecca Moon. New American Library. Paperback only.

SOON, ONE MORNING: NEW WRITING BY AMERICAN NEGROES 1940-1962. Edited by Herbert Hill. Alfred A. Knopf, 1963. Hardcover only.

TALES AND STORIES FOR BLACK FOLKS: WRITTEN BY BLACK AUTHORS. Edited by Toni Cade Bambara. Doubleday, 1971. Paperback only.

TEN TIMES BLACK: STORIES FROM THE BLACK EXPERIENCE. Edited by Julian Mayfield. Bantam, 1972. Paperback only.

THREE HUNDRED & SIXTY DEGREES OF BLACKNESS COMING AT YOU. Edited by Sonia Sanchez. Broadside Press, 1971. Paperback only.

VOCES DEL BARRIO. Edited by H. Snyder. Holt, Rinehart & Winston, 1974. Paperback textbook edition only.

VOICES OF AZTLAN: CHICANO LITERATURE OF TODAY. Edited by Dorothy Harth and Lewis M. Baldwin. New American Library, 1974. Paperback only.

THE WAY: AN ANTHOLOGY OF AMERICAN INDIAN LITERATURE. Edited by Stan Steiner and Shirley H. Witt. Alfred A. Knopf, 1972. Hardcover edition. Random House, 1972. Paperback edition.

WE ARE CHICANOS: AN ANTHOLOGY OF CHICANO LITERATURE. Edited by Philip Ortego. Washington Square Press, 1973. Paperback only.

WHAT WE MUST SEE: YOUNG BLACK STORYTELLERS. Edited by Orde Coombs. Apollo Editions, 1971. Paperback only.

Science Fiction

AGAIN DANGEROUS VISIONS. Science fiction edited by Harlan Ellison. Two volumes. New American Library, 1973. Paperback only.

AND NOW WALK GENTLY THROUGH THE FIRE & OTHER SCIENCE FICTION STORIES. Edited by Roger Elwood. Chilton, 1972. Hardcover only.

ANDROIDS, TIME MACHINES, AND BLUE GIRAFFES. Science fiction edited by Roger Elwood and Victor Ghidalia. Follett, 1973. Hardcover only.

ASTOUNDING: THE JOHN W. CAMPBELL MEMORIAL ANTHOLOGY OF SCIENCE FICTION. Edited by Harry Harrison. Random House, 1973. Hardcover only.

BEST SCIENCE FICTION. Annual volumes. Editors and publishers vary. Hardcover and paperback.

CHAINS OF THE SEA: THREE ORIGINAL NOVELLAS OF SCIENCE FICTION. Edited by Robert Silverberg. Nelson, 1973. Hardcover only.

CRISIS: TEN ORIGINAL STORIES OF SCIENCE FICTION. Edited by Roger Elwood. Nelson, 1974. Hardcover only.

DEEP SPACE: EIGHT STORIES OF SCIENCE FICTION. Edited by Robert Silverberg. Nelson, 1973. Hardcover only.

FUTURE CITY. Science fiction edited by Roger Elwood. Trident, 1973. Hardcover only.

HUMAN MACHINES: AN ANTHOLOGY OF STORIES ABOUT CYBORGS. Edited by Thomas N. Scortia and George Zebrowski. Vintage, 1975. Paperback only.

IN THE WAKE OF MAN: A SCIENCE FICTION TRIAD. By R.A. Lafferty et al. . Bobbs-Merrill, 1975. Hardcover only.

NEBULA AWARD STORIES. Annual volumes compiled by noted science fiction authors. Various publishers. Hardcover and paperback.

THE NEW ATLANTIS AND OTHER NOVELLAS OF SCIENCE FICTION. Three novellas. Edited by Robert Silverberg. Hawthorn, 1975. Hardcover only.

NEW DIMENSIONS. A series of annual anthologies. Edited by Robert Silverberg. Publishers vary. Hardcover and paperback.

NEW WORLDS. Edited by Michael Moorcock and Charles Platt. Avon, 1974. Paperback only.

OTHER WORLDS, OTHER GODS. Edited by Mayo Mohs. Avon, 1974. Paperback only.

POLITICAL SCIENCE FICTION. Edited by Martin H. Greenberg and Patricia Warrick. Prentice-Hall, 1974. Hardcover and paperback textbook edition.

SCIENCE FICTION HALL OF FAME. Vol. I edited by Robert Silverberg. Doubleday, 1974. Hardcover only. Vol. II edited by Ben Bova. Avon, 1974. Paperback only.

THE SCIENCE FICTION HONOR ROLL. Edited by Frederick Pohl. Random House, 1975. Hardcover only.

SURVIVAL PRINTOUT: SCIENCE FACT, SCIENCE FICTION. Edited by Total Effect. Random House, 1973. Paperback only.

TOMORROW'S ALTERNATIVES. Science fiction edited by Roger Elwood. Macmillan, 1973. Paperback only.

UNIVERSE. A series of annual anthologies. Edited by Terry Carr. Publishers vary. Hardcover and paperback.

WINDOWS INTO TOMORROW. Science fiction edited by Robert Silverberg. Hawthorn, 1974. Hardcover only.

Fiction Criticism

There are a total of 90 works of criticism listed alphabetically by title in two sections.

The first section, "Fiction Criticism: Reference," lists 13 reference works excerpting or indexing book reviews, essays, and book-length studies on contemporary American fiction. Most of these reference works are multi-volume editions priced for library purchase and designed for library use. However, prices have been included for publications costing $15 or less.

The second section, "Fiction Criticism: General," lists 76 books of criticism. Prices for these have not been included.

Many other critical works on contemporary American fiction may be found in libraries or book stores, but we have included only those which are in print and can be ordered from the publisher. Publishers' addresses can be found in *Books In Print*, which is available at book stores and libraries. Books published by small presses are listed with the name and address of a distributor.

This list is not complete. Suggestions for additional titles are welcome.

Fiction Criticism: Reference

AMERICAN LITERARY SCHOLARSHIP: 1963-1972. Duke University Press, 1974. This work, updated annually, provides running commentary on literary criticism published each year. It includes sections on fiction and poetry from 1930 to the present.

ARTICLES ON TWENTIETH CENTURY LITERATURE: AN ANNOTATED BIBLIOGRAPHY 1954-1970. Edited by David E. Pownall. Kraus Reprints, 1973. 7 volumes are now available; 16 volumes in all are planned. This is a massive project attempting to provide complete bibliographies on all authors living and writing in the 20th century. The first seven volumes, arranged alphabetically by author and extending through authors whose names begin with *I*, contain over 10,000 articles.

BOOK REVIEW DIGEST. Published annually since 1905 by H.W. Wilson. This is the standard source for reviews in literature and other fields. About 6,000 books a year are listed by author with excerpts from reviews as well as book prices, publishers, and descriptions.

BOOK REVIEW INDEX. Edited by Robert C. Thomas. Gale Research Co., annual. The *Book Review Index* indexes all reviews in 235 English language periodicals including many literary magazines. Entries are arranged alphabetically by author with a cumulative index published in every second issue.

CONTEMPORARY LITERARY CRITICISM: EXCERPTS. 4 volumes. Gale Research Co. This work contains excerpts of criticism on contemporary creative writers, i.e. those writers living as of 1960. Each volume contains cumulative indices of the previous volumes.

THE CONTEMPORARY NOVEL: A CHECKLIST OF CRITICAL LITERATURE ON THE BRITISH AND AMERICAN NOVEL SINCE 1945. By Irving Adelman and Rita Dworkin. Scarecrow Press, 1972. Hardcover only: $15. This is an excellent reference source for locating criticism on well-known authors.

EXTRAPOLATION. Begun in 1969, this is a semiannual periodical publishing criticism and bibliographies of science fiction. Subscriptions are $3 a year from *Extrapolation*, Box 3186, College of Wooster, Wooster, Ohio 44691.

MODERN BLACK NOVELISTS: A COLLECTION OF CRITICAL ESSAYS. Edited by Michael Cooke. Prentice-Hall, 1971. Hardcover: $5.95. Paperback: $1.95. This is a compendium of pamphlets published separately by Prentice-Hall in the series *Twentieth Century Views*.

MODERN LANGUAGE ASSOCIATION BIBLIOGRAPHY OF BOOKS AND ARTICLES ON THE MODERN LANGUAGES AND LITERATURES. 21 volumes, 1921-1968. Kraus Reprints. This work is mentioned here for its section on 20th century American literature. Each volume is indexed for the names of all authors and editors appearing in that volume. Cumulative indices are also published from time to time.

SCIENCE FICTION BOOK REVIEW INDEX. Edited by H.W. Hall. Gale Research Co., 1975. Reviews are indexed alphabetically by author with cross-referencing for pseudonyms. Also indexed are the titles of books and magazines in which reviews appeared and the magazines' editors. This is a good source for hard-to-find reviews.

SCIENCE FICTION CRITICISM: AN ANNOTATED CHECKLIST. By Thomas D. Clareson. Kent State University Press, 1972, Hardcover only: $7. This reference work indexes science fiction criticism in many American, British, and European periodicals which are not exclusively devoted to science fiction criticism or to literature. It is therefore a good source for hard-to-find articles. Many

books containing science fiction criticism are also indexed. The focus is on critical studies of the field in general. Professor Clareson did not include studies concentrating on the work of a single well-known author, items from science fiction magazines, or critical notes on anthologies. The volume is indexed by critics and authors. It is divided into nine categories, such as General Studies, Publishing, The Visual Arts, and Specialist Bibliographies.

TWENTIETH-CENTURY SHORT STORY EXPLICATION. Edited by Warren S. Walker. Shoe String Press, 1968. Hardcover only: $10.00. This work, with its supplements, contains critical interpretations published between 1900 and 1972 on short fiction written since 1800. Supplements are published every three years. Prices for the supplements vary.

WOMEN STUDIES ABSTRACTS. By Sara S. Whaley. Rush Publishing Co., 1972 to the present. A quarterly, *Women Studies* abstracts and lists articles and book reviews in the field of women's studies, including literary works, biography, and criticism. An index is published annually. Distributed at $10 a year or $3 an issue by Rush Publishing Co., P.O. Box 1, Rush, N.Y. 14543.

Fiction Criticism: General

ABSURD HERO IN AMERICAN FICTION: UPDIKE, STYRON, BELLOW, SALINGER. Edited by David D. Galloway. University of Texas Press, 1970. Hardcover only.

ADVERSITY AND GRACE: STUDIES IN RECENT AMERICAN LITERATURE. Edited by Nathan A. Scott, Jr. University of Chicago Press, 1968. Hardcover only.

AFTER ALIENTATION. By Marcus Klein. Books for Libraries, 1964. Hardcover only.

AMERICAN CITY NOVEL. By Blanche H. Gelfont. University of Oklahoma Press, 1974 (reprint of 1954 edition). Hardcover only.

AMERICAN NOVEL SINCE WORLD WAR TWO. Edited by Marcus Klein. Fawcett World, 1969. Paperback only.

BEYOND THE WASTE LAND: A STUDY OF THE AMERICAN NOVEL IN THE NINETEEN-SIXTIES. By Raymond M. Olderman. Yale University Press, 1972. Hardcover and paperback.

BILLION YEAR SPREE: THE TRUE HISTORY OF SCIENCE FICTION. By Brian W. Aldiss. Hardcover: Doubleday, 1973. Paperback: Schocken, 1974.

BLACK FICTION. By Roger Rosenblatt. Harvard University Press, 1974. Hardcover only.

BLACK HUMOROUS FICTION OF THE SIXTIES: A PLURALISTIC DEFINITION OF MAN AND HIS WORLD. By Max F. Schulz. Ohio University Press, 1973. Library binding only.

THE BLACK NOVELIST. By Robert Hemenway. Charles E. Merrill, 1970. Hardcover and paperback.

BRIGHT BOOK OF LIFE: AMERICAN NOVELISTS AND STORYTELLERS FROM HEMINGWAY TO MAILER. By Alfred Kazin. Little, Brown & Co., 1973. Hardcover. Dell, 1974. Paperback.

A CASEBOOK ON THE BEAT. Edited by Thomas Francis Parkinson. T.Y. Crowell, 1961. Paperback textbook edition.

CELEBRATION IN POSTWAR AMERICAN FICTION 1945-1967. By Richard H. Rupp. University of Miami Press, 1970. Hardcover only.

CITY OF WORDS: AMERICAN FICTION, 1950-1970. By Tony Tanner. Harper & Row, 1971. Hardcover only.

CLASSICS AND COMMERCIALS. By Edmund Wilson. Farrar, Straus & Giroux, 1950. Paperback only.

COLLECTED ESSAYS OF LESLIE FIEDLER. 2 Volumes. By Leslie Fiedler. Stein & Day, 1971. Hardcover only.

THE CONFUSION OF REALMS. By Richard Gilman. Random House, 1970. Hardcover and paperback.

CONTEMPORARY AMERICAN-JEWISH LITERATURE: CRITICAL ESSAYS. Edited by Irving Malin. Indiana University Press, 1973. Hardcover only.

CONTEMPORARY AMERICAN LITERATURE, 1945-1972: AN INTRODUCTION. By Ihab Hassan. Ungar Publishing Co., 1973. Hardcover and paperback.

CONTEMPORARY AMERICAN NOVELISTS. Edited by Harry T. Moore. Southern Illinois University Press, 1964. Hardcover only.

CONTEMPORARY WRITER: INTERVIEWS WITH 16 NOVELISTS AND POETS. Edited by L.S. Dembo and Cyrena N. Pondrom. University of Wisconsin Press, 1972. Hardcover and paperback.

THE CREATIVE PRESENT: NOTES ON CONTEMPORARY AMERICAN FICTION. By Nona Balakian and Charles Simmons. Gordian Press, 1972 (revised edition, reprinted from 1963 textbook edition). Hardcover only.

THE CRITICAL POINT: ON LITERATURE AND CULTURE. By Irving Howe. Horizon Press, 1973. Hardcover only.

DESPERATE FAITH: A STUDY OF BELLOW, SALINGER, MAILER, BALDWIN & UPDIKE. By Howard M. Harper, Jr. University of North Carolina Press, 1968. Paperback only.

THE DISMEMBERMENT OF ORPHEUS: TOWARD A POSTMODERN LITERATURE. By Ihab Hassan. Oxford University Press, 1971. Paperback textbook edition.

FACES OF THE FUTURE: THE LESSONS OF SCIENCE FICTION. By Brian Ash. Prometheus Books, 1975. Hardcover only.

THE FEMALE IMAGINATION. By Patricia M. Spacks. Alfred A. Knopf, 1975. Hardcover only.

FICTION AND THE FIGURES OF LIFE. By William Grass. Alfred A. Knopf, 1971. Hardcover only.

THE FIFTIES: FICTION, POETRY, DRAMA. Compiled by Warren G. French. Everett/Edwards, 1971. Hardcover only.

GIVE BIRTH TO BRIGHTNESS: A THEMATIC STUDY IN NEO-BLACK LITERATURE. By Sherley A. Williams. Dial, 1972. Harcover and paperback.

HARVEST OF A QUIET EYE: THE NOVEL OF COMPASSION. By James Gindin. Indiana University Press, 1971. Hardcover only.

HUMANISM AND THE ABSURD IN THE MODERN NOVEL. By Naomi Lebowitz. Northwestern University Press, 1971. Hardcover only.

THE ILLUSION: AN ESSAY ON POLITICS, THEATRE AND THE NOVEL. By David Caute. Harper & Row, 1972. Hardcover library binding only.

IN SEARCH OF HERESY. By John W. Aldridge. Greenwood, 1974. Hardcover only.

INTERVIEWS WITH BLACK WRITERS. Edited by John O'Brien. Liveright, 1973. Hardcover and paperback.

LANDSCAPE OF NIGHTMARE: STUDIES IN THE CONTEMPORARY AMERICAN NOVEL. By Jonathan Baumbach. New York University Press, 1965. Hardcover and paperback.

THE LIBERAL IMAGINATION: ESSAYS ON LITERATURE & SOCIETY. By Lionell Trilling. Viking Press, 1974. Paperback only.

LITERARY DISRUPTIONS: THE MAKING OF A POST-CONTEMPORARY AMERICAN FICTION. By Jerome Klinkowitz. University of Illinois Press, 1975. Hardcover only.

LITERARY HORIZONS: A QUARTER CENTURY OF AMERICAN FICTION. By Granville Hicks. New York University Press, 1970. Hardcover only.

THE LITERATURE OF SILENCE: HENRY MILLER AND SAMUEL BECKETT. By Ihab Hassan. Random House, 1967. Paperback textbook edition.

LONG BLACK SONG: ESSAYS IN BLACK AMERICAN LITERATURE & CULTURE. By Houston A. Baker, Jr. University Press of Virginia, 1972. Hardcover only.

LOVE AND DEATH IN THE AMERICAN NOVEL. By Leslie A. Fiedler. Stein & Day, 1966. Hardcover only.

MODERN AMERICAN POLITICAL NOVEL 1900-1960. By Joseph Blotner. University of Texas Press, 1966. Hardcover only.

MODERN BLACK NOVELISTS: A COLLECTION OF CRITICAL ESSAYS. Edited by Michael Cooke. Prentice-Hall, 1972. Paperback only.

MODERN FICTION: A FORMALIST APPROACH. By William J. Handy. Southern Illinois University Press, 1971. Hardcover only.

NATIVE SONS: A CRITICAL STUDY OF 20TH CENTURY NEGRO-AMERICAN AUTHORS. By Edward Margolis. Lippincott, 1969. Hardcover and paperback.

NEGRO NOVEL IN AMERICA. By Robert A. Bone. Yale University Press, 1965 (revised edition). Hardcover and paperback.

NEGRO NOVELIST: A DISCUSSION OF THE WRITINGS OF AMERICAN NEGRO NOVELISTS, 1940-1950. By John M. Hughes. Books for Libraries, 1953 (facsimile edition).

NEW AMERICAN GOTHIC. By Irving Malin. Southern Illinois University Press, 1962. Hardcover only.

THE NEW FICTION: INTERVIEWS WITH INNOVATIVE AMERICAN WRITERS. By Joe David Bellamy. University of Illinois Press, 1974. Hardcover and paperback.

THE NEW NOVEL IN AMERICA: THE KAFKAN MODE IN CONTEMPORARY FICTION. By Helen Weinberg. Cornell University Press, 1970. Hardcover only.

NEW WORLDS FOR OLD: THE APOCALYPTIC IMAGINATION, SCIENCE FICTION & AMERICAN LITERATURE. By David Ketterer. Hardcover: Indiana University Press, 1974. Paperback: Doubleday, 1974.

ON CONTEMPORARY LITERATURE: AN ANTHOLOGY OF CRITICAL ESSAYS ON THE MAJOR MOVEMENTS & WRITINGS OF CONTEMPORARY LITERATURE. Edited by Richard Kostelanetz. Books for Libraries (reprint of 1964 edition). Hardcover only.

THE OPEN DECISION. By Jerry H. Bryant. Free Press, 1970. Hardcover only.

PARACRITICISMS: SEVEN SPECULATIONS OF THE TIMES. By Ihab Hassan. University of Illinois Press, 1975. Hardcover only.

THE PERFORMING SELF: COMPOSITIONS AND DE-COMPOSITIONS IN THE LANGUAGE OF CONTEMPORARY LIFE. By Richard Poirier. Oxford University Press, 1971. Hardcover only.

PIONEERS & CARETAKERS: A STUDY OF NINE AMERICAN WOMEN NOVELISTS. By Louis Auchincloss. University of Minnesota Press, 1965. Hardcover only.

QUESTS SURD AND ABSURD: ESSAYS IN AMERICAN LITERATURE. By James Edwin Miller, Jr. University of Chicago Press, 1967. Hardcover only.

RADICAL INNOCENCE: STUDIES IN THE CONTEMPORARY AMERICAN NOVEL. By Ihab Hassan. Princeton University Press, 1971. Hardcover and paperback.

RADICAL SOPHISTICATION: STUDIES ON CONTEMPORARY JEWISH-AMERICAN NOVELISTS. By Max F. Schulz. Ohio University Press, 1969. Hardcover and paperback.

READING MYSELF AND OTHERS. By Philip Roth. Farrar, Straus & Giroux, 1975. Hardcover only.

THE RED HOT VACUUM AND OTHER PIECES ON THE WRITING OF THE SIXTIES. By Theodore Solotaroff. Atheneum, 1970. Hardcover and paperback.

RETURN OF THE VANISHING AMERICAN. By Leslie A. Fiedler. Stein & Day, 1969. Paperback only.

THE SCIENCE FICTION BOOK: AN ILLUSTRATED HISTORY. By Frank Rottensteiner. Continuum, 1975. Hardcover only.

SCIENCE FICTION NOVEL: IMAGINATION & SOCIAL CRITICISM. By Basil Davenport et al. Advent, 1969. Hardcover and paperback.

SCIENCE FICTION: THE FUTURE. By Dick Allen. Harcourt Brace Jovanovich, 1971. Paperback textbook edition only.

SCIENCE FICTION, TODAY AND TOMORROW: A DISCURSIVE SYMPOSIUM. By Reginald Bretnor. Penguin, 1975. Paperback only.

SEVEN CONTEMPORARY AUTHORS: ESSAYS ON COZZENS, MILLER, WEST, GOLDING, HELLER, ALBEE AND POWERS. Edited by Thomas B. Whitbread. University of Texas Press, 1966. Hardcover only.

SEVEN MODERN AMERICAN NOVELISTS: AN INTRODUCTION. Edited by William V. O'Connor. University of Minnesota Press, 1964. Hardcover only.

THE SEXUAL REVOLUTION IN MODERN AMERICAN LITERATURE. By Charles Irving Glicksberg. International Publications Service, 1971. Humanities, 1971. Both paperback only.

SHAKE IT FOR THE WORLD SMARTASS. By Seymour Krim. Dell, 1971. Paperback only.

SHRIVEN SELVES: RELIGIOUS PROBLEMS IN RECENT AMERICAN FICTION. By Wesley A. Kort. Fortress Press, 1972. Paperback only.

SINGERS OF DAYBREAK: STUDIES IN BLACK AMERICAN LITERATURE. By Houston A. Baker, Jr. Howard University Press, 1974. Hardcover only.

SURFICTION: FICTION NOW AND TOMORROW. Edited by Raymond Federman. Swallow Press, 1973. Hardcover only.

TIME TO MURDER AND CREATE: THE CONTEMPORARY NOVEL IN CRISIS. By John W. Aldridge. Books for Libraries (reprint of 1966 edition). Hardcover only.

TOWARD A NEW EARTH: APOCALYPSE IN THE AMERICAN NOVEL. By John R. May. University of Notre Dame Press, 1972. Hardcover textbook edition.

Poetry Anthologies

Only anthologies containing contemporary American poetry are included. If the major part of an anthology consists of British poetry or fiction written before the Second World War, the book has not been included.

There are a total of 192 anthologies listed alphabetically by title under five headings: General (54); Younger Poets (14); Ethnic Poets (61); Topics, Regions, and Special Forms (52); and Women Poets (11).

Many other anthologies of contemporary American poetry may be found in libraries or book stores, but we have listed only those which are in print and can be ordered from the publisher. Publishers' addresses can be found in *Books In Print*, which is available in book stores and libraries. Anthologies published by small presses are listed with the name and address of a distributor.

General

AN ACTIVE ANTHOLOGY. Edited by George Quasha. Sumac, 1975. Paperback only. Distributed by The Book Organization, Elm St., Millerton, N.Y. 12546.

AMERICA A PROPHECY: A NEW READING OF AMERICAN POETRY FROM PRE-COLUMBIAN TIMES TO THE PRESENT. Edited by Jerome Rothenberg and George Quasha. Random House, 1973. Hardcover and paperback.

AMERICAN POEMS: A CONTEMPORARY COLLECTION. Edited by Jascha Kessler. Southern Illinois University Press, 1964. Hardcover.

ASTROLABES. Three poets: Nellie Hill, David Hoag, and Elizabeth Keeler. Peace & Pieces Foundation, 1974. Distributed by Peace & Pieces Foundation, P.O. Box 99394, San Francisco, Calif. 94109.

THE BEST OF MODERN POETRY. Edited by Milton Klonsky. (Formerly titled SHAKE THE KALEIDOSCOPE.) Pocket Books, 1975. Paperback only.

BEST POEMS OF 1973: BORESTONE MOUNTAIN POETRY AWARDS OF 1974. Vol. 26. Edited by Lionel Stevenson. Pacific Books, 1974. Hardcover only.

BOTTEGHE OSCURE READER. Edited by George Garrett with the assistance of Katherine G. Biddle. Wesleyan University Press, 1974. Hardcover and paperback.

A CATERPILLAR ANTHOLOGY. Edited by Clayton Eshleman. From work first published in *Caterpillar* magazine. Doubleday-Anchor, 1971. Paperback only.

CHIEF MODERN POETS OF BRITAIN AND AMERICA. 2 volumes. Edited by Gerald DeWitt Sanders et al. Macmillan, 1970. Hardcover textbook edition and paperback.

CONTEMPORARIES: AN ANTHOLOGY OF CONTEMPORARY POETRY. Edited by William C. Duncan. Contemporary Literature Press, 1974. Hardcover.

THE CONTEMPORARY AMERICAN POET. Edited by Mark Strand. New American Library, 1971. Paperback.

CONTEMPORARY AMERICAN POETRY. Edited by Donald Hall. Penguin Books, 1972 (revised edition). Paperback.

CONTEMPORARY AMERICAN POETRY. 2nd Edition. Edited by Al Poulin, Jr. Houghton Mifflin, 1975. Paperback.

CONTEMPORARY AMERICAN POETS: AMERICAN POETRY SINCE 1940. Edited by Mark Strand. Hardcover: Norton, 1969. Paperback: New American Library, 1969.

A CONTROVERSY OF POETS: AN ANTHOLOGY OF CONTEMPORARY AMERICAN POETRY. Edited by Paris Leary and Robert Kelly. Doubleday-Anchor, 1965. Paperback.

DECADE: POEMS FROM THE FIRST TEN YEARS OF THE WESLEYAN POETRY PROGRAM. Edited by Norman Holmes Pearson. Wesleyan University Press, 1969. Hardcover and paperback.

THE DISTINCTIVE VOICE: TWENTIETH CENTURY AMERICAN POETRY. Compiled by William J. Martz. Scott, Foresman & Co., 1966. Paperback.

THE EAST SIDE SCENE: AMERICAN POETRY, 1960-1965. Edited by Allen De Loach. Doubleday-Anchor, 1972. Illustrated. Paperback.

GETTING INTO POETRY. Edited by Morris Sweetkind. Holbrook Press, 1972. Paperback textbook edition only.

THE GIST OF ORIGIN: AN ANTHOLOGY. Edited by Cid Corman. Grossman Publishers, 1975. Hardcover only.

THE LIVING UNDERGROUND: AN ANTHOLOGY OF CONTEMPORARY AMERICAN POETRY. Edited by Hugh Fox. Whitston Publishing Co., 1973. Hardcover only.

MAKING IT NEW: AMERICAN POEMS AND SONGS. Edited by William M. Chace and JoAn E. Chace. Canfield Press, 1973. Paperback textbook edition.

THE MENTOR BOOK OF MAJOR AMERICAN POETS. Edited by Oscar Williams and Edwin Honig. New American Library, 1962. Paperback.

50 MODERN AMERICAN AND BRITISH POETS, 1920-1970. Edited by Louis Untermeyer. David McKay, 1973. Hardcover and paperback.

MODERN AMERICAN POETRY. New and Enlarged Edition. Edited by Louis Untermeyer. Harcourt Brace Jovanovich, 1962. Hardcover textbook edition.

NAKED POETRY: RECENT AMERICAN POETRY IN OPEN FORMS. Edited by Stephen Berg and Robert Mezey. Bobbs-Merrill, 1969. Hardcover and paperback.

NEW AMERICAN AND CANADIAN POETRY. Edited by John Gill. Beacon Press, 1971. Hardcover and paperback.

NEW AMERICAN POETRY 1945-1960. Edited by Donald Allen. Grove Press, 1960. Paperback.

NEW DIRECTIONS 31. Latest in a series published semi-annually. Edited by James Laughlin and others. New Directions, 1975. Hardcover and paperback.

NEW MODERN POETRY: AN ANTHOLOGY OF AMER-ICAN & BRITISH POETRY SINCE WORLD WAR II. Edited by M.L. Rosenthal. Hardcover: Macmillan, 1966 and Oxford University Press, 1967. Paperback: Oxford University Press, 1969.

THE NEW POCKET ANTHOLOGY OF AMERICAN VERSE. Abbreviated Edition. Edited by Oscar Williams. New American Library, 1972. Paperback.

THE NEW YORKER BOOK OF POEMS: 1925-1969. Selected by editors of *The New Yorker*. William Morrow & Co., 1974. Paperback.

THE NORTON ANTHOLOGY OF MODERN POETRY. Edited by Richard Ellman and Robert O'Clair. W.W. Norton, 1973. Hardcover and paperback.

THE NOW VOICES. Edited by Angelo Carli and Theodore Kilman. Scribner's, 1971. Paperback textbook edition only.

100 AMERICAN POEMS. Revised Edition. Edited by Seldon Rodman. New American Library, 1972. Paperback.

THE OXFORD BOOK OF AMERICAN VERSE. Edited by F.O. Matthieson. Oxford University Press, 1950. Hardcover.

PEACE & PIECES: AN ANTHOLOGY OF CON-TEMPORARY AMERICAN POETRY. Edited by Maurice Custodio, Grace Harwood, David Hoag, and Todd S.J. Lawson. Peace & Pieces Press, 1975. Paperback. Distributed by Bookpeople, 2940 Seventh Ave., Berkeley, Calif. 94710.

PIONEERS OF MODERN POETRY. 2nd Edition. Edited by Robert L. Peters and George Hitchcock. Kayak Books, 1969. Paperback only. Distributed by Bookpeople, 2940 Seventh Ave., Berkeley, Calif. 94710.

POEMS OF OUR MOMENT: CONTEMPORARY POETS OF THE ENGLISH LANGUAGE. Edited by John Hollander. Pegasus, 1968. Hardcover and paperback.

POETRY SINCE NINETEEN THIRTY-NINE. Edited by Stephen Spender. Haskell, 1974. Hardcover only, library binding.

POETS ON THE PLATFORM. Edited by Robert McGovern and Richard Snyder. Ashland Poetry Press, 1970. Paperback only. Distributed by Ashland Poetry Press, Ashland College, Ashland, Ohio 44805.

POSSIBILITIES OF POETRY: AN ANTHOLOGY OF AMERICAN COMTEMPORARIES. Edited by Richard Kostelanetz. Dell Publishers, 1970. Paperback.

PREFERENCES: 51 AMERICAN POETS CHOOSE POEMS FROM THEIR OWN WORK AND FROM THE PAST. Edited by Richard Howard. Photographs by Thomas Victor. Viking, 1974. Hardcover only.

QUARTERLY REVIEW OF LITERATURE'S 30TH AN-NIVERSARY RETROSPECTIVE, VOL. XIX. Edited by T. Weiss and R. Weiss. Quarterly Review of Literature, 1975. Hardcover and paperback.

REVOLUTION OF THE WORD: A NEW GATHERING OF AMERICAN AVANT-GARDE POETRY, 1914-1945. Edited by Jerome Rothenberg. The Seabury Press, 1974. Hardcover only.

60 ON THE 60'S: A DECADE'S HISTORY IN VERSE. Edited by Robert McGovern and Richard Snyder, with a foreward by former Senator Eugene J. McCarthy. Ashland Poetry Press, 1970. Paperback only. Distributed by Ashland Poetry Press, Ashland College, Ashland, Ohio 44805.

TAKE HOLD: AN ANTHOLOGY OF PULITZER PRIZE WINNING POEMS. Compiled by Lee B. Hopkins. Nelson, 1974. Hardcover only.

TEN AMERICAN POETS. Edited by James Atlas. Dufour Editions, 1975. Paperback only.

A TEST OF POETRY. Edited by Louis Zukofsky. Jargon Books, 1975. Paperback only. Distributed by The Book Organization, Elm St., Millerton, N.Y. 12546.

TODAY'S POETS: AMERICAN AND BRITISH POETRY SINCE THE 1930'S. Edited by Chad Walsh. Scribner's, 1972. Paperback textbook edition.

TOWARDS WINTER. Edited by Robert Bonazzi. New Rivers Press, 1972. Paperback only. Distributed by Serendipity Books, 1790 Shattuck Ave., Berkeley, Calif. 94709.

TWENTIETH CENTURY POETRY: THE MODERN POETS. Edited by John Malcolm Brinnin and Bill Read. Includes 100 photographs of the poets by Rollie McKenna. McGraw-Hill, 1967. Hardcover. Textbook edition: THE MODERN POETS, 1970.

THE VOICE THAT IS GREAT WITHIN US: AN ANTHOL-OGY OF CONTEMPORARY AMERICAN POETRY. Edited by Hayden Carruth. Bantam Books, 1970. Paperback.

WHAT THERE IS LEFT: AN ANTHOLOGY. Edited by T.L. Kryss. Runcible Spoon, 1970. Paperback only. Distributed by Serendipity Books, 1790 Shattuck Ave., Berkeley, Calif. 94709.

Younger Poets

THE AMERICAN POETRY ANTHOLOGY: POETS UNDER 40. Edited by Daniel Halpern. Avon/Equinox, 1975. Paperback only.

ANOTHER WORLD. Edited by Anne Waldman. Works from the St. Mark's Poetry Project. Bobbs-Merrill, 1971. Hardcover and paperback.

AN ANTHOLOGY OF NEW YORK POETS. Poets from "The New York School." Edited by Ron Padgett and David Shapiro. Random House, 1970. Hardcover and paperback.

CONTEMPORARIES: AN ANTHOLOGY OF CON-TEMPORARY POETRY. Edited by William C. Duncan. Contemporary Literature, 1974. Hardcover.

EATING THE MENU: CONTEMPORARY AMERICAN POETRY 1970-1974. Edited by Bruce Edward Taylor. 28 new, young poets. Kendall/Hunt Publishing Company, 1974. Paperback.

JUST WHAT THE COUNTRY NEEDS, ANOTHER POETRY ANTHOLOGY. Edited by James McMichael and Dennis Saleh. 30 poets. Wadsworth Publishing Company, 1971. Paperback.

THE MAJOR YOUNG POETS. Edited by Al Lee. New American Library, 1971. Paperback.

NEW AMERICAN POETRY. Edited by Richard Monaco. Includes photographs of the poets. McGraw-Hill, 1973. Paperback.

NEW POETRY ANTHOLOGY I. Edited by Michael Anania. Swallow Press, 1969. Hardcover and paperback.

NEW VOICES IN AMERICAN POETRY. Edited by David Allen Evans. Winthrop Publishers, 1973. Paperback textbook edition only.

QUICKLY AGING HERE: SOME POETS OF THE 1970'S. Edited by Geof Hewitt. Doubleday-Anchor, 1969. Paperback.

SURVIVORS OF THE INVENTION: ANTHOLOGY OF NEW POETS. Edited by Isla Bonazzi. Latitudes Press, 1974. Hardcover and paperback. Distributed by Serendipity Books, 1790 Shattuck Ave., Berkeley, Calif. 94709.

31 NEW AMERICAN POETS. Edited by Ron Schreiber. Hill & Wang, 1969. Paperback.

THE WORLD ANTHOLOGY. Edited by Anne Waldman. Collected from work published at St. Mark's in the Bowery, N.Y.C. Bobbs-Merrill, 1970. Hardcover and paperback.

Ethnic Poets

AFRO-AMERICAN LITERATURE: POETRY. Edited by William Adams, Peter Conn, and Barry Slepian. Houghton Mifflin, 1970. Hardcover and paperback.

AIIIEEEEE! AN ANTHOLOGY OF ASIAN-AMERICAN WRITERS. Edited by J. Chan, F. Chin and L. Inada. Howard University Press, 1974. Hardcover.

AMERICAN INDIAN POETRY: AN ANTHOLOGY OF SONGS AND CHANTS. Edited by George W. Cronyn. Liveright Publishers, 1972: hardcover and paperback. Ballantine Books, 1972: paperback.

AMERICAN INDIAN PROSE AND POETRY: AN AN-THOLOGY. Edited by Margot Astrov. John Day, 1972. Hardcover. (Paperback title: THE WINGED SERPENT. Fawcett, 1973.)

AMERICAN INDIAN SPEAKS. Edited by John Milton. Dakota Press (University of South Dakota), 1969. Paperback.

AMERICAN NEGRO POETRY. Revised Edition. Edited by Arna Bontemps. Hill & Wang, 1974. Hardcover and paperback.

ARMENIAN-AMERICAN POETS: A BILINGUAL AN THOLOGY. Edited by Garig Basmadjian. Armenian General Benevolent Union, 1975. Paperback only. Distributed by Armenian General Benevolent Union, 22001 Northwestern Hwy., Southfield, Mich. 48075.

ARMENIAN-NORTH AMERICAN POETS: AN ANTHOL-OGY. Edited by Lorne Shiridian. Manna Publishers, 1975. Paperback only. Distributed by Manna Publishers, 428 rue Victor Hugo, Suite 10, St. Jean, Québec, Canada, J3A 1C7.

ASIAN-AMERICAN HERITAGE. Edited by David Hsin-Fu Wand. Washington Square Press, 1974. Paperback.

BETCHA AIN'T: POEMS FROM ATTICA. Edited by Celes Tisdale. Broadside Press, 1974. Hardcover and paperback. Distributed by Broadside Press, 12651 Old Mill Pl., Detroit, Mich. 48238.

THE BLACK AMERICAN WRITER, VOLUME II, POETRY AND DRAMA. Edited by C.W. Bigsby. Penguin Books, 1971. Paperback only.

BLACK FIRE: AN ANTHOLOGY OF AFRO-AMERICAN WRITING. Edited by LeRoi Jones and Larry Neal. William Morrow and Company, 1968. Paperback.

BLACK POETRY: A SUPPLEMENT TO ANTHOLOGIES WHICH EXCLUDE BLACK POETS. Edited by Dudley Randall. Broadside Press, 1969. Hardcover and paperback. Distributed by Broadside Press, 12651 Old Mill Pl., Detroit, Mich. 48238.

THE BLACK POETS. Edited by Dudley Randall. Includes listings of publishers of Black poetry, periodicals publishing Black poetry, phonograph records, tapes, videotapes, and films. Bantam Books, 1971. Illustrated. Paperback.

BLACKSPIRITS. Edited by Woodie King. Random House, 1972. Hardcover and paperback.

BLACK VOICES: AN ANTHOLOGY OF AFRO-AMER-ICAN LITERATURE. Edited by Abraham Chapman. New American Library, 1969. Paperback.

BROADSIDE ANNUAL 1972: INTRODUCING NEW BLACK POETS. Edited by Jill Witherspoon. Broadside Press, 1972. Paperback only. Distributed by Broadside Press, 12651 Old Mill Pl., Detroit, Mich. 48238.

BROADSIDE ANNUAL 1973. Edited by Jill Witherspoon. Broadside Press, 1973. Paperback only. Distributed by Broadside Press, 12651 Old Mill Pl., Detroit, Mich. 48238.

A BROADSIDE TREASURY 1965-1970. Edited by Gwendolyn Brooks. Broadside Press, 1971. Hardcover and paperback. Distributed by RPM Distributors, P.O. Box 1785, Rockville, Md. 20850.

CARRIERS OF THE DREAM WHEEL. Edited by Duane Niatum. Contemporary poetry by Native American poets. Harper & Row, 1974. Hardcover and paperback.

CHICANO POETRY ANTHOLOGY, 1968-1973. Edited by Juan Gomez Quinones and Teresa McKenna. Aztlan, Publications, UCLA, 1974.

THE CHICANOS: MEXICAN AMERICAN VOICES. Edited by Ed Ludwig and James Santibanez. Penguin Books, 1971: paperback. Peter Smith: hardcover.

COME TO POWER: WRITINGS BY AMERICAN INDIANS. Edited by Dick Lourie. The Crossing Press, 1974. Hardcover and paperback. Distributed by RPM Distributors, P.O. Box 1785, Rockville, Md. 20850.

DICES OR BLACK BONES: BLACK VOICES OF THE SEVENTIES. Edited by Adam David Miller. Houghton Mifflin, 1970. Paperback textbook edition.

FINDING THE CENTER: NARRATIVE POETRY OF THE ZUNI INDIANS. Translated by Dennis Tedlock. Dial Press, 1972. Paperback only.

THE FORERUNNERS: BLACK POETS IN AMERICA. Edited by Woodie King, Jr. Howard University Press, 1975. Hardcover only.

FOUR INDIAN POETS. Edited by John R. Milton. University of South Dakota Press, 1974. Paperback.

FROM THE BARRIO: A CHICANO ANTHOLOGY. Edited by L.O. Salinas and L. Faderman. Canfield Press, 1973. Paperback textbook edition.

FROM THE BELLY OF THE SHARK. POEMS BY CHICANOS, ESKIMOS, HAWAIIANS, INDIANS, PUERTO RICANS IN THE U.S. AND RELATED POEMS BY OTHERS. Edited by Walter Lowenfels. Vintage Books, 1973. Paperback.

"GET YOUR ASS IN THE WATER AND SWIM LIKE ME:" NARRATIVE POETRY FROM THE BLACK ORAL TRADITION. Edited by Bruce Jackson. Harvard University Press, 1974. Hardcover.

GIANT TALK: AN ANTHOLOGY OF THIRD WORLD WRITINGS. Edited by Quincy Troupe and Rainer Schulte. Random House, 1975. Hardcover and paperback.

IN A TIME OF REVOLUTION: POEMS FROM OUR THIRD WORLD. Edited by Walter Lowenfels. Random House, 1969. Paperback.

JAMBALAYA. Edited by Steve Cannon. Black, Hispanic, and Asian American writers. Reed, Cannon & Johnson, 1975. Paperback only. Distributed by Reed, Cannon & Johnson, 285 E. 3rd St., New York, N.Y. 10009.

KALEIDOSCOPE: POEMS BY AMERICAN NEGRO POETS. Edited by Robert Hayden. Harcourt Brace Jovanovich, 1967. Hardcover.

THE MAGIC WORLD: AMERICAN INDIAN SONGS AND POEMS. Edited by William Brandon. William Morrow & Company, 1971. Paperback only.

NATURAL PROCESS: AN ANTHOLOGY OF NEW BLACK POETRY. Edited by Ted Wilentz and Tom Weatherly. Hill & Wang, 1970. Hardcover and paperback.

THE NEW BLACK POETRY. Edited by Clarence Major. International Publishers, 1969. Hardcover and paperback.

NEW NEGRO POETS: USA. Edited by Langston Hughes. Indiana University Press, 1964. Hardcover and paperback.

NINETEEN NECROMANCERS FROM NOW. Edited by Ishmael Reed. Doubleday, 1970. Hardcover.

THE POETRY OF BLACK AMERICA: ANTHOLOGY OF THE 20TH CENTURY. Edited by Arnold Adoff. Harper & Row, 1973. Hardcover and paperback.

THE POETRY OF THE NEGRO, 1746-1970. Edited by Langston Hughes and Arna Bontemps. Doubleday, 1970, hardcover. New edition, 1973, paperback.

PRIDE AND PROTEST: AN ANTHOLOGY OF AMERICAN ETHNIC LITERATURE. Edited by Jay Schulman, Aubrey Shatter, and Rosalie Ehrlich. Dell Publishing Company, 1975. Paperback.

THE PUERTO RICAN POETS/LOS POETAS PUERTORIQUENOS. Edited by Alfredo Matilla and Ivan Silen. Bantam Books, 1972. Bilingual. Paperpack.

QUETZAL. By Amilcar Lobos and Leland Mellott. Edited by Rolando Castellon and Carlos Perez. Glide Publications, 1973. Paperback only. Distributed by Bookpeople, 2940 Seventh Ave., Berkeley, Calif. 94710.

RUN TOWARD THE NIGHTLAND: MAGIC OF THE OKLAHOMA CHEROKEES. Edited by Anna and Jack Kilpatrick. Medicine and magic rituals, with melodies and words (translated). Southern Methodist University Press, 1967. Hardcover.

SHAKING THE PUMPKIN: TRADITIONAL POETRY OF THE INDIAN NORTH AMERICAS. Edited by Jerome Rothenberg. Doubleday, 1972. Hardcover and paperback.

THE SKY CLEARS: POETRY OF THE AMERICAN INDIANS. Edited by A. Grove Day. University of Nebraska Press, 1964. Paperback textbook edition.

SOULSCRIPT. Edited by June Jordan. An anthology of new Black poetry. Doubleday, 1970. Hardcover and paperback. (Teachers' manual, by C.P. Eagleson, $.50).

SPEAKING FOR OURSELVES: AMERICAN ETHNIC WRITING. 2nd Edition. Edited by Lillian Faderman and Barbara Bradshaw. Scott, Foresman & Co., 1975. Paperback textbook edition only.

SURVIVING IN AMERICA. Edited by Sam Hamod. Vol. 1 (1971), Vol. 2 (1973), and Vol. 4 (1975) are contemporary American poetry. Cedar Creek Press. Paperback only. Distributed by Serendipity Books, 1790 Shattuck Ave., Berkeley, Calif. 94709.

TECHNICIANS OF THE SACRED. Edited by Jerome Rotheberg. A range of poetries from Africa, America, Asia and Oceania. Doubleday, 1968. Paperback.

TIME TO GREEZ! INCANTATIONS FROM THE THIRD WORLD. Edited by Janice Mirikitani and others. Glide Publications, 1975. Paperback only.

VOICES FROM WAH'KON-TAH: CONTEMPORARY POETRY OF NATIVE AMERICANS. Edited by Robert K. Dodge and Joseph B. McCullough. International Publishers, 1974. Hardcover and paperback.

VOICES OF THE RAINBOW: CONTEMPORARY POETRY OF THE AMERICAN INDIANS. Edited by Kenneth Rosen. Viking Press, 1975. Hardcover.

WALK IN YOUR SOUL: LOVE INCANTATIONS OF THE OKLAHOMA CHEROKEES. Edited by Anna and Jack Kilpatrick. Southern Methodist University Press, 1965. Hardcover.

WE ARE CHICANOS: AN ANTHOLOGY OF MEXICAN-AMERICAN LITERATURE. Edited by Philip D. Ortego. Washington Square Press, 1973. Paperback only.

WE SPEAK AS LIBERATORS: YOUNG BLACK POETS. Edited by Orde Coombs. Dodd, Mead & Company, 1970: hardcover. Apollo Editions, 1971: paperback.

YARDBIRD READER, VOLUME 2. Edited by Al Young. Poetry and prose by Blacks, Asian-Americans, and others. Yardbird Publishing Company, 1973. Paperback only. Distributed by Serendipity Books, 1790 Shattuck Ave., Berkeley, Calif. 94709.

YARDBIRD READER, VOLUME 3. Edited by Frank Chin, Shawn Wong, and Bob Onodera. Yardbird Publishing Company, 1975. Paperback only. Distributed by Serendipity Books, 1790 Shattuck Ave., Berkeley, Calif. 94709.

YARDBIRD READER, VOLUME 4. Edited by William V. Lawson. Emphasis on African, Black American, and Caribbean artists and writers. Yardbird Publishing Company, 1975. Paperback only. Distributed by Serendipity Books, 1790 Shattuck Ave., Berkeley, Calif. 94709.

YOU BETTER BELIEVE IT: BLACK VERSE IN ENGLISH. Edited by Paul Breman. Penguin Books, 1973. Paperback.

Topics, Regions, and Special Forms

AN ANTHOLOGY. Edited by Lamont Young. A collection of visual poetry, "concrete poetry," and related art. Heiner Friedrich, 1963. Paperback only. Distributed by Heiner Friedrich, 141 Wooster St., New York, N.Y. 10012.

AN ANTHOLOGY OF CONCRETE POETRY. Edited by Emmett Williams. Something Else Press, 1967. Hardcover and paperback. Distributed by Serendipity Books Distribution, 1790 Shattuck Ave., Berkeley, Calif. 94709.

ANTHOLOGY OF CONCRETISM. 2nd enlarged edition. Edited by Eugene Wildman. Swallow Press, 1969. Hardcover and paperback.

ANTHOLOGY OF GAY POETRY. Edited by Winston Leyland. Panjandrum Press, 1975. Paperback. Distributed by Bookpeople, 2940 Seventh Ave., Berkeley, Calif. 94710.

ANTHOLOGY OF L.A. POETS. Edited by Charles Bukowski, Neeli Cherry, and Paul Vangelisti. Red Hill Press, 1972. Paperback. Distributed by Serendipity Books, 1790 Shattuck Ave., Berkeley, Calif. 94709.

THE BERKSHIRE ANTHOLOGY. Edited by Gerald Hausman and David Silverstein. Bookstore Press, 1972. Paperback only. Distributed by RPM Distributors, P.O. Box 1785, Rockville, Md. 20850.

THE BLUES LINE: A COLLECTION OF BLUES LYRICS. Compiled by Eric Sackheim. Schirmer Books, 1975. Paperback only.

BREWING: 20 MILWAUKEE POETS. Edited by Martin J. Rosenblum. Giligia Press, 1972. Paperback only. Distributed by Giligia Press, East Chatham, N.Y. 12060.

CAPTIVE VOICES: AN ANTHOLOGY OF FOLSOM PRISON WRITERS. DustBooks, 1975. Paperback only. Distributed by DustBooks, P.O. Box 1056, Paradise, Calif. 95969.

CITY LIGHTS ANTHOLOGY. Edited by Lawrence Ferlinghetti. City Lights, 1974. Paperback only.

CONCRETE POETRY: A WORLD VIEW. Edited by Mary Ellen Solt and Willis Barnstone. Indiana University Press, 1969. Hardcover and paperback.

THE DOCTOR GENEROSITY POETS: NEW YORK CITY—NEW AMERICAN POETRY/ INTO THE 80'S. Edited by Charles Shahoud Hanna. Damascus Road Press, 1975. Paperback only.

DOWN AT THE SANTA FE DEPOT: 20 FRESNO POETS. Edited by David Kheridian and James Baloian. The Giligia Press, 1970. Paperback only. Distributed by The Giligia Press, East Chatham, N.Y. 12060.

EIGHT LINES AND UNDER. AN ANTHOLOGY OF SHORT POEMS. Edited by William Cole. Macmillan, 1967. Paperback.

FOR NERUDA, FOR CHILE. Edited by Walter Lowenfels. Beacon Press, 1975. Hardcover and paperback.

4-TELLING: FOUR NEW YORK CITY POETS. Marge Piercy, Dick Lourie, Robert Hershon, and Emmett Jarrett. The Crossing Press, 1971. Paperback. Distributed by RPM Distributors, P.O. Box 1785, Rockville, Md. 20850.

40 POEMS TOUCHING ON RECENT AMERICAN HISTORY. Edited by Robert Bly. Beacon Press, 1970. Hardcover and paperback.

GROUP 74: POEMS FROM THE NEW YORK POETS' COOPERATIVE. Edited by Coop members. New York Poets' Cooperative, 1974. Distributed by Robert Kramer, 3900 Graystone Ave., Bronx, N.Y. 10463. Paperback only.

THE HAIKU ANTHOLOGY: ENGLISH LANGUAGE HAIKU BY CONTEMPORARY AMERICAN AND CANADIAN POETS. Edited by Cor Van Den Heuvel. Doubleday-Anchor, 1973. Paperback.

I REALLY WANT TO FEEL GOOD ABOUT MYSELF: POEMS BY FORMER ADDICTS. Edited by Lee B. Hopkins and Sunna Rasch. Nelson, 1974. Hardcover.

JUMP BAD: A NEW CHICAGO ANTHOLOGY. Edited by Gwendolyn Brooks. Broadside Press, 1971. Hardcover and paperback. Distributed by Broadside Press, 12651 Old Mill Pl., Detroit, Mich. 48238.

KENNETH PATCHEN: A BOOK OF TRIBUTES BY VARIOUS HANDS. By Lawrence Ferlinghetti and others. Enitharmon Press, 1975. Distributed by Serendipity Books, 1790 Shattuck Ave., Berkeley, Calif. 94709.

LIVE POETRY: THOUGHTS FOR THE SEVENTIES. Edited by Kathleen Koppell et al. Holt, Rinehart & Winston, 1971. Paperback textbook edition.

LOVES. ETC. Edited by Marguerite Harris. Contemporary American and British poems on love. Doubleday-Anchor, 1973. Paperback.

THE MALE MUSE: A GAY POETRY ANTHOLOGY. Edited by Ian Young. The Crossing Press, 1973. Hardcover and paperback. Distributed by RPM Distributors, P.O. Box 1785, Rockville, Md. 20850.

MARK IN TIME: PORTRAITS AND POETRY/SAN FRANCISCO. Edited by Nick Harvey. Eighty photographs and poems by Christa Fleischmann, usually selected by the poet. Glide Publications, 1971. Hardcover. Distributed by Bookpeople, 2940 Seventh Ave., Berkeley, Calif. 94710.

MODERN POETRY OF WESTERN AMERICA. Edited by Clinton Larson and William Stafford. Brigham Young University Press, 1975. Hardcover and paperback.

MOONSTRUCK: AN ANTHOLOGY OF LUNAR POETRY. Edited by Robert Phillips. Vanguard, 1974. Hardcover only.

THE NEW NAKED POETRY: RECENT AMERICAN POETRY IN OPEN FORMS. Edited by Stephen Berg and Robert Mezey. Includes photographs of poets. Bobbs-Merrill, 1976. Paperback only.

NEW SOUTHERN POETS: SELECTED POEMS FROM SOUTHERN POETRY REVIEW. Edited by Guy Owen and Mary C. Williams. University of North Carolina Press, 1975. Hardcover and paperback.

NORTH CAROLINA POETRY: THE SEVENTIES. Edited by Guy Owen and Mary C. Williams. Southern Poetry Review Press, 1975. Paperback only.

ON THE MESA: AN ANTHOLOGY OF BOLINAS WRITINGS. Edited by Joel Weishaus. City Lights Books, 1971. Paperback only.

OPEN POETRY: FOUR ANTHOLOGIES OF EXPANDED POEMS. Edited by Ronald Gross et al. Simon & Schuster, 1972. Hardcover.

POEMS OF WAR RESISTANCE. Edited by Scott Bates. Grossman Publishers, 1969. Paperback.

POEMS ONE LINE AND LONGER. Edited by William Cole. Grossman, 1973. Paperback.

POET'S CHOICE. Edited by Paul Engle and Joseph Langland. Dial Press, 1963. Hardcover and paperback.

POETS OF THE CITIES: NEW YORK AND SAN FRANCISCO, 1950-65. Edited by Neil A. Chassman and Robert Murdock. Dutton, 1975. Paperback only.

POETS WEST: AN ANTHOLOGY OF CONTEMPORARY POEMS FROM ELEVEN WESTERN STATES. Edited by Lawrence P. Springarn and Harold Norse. Perivale Press, 1975. Paperback only.

THE SAN FRANCISCO POETS. Edited by David Meltzer. Wingbow Press, 1975. Hardcover and paperback. Distributed by Bookpeople, 2940 Seventh Ave., Berkeley, Calif. 94710.

THE SECOND BERKSHIRE ANTHOLOGY. Edited by Dana Collins. Bookstore Press, 1975. Paperback, boxed. Distributed by The Book Organization, Elm Street, Millerton, N.Y. 12546.

SONGS OF THE OPEN ROAD: FOLK ROCK LYRICS. Edited by Bob Atkinson. New American Library, 1974. Paperback only.

SOUNDS AND SILENCES: POETRY FOR NOW. Poems on social-psychological themes. Edited by Richard Peck. Delacorte, 1970: hardcover. Dell, 1970: paperback.

SOUTHERN WRITING IN THE SIXTIES: POETRY. Edited by John William Corrington and Miller Williams. Louisiana State University Press, 1967. Paperback.

SPECIMEN 73: A CATALOG OF POETS FOR THE SEASON 1973-74. Poets of the Los Angeles Basin. Edited by Paul Vangelisti and the Pasadena Museum of Art. Red Hill, 1973. Paperback only. Distributed by Serendipity Books, 1790 Shattuck Ave., Berkeley, Calif. 94709.

THE STRONG VOICE. Annual volumes from 1972 collecting work by Ohio poets. Edited by Robert McGovern and Richard Snyder. Ashland Poetry Press. Distributed by Ashland Poetry Press, Ashland College, Ohio 44805.

THIS BOOK IS A MOVIE: AN EXHIBITION OF LANGUAGE ARTS AND VISUAL POETRY. Edited by Jerry G. Bowles and Tony Russell. Dell Publishers, 1971. Paperback.

TRAVOIS: AN ANTHOLOGY OF CONTEMPORARY TEXAS POETRY. Edited by Paul Foreman and Joanie Whitebird. Thorp Springs Press, 1976. Paperback only. Distributed by Thorp Springs Press, 2311-C Woolsey, Berkeley, Calif. 94705.

25 TIMES IN THE SAME PLACE. . .: AN ANTHOLOGY OF SANTA BARBARA POETRY. Painted Cave Books, 1973. Paperback only. Distributed by Bookpeople, 2940 Seventh Ave., Berkeley, Calif. 94710.

WHERE IS VIETNAM: AMERICAN POETS RESPOND. An anthology of new work by 87 poets. Edited by Walter Lowenfels. Doubleday, 1967: paperback. Peter Smith: hardcover.

WOKE UP THIS MORNIN,: POETRY OF THE BLUES. Edited by A.X. Nicholas. Bantam Books, 1973. Paperback.

WORDS FROM THE HOUSE OF THE DEAD: AN ANTHOLOGY OF PRISON WRITINGS FROM SOLEDAD 2nd facsimile edition. Edited by Joseph Bruchac and William Witherup. The Crossing Press, 1973. Illustrated. Hardcover and paperback. Distributed by Bookpeople, 2940 Seventh Ave., Berkeley, Calif. 94710.

THE WRITING ON THE WALL: 108 AMERICAN POEMS OF PROTEST. Edited by Walter Lowenfels. Doubleday, 1969. Hardcover and paperback.

Women Poets

FOUR YOUNG LADY POETS. Edited by Leroi Jones. Corinth Books, 1962. Paperback only. Distributed by RPM Distributors, P.O. Box 1785, Rockville, Md. 20850.

KANSAS CITY REJECTS. By Joan Howlett, Dottie LeMieux, Alice Rogoff, Phyllis Speros, and Lou Jane Temple. Peace & Pieces Press, 1975. Paperback only.

MOUNTAIN MOVING DAY: POEMS BY WOMEN. Edited by Elaine Gill. The Crossing Press, 1973. Hardcover and paperback. Distributed by RPM Distributors, P.O. Box 1785, Rockville, Md. 20850.

MOVING TO ANTARCTICA. Edited by Margaret Kaminski. DustBooks, 1975. Hardcover and paperback. Distributed by DustBooks, P.O. Box 1056, Paradise, Calif. 95969.

NEW POETS: WOMEN. Edited by Terry Wetherby. Includes photographs of all 41 contributors. Les Femmes Publishing, 1976. Paperback only. Distributed by Les Femmes Publishing, 231 Adrian Rd., Millbrae, Calif. 94030.

NO MORE MASKS! AN ANTHOLOGY OF POEMS BY WOMEN. Edited by Florence Howe and Ellen Bass. Doubleday-Anchor, 1973. Paperback.

PSYCHE: THE FEMININE POETIC CONSCIOUSNESS. Edited by Barbara Segnitz and Carol Rainey. Dial Publishers, 1973: hardcover. Dell Publishers, 1973: paperback.

RISING TIDES: 20TH CENTURY AMERICAN WOMEN POETS. Edited by Laura Chester and Sharon Barba. Washington Square Press, 1973. Paperback only.

THIS IS WOMEN'S WORK: AN ANTHOLOGY OF WOMEN'S POETRY, PROSE AND GRAPHICS. Edited by Susan Efros. Panjandrum Press, 1974. Paperback only. Distributed by Bookpeople, 2940 Seventh Ave., Berkeley, Calif. 94710.

WE BECOME NEW: POEMS BY CONTEMPORARY AMERICAN WOMEN. Bantam Books, 1975. Paperback only.

WHAT, WOMAN, AND WHO, MYSELF, I AM. Edited by Rosalie Sorrels. Poems and songs by distinguished contemporary American women poets. Wooden Shoe, 1975. Paperback. Distributed by Bookpeople, 2940 Seventh Ave., Berkeley, Calif. 94710.

Poetry Criticism

There are a total of 72 works of criticism listed alphabetically by title in two sections.

The first section, "Poetry Criticism: Reference," lists 6 reference works excerpting or indexing book reviews, essays, and book-length studies on contemporary American poetry. Prices have been included for those which are under $15.

The second section, "Poetry Criticism: General," lists 66 works of criticism. Prices for these have not been included.

Many other critical works on contemporary American poetry can be found in libraries and book stores, but we have included only those which are in print and can be ordered from the publisher. Publishers' addresses can be found in *Books In Print*, which is available at book stores and libraries. Books published by small presses are listed with the name and address of a distributor.

This list is not complete. Suggestions for additional titles are welcome.

Poetry Criticism: Reference

ARTICLES ON TWENTIETH CENTURY LITERATURE: AN ANNOTATED BIBLIOGRAPHY 1954-1970. Edited by David E. Pownall. Kraus Reprints, 1973. 7 volumes are now available; 16 volumes in all are planned. This is a massive project attempting to provide complete bibliographies on all authors living and writing in the 20th century. The first seven volumes, arranged alphabetically by author and extending through authors whose names begin with *I*, contain over 10,000 articles.

BOOK REVIEW DIGEST. Published annually since 1905 by H.W. Wilson. This is the standard source for reviews in literature and other fields. About 6,000 books a year are listed by author with excerpts from reviews as well as book prices, publishers, and descriptions.

AN INDEX TO CRITICISMS OF BRITISH AND AMERICAN POETRY. By Gloria Cline and Jeffrey A. Baker. Scarecrow, 1973. Hardcover only. All periods are covered. This is a good source for criticisms of individual poems, which are listed by title, author, and first line; but it is not limited to contemporaries.

MODERN LANGUAGE ASSOCIATION BIBLIOGRAPHY OF BOOKS AND ARTICLES ON THE MODERN LANGUAGES AND LITERATURES. 21 volumes, 1921-1968. Kraus Reprints. This work is mentioned here for its section on 20th century American literature. Each volume is indexed for the names of all authors and editors appearing in that volume. Cumulative indices are also published from time to time.

PRINCETON ENCYCLOPEDIA OF POETRY AND POETICS. Revised Edition. Edited by Alex Preminger et al. Princeton University Press, 1974. Hardcover and paperback. This reference work deals with all aspects of poetry. It is arranged by topics (e.g., "Projective Verse" or "Sestina"), not individual poets. However, it is a standard work.

WOMEN STUDIES ABSTRACTS. By Sara S. Whaley. Rush Publishing Co., 1972 to the present. A quarterly, *Women Studies* abstracts and lists articles and book reviews in the field of women's studies, including literary works, biography, and criticism. An index is published annually. Distributed at $10 a year or $3 an issue by Rush Publishing Co., P.O. Box 1, Rush, N.Y. 14543.

Poetry Criticism: General

ADDITIONAL PROSE: A BIBLIOGRAPHY ON AMERICA, PROPRIOCEPTION & OTHER NOTES & ESSAYS. Charles Olson. Four Seasons Foundation, 1974. Hardcover and paperback. Distributed by Serendipity Books, 1790 Shattuck Ave., Berkeley, Calif. 94709.

ALLEN VERBATIM: LECTURES ON POETRY, POLITICS, CONSCIOUSNESS. Allen Ginsberg. Edited by Gordon Ball. McGraw-Hill, 1974. Hardcover only.

ALONE WITH AMERICA: ESSAYS ON THE ART OF POETRY IN THE UNITED STATES SINCE 1950. By Richard Howard. Atheneum, 1971. Hardcover and paperback.

AMERICAN POETRY IN THE TWENTIETH CENTURY. By Kenneth Rexroth. The Seabury Press, 1973 (new edition). Paperback only.

AMERICAN POETRY SINCE 1945. By Stephen Stepanchev. Harper & Row, 1965. Hardcover only.

AMERICAN POETRY SINCE 1960: A CRITICAL SURVEY. By Robert B. Shaw. Carcanet Press, 1973. Distributed by Dufour Editions, Chester Springs, Pa. 19425.

AMERICAN POETS 1976. Edited by William Heyen. Essays by 27 poets quoting and interpreting their own work. Illustrated with photographs of the poets. Bobbs-Merrill, 1975. Hardcover and paperback textbook edition.

BABEL TO BYZANTIUM: POETS & POETRY NOW. James Dickey. Library binding: Octogon, 1973. Paperback: Grosset & Dunlap, 1971.

BLACK POETRY IN AMERICA: TWO ESSAYS IN HISTORICAL INTERPRETATION. Edited by Blyden Jackson and Louis D. Robertson. Louisiana State University Press, 1975. Hardcover only.

A CASEBOOK ON THE BEAT. Edited by Thomas Parkinson. Thomas Y. Crowell, 1961. Paperback textbook edition.

CAUSAL MYTHOLOGY. Charles Olson. Four Seasons Foundation, 1969. Paperback only. Distributed by Serendipity Books, 1790 Shattuck Ave., Berkeley, Calif. 94709:

THE CONFESSIONAL POETS. By Robert Phillips. Southern Illinois University Press, 1973. Hardcover only.

THE CONTEMPORARY POET AS ARTIST AND CRITIC. Edited by Anthony Ostroff. Little Brown and Co., 1964. Hardcover only.

CONTEMPORARY POETRY IN AMERICA: ESSAYS AND INTERVIEWS. Edited by Robert Boyers. Schocken Books, 1975. Hardcover and paperback.

CONTEMPORARY POETS IN AMERICA: ESSAYS AND INTERVIEWS. Edited by Robert Boyers. Schocken Books, 1975. Hardcover and paperback.

CONTEMPORARY WRITER: INTERVIEWS WITH 16 NOVELISTS AND POETS. Edited by L.S. Dembo and Cyrena N. Pondrom. University of Wisconsin Press, 1972. Hardcover and paperback.

CONTEXTS OF POETRY: INTERVIEWS 1961-1971. Robert Creeley. Edited by Donald Allen. Four Seasons Foundation, 1973. Paperback only. Distributed by Serendipity Books, 1790 Shattuck Ave., Berkeley, Calif. 94709.

THE CONTINUITY OF AMERICAN POETRY. By Roy Harvey Pearce. Princeton University Press, 1961. Hardcover only.

THE CRAFT OF POETRY: NEW YORK QUARTERLY INTERVIEWS. Edited by William Packard, with photographs of poets by Layle Silbert. Doubleday, 1974. Hardcover and paperback textbook edition.

CROWELL'S HANDBOOK OF CONTEMPORARY AMERICAN POETRY. By Karl Malkoff. Thomas Y. Crowell, 1973. Hardcover only.

CRY OF THE HUMAN: ESSAYS ON CONTEMPORARY AMERICAN POETRY. By Ralph J. Mills, Jr. University of Illinois Press, 1975. Hardcover only.

JAMES DICKEY: SELF-INTERVIEWS. Recorded and edited by Barbara and James Reiss. Dell, 1972. Paperback only.

EARTH HOUSE HOLD: TECHNICAL NOTES & QUERIES TO FELLOW DHARMA REVOLUTIONARIES. Gary Snyder. New Directions, 1969. Paperback only.

THE FREEDOM OF THE POET: COLLECTED ESSAYS. John Berryman. Farrar, Straus, Giroux, 1976. Hardcover only.

HUMAN UNIVERSE & OTHER ESSAYS. Charles Olson. Edited by Donald Allen. Grove Press, 1968. Paperback only.

IN RADICAL PURSUIT: CRITICAL ESSAYS AND LECTURES. W.D. Snodgrass. Harper & Row, 1974. Hardcover only.

LETTERS FROM ORIGIN 1950-1956. Charles Olson. Edited by Albert Glover. Grossman Publishers, 1970. Hardcover and paperback.

LETTERS HOME; CORRESPONDENCE 1950-1963. By Sylvia Plath. Selected and edited by Aurelia Schober Plath. Harper & Row, 1975. Hardcover only.

LITERATURE OF THE AMERICAN INDIANS: Views and Interpretations. Edited by Abraham Chapman. New American Library, 1975. Paperback only.

THE LIVING UNDERGROUND: A CRITICAL OVERVIEW. By Hugh Fox. Whitston Publishing Co., 1970. Hardcover only.

THE LOGIC OF POETRY. By Richard Monaco and John Briggs. Illustrated with photographs of the poets. McGraw-Hill, 1974. Paperback textbook edition only.

MAKING IN ALL ITS FORMS: CONTEMPORARY AMERICAN POETICS AND CRITICISM. Edited by A. Poulin, Jr. E.P. Dutton & Co., 1974. Paperback only.

MANIFESTOS. By John Giorno, Dick Higgins, Jerome Rothenberg, Emmett Williams, and artists associated with them. Something Else Press, 1966. Paperback only. Distributed by Serendipity Books, 1790 Shattuck Ave., Berkeley, Calif. 94709.

A MAP OF MISREADING. By Harold Bloom. Oxford University Press, 1975. Hardcover only.

THE MAYAN LETTERS. Charles Olson. Edited by Robert Creeley. Grossman Publishers, 1968. Hardcover only.

MEAT SCIENCE ESSAYS. Michael McClure. City Lights, 1963 (second enlarged edition). Paperback only.

MEMOIRS AND OPINIONS. Allen Tate. Swallow Press, 1975. Hardcover only.

MODERN AMERICAN POETRY: ESSAYS IN CRITICISM. Edited by Jerome Mazzaro. David McKay Co., 1970. Hardcover and paperback.

THE MODERN POETS: A CRITICAL INTRODUCTION. By M.L. Rosenthal. Oxford University Press, 1965. Paperback only.

THE NEW POETS: AMERICAN AND BRITISH POETRY SINCE WORLD WAR II. Edited by M.L. Rosenthal. Oxford University Press, 1967. Paperback only.

NOTEBOOKS OF DAVID IGNATOW. Edited by Ralph J. Mills, Jr. Swallow Press, 1973. Hardcover only.

CHARLES OLSON READING AT BERKELEY. Transcribed by Zoe Brown. Illustrated with photographs of the poet. Coyote Press, 1966. Paperback only. Distributed by Bookpeople, 2940 Seventh Ave., Berkeley, Calif. 94710.

ON THE POET AND HIS CRAFT: SELECTED PROSE OF THEODORE ROETHKE. Edited by Ralph J. Mills, Jr. University of Washington Press, 1966. Hardcover and paperback.

POET IN THE WORLD. Denise Levertov. New Directions, 1973. Hardcover and paperback.

THE POETICS OF THE NEW AMERICAN POETRY. Edited by Donald Allen and Warren Tallman. Grove Press, 1973. Hardcover and paperback.

POETRY AND THE AGE. Randall Jarrell. Library binding: Octogon, 1972. Paperback: Farrar, Straus, Giroux, 1972.

POETRY AND THE COMMON LIFE. By M.L. Rosenthal. Oxford University Press, 1974. Hardcover only.

POETRY AND TRUTH: THE BELOIT POETRY LECTURES AND POEMS. Charles Olson. Transcribed and edited by George F. Butterick. Four Seasons Foundation, 1971. Hardcover and paperback. Distributed by Serendipity Books, 1790 Shattuck Ave., Berkeley, Calif. 94709.

THE POETRY OF POP. By Joe Bruchac. Dustbooks, 1975. Hardcover and paperback. Distributed by Dustbooks, P.O. Box 1056, Paradise, Calif. 95969.

THE POETRY WRECK. Karl Shapiro. Random House, 1975. Hardcover only.

POETS IN PROGRESS: CRITICAL PREFACES TO THIRTEEN CONTEMPORARY AMERICANS. By Edward B. Hungerford. Northwestern University Press, 1967. Paperback only.

POETS ON POETRY. Edited by Howard Nemerov et al. Basic Books, 1966. Hardcover only.

A QUICK GRAPH: COLLECTED NOTES AND ESSAYS. Robert Creeley. Edited by Donald Allen. Four Seasons Foundation, 1970. Hardcover and paperback. Distributed by Serendipity Books, 1790 Shattuck Ave., Berkeley, Calif. 94709.

RESPONSES. Richard Wilbur. Harcourt, Brace, Jovanovich, 1976. Hardcover only.

SELECTED LETTERS OF THEODORE ROETHKE. Edited by Ralph J. Mills, Jr. University of Washington Press, 1968. Hardcover only.

SELECTED WRITINGS OF CHARLES OLSON. Edited by Robert Creeley. New Directions, 1967. Hardcover and paperback.

SEVEN AMERICAN POETS FROM MACLEISH TO NEMEROV. Edited by Dennis Donoghue. Collected from the American Writers pamphlet series. University of Minnesota Press, 1975. Hardcover only.

SIX SAN FRANCISCO POETS. By David Kherdian. The Giligia Press, 1969. Hardcover and paperback. Distributed by Bookpeople, 2940 Seventh Ave., Berkeley, Calif. 94710.

SOME POEMS/POETS: STUDIES IN UNDERGROUND POETRY SINCE 1945. Samuel Charters. Illustrated with photographs of poets. Oyez Press, 1971. Hardcover and paperback. Distributed by Serendipity Books, 1790 Shattuck Ave., Berkeley, Calif. 94709.

SORTIES: JOURNALS & NEW ESSAYS. James Dickey. Doubleday, 1971. Hardcover only.

THE SPECIAL VIEW OF HISTORY. Charles Olson. Edited by Ann Charter. Oyez Press, 1970. Hardcover and paperback. Distributed by Serendipity Books, 1790 Shattuck Ave., Berkeley, Calif. 94709.

STRAW FOR THE FIRE: FROM THE NOTEBOOKS OF THEODORE ROETHKE 1943-1963. Edited by David Wagoner. Doubleday & Co., 1972. Hardcover only.

THE TRUTH & LIFE OF MYTH: AN ESSAY IN ESSENTIAL AUTOBIOGRAPHY. By Robert Duncan. Sumac, 1968. Paperback only. Distributed by Bookpeople, 2940 Seventh Ave., Berkeley, Calif. 94710.

VISION AND RESONANCE: TWO SENSES OF THE POETIC FORM. By John Hollander. Oxford University Press, 1975. Hardcover only.

WRITERS AT WORK: THE PARIS REVIEW INTERVIEWS. The Viking Press: First Series, 1958; Second Series, 1965; Third Series, 1968; Fourth Series, 1974. Hardcover and paperback.

THE YAGE LETTERS. Allen Ginsberg with William Burroughs. City Lights, 1963. Paperback only.

Resources for Creative Writing Teachers

The following is a list of publications and filmstrips which are suggested for use in creative writing classes. Entries are organized alphabetically by title. Addresses of small publishers are included. Books published by commercial presses can be ordered through local book stores. Only a few of the many teaching materials available from state arts councils are mentioned here. For further listings, write to the arts councils (addresses can be found in the Sponsors Listing of this directory).

AMERICAN POETRY REVIEW'S POETS-IN-THE-SCHOOLS SUPPLEMENT. Each issue of *APR*, a 48-page tabloid of poetry, interviews, and criticism, contains several pages of essays by poets on teaching poetry in elementary and high schools. *APR* is published six times a year. Subscription rates are one year: $5, two years: $9, three years: $13. Single copies are $1. Write to *The American Poetry Review*, Dept. S, 401 S. Broad St., Philadelphia, Pa. 19147.

ANGWAMAS MINOSEWAG ANISHINABEG (Time of the Indian). A continuing magazine of writings by Indian children. Free, from Molly LaBerge, Minnesota Poets-in-the-Schools, COMPAS (Community Programs in the Arts and Sciences), 75 West 5th St., St. Paul, Minn. 55102.

ANKH: GETTING IT TOGETHER. Edited by Lorenzo Thomas. Houston: Hope Development, Inc., 1974. Writings from the creative communications workshop Ethnic Arts Program of the Black Arts Center in Houston, Texas. Black Arts Center, Hope Development, Inc., 2801 Lyons Ave., Houston, Tex. 77026. $2.50.

THE ANT'S FOREFOOT publishes adult poetry by poet-teachers, accompanied by poems of young (12 and under) students they have been working with for at least a year. To contribute, send 10 poems by the student *only*. If accepted, you will be asked to contribute a comparable number of poems yourself. Send manuscripts to David Rosenberg, 29 St. Mark's Pl., New York, N.Y. 10003.

ARROWS FOUR: PROSE AND POETRY BY YOUNG AMERICAN INDIANS. Edited by T.D. Allen. Washington Square Press, 1974. $.95.

ART RESOURCES FOR TEACHERS AND STUDENTS, INC. Booklets on the Chinese and Puerto Rican cultures by students* and the staff of ARTS, Inc. Titles include: *Arriving: NYC,* * *Chinese Folk Songs*, *Chinese Children's Games,* * *Chinese Lanterns*, *Christmas in Puerto Rico*, *Chinese Heroines*, *Songs of My Island* (Puerto Rican folk songs), and *Children of the Yellow River*. All booklets are $.50 each ($.50 handling on orders less than $5). Order from ARTS, Inc., 32 East 58th St., New York, N.Y. 10022.

BAKER & TAYLOR'S AUDIO VISUAL SERVICES DIVISION is the largest single source for educational media by over 500 producers in the U.S. A computerized inventory system lists over 120,000 titles in a great variety of subject areas and media formats, including film, videotape, filmstrips, records, tapes, charts, slides, etc. A catalog of titles in literature and related areas is available free under the title *Books in Media: A/V Quicklist K-6*. The catalog contains an order form and complete ordering information. Write or call The Baker & Taylor Co., Audio Visual Services Division, Box 230, Momence, Ill. 60954, (815) 472-2444.

BEING WITH CHILDREN: A HIGH-SPIRITED ACCOUNT OF TEACHING WRITING, THEATER, AND VIDEOTAPE. By Phillip Lopate. Doubleday, 1975. $7.95 (hardcover).

BLACK OUT LOUD: AN ANTHOLOGY OF MODERN POEMS BY BLACK AMERICANS. Edited by Arnold Adoff. Macmillan, 1970. $4.95 (hardcover). An anthology for children in grade 4 and older.

BLOODLINE, the novel by Ernest Gaines, is available with taped lessons on cassettes and a teacher's guide. The kit costs $45.50 from Paul S. Amidon and Associates, Inc., 1329 Nicollet Ave. S., Minneapolis, Minn. 55409.

A DAY DREAM I HAD AT NIGHT. By Roger Landrum. A collection of oral literature from children who were not learning to read well or write competently or feel a sense of satisfaction in school. The author describes how he worked with two elementary school teachers, made class readers out of the children's own work, recorded the readers in a tape library, and designed a set of language exercises based on the readers. Available for $3 from Teachers & Writers Collaborative (address under TEACHERS & WRITERS COLLABORATIVE NEWSLETTER).

DISCOVERY: TO SEE. A filmstrip with accompanying record and teaching materials for teaching poetry to children. Purchase only: $20. Media Plus, Inc., 60 Riverside Dr., Suite 11D, New York, N.Y. 10024.

DREAMS AND INNER SPACES. A newsletter for getting in touch with your dreams; and guide materials for teachers. Send a legal sized, stamped, self-addressed envelope to Dreams and Inner Spaces, Edendale P.O. Box 26556, Los Angeles, Calif. 90026 for a free sample copy.

ENGLISH JOURNAL. The official high school publication of the National Council of Teachers of English, 1111 Kenyon Rd., Urbana, Ill. 61801, (217) 328-3870. $15 per year, or $2 for single copies.

EXHIBITS OF CHILDREN'S ART & WRITING are available from The Touchstone Center for Children, Inc., 141 E. 88 St., New York, N.Y. 10028. Titles of the exhibits are: *I Breathe a New Song: Poems and Artwork by Eskimos; Between Earth and Sky: Paintings and Poems by Children of New Zealand;* and *My Roots Be Coming Back: Art and Writing by Children in New York Hospitals*. Two other exhibits produced by the Center are available through the Gallery Association of New York State, 14 Prentice St., Norwich, N.Y. 13815. They are *Prints and Poems by Children of Japan* and *Haiku*.

FAMOUS WRITERS AT WORK SETS I AND II are collections of filmstrips with records or cassettes. Set I presents authors Frank Conroy, Bel Kaufman, and Piri Thomas. Set II presents James T. Farrell, Penelope Gilliatt, and Charles Gordon. The sets are $56 each with records or $66 with cassettes. Order from Schloat Productions, 150 White Plains Rd., Tarrytown, N.Y. 10591.

A FEEL FOR WORDS: MAKING POETRY IN THE PUBLIC SCHOOLS. By Richard Fricks. A handbook for teachers and parents by Chattanooga's Poets-in-the-Schools, 1971-73. Tennessee Arts Commission, 222 Capitol Hill Bldg., Nashville, Tenn. 37219. $3.50 (paperback).

FILMS KIDS LIKE. Edited by Susan Rice. New York: Center for Understanding Media, Inc., 75 Horatio St., New York, N.Y. 10014, (212) 989-1000. $4.95. A number of other publications on media use for children are available from the Center—inquire for a list of publications.

THE FILM USER'S HANDBOOK. By George Rehrauer. A guide to building a film service in the library, school, or community. The selection and maintenance of equipment is discussed in detail. R.R. Bowker Company, 1975. Paperback only: $14.95. To order, write to R.R. Bowker Order Dept., P.O. Box 1807, Ann Arbor, Mich. 48106.

FIVE TALES OF ADVENTURE. A classroom reader featuring short novels written by elementary school children. An introduction describes how the tales were written. $3 from Teachers & Writers Collaborative (address under TEACHERS & WRITERS NEWSLETTER).

4TH STREET I. Edited by Freddy Gonzales. A magazine of writing by Puerto Rican students from Manhattan's Lower East Side. Write to 4th Street I, có Box 13, 56 Avenue B, New York, N.Y. 10009, (212) 437-8908. $1 per issue (published quarterly).

FOXFIRE. A magazine published quarterly in a small Georgia town by high school students. Subscriptions are $6 a year. Write Foxfire, Rabun Gap, Ga. 30568, (404) 746-2561.

HOMEMADE POEMS is an illustrated handbook by poet Daniel Lusk on imaginative techniques for teaching poetry-writing to children, adults, old people and the handicapped. $2.50 from Lame Johnny Press & Associates, Hermosa, S. Dak. 57744.

HOW A BOOK IS MADE. A filmstrip with Elizabeth Bishop, explaining bookmaking from desire to dustjacket. With 3 records & book, purchase only: $48. Media Plus, 60 Riverside Dr., Suite 11D, New York, N.Y. 10024.

I AM THE DARKER BROTHER. Edited by Arnold Adoff. Macmillan, 1968. $4.95 (hardcover), $1.95 (paperback). Black poetry anthology for children in grade 7 and older.

IMAGINARY WORLDS. By Richard Murphy. Account of an attempt to find themes of sufficient breadth and interest to allow sustained, independent writing by students. Children are asked to invent utopias, different schools, new religions, new ways of fighting wars and making peace. Incorporates the children's writings. Available for $3 from Teachers & Writers Collaborative (address under TEACHERS & WRITERS NEWSLETTER).

THE INDIVIDUAL VOICE is a student poetry anthology available free from the Indiana Arts Commission, 155 E. Market St., Suite 614, Indianapolis, Ind. 46204. Work contained is by elementary and high school students who studied in Poets-in-the-Schools programs during 1973-74.

JOURNEYS. Edited by Richard Lewis. Simon and Schuster, 1969. Prose by children of the English-speaking world. $4.95.

LOTUS PRESS BROADSIDES feature work by Black poets (Gloria Oden, Raymond R. Patterson, Dudley Randall, and others) printed on twenty 8-inch by 14-inch colored posters to appeal to students in elementary school.

The collection is titled *Deep Rivers, A Portfolio: 20 Contemporary Black American Poets.* $5.95 plus $.50 postage from Lotus Press, P.O. Box 601, College Park Station, Detroit, Mich. 48221. A 15-page teacher's guide by poet Naomi Madgett is included.

MATH, WRITING, AND GAMES IN THE OPEN CLASSROOM. By Herbert R. Kohl. Vintage Books, 1973. Practical suggestions and techniques for teaching math and writing to children. Distributed by New York Review, 250 W. 57 St., New York, N.Y. 10019. $6.95 (hardcover), $2.45 (paperback).

THE ME NOBODY KNOWS. Edited by Steven Joseph. A collection of prose and poetry from ghetto children in New York. Avon, 1969. $.95 (paperback).

MIRACLES. Edited by Richard Lewis. Simon and Schuster, 1966. Poems by children of the English-speaking world. $5.95 (hardcover).

MY ROOTS BE COMING BACK. Edited by Nancy Lewis. A selection of art and written material from children in hospitals. New York: Touchstone Center for Children, 1973. $1. Address: 141 E. 88 St., New York, N.Y. 10028.

MY SISTER LOOKS LIKE A PEAR: AWAKENING THE POETRY IN YOUNG PEOPLE. By Doug Anderson. Hart Publishing, 1974. $7.50 (hardcover), $2.95 (paperback).

THE NEW KIDS. A magazine by and for children. Individual subscriptions are $7 for 8 issues. Write to Kids Magazine, 747 Third Ave., New York, N.Y. 10017.

OUT OF MY BODY. Edited by Nancy Lewis. Contains work in various media by children in pediatrics wards of New York hospitals. A companion volume to *My Roots Be Coming Back* (see that listing). $1 from The Touchstone Center for Children, Inc., 141 E. 88 St., New York, N.Y. 10028.

POET TO TEACHER TO STUDENT. Edited by Richard Snyder, 1971. A talk to teachers and a supplement to building an audience for poetry. The Ashland Poetry Press, Ashland College, Ashland, Ohio 44805. $1 (paperback).

A POETRY RITUAL FOR GRAMMAR SCHOOLS by Robert McGovern is a manual for teachers and teacher-training. It proposes the routine use of adult poetry to begin the children's day. A small anthology of likely poems is appended. $1 from The Ashland Poetry Press, Ashland College, Ashland, Ohio 44805 (paperback).

PROFILES IN LITERATURE is a series of 23 black and white, half-hour videotaped interviews with leading children's authors, editors, and illustrators, for use in secondary and adult level children's literature classes. Authors and editors interviewed include Richard Lewis, Pura Belpre, Arna Bontemps, Kristin Hunter, Eve Merriam, and Letta Schatz. A special 20 minute preview tape of the series is available on 2-day loan for $1 (format: half-inch EIAJ). Individual tapes are available at a duplication charge of $25 each (any format), or the tapes can be purchased as half-inch EIAJ at $20 per half-hour and $30 per hour of tape combining any segments. Information is available on quantity rates and on a teachers' guide for using the tapes. Send inquiries to *Profiles in Literature,* Temple University, Office of Television Services, Tomlinson Hall 214, Philadelphia, Pa. 19122. Make checks payable to the Office of Television Services.

RESOURCES FOR THE TEACHING OF ENGLISH AND THE LANGUAGE ARTS. A comprehensive guide to publications, maps, filmstrips and recordings for classroom use. Free from the Editor, Resources for the Teaching of English, National Council of Teachers of English, 1111 Kenyon Rd., Urbana, Ill. 61801, (217) 328-3870.

A ROAD NOT TAKEN: AN APPROACH TO TEACHING POETRY. By David Verble. Classroom experiences of Nashville's Poet-in-the-Schools, 1971-72. $2 (paperback). Write to Tennessee Arts Commission, 222 Capitol Hill Bldg., Nashville, Tenn. 37219.

ROSE, WHERE DID YOU GET THAT RED? By Kenneth Koch. Teaching great poetry to children. Random House, 1973. $7.95 (hardcover, $2.45 (paperback). For Kenneth Koch's videotape of the same title, see *Camera Three* in the Distributors Listing under *Videotapes* in the Service Section of this directory.

SOMEBODY TURNED ON A TAP IN THESE KIDS. Edited by Nancy Larrick. A textbook anthology of writing by Florence Howe, June Jordan, Richard Lewis, Eve Merriam, students, and others. The greater portion of the book is made up of talks, papers, and discussions taped at the Poetry Festival at Lehigh University in the spring of 1969. Delacorte Press, 1971. $5.95 (hardcover), $2.45 (paperback).

SOULSCRIPT. Edited by June Jordan. Doubleday & Company, 1970. An anthology for teaching use, containing work by black poets. Grade 7 and up. $3.95 (hardcover), $1.75 (paperback). Teacher's manual by C.P. Eagleson: $.50.

SPICY MEATBALL. The annual literary magazine of P.S. 75, N.Y.C., which anthologizes poetry and fiction by elementary school children. $1 from Teachers & Writers Collaborative (see address under TEACHERS & WRITERS COLLABORATIVE NEWSLETTER).

STONE SOUP. William Rubel, Editor. Poetry, prose and art from children worldwide. $4.95 for 3 issuesyear. $2.00 for single copies. Write Stone Soup, Box 83, Santa Cruz, Calif. 95063, (408) 426-5557.

TALKIN' ABOUT US. Edited by Bill Wertheim. Irvington Books, 1970. Distributed by Hawthorn Books. Poems and stories from Black, Puerto Rican, Indian, Chicano, and Appalachian students. $4.45.

THE TEACHER PAPER. "The only magazine to print only work by teachers." A magazine published 5 times a year in October, December, February, April and June, written by and for teachers. $8 per year, $1.75 per copy. The Teacher Paper, 2221 N.E. 23 St., Portland, Oreg. 97212.

TEACHERS & WRITERS COLLABORATIVE NEWSLETTER. Contains diary excerpts and articles by professional writers and other artists who are working in classrooms on a regular basis with teachers and students. Also includes student work and outside contributions. Subscriptions are $5 for 3 issues, $2 for single issues. Write to Teachers & Writers Collaborative, 186 W. 4 St., New York, N.Y. 10014.

THERE ARE TWO LIVES. Edited by Richard Lewis. A collection of translated poems by Japanese school children. Simon & Schuster, 1970. $4.95 (hardcover).

THE TURTLIE AND THE TEACHER: A DIALOGUE BETWEEN POETS AND STUDENTS. Edited and compiled by Ruby Lee Norris and Sally Harris Sange. The poets are Michael Mott, Dabney Stuart, and Sylvia Wilkinson. Their conversations with elementary through high school students in the Virginia school system are recounted, alongside some of the resultant student writing. $2 from The Humanities Center, One W. Main St., Richmond, Va. 23220.

VOICE OF THE CHILDREN. Collected by June Jordan and Terri Bush. Poetry by black and Puerto Rican junior high school students. Holt, Rinehart & Winston, 1970. $3.95 (hardcover), $1.95 (paperback). And Washington Square Press, $.95 (paperback).

WHAT'S INSIDE YOU IT SHINES OUT OF YOU. By Marc Kaminsky. Horizon Press, 1974. A young poet's description of poetry writing with a group of older people, plus an anthology of their work. Write to Horizon Press, 156 Fifth Ave., New York, N.Y. 10010.

THE WHISPERING WIND: POETRY BY YOUNG AMERICAN INDIANS. Edited by Terry Allen. Doubleday, 1972. $1.95 (paperback).

THE WHOLE WORD CATALOGUE. Edited by Rosellen Brown, Marvin Hoffman, Martin Kushner, Phillip Lopate, and Sheila Murphy. A practical collection of assignments for stimulating student writing, for both elementary and secondary students. Contains an annotated bibliography. $3 from Teachers & Writers Collaborative (address under TEACHERS & WRITERS COLLABORATIVE NEWSLETTER).

WISHES, LIES, AND DREAMS: TEACHING CHILDREN TO WRITE POETRY. By Kenneth Koch and the students of P.S. 61 in New York City. Ideas on stimulating children to write that challenge more conventional techniques. A pioneer book in this field by a master teacher-poet. Includes many poems by the children of P.S. 61 which have proven most stimulating to students. Chelsea House Publishers, distributed by Random House. $7.95 (hardcover), $1.95 (paperback). For a related film and videotape, see Kenneth Koch under *Films* and *Videotapes* in the Service Section of this directory.

WORD MAGIC: HOW TO ENCOURAGE CHILDREN TO WRITE AND SPEAK CREATIVELY. By Charleen Whisnant and Jo Hassett. Doubleday & Company, 1974. $6.95 (hardcover).

WRITERS AS TEACHERS/TEACHERS AS WRITERS. Edited by Jonathan Baumbach. Holt, Rinehart & Winston, 1970. Essays by professional writers such as Denise Levertov and Grace Paley about their work in college writing programs. $2.45 (paperback).

THE YOUNG VOICE, THE YOUNG VOICE II, and THE YOUNG VOICE III. Robert McGovern and Richard Snyder. Poems by Ohio high school students at the fifth annual The Voice and The Word Poetry Festival. Write to The Ashland Poetry Press, Ashland College, Ashland, Ohio 44805. $1 each (paperback).

Films

Films are listed alphabetically by author and coded to a list of distributors which follows. When more than one author is seen in a film, the complete listing appears under the author whose name comes first in alphabetical sequence. Many films are annotated by a viewer or described with a paragraph from the distributor's catalogue. In no case do the comments represent the opinion of Poets & Writers, Inc. or the Literature Program of the National Endowment for the Arts.

We have not listed popular screen adaptations of novels or films for which an author wrote the screenplay. Listings of films on novelists and on authors from outside the U.S. are not intended to be complete.

Rental customers are urged to borrow films through a local library whenever possible. In addition to saving time and postage, this encourages the library to buy and maintain literature films.

When purchase is offered, the rental fee is usually applicable toward it. Preview services are available only to purchase customers. Admission may not be charged to audiences of either rented or purchased films without permission from holder of copyright. Additional information on customer policies and discount rates should be requested when ordering.

This section contains 120 films on 120 authors and addresses of 37 distributors.

Daisy Aldan and others. ONCE UPON AN EL. Eighteen poets and painters as they were in 1955 during the demolition of the Third Avenue El in New York City. Includes Daisy Aldan, John Ashbery, Frank O'Hara, James Schuyler, Chester Kallman, James Broughton, and Kenward Elmslie. 8mm color, sound track on separate tape. Rental only: $25. For availability in 16mm format, inquire. (FE)

Brother Antoninus (William Everson) and Michael McClure. Michael McClure, introduced as a "beat" poet, talks about his craft and the influence of consciousness-expanding drugs on his life and experimental art. He reads several poems and performs some of his sound-poem Ghost Tantras, one in a zoo to an audience of lions. We first see Brother Antoninus in tight close-up confronting us—attempting, as he says later, to "open you up in myself." The poet in performance, reading and speaking with great energy and pain, is intercut with scenes at the Dominican monastery where Brother Antoninus, who now uses his given name William Everson, still lived in 1966 when the film was made. (Annotated by Honor Moore.) Produced in 1966 by Brice Howard for National Educational Television. 16mm B/W, 30 min. Rental: $9.50 for one to five days. Purchase: $165. For videotape of this film see Indiana University under *Videotapes* in the Service Section of this directory. For another film on Brother Antoninus, see listing under William Everson in this section of the directory. (IU)

John Ashberry. See Daisy Aldan.

James Baldwin. JAMES BALDWIN'S HARLEM. "My life had begun. . .in the invincible and indescribable squalor of Harlem. . .here in the ghetto I was born." James Baldwin speaks of the poverty, despair, and his father's hatred which led him to despise both white and black people alike. (Description from catalogue). 16mm B/W, 25 min. Rental: $25 for one showing. Purchase: $230. 8mm sound cartridge rates are the same (specify projector). (BF)

Eric Barker. POET AT LOBOS. Robinson Jeffers described the English-born poet Eric Barker as among the best of the nature poets. Barker has also been described as a poet who lives as a poet should—simply and with nature. Cinematographer Robert Blaisdell follows Barker as he walks the trails of his favorite place, Point Lobos, on the Northern California Coast. Barker recites poems from his volumes *Looking for Water* and *Directions in the Sun*. (Description from catalogue.) 16mm color, 13 min. Rental: $12 for one day. Purchase: $155. (LL)

Saul Bellow. THE WORLD OF THE DANGLING MAN. Norman Podhoretz of *Commentary* Magazine discusses the common literary theme of alienation and Saul Bellow's repudiation of alienation. Works discussed include *The Dangling Man, The Victim, The Adventures of Augie March, Seize the Day, Henderson the Rain King,* and *Herzog*. (Description from catalogue.) Produced by Jack Sameth in 1966 for National Educational Television. 16mm B/W, 29 min. Rental: $9.50 for one to five days. Purchase: $165. For a videotape of this film see Indiana University under *Videotapes* in the Service Section of this directory. (IU)

John Berryman. I DON'T THINK I WILL SING ANY MORE JUST NOW. A documentary tracing the life and work of John Berryman. Through photographs, readings, and interviews, the film examines his personal history and reviews his career as teacher, scholar, poet, and winner of the National Book Award and the Pulitzer Prize. Much of the film is devoted to interviews with his friends and close associates; author Saul Bellow, book reviewer Walter Clemons, and publisher Robert Giroux. Berryman's wife Kate describes the excitement and confusion of his life. Particular attention is paid to Berryman's exhausting struggle with alcoholism. (Description from catalogue.) Produced by Carol Johnsen. 16mm color, 30 min. Rental: $12.80 for one to five days. Purchase: $390. (AV)

John Berryman. Shot at the Spoleto Festival in 1967, this film shows Berryman reading from *77 Dream Songs* and talking about the main characters in these poems, Henry and Mr. Bones. Visually rather boring but invaluable for Berryman's own reading of the poems. (Annotated by Cheri Fein.) 16mm B/W, 20 min. Purchase only: $95. (BP)

Jorge Luis Borges. THE INNER WORLD OF JORGE LUIS BORGES. Borges' personality emerges as he is interviewed and shown in Buenos Aires, in his library, with his family. Sound track is blurred at times when Borges is speaking, but a valuable film for its glimpse of Borges as he goes about his daily life. (Annotated by Nash Cox.) Narrated by Jorge Luis Borges and Joseph Wiseman. 16mm color, 28 1/2 min. Rental: $35 for one day. Purchase: $340. For videotape of this film, see Films for the Humanities under *Video* in the Service Section of this directory. (FH)

Ray Bradbury. STORY OF A WRITER. About and with Ray Bradbury and high school students. (Description from distributor.) 16mm B/W, 25 min. Rental through various university film libraries—list available from SE. Purchase: $185. (SE)

Henry Braun and others. THESE DAYS. Examines the lives and work of Ted Enslin, Constance Hunting, and Henry Braun. Straight documentary material complements the poets' voiced-over readings. (Description from catalogue.) Produced by William Kenda in 1974. 16mm B/W, 30 min. Rental: $30. Purchase: $265. (WK)

Gwendolyn Brooks. The poet reading her poems is intercut with scenes of the Chicago community that has inspired her. Gwendolyn Brooks talks movingly about her craft, winning the Pulitzer Prize for poetry in 1950, her family, and the lives of the poor Black people she writes about. This 1966 film predates Brooks' later strong involvement with the Black Arts Movement. (Annotated by Honor Moore.) Directed by Aida Aronoff and produced by Roger Smith in 1966 for National Educational Television. 16mm B/W, 30 min. Rental: $9.50 for one to five days. Purchase: $165. For a videotape of this film see Indiana University under *Videotapes* in the Service Section of this directory. (IU)

James Broughton. FOUR IN THE AFTERNOON. The poet reads his poetry while his camera studies dancer Ann Halprin. (Description from distributor.) Produced by James Broughton. 16mm B/W, 14 min. Rental only: $20 for three days. (HB)

James Broughton. HIGHKUKUS. In this film produced by Broughton, he reads 14 of his haiku in tribute to the 17th century Japanese poet, Basho, who was the first noted practitioner of the form. Images of a pool of water accompany the reading. (Description from distributor.) 16mm B/W, 14 min. Rental only: $6 for three days. (HB)

James Broughton. TESTAMENT. This autobiographical film by Broughton pays tribute to the French filmmaker and poet, Jean Cocteau. Family photographs of Broughton and surrealist film techniques are combined. (Description from distributor). Produced by James Broughton. 16mm color, 10 min. Rental only: $20 for three days. (HB)

James Broughton. THIS IS IT! In this film by Broughton, he reflects poetically on the book *THIS IS IT!* by the distinguished student of Zen Buddhism, Alan Watts. The film follows a two-year-old child in pursuit of his fantasy, while on the soundtrack Broughton reads (his own) Zen poems. (Description from distributor.) 16mm color, 9-1/2 min. Rental only: $15 for three days. (HB)

James Broughton. See Daisy Aldan.

Charles Bukowski. Bukowski's Rabelaisian personality dominates this highly personal film. He freely discusses his writing, women, drinking, why he plays the horses. He is shown at the track, at a reading at City Lights Bookstore, at home. Two women in his life perceptively discuss their relationship with him. A marvelously human film which seems to capture the essence of Bukowski. (Annotated by Nash Cox.) Produced and directed by Taylor Hackford. 16mm B/W, 58 min. No distributor at this writing, but inquiries may be sent to KCET-TV, 4400 Sunset Dr., Los Angeles, Calif. 90027, Attention: Taylor Hackford, (213) 666-6500.

Truman Capote. THE NONFICTION NOVEL—A VISIT WITH TRUMAN CAPOTE. The author is shown at his Long Island summer home and his Manhattan apartment. He discusses his book *In Cold Blood*, which he considers a new art form that he terms the nonfiction novel. He comments on how and why he came to write the book, describes the characters and his relationship to them, and reads certain episodes from the book. (Description from catalogue.) Produced by Jack Sameth in 1966 for National Educational Television. 16mm B/W, 30 min. Rental: $9.50 for one to five days. Purchase: $165. For videotape of this film see Indiana University under *Videotapes* in the Service Section of this directory. (IU)

R. V. Cassill. See Bruce Jay Friedman.

John Ciardi and others. POET. An interview with three American poets to discover why they write poetry. Questions are asked on whether the poet performs a worthwhile task or is a nonproductive member of society. Opinions are offered concerning the poet's function, choice of subjects, and why much of today's poetry seems incomprehensible. Features John Ciardi, Richard Eberhart, and Kenneth Rexroth. (Description from catalogue.) Produced for KCET-TV. 16mm B/W, 29 min. Rental: $9.50 for one to five days. Purchase: $165. For a videotape of this film see Indiana University under *Videotapes* in the Service Section of this directory. (IU)

Leonard Cohen. LADIES AND GENTLEMEN, MR. LEONARD COHEN. Scences of the poet as he walks around Montreal cafes and parks and in his home. He also reads a few of his poems. (Annotated by Galen Williams.) Produced in 1966 by the National Film Board of Canada. 16mm B/W, 54 min. Rental: $16 for one day. (MH) Purchase: $308. (CMC)

Leo Connellan and Walter Lowenfels. Filmed at Lowenfels' house in Peekskill, New York. Both poets read their work and discuss their philosophy of poetry. (Description from distributor.) 16mm color, 28 min. Rental: $40. Purchase: $350. (LP)

Gregory Corso and others. PULL MY DAISY. Jack Kerouac narrates his own prose poem about the comic afternoon visit of a Buddhist bishop and his mother to a downtown loft full of young poets and artists. The all-star cast (Delphine Seyrig; poets Allen Ginsberg, Peter Orlovsky, Gregory Corso; painters Larry Rivers and Alice Neal; composer David Amram who also provided the music) improvise and cavort. The film's dated attitudes toward women mitigate its charm as a period piece. (Annotated by Honor Moore.) Produced and directed by Robert Frank and Al Leslie. 16mm B/W, 29 min. Rental only: $60 for classroom showing; $100 for public showing. (NY)

Robert Creeley. Robert Creeley is shown with his wife, Bobbie, and their two young daughters in the adobe-like house they shared in 1966 while he was poet-in-residence at the University of New Mexico. Creeley speaks articulately about his craft, specifically the influence of Charles Olson, and reads several poems. This footage about the poet's work is gracefully intercut with his account of growing up in New England. (Annotated by Honor Moore.) Produced in 1966 by Richard Moore for National Educational Television. 16mm B/W, 30 min. Rental: $9.50 for one to five days. Purchase: $165. For a videotape of this film see Indiana University under *Videotapes* in the Service Section of this directory. (IU)

e. e. cummings. THE MAKING OF A POET. Based primarily on still photographs tracing cummings' life. Narration by the poet adapted from his recording of *i: six nonlectures*. Fascinating drawings and watercolors by cummings. However, lack of action presents an incomplete image of the man and the poet. (Annotated by Nash Cox.) Produced by Harold Mantell. 16mm color, 24 min. Rental: $30 for one day. Purchase: $325. For videotape of this film, see Films for the Humanities under *Videotapes* in the Service Section of this directory. (FH)

Ann Darr and others. WHAT IS A POET? Ann Darr, George Garrett, Carolyn Kizer, William Stafford, David Wagoner, Richard Wilbur, and Miller Williams reading their work in various settings. (Description from filmmaker.) 16mm color, 17 min. Purchase and rental information on request. (MM)

James Dickey. LORD, LET ME DIE BUT NOT DIE OUT. A warm and human picture of James Dickey and how he fashions poetry out of the fabric of his own experiences and observations. Especially revealing scenes of the poet at readings before college audiences, discussing poetry with a New York taxi driver and Robert Lowell, and in the field in hunting garb with bow and arrow. (Annotated by Nash Cox.) Produced in collaboration with Clifton Fadiman for the Encyclopaedia Britannica Educational Humanities Program. 16mm color, 37 min. Rental: $22 for three days. Purchase: $450. (EB)

Robert Duncan And John Wieners. . We look over Robert Duncan's shoulder as he writes parts of a long work-in-progress called "Passages Nigh" in this 1966 film. The poet, shown in his San Francisco home, talks in fascinating detail about his writing process and his theory of poetry. In the second half of the film, duncan introduces us to John Wieners and we go with the two poets to a torn-up room in the then-to-be-torn-down Hotel Wentley in San Francisco. There, "on location," Wienres movingly reads the first of his famous Hotel Wentley poems. (Annotated by Honor Moore.) Produced by Brice Howard in 1966 for National Education Television. 16mm B/W, 30 min. Rental: $9.50 for one to five days. Purchase: $165. For videotape of this film, see either San Francisco Poetry Center VideoTape Library or Indiana University under *Videotapes* in the Service Section of this directory. (IU)

Richard Eberhart. IF ONLY I COULD LIVE AT THE PITCH THAT IS NEAR MADNESS. A documentary in Maine, New Hampshire, and other settings. Footage includes Eberhart aboard the cruiser "Reve" in Maine, at his daughter's wedding, as Visiting Professor of English at the University of Washington, at a street fair, etc. Eberhart reads "The Groundhog," "The Fury of Aerial Bombardment," "Froth," "Horse Chestnut Tree," and other poems. (Description from distributor.) Produced in 1973-74 by Irving Broughton. 16mm B/W, 17 min. Purchase and rental information on request. (MM)

Richard Eberhart. Filmed on location at Dartmouth where Eberhart teaches and resides. Through pictures and personal memoirs he tells his story, reads his poetry, and discusses his life work. (Description from distributor.) 16mm color, 26 min. Rental: $40. Purchase: $350. (LP)

Richard Eberhart. See John Ciardi. **Larry Eigner and Allen Ginsberg.** GETTING IT TOGETHER. Eigner, who is severely handicapped, reads his poems with Allen

Ginsberg's help. Comments are offered by Ginsberg on Eigner's hardship and courage. (Description from distributor.) Produced by Leonard M. Henry. 16mm color, 20 min. Rental only: $20 for three days. (HB)

T. S. Eliot. THE MYSTERIOUS MR. ELIOT. Reminiscences from some of Eliot's closest friends (Robert Lowell, Stephen Spender, I. A. Richards, Laurens Van Der Post) and his second wife. Valerie Fletcher. Matched with these interviews are film footage of Eliot reading from *The Four Quartets, Murder in the Cathedral* and from such rarely performed plays as *Sweeney Agonistes* and *The Family Reunion.* Also footage of Burnt Norton, East Coker, Little Gidding. (Description from catalogue.) Narrated by Keir Dullea. Produced jointly by the BBC and Channel 13WNET. In two parts. 16mm color, 62 min. Rental: $50 for one day. Purchase: $750. (MH)

T. S. Eliot. PRUFROCK AND AFTER. A tribute to Eliot, featuring Eliot's voice in readings from tapes, and discussion of his work by E. Martin Brown, Rev. Martin D'Arcy, Paul Horgan, and Robert Speaght. 1965. 16mm color, 30 min. Purchase only: $300. (CBS)

Ralph Ellison. RALPH ELLISON ON WORK IN PROGRESS. A 1966 interview with Ralph Ellison in his New York apartment in which he describes the genesis of his famous novel *The Invisible Man*, discusses his craft, and talks about his life. During the course of the interview, Ellison reads a short section of a work-in-progress. This simple film would be useful in conjunction with reading Ellison's work. (Annotated by Honor Moore.) Produced and directed by Robert Hughes in 1966 for National Educational Television. 16mm B/W, 30 min. Rental: $9.50 for one to five days. Purchase: $165. For videotape of this film see Indiana University under *Videotapes* in the Service Section of this directory. (IU)

Kenward Elmslie. See Daisy Aldan.

Ted Enslin. See Henry Braun.

William Everson (Brother Antoninus). BIRTH OF A POET. The former Brother Antoninus mediates on his life's cyclic process of withdrawal to wilderness and return to society and reads from his work. (Description from distributor.) Produced by David Eberling. 16mm color, 15 min. Rental only: $12 for three days. For another film on William Everson, see listing under Brother Antoninus in this section. (HB)

William Everson. Same as Brother Antoninus. See that listing also.

Harry Fainlight. See Gregory Corso (WHOLLY COMMUNION).

Lawrence Ferlinghetti. ASSASSINATION RAGA. Ferlinghetti reads his poetry with sitar accompaniment to collage visuals of the assassinated "Who's Who" of our time, from Ghandi to Martin Luther King. (Description from distributor.) Produced by Max Cosley. 16mm B/W, 13 min. Rental only: $25 for three days. (HB)

Lawrence Ferlinghetti. See Allen Ginsberg.

Leslie A. Fiedler. See Bruce Jay Friedman.

Edward Field and others. POETRY IS ALIVE AND WELL AND LIVING IN AMERICA. A set of 3 films on Edward Field, G.C. Oden, and May Swenson reading their poetry, and discussing themselves and their work. Field reads "Frankenstein,' and "The Sleeper;" Oden reads "The Way It Is" and "Speculation;', Swenson reads "Still Turning" and ',The Pregnant Dream." (Description from catalogue.) 16mm color, 10 min. each Rental: $30 (set of three). Purchase: $150 each; $425 set of three. Prices include follow-up mini-lessons on Lp records, tapes or tape cassettes, plus teacher's guide. Also available for purchase as 10 min. color, sound filmstrips with mini-lessons, Lp records and guide for $90 (set of six). (MP)

Bruce Jay Friedman. BRUCE JAY FRIEDMAN AND BLACK HUMOR. The black humorist's rationale for coping with some of the horrors of our day. Novelist-critic Leslie A. Fiedler, novelist George Mandell, and author R.V. Cassill discuss Friedman's novel *Stern* and black humor in general. (Description from catalogue.) Produced in 1968 by Jerome Tookin for National Educational Television. 16mm B/W, 30 min. Rental: $9.50 for one to five days. For a videotape of this film see Indiana University under *Videotapes* in the Service Section of this directory. (IU)

Robert Frost. AUTUMN: FROST COUNTRY. Beautiful scenes of nature shown with a sound track of Robert Frost reading "The Road Not Taken" and "Reluctance." Photography and music create a rich, colorful fall tapestry, though the poetry seems almost incidental. (Annotated by Nash Cox.) 16mm color, 9 min. Rental: $10 for three days. Purchase: $125. (BFA)

Robert Frost. A FIRST ACQUAINTANCE. Largely photographed at the Frost Farm in Derry, New Hampshire, where his daughter Lesley lived as a child. Lesley retraces the origins and locales of her father's poems at various sites on the farm. Poems read by Robert and Lesley are interpreted through the actions of children. (Description from catalogue.) Produced by Harold Mantell. 16mm color, 16 min. Rental: $22.50 for one day. Purchase: $225. For a videotape of this film see Films for the Humanities under *Videotapes* in the Service Section of this directory. (FH)

Robert Frost. A LOVER'S QUARREL WITH THE WORLD. Robert Frost in a reading at Sarah Lawrence toward the end of his life is intercut with scenes at his farm and with John Kennedy and others. A warm, candid Frost is shown, full of homey wisdom, though his darker side is never far from the surface. An important film for its balanced portrait of Frost and the effect he had on audiences and individuals. (Annotated by Nash Cox.) Directed by Shirley Clarke. 16mm B/W, 40 min. Rental: $24 for three days. Purchase: $290. (BFA)

Robert Frost. Frost discusses his life and work at his farm home in Vermont. A lifelong critic of regimentation in schools and universities, he recalls the wide range of personal experiences—mill worker, country school teacher, cobbler, small-town editor, and farmer—that furnished the background for his poetry. He reads "Stopping by Woods on a Snowy Evening" and "The Drublin Woodchuck." (Description from catalogue.) 16mm B/W, 30 min. Rental: $14 for one day. (LL)

George Garrett. See Ann Darr.

Allen Ginsberg. SEPTEMBER ON JESSORE ROAD. Allen Ginsberg filmed travelling through Bangladesh in 1971 with a soundtrack of Ginsberg reading/singing "September on Jessore Road." Shot in 8mm and blown up to 16mm, which results in a fuzzy picture. Nevertheless, a fascinating glimpse of the beardless Ginsberg. (Annotated by Nash Cox.) 16mm color, 10 min. Rental: $25. Purchase: $100. (GI)

Allen Ginsberg and Lawrence Ferlinghetti. The first portion deals with Allen Ginsberg and documents his way of life—at his home, in San Francisco's City Lights Bookshop, and in the studio of painter Bob Levyne. He reads "Who To Be Kind To," "From New York to San Fran," and "The Guru" and also excerpts from *Howl and Other Poems* and "Notes for Howl and Other Poems." Lawrence Ferlinghetti is the principal owner and editor of City Lights Booksellers and Publishers, San Francisco. He is filmed in his office and on the streets of San Francisco where he reads his own poetry, including "Dog" and an excerpt from "The Situation in the West." (Description from catalogue.) Produced in 1966 by Brice Howard for National Educational Television. 16mm B/W, 30 min. Rental: $9.50 for one to five days. For a videotape of this film see Indiana University under *Videotapes* in the Service Section of this directory. (IU)

Allen Ginsberg and Peter Orlovsky. ME AND MY BROTHER. Only a quarter of this overlong film deals directly with the effort poets Peter Orlovsky and Allen Ginsberg made to care for the former's schizophrenic brother Julius outside a hospital; these parts are often very moving. The rest of the film, though occasionally imagistically brilliant, is confusing and full of scenes that seem irrelevant. In fiction passages that filmmaker Robert Frank has intercut with documentary footage, actor Joseph Chaikin plays Julius. In these sections, many aspects of the poets' world are explored in detail, including trips to the dentist, reading tours, and sexual encounters. (Annotated by Honor Moore.) 16mm color, 93 min. Rental only: $60 for classroom use; $100 for public showing. (NY)

Allen Ginsberg. See Gregory Corso (PULL MY DAISY). Also see Larry Eigner.

Gunter Grass. An introduction to the prose, poetry, personality, and politics of German writer Gunter Grass. He reads a short excerpt from his novel *The Tin Drum.* He is also shown reading his poem ,'Metz" to a book store audience and his unpublished work "Advent" to the men at a German airbase. A speech by Grass advocating that young voters not vote for the Neo-Nazi party is the focus of a political rally. Grass is also visited in his studio where he discusses his background and political sympathies. (Description from catalogue.) Produced and directed in 1966 by Michael Blackwood for National Educational Television. 16MM B/W, 30 min. Rental: $9.50 for one to five days. Purchase: $165. For a videotape of this film see Indiana University under *Videotapes* in the Service Section of this directory. (IU)

Arthur Gregor. THINGS THAT ABIDE. The poet reading and discussing his work. (Description from distributor.) Produced by CBS-TV in 1973. 16mm color, 30 min. Purchase only: $300. (CBS)

Lorraine Hansberry. TO BE YOUNG, GIFTED, AND BLACK. Portrays Lorraine Hansberry's struggles, from her first visit to the South, to the streets of Harlem. Much of the script is in her own words drawn from plays, letters, and diaries written prior to her premature death from cancer at the age of 34. (Description from catalogue.) Produced in 1972 by Robert M. Fresco and directed by Michael A. Schultz for National Educational Television. 16mm color, 90 min. Rental: $27 for one to five days. Purchase: $665. For a videotape of this film see Indiana University under *Videotapes* in the Service Section of this directory. (IU)

Seamus Heaney. POET IN LIMBOLAND. A powerful film about a poet greatly affected by the conflict in Northern Ireland. Narrator and Heaney explore his roots in the country and influences on his poetry. Scenes of the civil war intercut with Heaney reading poetry make the tragedy vividly real. A moving account of the influence of the war on a sensitive man living in "the country of the damned." (Annotated by Nash Cox.) Produced by London Weekend Television. 16mm color, 28 1/2 min. Rental: $35 for one day. Purchase: $340. For videotape of this film see Films for the Humanities under *Videotapes* in the Service Section of this directory. (FH)

Ernest Hemingway. HEMINGWAY. Using old footage and stills, this movie shows how Hemingway's boyhood in America and his adventures overseas provided the material for his most important novels and short stories. The contrast between Hemingway's hatred of war and his life-long love of bull-fighting and hunting is examined in detail, along with the influences of such friends as James Joyce, F. Scott Fitzgerald, and, above all, Gertrude Stein. (Description from catalogue.) narrated by Chet Huntley. In two parts. 16mm B/W, 54 min. Rental: $30 for one day. Purchase: $410. (MH)

Ernest Hemingway. HEMINGWAY'S SPAIN. In this trilogy, the country and people who play so powerful a role in Hemingway's imagination are recaptured by the camera. Actors Rod Steiger and Jason Robards read from Hemingway's works. (Description from catalogue.) 16mm color, 52 min. total. In three parts, separately titled and priced. FOR WHOM THE BELL TOLLS (Rental: $15 for one day. Purchase: $305). DEATH IN THE AFTERNOON (Rental: $15. Purchase: $240). THE SUN ALSO RISES (Rental: $15. Purchase: $275). (MH)

Constance Hunting. See Henry Braun.

Lawson Inada. I TOLD YOU SO. A portrait of Asian American poet, Lawson Inada, which travels from his past as a child in Fresno, California to his present as a professor of English at Southern Oregon University. The film examines the multicultural influences which have created a unique artist. (Description from catalogue.) 16mm B/W, 18 min. Rental: $20 plus postage. Purchase: $230. (AB)

Robinson Jeffers. ROBINSON JEFFERS: GIVE YOUR HEART TO THE HAWKS. The poet Robinson Jeffers died five years before this film project got underway, but filmmaker David Myers had access to several tape recordings in which Jeffers reads from his works, and to his home and study, Tor House and Hawk Tower, in Carmel, California. Dame Judith Anderson reads a speech from *The Tower Beyond Tragedy* in the ideal setting of Hawk Tower and portrays Clytemnestra. Walter Van Tilburg Clark comments on the poet's philosophy and vision, his hatred of urban civilization, and his belief that we have betrayed our roots in nature. Although the 1941 recordings

of Jeffers are not flawless, this literary analysis of his work is honest and effective, and the film is an aesthetic triumph. (Description from catalogue.) 16mm B/W, 30 min. Rental: $13 for one day. (LL)

Robinson Jeffers. Snapshots from the Jeffers' family album provide an intimate glimpse of his family life. Recordings of his works made in 1914 by Jeffers are matched to illustrative scenes. An assessment of the poet and his works is given by novelist Walter Van Tilburg Clark and Dame Judith Anderson. Dame Anderson dramatically presents a passage from Jeffers' "The Power Beyond Tragedy." (Description from catalogue.) Produced and directed in 1967 by David Myers for National Educational Television. 16mm B/W, 30 min. Rental: $9.50 for one to five days. Purchase: $165. For a videotape of this film see Indiana University under *Videotapes* in the Service Section of this directory. (IU)

James Jones. THE PRIVATE WORLD OF JAMES JONES. Jones is seen participating in varied activities from skeet-shooting to shopping with his wife, and socializing with friends. He discusses his past, his approach to writing, and expounds on many subjects as varied as sexual frustration and the Viet Nam war. (Description from catalogue.) Produced and directed in 1967 by Allan King for National Educational Television. 16mm B/W, 30 min. Rental: $9.50 sor one to five days. Purchase: $165. For a videotape of this film see Indiana University under *Videotapes* in the Service Section of this directory. (IU)

Norman Jordan. DEAD ENDS AND NEW DREAMS. As seen through Jordan's imagery of the Cleveland ghetto, he urges black youths to express their innermost feelings and use words as their weapons. He sensitizes whites to the pride and problems of America's black people. (Description from catalogue.) 16mm color, 25 min. Rental: $30. Purchase: $330. (MH)

James Joyce. FAITHFUL DEPARTED. From a collection of 40,000 rare period photographs, director Kieran D. Hickey has drawn a vivid film portrait of Dublin as it was in 1904—the setting for James Joyce's novel *Ulysses*. Here are the scenes of Joyce's childhood and adolescence, and his meeting with Nora Barnacle on June 16, 1904—the day when time stood still for Dedalus and Bloom. The music, drawn from the songs referred to in *Ulysses*, and the narration by Dublin-born actor Jack MacGowran evoke the mood of Dublin and its people as they were in Joyce's youth. (Description from catalogue.) 16mm B/W, 10 min. Rental: $12.50 for one day. Purchase: $145. (MH)

James Joyce. SILENCE, EXILE AND CUNNING. Similar to an illustrated lecture focused on Joyce's birthday. Anthony Burgess recreates the world of Joyce through pictures, revisiting places important to Joyce, emphasizing influences on his life: Dublin and Roman Catholicism. Narrator reads passages from Joyce's work. Reverent attitude toward Joyce results in a pedantic and pretentious film. (Annotated by Nash Cox.) 16mm B/W, 30 min. Rental: $40 for three days. Purchase: $385. (TL)

Gylan Kain and others. RIGHT ON: POETRY BY THE LAST POETS. Written and performed by Gylan Kain, Felipe Luciano, and David Nelson. Black poetry which fuses gospel, soul music, street theater, and ritual. Shot in the streets of New York in 1971. (Description from distributor.) Produced by Woodie King, Jr. 16mm and 35mm color, 72 min. Rental: $125. Purchase: $1,100, subject to negotiation for groups. (NL)

Chester Kallman. See Daisy Aldan.

Jack Kerouac. See Gregory Corso (PULL MY DAISY).

Carolyn Kizer. See Ann Darr.

Kenneth Koch. WISHES, LIES AND DREAMS. TEACHING CHILDREN TO WRITE POETRY. A film about the poet teaching writing to fifth and sixth graders at P.S. 61 in New York City. Made by the National Endowment for the Arts. (Description from distributor.) 16mm color, 30 min. Purchase only: $99.50. (NAV)

Philip Lamantia. MAN IS IN PAIN. Set to a poem by Lamantia, it depicts an empty room as experienced by a hand reaching out, touching and grasping objects in the room and moving through it. (Description from catalogue.) Produced by Larry Jordan, 1955. 16mm B/W, 6 min. Rental only: $7.50. (ABF)

D.H. Lawrence. D.H. LAWRENCE IN TAOS. Taos, New Mexico, is the desert town where Lawrence lived in the 1920's and where his ashes repose today. British director Peter Davis focuses his cameras on the townspeople and friends who still revere Lawrence, including artist Dorothy Brett, who vied for Lawrence's affections nearly half a century ago. Combines contemporary interviews with rare old photographs and excerpts from Lawrence's writings and lectures. (Description from catalogue.) 16mm color, 41 min. Rental: $30 for one day. Purchase: $570. (MH)

D.H. Lawrence. AMERICAN INDIANS AS SEEN BY D.H. LAWRENCE. At the Lawrence ranch near Taos, New Mexico, where Lawrence spent most of his later years, his wife Frieda speaks intimately about his beliefs and thoughts. Aldous Huxley presents selections from Lawrence on the religious and ceremonial impulses of Indian culture as shown by various ritual dances. (Description from catalogue.) 16mm color, 13 1/2 min. Rental: $10 for three days; (MF). Purchase: $164 for color print; (CIF).

Robert Lax. NEW FILM. A film based on Lax's book *New Poems*. Produced by Emil Antonucci. 16mm B/W, 20 min. Rental: $25. Purchase: $175. (JP)

Robert Lax. RED & BLUE. A film of three Robert Lax poems, "Red & Blue," "Slap Bank," and "Sleeping Waking." Produced by Emil Antonucci. 16mm color, 25 min. Rental: $25. Purchase: $200. (JP)

Robert Lax. SHORTS. Many short Lax poems. Produced by Emil Antonucci. 16mm color, 20 min. Rental: $25. Purchase: $200. (JP)

Denise Levertov and Charles Olson. Denise Levertov is seen in her home, where she reads "Life at War," "Losing Track," "The Ache of Marriage," "Two Angels." She also discusses her reasons for being a poet and her methods of work. Charles Olson, also seen at home, describes his concept of open-verse composition and recites "The Leap, "She Said. . .," "Maximus to Dogtown," "Letter 27," and "The Librarian." (Description from catalogue.) Produced in 1966 by Richard Moore for National Educational Television. 16mm B/W, 30 min. Rental: $9.50 for one to

five days. Purchase: $165. For Olson section on videotape see Cable Arts under *Videotapes* in the Service Section of this directory. For videotape of entire film see Indiana University under *Videotapes* in the Service Section of this directory. (IU)

Robert Lowell and Richard Wilbur. In his Portland, Connecticut home, Richard Wilbur reads "On the Marginal Way," "Love Calls Us to the Things of this World," and "Advice to a Prophet." In his New York studio, Robert Lowell reads "Water," "Soft Wood," "A Flaw," "Fall 1961," and "The Opposite House." (Description from catalogue.) Produced in 1966 by Richard Moore for National Educational Television. 16mm B/W, 30 min. Rental: $9.50 for one to five days. Purchase: $165. For Lowell section on videotape see Cable Arts under *Videotapes* in the Service Section of this directory. For entire film on videotape see Indiana University under *Videotapes* in the Service Section of this directory. (IU)

Robert Lowell. See James Dickey.

Walter Lowenfels. See Leo Connellan.

Felipe Luciano. See Gylan Kain.

Toby Lurie. INNOCENCE. Animation and live action are combined for a reflection on the topic of war. The poet is heard reading his poetry but does not appear in the film. (Description from distributor.) Produced by Steve Michaels. 16mm color, 3-1/2 min. Rental only: $5 for three days. (HB)

George Mandel. See Bruce Jay Friedman.

Vladimir Mayakovsky. MAYAKOVSKY: THE POETRY OF ACTION. A fascinating study of Mayakovsky, focusing on his life as a revolutionary. Despite a melodramatic narrator and distracting music, the film captures his passion. Mayakovsky is shown in his milieu with many photographs of the poet and his art, relevant old film clips, and even a rare recording of Mayakovsky reading his poetry. Not only a portrait of the poet, but a vivid glimpse of his world. (Annotated by Nash Cox.) Produced by Harold Mantell. 16mm color, 22 min. Rental: $27.50 for one day. Purchase: $300. For a videotape of this film see Films for the Humanities under *Videotapes* in the Service Section of this directory. (FH)

Michael McClure. See Brother Antoninus.

Arthur Miller. PSYCHOLOGY AND ARTHUR MILLER. Part I (50 min.): Playwright Arthur Miller discusses conceptions of motivation and his own reactions to the psychoanalysis of an author through his work. Part II (55 min.): Miller's reactions to major personality theories, art vs. science and his own reflections on contemporary problems. (Description from catalogue.) 16mm B/W. Parts can be ordered separately. Rental (each): $17.50 for one showing. Purchase (each): $275. (ABF)

Henry Miller. HENRY MILLER ASLEEP AND AWAKE. Henry Miller is in the film but otherwise no description is available at this writing. Produced by Tom Schiller. 16mm color, 30 min. Rental: $40 for classroom showing; $75 for public showing. Purchase: $395. (NY)

Henry Miller. THE HENRY MILLER ODYSSEY. Among other things, Miller reminisces. (Further description unavailable at this writing.) Produced and directed by Robert Snyder. 16mm B/W with color sequences, 110 min. Rental: $150. Purchase: $1,350. (GP)

Vladimir Nabokov. Living with his wife in Montreux, Switzerland, naturalized American novelist Vladimir Nabokov holds his first filmed interview. He talks of his life and work including a novel in progress. As he discusses his past, scenes illustrative of his early life in Europe and America are shown. His comments on contemporary novelists include tart observations about the public's acceptance of works by Mann, Faulkner, and Pasternak. (Description from catalogue.) Directed by Robert Hughes and Terence Macarthy in 1966 for National Educational Television. 16mm B/W, 29 min. Rental: $9.50 for one to five days. Purchase: $165. For a videotape of this film see Indiana University under *Videotapes* in the Service Section of this directory. (IU)

John G. Neihardt. PERFORMING THE VISION. John G. Neihardt, poet and author of *Black Elk Speaks*, tells of his relationship with Black Elk and reads from his own poetry. In addition to interview material, the film successfully attempts to document the sources and spirit of Neihardt's work through the use of landscape imagery and stunning 19th century photographs of North American Indians. Valuable, too, as a record of an older poet. (Annotated by Janet Sternburg.) Directed by Bob Dyer and Michael Welber. 16mm color, 20 min. Rental: $20. Purchase: $300. (FF)

David Nelson. See Gylan Kain.

Pablo Neruda. I AM PABLO NERUDA. Scenes of Neruda's surroundings in Chile, such as the market place, zoo, and his seaside home. Anthony Quayle narrates and reads translations of his poetry relevant to the scenes. Neruda shown as a warm human figure, though politics are not mentioned. The origins of his poetry, deeply rooted in his life in Chile, are vividly conveyed. (Annotated by Nash Cox.) Produced by Harold Mantell. 16mm B/W, 28 1/2 min. Rental: $25 for one day. Purchase: $240. For a videotape of this film see Films for the Humanities under *Videotapes* in the Service Section of this directory. (FH)

Anais Nin. BELLS OF ATLANTIS. A film based on Anais Nin's prose poem, *The House of Incest*, and the line, "I remember my first birth in water." Performed by and commentary spoken by Anais Nin. (Description from catalogue.) Produced and photographed by Ian Hugo. 16mm color, 10 min. Rental: $20. Purchase: $190. (FI)

Anais Nin. ANAIS OBSERVED: A FILM PORTRAIT OF A WOMAN AS ARTIST. The famous writer at home. She talks with students about her life, the lives of the many famous people she has known, and writing as a profession. Film technique unfortunately interferes in an overstatement of the artist's 'visionary' stance. But, finally, a person of remarkable bearing, and the film is therefore well worth seeing. (Annotated by Cheri Fein.) Produced and directed by Robert Snyder. 16mm color, 68 min. Rental: $150. Purchase: $1,000. (GP)

G.C. Oden. See Edward Field.

Frank O'Hara and Ed Sanders. O'Hara, shown in his workshop, reads from "The Day Lady Died," "Song," "Having a Coke With You," and a film script. Sanders discusses pacifism and reads from "Cemetery Hill" while sitting in his bookstore on New York's lower east side. Part of his night club act as a rock-and-roll singer is shown. (Description from catalogue.) Produced by Richard Moore in 1966 for National Educational Television. 16mm B/W, 30 min. Rental: $9.50 for one to five days. Purchase: $165. For the O'Hara section on videotape see Cables Arts under *Videotapes* in the Service Section of this directory. For the entire film on videotape see Indiana University under *Videotapes* in the Service Section of this directory. (IU)

Frank O'Hara. See Daisy Aldan.

Charles Olson. MAXIMUS TO HIMSELF. Filmed at Olson's home in Gloucester, Mass. (No further description available at this writing.) Produced by Theodora Cichy and William David Sherman. 1967. 16mm B/W with color sequences. 5 min. Rental only: $10, plus $4 for handling, for one showing. (FC)

Charles Olson. See Denise Levertov.

Peter Orlovsky. See Gregory Corso (PULL MY DAISY). Also see Allen Ginsberg (ME AND MY BROTHER).

Kenneth Patchen. PLAGUE SUMMER. Based on *The Journal of Albion Moonlight*. A record of the journey of six allegorical characters through landscapes brutalized by war. Uses drawings (whether Patchen's own, the catalogue does not say) to reflect the mental climate of a sensitive artist in the war-torn summer of 1940. (Description from catalogue.) Produced by Chester Kessler in 1951. 16mm B/W, 17 min. Rental only: $15. (ABF)

S.J. Perelman. Perelman is seen at his home in Pennsylvania discussing the authors who have influenced him and the reasons why a writer must imitate somebody. He then goes on to talk about F. Scott Fitzgerald and Nathanael West, among other writers and topics. (Description from catalogue.) Produced by Jerome Tookin in 1966 for National Educational Television. 16mm B/W, 30 min. Rental: $9.50 for one to five days. Purchase: $165. For a videotape of this film see Indiana University under *Videotapes* in the Service Section of this directory. (IU)

Ezra Pound. A profile of Ezra Pound at his daughter's castle in Italy. He speaks of his life and quotes from his poetry. (Description from distributor.) Originally produced for BBC. 16mm B/W, 15 min. Rental: $12.50 for one day. Purchase: $140. (MH)

Ezra Pound. EZRA POUND: POET'S POET. Focuses on Pound's influence on modern poetry as a poet and a mentor of major literary figures. Scenes of Pound toward the end of his life reading his poetry and talking, interspersed with old photographs and film clips explained by a narrator. A sanitized introduction to a controversial figure—lacking depth for those who know his life and work. (Annotated by Nash Cox.) Produced by Harold Mantell. 16mm B/W, 28 1/2 min. Rental: $25 for one day. Purchase: $240. For a videotape of this film see Films for the Humanities under *Videotapes* in the Service Section of this directory. (FH)

Ezra Pound. Shot at the Spoleto Festival in 1965, this film shows Pound sitting at lunch with Olga Rudge and other friends. He spontaneously recites "Canto I" in a quavering but clear voice while on screen are images of his face and scenes of strolls through Spoleto. A touching film. (Annotated by Cheri Fein.) 16mm B/W, 8 min. Purchase only: $80. For a videotape of this film see Blackwood Productions under *Videotapes* in the Service Section of this directory. (BP)

Kenneth Rexroth. See John Ciardi.

Theodore Roethke. IN A DARK TIME is an extraordinary and vivid portrait of Theodore Roethke made just before his death in 1963. The poet's readings of his poems (including "In A Dark Time," "Papa's Waltz," and "Elegy for Jane") intersect his reflections on poetry and his life as a poet and teacher. Visually the film combines evocative footage of the Washington State coast and countryside Roethke loved with a documentary record of the poet teaching, reading his work, and writing. (Annotated by Honor Moore.) 16mm B/W, 27-1/2 min. Rental: $15 for one day. Purchase: $190. (MH)

Ted Rosenthal. HOW COULD I NOT BE AMONG YOU. An articulate, very personal film about a young poet who discovers he has a fatal illness and only a short time to live. A rare and real look at death—avoids sentimentality and excess emotion. (Annotated by Nash Cox.) 16mm color, 28 min. Rental: $35. Purchase: $390. (H)

Henry Roth. A series of interviews between Henry Roth, author of *Call It Sleep*, and John Williams, another American novelist, during which Roth discusses his first novel and its effect upon his life. Stills are used to depict scenes from Roth's past. Thirty years were required for his first novel to be acclaimed a success. Roth discusses how this affected his further attempts to write and talks about himself in general. (Description from catalogue.) Produced by Eliot Tozer and John Williams in 1966 for National Educational Television. 16mm B/W, 30 min. Rental: $9.50. Purchase: $165. For a videotape of this film see Indiana University under *Videotapes* in the Service Section of this directory. (IU)

Philip Roth. Roth discusses his stories and plays with Jerre Mangione and explains the covert and ostensible meanings of his works. The interview takes place in Roth's apartment in Greenwich Village, New York. The relationship of his work to that of Saul Bellow and Roth's reactions to critics' reviews are also discussed. (Description from catalogue.) Produced by Jerome Tookin in 1966 for National Educational Television. 16mm B/W, 30 min. Rental: $9.50 for one to five days. Purchase: $165. For a videotape of this film see Indiana University under *Videotapes* in the Service Section of this directory. (IU)

James Salter. A filmmaker, director, film writer, and novelist, James Salter has won international acclaim for his novel, *A Sport and A Pastime* and films, *Downhill Racer* and *Three*. Actor Robert Redford, star of *Downhill Racer*, describes him as a writer and director who "backs off a bit and makes room for spontaneous behavior." In this film Salter is seen in the resort community of Aspen, Colorado, a retreat from the stimulating chaos of New York, his other spiritual home. (Description from catalogue.) 16mm color, 30 min. Rental: $12.50 for one to five days. Purchase: $315. (IU)

Carl Sandburg. THE BEST OF SANDBURG. A tribute to Carl Sandburg with clips from televised appearances with Edward R. Murrow and H.K. Smith. Produced by CBS-TV in 1966. 16mm B/W, 30 min. Purchase only: $300. (CBS)

Carl Sandburg. CARL SANDBURG DISCUSSES HIS WORK. Filmed at his farm in North Carolina, Sandburg speaks of his early years, his struggle to gain fame, and his philosophy. He comments on his writing and reads passages from *The People, Yes*, and *Remembrance Rock*. (Description from catalogue.) Produced in cooperation with CBS from an interview with Edward R. Murrow. 16mm B/W, 13 1/2 min. Rental only: $10 for three days. (MF)

Carl Sandburg. THE WORLD OF CARL SANDBURG. Based on the stage presentation by Norman Corwin. An exploration of Carl Sandburg's love affair with America—as gleaned from his poetry, his collections of American folk music and humor and his towering biography of Lincoln. Corwin has drawn upon Sandburg's ten published volumes as well as several never-published pieces. Sandburg himself chose the music performed by balladeers Carolyn Hester and the Tarriers. He is also heard in a memorable poetry recording. Uta Hagen and Fritz Weaver handle the other readings. (Description from catalogue.) Produced by National Educational Television. In two parts. 16mm B/W, 59 min. Rental: $30 for one day. Purchase: $405. (MH)

Ed Sanders. See Frank O'Hara.

James Schuyler. See Daisy Aldan.

Armand Schwerner. Reading some of the *Tablets* at a site overlooking the Verrazzano Bridge in New York on the Wagner College Campus. Produced by Phil Niblock. 16mm color, 11 min. No distributor at this writing, but inquiries may be sent to Phil Niblock, 224 Centre St., New York, N.Y. 10013, (212) 431-5127.

Leopold Sedar Senghor. An introduction to Leopold Sedar Senghor, his poetry, and the environment which his poems reflect. President Senghor also discusses his philosophy concerning the blending of the African and the Western culture traditions. Leopold Senghor is the poet laureate and the president of the republic of Senegal. Maurice Sonnar Senghor, director of the National Theater of Senegal, reads five of President Senghor's poems in English. During the poetry readings the locales described in the poetry are shown. (Description from catalogue.) Produced by Henry Dore for National Educational Television. 16mm B/W, 30 min. Rental: $9.50 for one to five days. Purchase: $165. (IU)

Anne Sexton. This film provides a candid view of Anne Sexton in her home and introduces her poetry. She explains how seeing a television program in which I.A. Richards lectured on the sonnet form ". . .turned me on." After viewing the program she began to construct sonnets and went from there to other forms of poetry. She is seen in various rooms of her house and outdoors in the yard as she reads her poems "Her Kind," "Self in 1958," "Ringing the Bells," "The Addict," "Young," "Those Times," "Little Girl," "My String Bean," "My Lovely Woman," and "Live." She also describes her family tree and talks briefly about her life in a mental hospital. (Description from catalogue.) Produced by Richard Moore for National Educational

Television. 16mm B/W, 30 min. Rental only: $9.50 for one to five days. For a videotape of this film see Indiana University under *Videotapes* in the Service Section of this directory. (IU)

Isaac Bashevis Singer. ISAAC SINGER'S NIGHTMARE & MRS. PUPKO'S BEARD. Based on the short story, *Beard*, by Isaac Bashevis Singer. Narrated by the author (description from distributor). Produced by Bruce Davidson. 16mm color, 30 min. Rental: $60 for classroom use, $100 for public rental. (NY)

Gary Snyder and Philip Whalen. While Whalen reads his work "Homage to Rodin," the film shows the Palace of the Legion of Honor and Rodin's sculptures. Gary Snyder, in a student uniform brought from Japan, reads "Hay for the Horses," "Above Pate Valley," and "The Market." (Description from catalogue.) Produced by Brice Howard in 1966 for National Educational Television. 16mm B/W, 30 min. Rental: $9.50 for one to five days. Purchase: $165. For a videotape of this film see Indiana University under *Videotapes* in the Service Section of this directory. (IU)

William Stafford. See Ann Darr.

Frank Stanford. IT WASN'T A DREAM: IT WAS A FLOOD. About the creative process and use of the subconscious and dreams in the poetry of Stanford. The film is the poet's dreams, and includes imagery filmed on location in Arkansas, Mississippi, and Missouri. Also, Stanford reads from his work. (Description from filmmaker.) 16mm B/W, 26 min. Rental and purchase information on request. (MM)

Gertrude Stein. WHEN THIS YOU SEE, REMEMBER ME. Rare photographs and documentary footage recreate Gertrude Stein's Paris and her circle of admirers, both French and American. Interviews with Jacques Lipschitz, Virgil Thomson, Janet Flanner and Bennett Cerf. Readings from Gertrude Stein's own works—and her reflections on such friends as Hemingway, F. Scott Fitzgerald and Sherwood Anderson—round out a portrait of this legendary woman as author, hostess, art collector and, above all, cultural catalyst. (Description from catalogue.) Produced and directed by Perry Miller Adato. In three parts. 16mm color, 89 min. Rental: $50 for one day. Purchase: $985. (MH) (LL)

Ruth Stone. THE EXCUSE: THE POETRY OF RUTH STONE. In this simply made and moving film, Ruth Stone reads several of her poems, speaks of her development as a poet, and recounts her struggle to come to terms with her husband's suicide. Filmed in and around her home, the film conveys the immediacy of a visit with a friend who is sharing her thoughts and her work. (Annotated by Janet Sternburg.) Directed by Sidney Wolinsky. 16mm color, 20 min. Inquire for rental and purchase prices. (LL)

May Swenson. See Edward Field.

Nathaniel Tarn. THE GREAT ODOR OF SUMMER. A film interpretation of Tarn's poem, "The Great Odor of Summer," written shortly after the killing of four Kent State University students on May 4, 1970. With Terry Riley's musical composition, *In C./*. Produced by David Lenfest. (Description from catalogue.) 16mm color, 9 min. Rental: $20. Purchase: $150. (FI)

Dylan Thomas. A BRONZE MASK. Lack of unity spoils what could have been a fine film. Thomas reads a series of poems linked by visual images and a narrator explaining the poet's view. Images are often distracting. Absence of an imaginative approach and the overexposed color of the print make this film particularly disappointing. (Annotated by Nash Cox.) Produced by BBC-TV. 16mm color, 30 min. Rental: $45 for three days. Purchase: $385. For videocassette of this film see Time-Life Films under *Videotapes* in the Service Section of this directory. (TL)

Dylan Thomas. A CHILD'S CHRISTMAS IN WALES. Thomas' own reminiscences of his Welsh childhood. Narrated by the poet accompanied by Welsh harp music. (Description from catalogue.) 16mm B/W, 26 min. Rental: $20 for one day. Purchase: $240. (MH)

Dylan Thomas. THE DAYS OF DYLAN THOMAS. Rare photographs recapture Thomas' childhood on the Welsh sea coast, his youthful fling in London, his two visits to the U.S. and his on-again, off-again bouts with the extremes of happiness and despair. Interspersed throughout are candid remarks as well as readings by Thomas himself from many of his works. (Description from catalogue.) 16mm B/W, 21 min. Rental: $15 for one day. Purchase: $200. (MH)

Dylan Thomas. A DYLAN THOMAS MEMOIR. The voice of the great Welsh poet, recorded at various poetry readings before his death in 1953, narrates much of this film, while the camera visualizes the places and people he knew and wrote about. The candor of his wife Caitlin's reminiscences and the black and white photographs of the poet at home, with his wife, in pubs, and on lecture tours put us in touch with both the man and poet. Poems in the film include "Sonnet," "In My Craft or Sullen Art," "Over St. John's Hill." Prose selections are excerpted from "Reminiscences of Childhood" and "A Visit to America." (Description from catalogue.) Produced by Bayley Silleck. 16mm or 8 mm color, 28 min. Rental: $25 for one day. Purchase: $350. For a videotape of this film see Pyramid Films under *Videotapes* in the Service Section of this directory. (PF)

Piri Thomas. THE WORLD OF PIRI THOMAS. Piri Thomas is a painter, ex-con, poet, and ex-junkie. He is also the author of the book *Down These Mean Streets*. In this film, Thomas takes the viewer on a tour of Spanish Harlem. (Description from catalogue.) Produced by Richard McCutchen in 1968 for National Educational Television. Special Segment Director: Gordon Parks. 16mm color or B/W, 60 min. Rental: $20.75 (color), $15.25 (B/W). Purchase: $550 (color), $265 (B/W). For a videotape of this film see Indiana University under *Videotapes* in the Service Section of this directory. (IU)

R.S. Thomas. R.S. THOMAS: PRIEST AND POET. The Welsh poet reads 4-5 poems and discusses his relationship to his parish and to the Welsh countryside as these influence his writing. (Description from distributor.) Produced by John Ormond for BBC, Wales. 16mm color, 28 min. Available for free preview only. (CIE)

Dalton Trumbo. Dalton Trumbo, the once-blacklisted author and screenwriter, recalls his 1947 appearance before the House Committee on Un-American Activities and discusses his subsequent conviction for contempt of

Congress. Noting the changing attitudes toward dissent and filmmaking, Trumbo explains his decision to make *Johnny Got His Gun*, his controversial anti-war novel, into a feature film. Trumbo expresses his fears for the United States and his strong sense of obligation to actively help his country. (Description from distributor.) Produced by Barbara Gordon in 1971 for National Educational Television. 16mm B/W, 10 min. Rental: $5.25. Purchase: $85. (IU)

John Updike. Filmed interviews in which the writer discusses beliefs, concepts, and attitudes which have influenced his novels. He is seen at his home in Ipswich, Massachusetts, reading selections from several of his short stories, including "My Grandmother's Thimble," and "Packed Dirt" from *Pigeon Feathers*. (Description from catalogue.) Produced by Jack Sommers in 1966 for National Educational Television. 16mm B/W, 30 min. Rental: $9.50 for one to five days. Purchase: $165. For a videotape of this film see Indiana University under *Videotapes* in the Service Section of this directory. (IU)

Kurt Vonnegut. BETWEEN TIME AND TIMBUKTOO—A SPACE FANTASY. Incorporates excerpts from about six novels and one play by Vonnegut. (Description from distributor.) 16mm color, 90 min. Rental: $250 for one week. Purchase: $1,250, subject to negotiation for groups. For a videotape of this film, see New Lines Cinema under *Videotapes* in the Service Section of this directory. (NL)

Kurt Vonnegut, Jr. KURT VONNEGUT, JR.: A SELF-PORTRAIT. The novelist speaks candidly about his self-discovery as a writer; his themes and their meaning; his relationship to other writers, past and present; his problems in sustaining his special vision of American life in his novels and plays. Vonnegut discusses and illustrates some of his famous novels. Intended for high school, college and library audiences and for use in courses in modern American literature, the 20th century novel, language arts, and creative writing. (Description from news release.) Produced and directed by Harold Mantell. 16mm color, 29 min. Rental: $37.50. Purchase: $380. (FH)

David Wagoner. See Ann Darr.

Philip Whalen. See Gary Snyder.

Walt Whitman. THE NEIGHBORING SHORE. The United States as interpreted visually through more than 100 striking woodcuts by artist Antonio Frasconi and narrated with selections from the poetry of Walt Whitman. (Description from catalogue.) Narrated by Pat Hingle. Produced in 1960 by Sidney Meyers and others. 16mm color, 15 min. Rental: $15 for one showing. Purchase: $200. (ABF)

John Wieners. See Robert Duncan.

Richard Wilbur. See Ann Darr. Also see Robert Lowell.

Thornton Wilder. A biography. Interviews with his brother and sisters, family snapshots, and other still photographs tell the story of Wilder's life and family background. This account is supplemented with recorded excerpts from his speeches, quotations from his writings, and film clips. The themes of several of his works are briefly analyzed for social meaning. (Description from catalogue.) Produced by Virginia Kassel in 1967 for National Educational Television. 16mm B/W, 30 hin. Rental: $9.50 for one to five

days. Purchase: $165. For a videotape of this film see Indiana University under *Videotapes* in the Service Section of this directory. (IU)

Thornton Wilder. This documentary ranges from Grover's Corners, New Hampshire, to Peru; from Germany to Broadway and the author's home in Hamden, Connecticut. Included are sequences of Wilder with the German director Max Reinhardt and the writer Gertrude Stein. Wilder himself reads excerpts from his plays and novels, including *The Ides of March*, and discloses his views on the craft of writing and on the importance of ideas in literature. (Description from catalogue.) Narrated by actor David Wayne. Produced by Harold Mantell. 16mm B/W, 24 min. Rental: $22.50 for one day. Purchase: $225. For a videotape of this film see Films for the Humanities under *Videotapes* in the Service Section of this directory. (FH)

Emmett Williams and others. CONCRETE POETRY. Concrete poetry brought alive with image and sound. Not every poem is successfully animated, but many are fresh and fun to watch. A teacher's manual is available. (Annotated by Nash Cox.) Produced by Michael Warshaw and Rainy Day Films. 16mm or 8mm color, 12 min. Rental: $15. Purchase: $150. For a videotape of this film, see Pyramid Films under *Videotapes* in the Service Section of this directory. (PF)

John Williams. OMOWALE: CHILD RETURNS HOME. Visiting Badagary, the slave port in Nigeria where his ancestors departed for America, Mississippi-born novelist John Williams sees the chains used long ago to fetter slaves. In Yoruba, one of the languages of Nigeria, he would be called *Omowale*, or "the child returns home." Williams explores the relationship of the American Negro to Africa. He observes tribal religious ceremonies in which his ancestors participated and interviews Nigerian novelist and fellow-Mississippian James Meredith, then at the University of Ibadan. He concludes, "Once you understand your roots and place them in proper perspective, you really have no reason to go home again—especially to one seven generations removed from you. (Description from catalogue.) 16mm B/W, 30 min. Rental: $13 for one day. (LL)

Miller Williams. See Ann Darr.

William Carlos Williams. Selected readings from letters, poems, and the autobiography of the poet are accompanied by illustrative scenes. Dr. Williams' son is shown in tasks similar to those of his father, who practicedmedicine in the same town and the same office. Still photographs show scenes of the poet as a young man and in his later years. (Description from catalogue.) Produced by Brice Howard in 1966 for National Educational Television. 16mm B/W, 30 min. Rental: $9.50 for one to five days. Purchase: $165. For a videotape of this film see Indiana University under *Videotapes* in the Service Section of this directory. (IU)

Virginia Woolf. THE MOMENT WHOLE. Marian Seldes reads selections from Virginia Woolf about writing and women with lovely background photography of beach and ocean off Long Island. Focal point is a room at Montauk that successfully evokes the mood of Woolf, especially *To The Lighthouse*. (Annotated by Nash Cox.) Includes photographs of Virginia Woolf. Produced and Directed by

Janet Sternburg for National Educational Television. 16mm color, 10 min. Rental through various university film libraries—list available from ACI. Purchase: $160. (ACI)

W.B. Yeats. A TRIBUTE. On the life and work of the Irish poet, playwright, and patriot. Yeats' poetry is spoken by Michael MacLiammor and Siobhan McKenna. (Description from catalogue.) Produced by the National Film Institute of Ireland in 1950. Rental: $7.50 for one showing. Purchase: $125. (ABF)

Yevgeny Yevtushenko. A POET'S JOURNEY. This film focuses on Yevtushenko's readings and glimpses of places important in his poems: Babi Yar, Zima Junction. Intense excitement at his readings is conveyed by the response of audiences; but narrator, reading in English, prevents the viewer from the direct experience of Yevtushenko reading in Russian. The poet's credo of a world living together in peace comes across clearly. (Annoted by Nash Cox.) Narrated by Kenneth Haigh. 16mm B/W, 28 1/2 min. Rental: $25 for one day. Purchase: $240. For a videotape of this film see Films for the Humanities under *Videotapes* in the Service Section of this directory. (FH)

Louis Zukofsky. A filmed interview, during which he explains the underlying form and philosophy of his poetry and reads "A Poem Beginning 'The'" and passages taken from *A* and his translations. (Description from catalogue.) Produced in 1966 by Richard Moore for National Educational Television. 16mm B/W, 30 min. Rental: $9.50 for one to five days. Purchase: $165. For a videotape of this film see Indiana University under *Videotapes* in the Service Section of this directory. (IU)

Distributors

AB
Amerasia Bookstore, 338 East 2nd Street, Los Angeles, California 90012, (213) 680-2888.

ABF
Audio Brandon Films, Inc., 34 MacQueston Parkway South, Mount Vernon, New York 10550, (914) 664-4277.

ACI
ACI Films, 35 West 45 Street, New York, New York 10036, (212) 582-1918.

AV
Audiovisual Library Service, 3300 University Avenue, S.E., Minneapolis, Minnesota 55414, (612) 373-3810.

BF
Benchmark Films, Inc., 145 Scarborough Road, Briarcliff Manor, New York 10510, (914) 762-3838.

BFA
BFA Educational Media, Inc., 2211 Michigan Avenue, Santa Monica, California 90404, (213) 829-2901.

BP
Blackwood Productions, Inc., 58 West 58 Street, New York, New York 10019, (212) 688-0930.

CBS
CBS Publishing Group, 383 Madison Avenue, New York, New York 10017, (212) 688-9100.

CIE
Centre for Internationalising the Study of English, 628 Grand Avenue, St. Paul, Minnesota 55105, (612) 222-2096.

CIF
Coronet Instructional Films, Coronet Building, 65 East South Water Street, Chicago, Illinois 60601, (312) 332-7676.

CMC
Center for Mass Communications, 562 West 103 Street, New York, New York 10025, (212) 865-2000 (ext. 713).

CW
Division of Instructional Support, Case Western Reserve University, 10900 Euclid Avenue, Cleveland, Ohio 44106, (216) 368-2000.

EB
Encyclopaedia Brittanica Educational Corp., Dept. 10A, 425 North Michigan Avenue, Chicago, Illinois 60611, (312) 321-6800.

FC
Filmmakers Coop., 175 Lexington Avenue, New York, New York 10016, (212) 889-3820.

FE
Folder Editions, 325 East 57 Street, New York, New York 10022, (212) 759-7995.

FF
Frugal Films, 1616 Windsor, Columbia, Missouri 65201.

FH
Films for the Humanities, P.O. Box 378, Princeton, New Jersey 08540, (609) 921-2803.

FI
Film Images, Radim Films, Inc., 17 West 60 Street, New York, New York 10023, (212) 279-6653.

GI
Giorno Poetry Systems Institute, Inc., 222 Bowery, New York, New York 10012, (212) 925-6372.

GP
Grove Press, Film Division, 53 East 11 Street, New York, New York 10003, (212) 677-2400.

H
Horizons, Riverside Church, 490 Riverside Drive, New York, New York 10027, (212) 866-0266.

HB
Herman Berlandt, Director, Poetry Film Workshop, Box 7, Ocean Parkway, Bolinas, California 94924, (415) 868-0478.

IU
Indiana University Audio-Visual Center, Bloomington, Indiana 47401, (812) 337-8087.

JP
Journeyman Press, P.O. Box 4434, Grand Central Station, New York, New York 10017, (212) 745-6480.

LL
Lifelong Learning Films, University of California Extension Media Center, Berkeley, California 94720, (415) 642-0460.

LP
Living Poets Series, Living Poets Press, Inc., 838 Carroll Street, Brooklyn, New York 11215, (212) 638-3511.

MF
Modern Film Rentals, 45 Rockefeller Plaza, 14th Floor, New York, New York 10020, (212) 765-3100.

MH
Contemporary/McGraw-Hill Films, 1221 Avenue of the Americas, New York, New York 10020, (212) 997-6031. For rental, use one of the following regional film library addresses: Princeton Road, Hightstown, New Jersey 98520, (609) 448-1700; 828 Custer Avenue, Evanston, Illinois 60202, (312) 869-5010; 1714 Stockton Street, San Francisco, California 94133, (415) 362-3115.

MM
Mill Mountain Films, Irving Broughton, 1425 9th West, Seattle, Washington 98119, (206) 543-2660.

MP
Media Plus, Inc., Suite 11D, 60 Riverside Drive, New York, New York 10024, (212) 873-5543.

NAV
National Audio-Visual Center, G.S.A., Washington, D.C. 20409, (202) 763-5500.

NL
New Lines Cinema, 853 Broadway, 16th Floor, New York, New York 10003, (212) 674-7460.

NY
New Yorker Films, 43 West 61 Street, New York, New York 10023, (212) 247-6110.

PF
Pyramid Films, Box 1048, Santa Monica, California 90406, (213) 828-7577.

SE
Sterling Educational Films, 241 East 34 Street, New York, New York 10016, (212) 683-6300.

TL
Time-Life Films, 100 Eisenhower Drive, Paramus, New Jersey 07652, (201) 843-4545.

WK
William Kenda, English Dept., 265 Stevens Hall, University of Maine, Orono, Maine 04473, (207) 581-7379.

Videotapes

An alphabetical list of authors appears first, coded to a list of distributors which follows. For descriptions and additional ordering information, write to distributors.

This section lists 281 videotaped authors and 25 distributors.

Authors

Keith Abbott	PC
Oscar Zeta Acosta	FFC
Teresa Paloma Acosta	FFC
Aijaz Ahmad	WF
Ai	PC
Lloyd Alexander	TU
Alurista	FFC
Jorge Alvarez	FFC
Jack Anderson	CA,WF
Jon Anderson	PC,WF
Ronald Arias	FFC
Richard Armour	IU
Flora Arnstein	PC
Estevan Arrellano	FFC
John Ashbery	PC,WF
Tomas Atencio	FFC
W.H. Auden	PF
Richard Avery	AIT
Richard Barnes	PC
John Batki	EM
Marvin Bell	PT
Saul Bellow	IU
Pura Belpre	TU
Michael Benedikt	CA
William Benton	PC
Carol Berge	PC
Bill Berkson	PC
Ted Berrigan	PC
Wendell Berry	PT
John Berryman	BP,WF
Jeronimo Blanco	FFC
Douglas Blazek	AIT
Robert Bly	PT,PV,WF
Arna Bontemps	TU
Ray Bradbury	IU
John Malcolm Brinnin	WF
Gwendolyn Brooks	IU
James Broughton	PC
Lennart Bruce	PC
Charles Bukowski	PC
William Burroughs	PC
Truman Capote	IU
Jim Carroll	PC
R.V. Cassill	IU
Olivia Castellano	FFC
Vibiana Chamberlain	FFC
Laura Chester	PC
John Ciardi	IU
Josephine Clare	EM
Tom Clark	PC
Andrei Codrescu	EM,PC
Horace Coleman	OU
Juan Contreras	FFC
Jane Cooper	PC
Jayne Cortez	CA
Robert Creeley	IU,PV,WF
ee. cummings	FH

Veronica Cunningham	FFC
Beverly Dahler	PC
William Demby	WF
Benjamin DeMott	WF
James Dickey	PV,WF
William Dickey	PC
Diane Di Prima	PC
Stephen Dobyns	WF
Ed Dorn	PC
Ree Dragonette	VE
Robert Duncan	IU,PC
Richard Eberhart	IU,WF
Ralph Ellison	IU
Kenward Elmslie	PC
Paul Engle	WF
William Everson (Brother Antoninus)	IU,PC,WF
Larry Fagin	PT
Lawrence Ferlinghetti	IU,PV,WF
Leslie Fiedler	IU
Kathleen Fraser	PC
Bruce Jay Friedman	IU
Norman Friedman	WF
W.M. Frohock	WF
Robert Robert Frost	IU,FH
Ernest Gaines	WF
Dick Gallup	CA
Philip Garrison	PC
Allen Ginsberg	IU,PC,PV,VE,WF
Louis Ginsberg	PC
John Giorno	MMA,GI,PC
Daniela Gioseffi	IV
Madeline Gleason	PC
Patricia Goedicke	WF
Michael Goldman	CA
David Gomez	FFC
Juan Gomez-Quinones	FFC
Jorge Gonzalez	FFC
Nadine Gordimer	WF
Judy Grahn	PC
Gunter Grass	IU
Daryl Gray	EM
Ronald Gross	WF
Barbara Guest	PC
Donald Hall	PT
Lorraine Hansberry	IU
Ihab Hassan	WF
Bobbie Louise Hawkins	PC
Robert Hayden	PT,WF
Seamus Heaney	FH
Anthony Hecht	WF
Sheila Heldenbrand	EM
Lyn Hejinian	PC
Barbara Hernandez	FFC
Juan Felipe Herrera	FFC
William Heyen	WF
Granville Hicks	WF
R.R. Hinojosa-Smith	FFC
George Hitchcock	PC
Barbara Holland	OS
Joyce Holland	EM
John Hollander	WF
Anselm Hollo	EM
Robert Horan	PC
Richard Howard	WF
Andrew Hoyem	PC
Kristin Hunter	TU
Elias Hruska-Cortes	FFC
Richard Hugo	PC,WF
David Ignatow	WF
Robinson Jeffers	IU
James Jones	IU
Erica Jong	CA,WF
Donald Justice	WF
Gylan Kain	NL
Allen Katzman	VE
Shirley Kaufman	PC
Ezra Jack Keats	NL
Hugh Kenner	WF
W. Bliem Kern	CA,CT
Faye Kicknowsway	PC
Galway Kinnell	C,PT,PV,VE,WF
Carolyn Kizer	PC,PT,WF
Etheridge Knight	PC
Kenneth Koch	CT
Alan Kornblum	EM
Richard Kostelanetz	CT
Stanley Kunitz	PC,WF
Joanne Kyger	PC
Enrique LaMadrid	FFC
Ruth Lechlitner	PC
Denise Levertov	IU,PV,WF
Philip Levine	PC
Janet Lewis	PC
John Lexau	TU
John Logan	PV,WF
Robert Lowell	CA,IU
Audre Lorde	CA,PC
Felipe Luciano	NL
Benjamin Rochin Luna	FFC
David Lunde	WF
Archibald MacLeish	WF
Lewis MacAdams	PC
Susan MacDonald	TS
George Mandel	IU
Peter Marchant	WF
E.A. Mares	FFC
Paul Mariah	PC
John Marron	PC
Jack Marshall	PC
Harry Mathews	PC
Bill Matthews	PC
Jack Matthews	OU
George Mattingly	EM
Vladimir Mayakovsky	FH
Jerome Mazzaro	WF
Mark McCloskey	WF
Michael McClure	IU,PC
William Meredith	WF
Eve Eve Merriam	PC,TU
W.S. Merwin	PT
Josephine Miles	PC
Jose Montoya	FFC
Richard Moore	PC
Rosalie Moore	PC
Dorinda Moreno	CM
Dave Morice	EM
Alejandro Murguia	FFC
Vladimir Nabokov	FH
David Nelson	NL
Pablo Neruda	FH
Howard Norman	PT
Kathleen Norris	CA
Frank O'Hara	CA,IU
Charles Olson	CA,IU
George Oppen	PC
Joel Oppenheimer	VE

Peter Orlovsky	WF
Gregory Orr	PT
Antonio G. Ortiz	FFC
Javier Pacheco	FFC
Ron Padgett	PC
Thomas Parkinson	PC
S.J. Perelman	IU
Robert Perlman	EM
Joyce Peseroff	PT
Robert Peters	PC
Marge Piercy	WF
Stanley Plumly	WF
Ezra Pound	BP,FH
Holly Prado	PC
Jonathan Price	CT
Lawrence Raab	PT
Carl Rakosi	PC
Ishmael Reed	PC,WF
Kenneth Rexroth	IU,PC
Charles Reznikoff	PC
Stan Rice	PC
Adrienne Rich	PC,WF
Tomas Rivera	FFC
Lynne Romero	FFC
Henry Roth	IU
Philip Roth	IU
Jerome Rothenberg	PC,PT,WF
Ponce Javier Ruiz	FFC
Muriel Rukeyser	VE
Michael Ryan	PC
Thomas Salamun	EM
Omar Salinas	FFC
Raul Salinas	FFC
James Salter	IU
Carolee Sanchez	CM
Ricardo Sanchez	FFC
Sonia Sanchez	CA
Ed Sanders	IU
Peter Schjeldahl	PC
Dennis Schmitz	PC
Armand Schwerner	BC,PC
Hugh Seidman	PV,VE
Leopold Sedar Senghor	IU
Anne Sexton	IU,WF
Frederick Shroya	GBH
Frank Sifuentes	FFC
Jon Silkin	WF
Judith Johnson Sherwin	CA
Louis Simpson	PT,WF
Isaac Bashevis Singer	WF
John Sjoberg	EM
Knute Skinner	WF
W.D. Snodgrass	WF
Gary Snyder	IU,PV,WF
Stephen Spender	WF
Kathleen Spivack	PC
William Stafford	WF
Terry Stokes	CA
Mark Strand	WF
Lucien Stryk	WF
Mario Suarez	FFC
Hollis Summers	OU
Barry Targan	WF
Nathaniel Tarn	PC
Walter Tevis	OU
Dylan Thomas	PF,TL
Piri Thomas	IU
Stephen Toth	EM

Tomas Transtromer	PC
Marcela Trujillo	FFC
Dalton Trumbo	IU
Lewis Turco	WF
John Updike	IU
Nanos Valaoritis	PC
Avelardo Valdez	FFC
Roberto Vargas	FFC
Pedro Ortiz Vasquez	FFC
Kurt Vonnegut	NL
D.R. Wagner	AIT
Anne Waldman	GI,PC
Diane Wakoski	GI,PC
Phil Weidman	AIT
James Welch	PC
Philip Whalen	IU
Nathan Whiting	CA
Frances Whyatt	VE
John Wieners	IU,PC
Richard Wilbur	PV,WF
C.K. Williams	WF
Emmett Williams	PF
John Williams	IU
Miller Williams	WF
Keith Wilson	WF
James Wright	WF
Yevgeny Yevtushenko	FH

Distributors

AIT

Agency for Instructional Television. *Four Poets and Other Ideas* is a 20-minute color tape of poets Richard Avery, Douglas Blazek, D.R. Wagner, and Phil Weidman. They are shown reading their work in home and work environments and discussing poetry and science with a physicist. Available on video cassette, Ampex 1" tape, IVC 1" tape, or 1/2" EIAJ tape. Rental only: $37.50 plus $1.40 per 10,000 students (or portion thereof) up to 250,000, plus $.50 for each additional 10,000. Contact William B. Perrin, Director of Field Services, Agency for Instructional Television, Box A, Bloomington, Ind. 47401, (812) 339-2203.

BC

Brooklyn College Television Center produced the 30 min. *Armand Schwerner Show* for local television. Part One is from a film on Armand Schwerner by filmmaker Phil Niblock. Part Two is a live concert/reading. The tape is available in color on videocassette or 1/2" EIAJ tape for a handling and postage charge of $7.50 (customer provides raw stock). Contact Mark Rosenblatt, Assistant Producer, TV Center, Whitehead Hall, Brooklyn College, Bedford and Avenue H, Brooklyn, N.Y. 11210, (212) 780-5555.

BP

Blackwood Productions, Inc. *Ezra Pound*, 8 min., purchase only: $40. *John Berryman*, 20 min., purchase only: $80. Both on 3/4" B/W videocassette. For annotations and 16mm film format, see Ezra Pound and John Berryman under *Film* in the Service Section of this directory. Blackwood Productions, Inc., 58 W. 58 St., New York, N.Y. 10019, (212) 688-0930.

CA

Cable Arts Foundation, Inc. A series of readings moderated by Galen Williams. Also 3 tapes from the NET Film Series (Charles Olson, Robert Lowell, Frank O'Hara: for film formats, see these names under *Film* in the Service

Section of this directory). Available on 1" IVC or Ampex tape, 2" tape, or 3/4" color videocassette. For rental and purchase information, contact Claire Monaghan at Cable Arts, 171 W. 57 St., New York, N.Y. 10019, (212) 541-4666.

CM
Consilio Mujeres. Two videotapes on poetry in the context of the Latino/Chicano, Puerto Rican, and Native American issues as they affect women. *En Pia de Lucha* was produced by KCET-TV, Los Angeles, It shows poet and anthropologist Dorinda Moreno reading her poetry, in English with some Spanish, accompanied by interpretive Latin music and dance. Color, 30 min., 1/2" EIAJ. Rental only: $25 plus shipping. A copy of the script is available for an additional $2. A second tape, *Puppets & Politics*, shows La Raza women poets reading at Intersection Coffeehouse in San Francisco in 1974. The poets include Dorinda Moreno, Carolee Sanchez, and others, framed by a puppet performance and music. A nonprofessional community effort, the tape is the first record of the La Raza women,s movement in the arts. In English, 40 min., on B/W 1/2" EIAJ. Rental only: $20 plus shipping. Contact Dorinda Moreno, Project Director, Consilio Mujeres, 2588 Mission St., Room 201, San Francisco, Calif. 94110, (415) 826-1530.

CT
Camera Three. Tapes of two CBS-produced Camera Three programs are available from the New York State Department of Education. *Poetry to See, Poetry to Hear* is a 1/2 hour tape made in 1973 with poets W. Bliem Kern, Richard Kostelanetz, and Jonathan Price. *Rose, Where Did You Get That Red?* is a 1/2 hour tape on children,s poetry made in 1974 with poet Kenneth Koch. Color or B/W on videocassette, 1/2" EIAJ, 1" Ampex, or 2" Quadruplex. Customer must supply raw stock. Dubbing charge is $37.50 per 1/2 hour. For ordering information, write to The New York State Department of Education, Bureau of Mass Communications, Education Building Annex, Room 1061, Albany, N.Y. 12234, (518) 474-2241.

EM
Everson Museum of Art, Syracuse. *Iowa Writers' Workshop* is a series of one-hour, 1/2" EIAJ, B/W tapes, one per poet. Rental price: from $75-$100 per tape with royalties going to the poets. For purchase prices, contact Richard Simmons, Associate Curator of Video, Everson Museum of Art, Syracuse, N.Y. 13202, (315) 474-6064.

FFC
Festival Flor Y Canto. Televised expressions of the Chicano experience in literature. 38 1/2 hour videocassettes, color, 3/4". Purchase only: $200 per cassette. Contact Phil Rapa, University of Southern California Public Broadcasting, có VCI Studios, 201 N. Occidental Blvd., Los Angeles, Calif. 90026, (213) 380-2722, ext. 320 or 321.

FH
Films For The Humanities. All listings available as 16mm films through Films for the Humanities are also available as U-Matic videocassettes, purchase only. Inquire for prices. Films For The Humanities, P.O. Box 378, Princeton, N.J. 08540, (609) 921-2803. For lengths and descriptions, see listings by author under *Films* in the Service Section of this directory.

GBH
WGBH Educational Foundation. *Anne Sexton: Matters of Life and Death* is a 1/2 hour color videotape made by WGBH-TV, Channel 2, in Cambridge, Massachusetts, featuring Anne Sexton reading and discussing her work. On videocassette or 1/2" EIAJ. Purchase only: $130 plus postage and handling. Order from WGBH Educational Foundation, 125 Western Ave., Boston, Mass. 02134, (617) 868-3800.

GI
Giorno Poetry Systems Institute, Inc. Half-hour 1/2" B/W tapes of readings held in 1973. Purchase only: $25. 222 Bowery, New York, N.Y. 10012, (212) 925-6372.

IU
Indiana University. All titles listed by author under *Films* in the Service Section of this directory are also available in all videotape formats in color or B/W. Purchase only: prices same as B/W film purchase. (For most titles, $165. But some vary, so please refer to authors listings under *Films*.) For further information, contact Indiana University Audio-Visual Center, Bloomington, Ind. 47401, (812) 337-8087.

IV
International Videoletters. *Daniela Gioseffi* is a 10 min. videotape of the poet reading her work produced by Ann Volkes. B/W 1/2" EIAJ. Rental: $20. Purchase: $25. Prices include postage and handling. Contact Ann Volkes, International Videoletters, 74 Third Ave., New York, N.Y. 10003, (212) 246-6570.

MMA
Museum of Mott Art. Les Levine produced and directed *Suicide Sutra* by John Giorno. 30 min., 3/4" color videocassette. Purchase only: $225 plus transfer cost. Available from Les Levine, Museum of Mott Art, 181 Mott Street, New York, N.Y. 10012, (212) 925-0447.

NL
New Lines Cinema. Kurt Vonnegut's *Between Time and Timbuktoo—A Space Fantasy*: 90 min., rental only, $250 for one week. *Right On: Poetry by the Last Poets*: 72 min., rental only, $165 for one week. Both tapes are 3/4" color videocassette. Other video formats available upon inquiry. 121 University Pl., New York, N.Y. 10003. For 16mm color film format of both tapes, see Gylan Kain and Kurt Vonnegut under *Films* in the Service Section of this directory.

OS
Olivera Sajkovic. *Profile of a Poet* is a 1/2 hour videotape of poet Barbara Holland, including a reading and an interview, produced in 1972 by Olivera Sajkovic, poetry editor of *New Renaissance*. B/W 1/2" EIAJ. Rental only: $30. Contact Olivera Sajkovic, 39 Christopher St., New York, N.Y. 10014, (212) 929-8491.

OU
Ohio University. *The Ohio University Writers* is a series of 1/2 hour color videotapes each showing the author reading and being interviewed. Tapes on poets are *Horace Coleman: Mood Indigo* and *Hollis Summers: Start from Home*. Tapes on fiction writers are *Jack Mathews: Creation as Discovery* and *Walter Tevis: The Aesthetics of Gamesmanship*. Available in color videocassette or color 1/2" EIAJ. Rental: $25 per tape for 10 days. Contact Instructional Telecommunications, Radio/TV Building, Ohio University, Athens, Ohio 45701, (614) 594-2276.

PC
San Francisco Poetry Center Video Tape Library. Over 20 tapes of readings held at the Center in 1973-74. Length varies. Some are 3/4" color videocassettes; others are 1/2" EIAJ B/W. Rental only: $5 royalty fee per poet per showing plus cost of postage and handling. For further information, contact Gordon Craig, Technical Videotape Director, Poetry Center, San Francisco State University, 1600 Holloway, San Francisco, Calif. 94132, (415) 469-1056.

PF
Pyramid Films. Listings under Dylan Thomas (*A Dylan Thomas Memoir*) and Emmett Williams under *Films* in the Service Section of this directory are available in video-cassette format for the same prices. Pyramid Films, Box 1048, Santa Monica, Calif. 90406, (213) 828-7577.

PT
Poets Talking. A series consisting of fifteen 1/2 hour tapes, most of them interviews hosted by poet Donald Hall. Available for purchase only. Three formats: open reel B/W 1/2" EIAJ; 3/4" color videocassette; and 2" HB color. Prices available on request. Contact Lynn Kneer, Media Distribution Supervisor, University of Michigan Television Center, 400 S. Fourth St., Ann Arbor, Mich. 48102, (313) 764-8218.

PV
Poets on Videotape. Readings/interviews, for use in New York State only. B/W. Lengths vary between 1/2 and 1-1/2 hours. Customer must supply raw stock. Dubbing charge is $37.50 per 1/2 hour. Formats available are 1" and 2" Ampex, 1/2" EIAJ, and U-Matic videocassettes. Order forms available on request. Contact The New York State Education Department, Bureau of Mass Communications, Education Building Annex, Albany, N.Y. 12234, (518) 474-2241.

TL
Time-Life Films. *Dylan Thomas: A Bronze Mask*, 26 min., color, in any videotape format. Rental: $45 for 3 days. Purchase: $270 plus postage and handling. For annotation and 16mm film format, see *Dylan Thomas: A Bronze Mask* under *Films* in the Service Section of this directory. Time-Life Films, 100 Eisenhower Dr., Paramus, N.J. 07652, (201) 843-4545.

TS
Shera Thompson/Shelley Surpin. *Everything a Woman Could Want* is a 26 min. videotape including readings and discussions with poet Susan MacDonald and two other creative women on the subjects of marriage, divorce, lovers, children, roles and demands, and the development of creativity. B/W 1/2" EIAJ. Rental: $35 (applicable toward purchase). Purchase: $70. Prices for other formats are available on request. The producers, Shera Thompson and Shelley Surpin, are available for discussions about the contents and production of the tape. To order contact them at 514 Bryant St., ño1, Palo Alto, Calif. 94301, (415) 326-0734.

TU
Temple University. *Profiles in Literature* is a series of B/W 1/2 hour videotaped interviews with leading children's authors. A special 20 min. preview tape of series is available on 2-day loan for $1 (format: 1/2" EIAJ). Individual tapes available at duplication charge of $25 each (any format), or tapes can be purchased as 1/2" EIAJ at $20 per 1/2 hour and $30 per hour of tape combining any segments. Information is available on quantity rates and on a teachers' guide for using the tapes. Send inquiries to *Profiles in Literature*, Temple University, Office of Television Services, Tomlinson Hall 214, Philadelphia, Pa. 19122. Checks payable to Office of Television Services.

VE
Video Exchange, Inc. 463 West St., New York, N.Y. 10014, (212) 691-5035 or 242-3049. Edited 1/2" EIAJ B/W. For purchase or rental contact Michael Temmer. Prices available on request.

WF
Writers Forum. Over 80 1/2-hour and 1-hour videotapes of interviews conducted since 1967 with poets, fiction writers, and critics, are available free for use in New York State only. Contact The Writers Forum of the Department of English, State University College at Brockport, Brockport, New York 14420, (716) 395-2660 (Audio-Visual Department: Mr. Bemis or Mrs. Haskins). Postage and handling will be charged to the user.

Records and Tapes

In this section we have only included recordings of works read by the authors themselves. Records listed are 33-1/3 rpm unless stated otherwise. Recordings by children's authors are not listed in this section, but some can be found under *Resources for Creative Writing Teachers* in the Service Section of this Directory.

AKWESASNE NOTES. *Native Colours and Before*, a 60-minute tape, includes selected readings by Karoniaktatie. It is available in stereo or mono on open reel or cassette tapes at $10.00 for institutions and $5.00 for individuals. *The Poetry of Gary Snyder,* a 60-minute tape, features the poet reading many selections from *Turtle Island*, his book which won the Pulitzer Prize in 1975. The tape also includes Mohawk poet Peter Aroniawenrate Blue Cloud reading two of his poems. *Akwesasne Notes*, Mohawk Nation, via Rooseveltown, New York 13683, (518) 358-4697.

APPLAUSE PRODUCTIONS lists over 2,000 records, tapes, and cassettes of poetry, prose, and theater in their catalogue. This includes 62 volumes of readings by several hundred contemporary American and British poets. Prices are approximately $7.00 per record and $8.00 to $15.00 for a cassette or an open reel tape. Write to them at 85 Longview Rd., Port Washington, N.Y. 11050 or call (516) 883-7460.

ARCHIVE FOR NEW POETRY. Over 400 tapes of poetry readings produced by the University of California are available for listening in the Archive for New Poetry on the 8th floor of the Central University Library, University of California—San Diego, La Jolla, Calif. 92037, (714) 452-2533. The Archive is open from 10:00 to 5:00, Monday through Friday.

BLACK BOX is a magazine on cassettes published bi-monthly as a service of The New Classroom, a nonprofit educational cooperative. Volumes 1-6 are currently available. Robert Bly and Sonia Sanchez are represented in Volume 3; Julius Lester and Muriel Rukeyser in Volume 6.

Other volumes include 14-19 poets each. The subscription price is $20.00 for six issues; for institutions the price is $50.00. Single copies, when available, are $5.00 postpaid to subscribers, $10.00 postpaid to non-subscribers. Write Black Box, P.O. Box 4174, Washington, D.C. 20015, (202) 872-8685.

BROADSIDE VOICES. Over fifteen Black poets, including Gwendolyn Brooks, Jon Eckels, Keorapetse William Kgositsile, and Clarence Major, read their work on a series of tapes in open reel or cassette format for $5.00 each (purchase only). Also available is an album *Rappin' and Readin'* by Don L. Lee ($5.00). Broadside Press, 12651 Old Mill Pl., Detroit, Mich. 48238, (313) 935-1188.

CAEDMON RECORDS. Send for a catalogue of over 800 titles in cassette and Lp format, including children's and foreign language recordings. 505 Eighth Ave., New York, N.Y. 10018, (212) 594-3122.

CENTER FOR CASSETTE STUDIES. A catalogue is available listing cassette tapes of interviews with about 25 contemporary American poets and over 100 contemporary American fiction writers. Among authors included are Lawrence Durrell, Nora Ephron, Allen Ginsberg, Joseph Heller, Lillian Helman, Jerzy Kosinski, Henry Miller, Frank O'Hara, Katherine Anne Porter, Ed Sanders, Kurt Vonnegut, Jr., and John Williams. Lengths range from 1/2 hour to 1 hour. Write or call Center for Cassette Studies, 8110 Webb Avenue, North Hollywood, Calif. 91605, (213) 768-5040.

CHARLES SCRIBNER'S SONS has tapes of May Swenson reading from *To Mix With Time*; John Hall Wheelock reading from *By Daylight and in Dream*; and Robert Creeley reading from *For Love*. Individual cassettes are $7.50. Kits containing a cassette and a copy of the book are available for $9.95 (New York State residents add 8% sales tax and $.50 postage). Order from Customer Retail Service, Scribner Bookstore, 597 Fifth Ave., New York, N.Y. 10017, (212) 486-2700.

CMS RECORDS has a series of albums of American and foreign poets titled *The World's Great Poets, Volumes 1-7*. Poets included are Gregory Corso, Lawrence Ferlinghetti, Allen Ginsberg, and Ezra Pound (Vol 1). Also in the series are poets Rafael Albert, Homero Aridjis, and Jose Emilio Pacheco. Another album offered by CMS is *Word Music*, a reading by Toby Lurie. Cost is $6.98 per album. Contact CMS Records, 14 Warren St., New York, N.Y. 10007, (212) 964-3380.

CREDO. The Credo Series of records includes a reading and interview by James Baldwin with Studs Terkel (Credo #1); a lecture by R. Buckminster Fuller (Credo #2); and a reading and interview by Sylvia Plath with Peter Orr of the BBC (Credo #3). The albums are $6.98 each from Pathways of Sound, Inc., 102 Mount Auburn St., Cambridge, Mass. 02138, (617) 354-6190.

DUFOUR EDITIONS. A catalogue is available, listing about thirty 33 1/3 and 45 rpm poetry records produced on the *Jupiter, Claddagh, Listen, Aquilar, Marvell,* and *Argo* labels. Records include the English *Poets Reading* series and several records by Spanish and Irish poets. Prices vary, generally around $5 to $7. Dufour Editions, Chester Springs, Pa. 19425, (215) 458-5005.

EVERETT/EDWARDS offers a series of 30-minute cas-

settes titled *Contemporary American Poets Read Their Work*. The series features 12 poets including George Hitchcock, Guy Owen, and William Stafford. Each tape is $9.00 (no postage if prepaid). Another series, *Contemporary Women Writers*, includes cassettes of poets Rose Graubart Ignatow, Marge Piercy, and Diane Wakoski giving readings or interviews. Lengths and prices on this series are not available at this writing. To obtain a catalogue write or call Everett/Edwards, P.O. Box 1060, Deland, Fla. 32720, (904) 734-7458.

FESTIVAL FLOR Y CANTO. Cassettes are available of 38 Chicano authors (one per tape) reading at the Festival De Flor Y Canto. $6.00 each. For a catalog order form, contact Phil Rapa, University of Southern California Public Broadcasting, c/o VCI Studios, 201 North Occidental Blvd., Los Angeles, Calif. 90026, (213) 380-2722, ext. 320 or 321. For videotapes of the same authors, see FFC (Festival Flor Y Canto) under *Videotapes* in the Service Section of this directory.

FOLKWAYS RECORDS. Catalog lists almost 200 literature titles, including the *Spoken Word* series and many recordings of foreign authors. Most titles are available only on 12-inch monaural records, $6.98. Cassette format, at $9.95, is being offered for an increasing number of titles. Contact Folkways Records, 43 W. 61 St., New York, N.Y. 10023, (212) 586-7260.

GIORNO POETRY SYSTEMS. *Dial-a-Poem Poets* (a 2-Lp set), *Dial-a-Poem Poets DISCONNECTED* (a 2-Lp set), and *Biting Off the Tongue of a Corpse* (single Lp) each feature a large number of poets reading their work. *William S. Burroughs and John Giorno* (a 2-Lp set) contains one album by each of the two authors. Forthcoming are single albums by Anne Waldman and Frank O'Hara. The double Lp sets are $7.50, and the single albums are $4.98. Currently available albums may be purchased together (7 Lps) for $24.00. Order from Giorno Poetry Systems Institute, Inc., 222 Bowery, New York, N.Y. 10012, (212) 925-6372.

GREAT ATLANTIC RADIO CONSPIRACY. *Breaking Free: The Poetry of Repression, Resistance, and Liberation* is a 30-minute tape featuring Diane Di Prima, Erica Jong, and Gil Scott-Heron reading their own work. The purchase price for individuals is $5.00 for open reel and $3.50 for cassette. Prices vary for institutional buyers. Contact The Great Atlantic Radio Conspiracy, 2743 Maryland Ave., Baltimore, Md. 21218, (301) 243-6987.

HOUSATONIC REGIONAL VALLEY HIGH SCHOOL in Connecticut has tapes, made at the high school, of readings given by Mark Van Doren, Galway Kinnell, Kathleen Fraser, James Wright, William Meredith, W.D. Snodgrass, L.E. Sissman, Emmett Jarrett, Dick Lourie, Donald Hall, John Haines, Harold Bond, Carolyn Kizer, Halsey Davis, Gerald Housman, Donald Junkins, Ron Atkinson, Clarence Major, and Shirley Kaufman. Written permission from the poet (for poets' addresses, see *A Directory of American Poets*) must be sent with blank tape (reel or cassette) to Bill DeVoti, c/o Housatonic Regional Valley High School, Falls Village, Conn. 06031, (203) 824-5123. Copies are free except for postage and a minimal service charge. Lengths of tapes vary. Unedited and not of professional quality.

JEFFREY NORTON. A fully indexed catalogue is available, with a literature section listing over 150 tapes of writers and poets (one author per tape), including the YMHA Poetry Center series. All titles are available in cassette and open reel formats, priced the same (generally $11.75). Contact Jeffrey Norton Publishers, Inc., 145 E. 49 St., New York, N.Y. 10017, (212) 753-1783.

LAST WORD BOOKSHOP. A 20-minute cassette of *William D. Elliot Reading his Poetry at the Last Word Bookshop* is available for rental ($15.00) or purchase ($25.00). Contact James Tracy, Manager, Last Word Bookshop, 408 S. Third St., St. Peter, Minn. 56082, (507) 931-4120.

THE LIBRARY OF CONGRESS has albums of 31 English language and 3 Spanish authors available for purchase. Request catalogue from Recorded Sound section, Music Division, Library of Congress, Washington, D.C. 20540, (202) 426-5509.

LIFELONG LEARNING has tapes of readings by over 20 poets who have participated in poetry conferences at the University of California at Berkeley. Available in open reel or cassette format, the poets include Alta, Susan Griffin, Jessica Hagedorn, and Gary Snyder. Prices and lengths vary. A catalogue is available from Lifelong Learning, University of California Extension, Berkeley, Calif. 94720, (415) 642-5725.

LISTENING LIBRARY has a 3-volume *Album of American Poets* featuring 45 American poets. The volumes can be purchased separately at $6.50 for a record or $7.95 for a cassette tape. Also available are *The Isaac Asimov Cassette Library* (6 cassettes for $49.95); *William Faulkner* ($6.50 for a record, $7.95 for a cassette); *A Separate Peace* with John Knowles discussing and reading from his book (2 Lps $12.95, or cassettes $15.90); *Here's Will Saroyan* ($19.95 for 3 Lps, $22.95 for cassettes); and *The Ray Bradbury Cassette Library* (6 cassettes for $49.95). Most of the above records or tapes include text and/or teachers notes. A catalogue is available from Listening Library, Inc., 1 Park Ave., Old Greenwich, Conn. 06870, (203) 637-3616.

OUT LOUD PRODUCTIONS. A series of stereo Lp records of oral poetry produced by the poets themselves to high technical standards. Most of the work recorded is by Peter and Patricia Herleman. The rest is by Klyd and Linda Watkins and French oral poet Bernard Heidsieck. Nine Lps are available to date. Subscriptions cost $6 a year for three issues. Single issues are $3 and back issues $4. Write to Out Loud Productions, 39 Ridgetop Drive, St. Louis, Mo. 63117.

PANJANDRUM No. 1 is an album containing readings by 14 poets, including David Gitin, John Logan, and Nanos Valaoritis. It is available for $5.00 from Panjandrum Press, 99 Sanchez St., San Francisco, Calif. 94114.

REVUE OU is a periodical anthology of visual and sound poetry. Most issues consist of a "book-object" and a record. Featured writers have included Charles Amirkhanian, William Burroughs, Bryon Gysin, Tom Phillips, as well as many European writers and artists. Prices vary. Write to Review Ou, Henry Chopin, Editor, The Gate House, Station Lane, Ingatestone, Essex, England.

ROAD RUNNER PRESS. Doug Flaherty is offering a cassette of his poetry, recorded at Harvard, approximately 40 minutes long. Purchase: $5.00. Road Runner Press, 1525 Burdick, Oshkosh, Wis. 54901.

SCHOLASTIC AUDIO-VISUAL CENTER. While mostly teaching aids, the Scholastic A-V catalogue lists the 5-album Scholastic record series *Today's Poets: Their Poems-Their Voices*, the album *Anthology of Contemporary American Poetry* and several black literature albums. It also lists *Oral Anthology: Spanish-American Poetry of the 20th Century* (with bi-lingual text) and two albums of readings by Theodore Roethke. Address: 904 Sylvan Ave., Englewood Cliffs, N.J. 07632, (201) 567-7900.

1750 ARCH RECORDS. Seven poets are represented in *102:12 American Text Sound Pieces* illustrating "music composed from speaking not singing" (annotation from publisher). The poets are Charles Amirkhanian, John Cage, Clark Coolidge, Liam O'Gallagher, John Giorno, thony Gnazzo, and Aram Saroyan. The purchase price is $5.00 plus handling (U.S. $.75, overseas $1.50). Order from 1750 Arch Records, P.O. Box 9444, Berkeley, Calif. 94709, (415) 841-0216.

SPOKEN ARTS, INC. Send for a catalogue listing several hundred literature and related titles available in $6.98 record and $7.98 cassette and open reel formats. Address: 310 North Ave., New Rochelle, N.Y. 10801, (914) 636-5482.

STANFORD UNIVERSITY has produced seven albums of readings by J.V. Cunningham, John Hawkes, Janet Lewis, N. Scott Momaday, Adrienne Rich, Yvor Winters, and English poet Donald Davie. They are $7.00 each from Serendipity Books Distribution, 1790 Shattuck Ave., Berkeley, Calif. 94709, (415) 548-8204.

THOMAS MORE ASSOCIATES. A cassette, *Dark Came Early in That Country*, features Nelson Algren, author of *Walk on the Wild Side* and *Man with the Golden Arm*, reading selections from his work. It is 60 minutes long, and the price is $10.45 which includes postage. A second 60-minute cassette, *Harry Petrakis Reads Harry Petrakis*, is also available for $9.45 including postage. Contact Thomas More Associates at 180 N. Wabash, Chicago, Ill. 60601, (312) 332-1795.

TRAVELLING VOICES cassette tapes are available of the following poets reading from their own work: Neeli Cherry, Ed English, Jack Micheline, Irving Stettner, and Tommy Trantino. The tapes run 30-60 minutes. $7.50 (postage included) from Travelling Voices, 72 Thompson St., New York, N.Y. 10013.

UNIVERSITY OF ILLINOIS. *An Hour with W.S. Merwin* is a tape made by the University of Illinois for broadcast on their radio station WILL. It is available for sale only: $25. Contact Mike H. Mottler, WILL Recording Service, 228 Gregory Hall, University of Illinois, Urbana, Ill. 61801, (217) 333-0850.

UNIVERSITY OF MINNESOTA. Over 15 poets and fiction writers, including Robert Bly, Marya Mannes, and Tom McGrath, read and discuss their work on tapes produced by the University's radio station KUOM. They are available in cassette and open reel formats. Prices vary. Contact Lesley Jorbin, Senior Library Assistant, Audio Visual Library Service, 3300 University Ave. S.E., Minneapolis, Minn. 55414, (612) 373-4043.

Book Stores

The following 70 book stores consistently stock poetry and literary magazines. Most will also single-order poetry and fiction books. This list is not meant to include all fine book stores which stock poetry; it is a geographical sampling.

California
BOOKS PLUS, 3910 24th St., San Francisco, Calif. 94114
CHANGE OF HOBBIT, 1371 Westwood Blvd., Los Angeles, Calif. 90024
CHATTERTON'S BOOKSTORE, 1818 N. Vermont, Los Angeles, Calif. 90027
CITY LIGHTS BOOKS, 263 Columbus Ave., San Francisco, Calif. 94133
CODY'S BOOK STORE, 2454 Telegraph Ave., Berkeley, Calif. 94704
DISCOVERY BOOKSHOP, 245 Columbus Ave., San Francisco, Calif. 94133
KEPLER'S BOOKS, 825 El Camino Real, Menlo Park, Calif. 94025
MOE'S BOOKS, 2484 Telegraph Ave., Berkeley, Calif. 94704
NORTHTOWN BOOKS, 1604 G St., Arcata, Calif. 95521
PAPA BACH'S PAPERBACKS, 11317 Santa Monica Blvd., West Los Angeles, Calif. 90025
PUNTA DE LOS REYES, 11265 State Route #1, Point Reyes, Calif. 94956
PURPLE HERON BOOKSTORE, Bolinas, Calif. 94924
SAND DOLLAR BOOKS, 650 Colusa, Berkeley, Calif. 94707
SERENDIPITY BOOKS, 1790 Shattuck Ave., Berkeley, Calif. 94709
SHAKESPEARE & CO. BOOKS, 2499 Telegraph Ave., Berkeley, Calif. 94704
SHAMBALA BOOKSELLERS, 2482 Telegraph Ave., Berkeley, Calif. 94704
THE TIDES, 749 Bridgeway, Sausalito, Calif. 94965
A WOMAN'S PLACE BOOKSTORE, 5251 Broadway, Oakland, Calif. 94618

Colorado
KUGELMAN & BENT BOOKSTORE, 1028 E. 9th Ave., Denver, Colo. 80218

District of Columbia
DISCOUNT BOOK SHOP, 1342 Connecticut Ave., N.W., Washington, D.C. 20036
FOLIO BOOKS, 2000 P St., N.W., Washington, D.C. 20036
SAVILE BOOK STORE, 3236 P St., N.W., Washington, D.C. 20007

Illinois
CIRCLE BOOKSTORE, 1049 W. Taylor St., Chicago, Ill. 60607
GREAT EXPECTATIONS, 909 W. Foster, Evanston, Ill. 60201

Kansas
KANSAS UNION BOOKSTORE, University of Kansas, Lawrence, Kans. 66044

Massachusetts
GROLIERS, 6 Plympton St., Cambridge, Mass. 02138

LOGOS BOOK SHOP, 25 N. Pleasant St., Amherst, Mass. 01002
NEW WORDS, Somerville, Mass. 02184
PANGLOSS BOOKSHOP, 1284 Massachusetts Ave., Cambridge, Mass. 02138
PAPERBACK BOOKSMITH, 516 Commonwealth Ave., Boston, Mass. 02215
THE BOOKSTORE, Lenox, Mass. 02140

Michigan
ALLEN'S BOOK SHOP, 26 N. Division Ave., Grand Rapids, Mich. 49502

Minnesota
PERINE'S CAMPUS BOOK CENTER, 315 Fourteenth Ave. S.E., Minneapolis, Minn. 55414
RUSOFF & COMPANY, BOOKDEALERS, 1302 S.E. 4th St., Minneapolis, Minn. 55414
SAVRAN'S BOOKSTORES, 301 Cedar, Minneapolis, Minn. 55404

Missouri
PAUL'S BOOKS, 6691 Delmar Blvd., University City, Mo. 63130

New York City
ARMADILLO BOOKSHOP, 215 W. 10 St., New York, N.Y. 10014
BIG APPLE BOOKS, LTD., 282 Columbus Ave., New York, N.Y. 10023
EAST SIDE BOOK STORE, 34 St. Mark's Pl., New York, N.Y. 10009
E. S. WILENTZ'S EIGHTH STREET BOOKSHOP, 17 W. 8 St., New York, N.Y. 10011
GOTHAM BOOK MART, 41 W. 47 St., New York, N.Y. 10036
HART BOOK SHOP, INC. 137 Sullivan St., New York, N.Y. 10012
NEW YORKER BOOKSHOP, 250 W. 89 St., New York, N.Y. 10024
PAPYRUS BOOKSELLERS, 2915 Broadway, New York, N.Y. 10025
PARNASSUS BOOK SHOP, 216 W. 89 St., New York, N.Y. 10024
PHOENIX BOOK SHOP, 22 Jones St., New York, N.Y. 10014
SCIENCE FICTION BOOK SHOP, 56 Eighth Ave., New York, N.Y. 10001
WOMAN BOOKS, 255 W. 92 St., New York, N.Y. 10025

New York State
EVERYONE'S BOOK CO-OP, 3102 Main St., Buffalo, N.Y. 14214
ITHACA HOUSE, 108 N. Plain St., Ithaca, N.Y. 14850
KEENAN'S BOOKSTORE, 6 East Park Row, Clinton, N.Y. 13323
OXCART BOOKSHOP, 676 Monroe Ave., Rochester, N.Y. 14607

North Carolina
COMMUNITY BOOK STORE, 403 W. Franklin St., Chapel Hill, N.C. 27514

Ohio
ASPHODEL BOOKSHOP, 17192 Ravenna Rd., Burton, Ohio 44021

PAGES & PRINTS, 166 W. McMillan St., Cincinnati, Ohio 45219

Oregon
BRIAN THOMAS BOOKS, 822 S.W. 10th, Portland, Oreg. 97205
THE SOMETHING OWL BOOKSHOP, 7828 S.W. 35th, Portland, Oreg. 97219

Pennsylvania
LEAVES OF GRASS, 5314 Germantown Ave., Philadelphia, Pa. 19144
ROBIN'S BOOKSTORE, 6 N. 13 St., Philadelphia, Pa. 19107
SPRING CHURCH BOOK COMPANY, P.O. Box 127, Spring Church, Pa. 15686 (mail order only)

Texas
BROWN BOOK SHOP, 1219 Fannin, Houston, Tex. 77002
COLLOQUIUM BOOKS, INC., 202 Colorado, San Marcos, Tex. 78666
THE BOOKSELLER, 9751 N. Central Expressway, Dallas, Tex. 75231
THE BOOK MART, 3127 Broadway, San Antonio, Tex. 78209
UNIVERSITY COOP, 2246 Guadalupe, Austin, Tex. 78705

Virginia
OLD TOWN BOOK WORKS, The Small Mall, 118 King St., Alexandria, Va. 22314

Wisconsin
MADISON BOOK COOP, 660 1/2 State St., Madison, Wis. 53703

Canada
WILLIAM HOFFER BOOKS, 4529 W. 10th, Vancouver, B.C., Canada
RICHARD PENDER, 438 Richard, Vancouver, B.C., Canada
VILLAGE BOOK STORE, 29 Gerrard St. West, Toronto 2, Ont., Canada

Acknowledgments

We wish to express our gratitude to the following who gave us advice in compiling this Service Section: Jonathan Baumbach, fiction writer (*Reruns*, Fiction Collective, 1974); Harold Bond, poet (*Dancing on Water*, Cummington Press, 1970); Nash Cox, Executive Director, Kentucky Arts Commission; Honor Moore, poet and playwright (published in *We Become New: Poems by Contemporary American Women*; *Mourning Pictures*, a play produced on Broadway, November 1974); Raymond M. Olderman, critic (*Beyond the Wasteland: A Study of the Novel in the 1960's*, Yale University Press, 1973); Al Poulin, Jr., poet, anthologist, editor (of *Contemporary American Poetry, 2nd Edition:* Houghton-Mifflin, 1975); Steven Schrader, fiction writer (*Crime of Passion*, Inwood Press, 1975) and Executive Director, Teachers & Writers Collaborative; Norman Stock, librarian, Reference Division, Brooklyn Public Library.

Checklist:
How to Organize a Reading or Workshop

Hospitality:

1. Personal contact with authors should be made a week or two before arrival date in order to directly confirm last minute arrival and departure times, driving or transportation instructions, the general schedule, and fees. Inconveniences and misunderstandings can often be avoided in this way.

2. Ask faculty members or students to meet authors, show them around, and outline the details of their schedules. Be sure that writers are allowed sufficient time to rest and recharge.

3. Be sure to provide authors with meals. If they are to stay overnight, arrange for rooms in advance.

4. Make it easy for the *students* to talk informally to authors *outside of class*. Meals or an informal reception in a lounge are good situations for this contact.

5. Many authors have indicated that they prefer informal sessions with the students to parties with faculty members only. If there is to be a more formal reception, however, notify the guests well in advance, so they can arrange their schedules.

6. Have someone accompany authors to buses, trains, or planes. When authors have arrived by car, make sure they know the best route to their next destination.

7. Have checks ready when authors leave. Many authors count on the money for immediate use. (If Poets & Writers, Inc., has also supported the visit, there will be two checks: one from the Poets & Writers, Inc. funds and one from the host group.)

For Readings:

1. Publicize and advertise the event well in advance. It is demoralizing for both author and organizer to have a small audience in a large hall. Include newspapers, radio, television, posters, and flyers in your campaign. Contact the writer's publisher for a photograph and publicity information.

2. Select a day and time when there is not too much going on. One good way to get an audience is to have the writer visit classes *before the reading*.

3. If a small audience is anticipated, use a small room (if a large hall has been reserved, change the reservation).

4. Contact the community or college book store well in advance. They can have books on sale at the reading and/or available in their stock. If this is not possible, suggest that the author bring along extra books for sale immediately after the reading. Offer to make sales space available in the room where the reading will be held, and also offer to provide volunteer help for sales.

5. Gather information for a program sheet. It is an excellent idea to mimeograph some of the author's work and distribute it to the audience. Ask the author to suggest poems or prose that might be used. Favorable reviews and comments might also be included.

6. Appoint someone to introduce the author.

7. Make sure the microphone and sound equipment are working. This *must* be tested in advance. Last minute repairs are impossible.

8. Make sure there is enough light for the author.

9. Have an ashtray and water on stage, and offer the author coffee or a drink before the reading.

10. Agree in advance on the approximate length of the reading or talk. You might even ask the author *not* to read long poems. One poet writes "nothing is more deadly than one who drones on with very abstract poems."

11. Encourage authors to talk a bit between selections to give the audience a rest and to share a few of their experiences. One poet says, "People place such urgent value on experience and if an author talks about his work, the audience often responds to the poems as an immediate experience. It's not logical, but it seems to work that way."

12. Allow time for questions and discussions at the end of the reading. A few questions might be prepared beforehand, to begin this session.

For Workshops:

1. A good preparation for workshop participants is to read the author's work before the visit.

2. Informality should be encouraged—this includes the meeting place and the placement of chairs and tables.

3. The size of the workshop should be no more than 20 people. In some cases, the number of participants is determined by the author.

4. It is always advisable for the workshop to meet in a quiet room where there will be little interference with other activities and at a time when the workshop will not have to end abruptly because of the building's closing hours.

5. Your group may want to consider selecting works written by the participants for an anthology of their work. This can easily be typed, mimeographed or photocopied, and assembled in the form of a booklet.

For Class Visits (Authors' Suggestions):

1. A good preparation for students is to have studied the author's work before the visit.

2. Make copies of some of the author's work to distribute in class during the visit. Favorable publicity quotes and reviews can help students in preparing for a visit.

3. If the class is a writing class, students should be asked to bring in their work for discussion. If possible, copy and distribute student work, so that all students can participate in a critical discussion by the visiting writer.

4. Informality should be encouraged—this includes placement of chairs and tables.

5. Encourage students to ask questions of the authors. One poet writes, "Any question will do, like *How much money do you make?* or *How did you get into this anyway!*"

Alphabetical Index of All Writers

Abbey, Edward, 24
Abbott, Keith, 2
Abbott, Raymond H., 14
Abel, Robert H., 15
Abish, Walter, 24
Adler, Renata, 24
Albert, Mimi Abriel, 24
Alexander, Floyce, 45
Algren, Nelson, 19
Alta, 2
Amidon, Bill, 24
Anaya, Rudolfo, 20
Angell, Roger, 24
Angoff, Charles, 24
Antin, David, 2
Apple, Max, 43
Appleman, Philip, 12
Arias, Ron, 2
Arkin, Frieda, 24
Ascher, Sheila (Ascher/Straus), 24
Ashley, Franklin, 42
Asimov, Isaac, 24
Astrachan, Samuel, 46
Athas, Daphne, 39
Atwood, Margaret, 45
Auchincloss, Louis, 24
Awoonor, Kofi, 24

Baber, Asa, 11
Baker, Donald W., 12
Baker, Elliott, 46
Baldwin, James, 24
Ballard, J. G., 46
Banks, Russell, 19
Barba, Harry, 20
Barker, George, 46
Barnard, Mary, 45
Barolini, Helen, 20
Barrio, Raymond, 3
Barretto, Lefty, 24
Barth, John, 14
Barthelme, Donald, 24
Bartlett, Paul Alexander, 47
Batki, John, 21
Baumbach, Jonathan, 24
Beagle, Peter S., 3
Beal, M. F., 41
Beck, Warren, 11
Becker, Stephen, 15
Bell, Charles G., 20
Bellamy, Joe David, 21
Bellow, Saul, 11
Benedikt, Michael, 25
Bennett, Hal, 25
Berge, Carol, 17
Berger, Thomas, 25
Bergson, Deirdre Levinson, 25
Bergstein, Eleanor, 25
Bernard, Kenneth, 25
Bernays, Anne, 15
Berne, Stanley, 20
Berry, Wendell E., 13
Bethune, Lebert, 25

Betts, Doris, 39
Birnbaum, Ben, 44
Birstein, Ann, 25
Blecher, George, 25
Bloch, Robert, 3
Boles, Robert E., 15
Bonime, Florence, 25
Bontly, Thomas, 45
Borden, William, 40
Borenstein, Audrey F., 21
Bourjaily, Vance, 13
Bowers, John, 25
Bowles, Paul, 47
Boyle, Kay, 25
Bradbury, Ray, 3
Brand, Millen, 25
Brandi, John, 20
Brautigan, Richard, 3
Brawley, Ernest, 3
Brennan, Maeve, 25
Brickner, Richard P., 25
Bried, Hedi, (H. W. Blattner), 3
Brigham, Besmilr, 2
Brodkey, Harold, 25
Bromell, Henry, 13
Bromige, David, 3
Brookhouse, Christopher, 39
Brossard, Chandler, 46
Broughton, T. Alan, 44
Brower, Brock, 19
Brown, Cecil, 3
Brown, Claude, 25
Brown, Kenneth H., 25
Brown, Rita Mae, 10
Brown, Rosellen, 19
Brown, Wesley, 26
Brownstein, Michael, 26
Bruchac, Joseph, III, 21
Bryan, C. D. B., 9
Buchanan, Cynthia, 26
Buechner, Frederick, 26
Bukowski, Charles, 3
Bumpus, Jerry, 3
Burgess, Anthony, 47
Burland, Brian, 9
Burroughs, William S., 26
Burroughs, William S., Jr., 26
Busch, Frederick, 21

Cable, Mary, 20
Cady, Jack, 45
Caldwell, Erskine, 10
Calisher, Hortense, 21
Cannon, Steve, 26
Canzoneri, Robert, 40
Capote, Truman, 26
Carlisle, Henry, 9
Carpenter, Don, 26
Carver, Raymond, 3
Cassill, R. V., 42
Catala, Rafael E., 26
Chaffin, Lillie D., 13
Chambers, George, 11

Chan, Jeffrey Paul, 3
Chang, Diana, 26
Chappell, Fred, 39
Charyn, Jerome, 26
Chatain, Robert, 26
Cheever, John, 26
Cheifetz, Dan, 26
Cherry, Kelly, 21
Chianese, Merle Molofsky-, 26
Chin, Frank, 3
Clark, Eleanor, 9
Clark, L. D., 43
Clark, LaVerne Harrell, 2
Clay, Buriel, II, 3
Clayton, John Jacob, 15
Codrescu, Andrei, 3
Cohen, Arthur A(llen), 26
Cohen, Gerald, 21
Cohen, Marvin, 26
Cohoe, Grey, 20
Coleman, Arthur, 21
Connell, Evan S., 27
Cooper, Kent, 27
Coover, Robert, 27
Coppel, Alfred, 3
Corrington, John William, 14
Costello, Mark, 11
Cozzens, James Gould, 27
Cravens, Gwen, 27
Crawford, Max, 27
Crawford, Stanley, 20
Creeley, Robert, 4
Crews, Harry, 10
Crumley, James, 43
Cuelho, Art, Jr., 4
Cummins, Walter, 19
Cuomo, George, 15
Curley, Daniel, 11
Curley, Thomas, 27
Curry, Peggy Simson, 45

Dabney, Dick, 44
Dahl, Roald, 46
Dahlberg, Edward, 27
Dann, Jack, 21
Davenport, Guy, 13
Davis, Christopher, 41
Davis, George, 21
Davis, Hope Hale, 9
Davis, L. J., 27
Dawkins, Cecil, 20
Dawson, Fielding, 27
de Aparicio, Vibiana Chamberlin, 4
Deck, John, 4
Deemer, Charles, 14
DeFrees, Madeline, 18
Delany, Samuel R., 27
Delbanco, Nicholas, 21
De Leon, Nephtali, 43
Delillo, Don, 27
de Lima, Sigrid, 21
DeMott, Benjamin, 15
DeVeaux, Alexis, 9

DeVries, Peter, 27
Dick, Philip K., 4
Dickey, James, 42
Didion, Joan, 27
Dikeman, May, 27
Dillard, R. H. W., 44
Dillon, Millicent G., 4
di Prima, Diana, 4
Ditsky, John, 45
Dixon, Stephen, 27
Doctorow, E. L., 21
Dodson, Owen, 27
Dokey, Richard, 4
Donleavy, J. P., 15
Dorman, Sonya, 9
Douglas, Ellen, 17
Doulis, Thomas, 41
Downs, Robert C. S., 2
Drake, Albert Dee, 17
Drake, Barbara, 17
Drexler, Roslyn, 27
Duberstein, Helen, 27
Dulany, Harris, 47
Durham, Marilyn, 27
Dworkin, Martin S., 28
Dworzan, Helene, 28
Dybek, Stuart, 17

East, Charles, 14
Eastlake, William, 2
Eaton, Charles Edward, 9
Edwards, Margaret, 44
Edwards, Page, 15
Ehle, John, 28
Eisenstein, Sam A., 4
Elder, Gary, 4
Elevitch, M. D., 21
Elkin, Stanley, 18
Elliott, George P., 21
Elliott, William D., 17
Ellison, Harlan, 4
Ellison, Ralph, 28
Elman, Richard, 28
Elmslie, Kenward, 28
Ely, David, 47
Emiot, Israel, (Goldwasser), 21
Emshwiller, Carol, 21
Epstein, Leslie, 28
Epstein, Seymour, 9
Esfandiary, F. M., 28
Espey, John, 4
Espinosa, Rudy, 4
Evanier, David, 28
Everman, Welch D., 19
Exley, Frederick, 28

Fair, Ronald, 11
Farmer, Philip Jose, (Kilgore Trout), 11
Farrell, James T., 28
Faust, Irvin, 28
Federman, Raymond, 22
Feld, Ross, 28
Feldman, Alan, 15
Felton, B., 40
Fiedler, Leslie A., 22
Figueroa, John L., 4
Fisher, M. F. K., 4

Fitz Gerald, Gregory, 22
Flanagan, Richard, 15
Flanagan, Robert, 40
Flender, Harold, 28
Flynn, R. L., 43
Foote, Shelby, 28
Fox, Hugh B., 17
Fox, Lucia A., 17
Fox, Paula, 28
Frank, Sheldon, 11
Friedman, B. H., 28
Friedman, Bruce Jay, 28
Friedman, Paul, 12
Friedman, Sanford, 28
Fuchs, Daniel, 4
Fulton, Len, 4

Gaddis, William, 28
Gaines, Ernest J., 4
Gallant, Mavis, 47
Gangemi, Kenneth, 29
Gardner, John, 44
Gardner, Leonard, 29
Garrett, George, 14
Gass, William, 18
Gellhorn, Martha, 29
Gerald, John Bart, 15
Gerber, Dan, 17
Ghose, Zulfikar, 43
Giggord, Barry, 5
Gilbert, Sandra M., 5
Gildner, Gary, 13
Gill, Brendan, 29
Gilliat, Penelope, 29
Gilroy, Frank D., 5
Gioseffi, Daniela, 29
Giovannitti, Len, 29
Glaser, Isabel J., 42
Glass, Joanna, 29
Gloag, Julian, 29
Godwin, Gail, 29
Gold, Herbert, 5
Gold, Ivan, 15
Goldberg, Gerald Jay, 29
Goldfein, Alan, 29
Goldman, William, 29
Gonzalez, N. V. M., 5
Gonzalez, Rafael Jesus, 5
Goodman, Mitchell, 14
Goodwin, Stephen, 41
Gordon, Caroline, 43
Gottlieb, Elaine, (Hemley), 12
Gould, Lois, 29
Gover, Robert, 5
Goyen, William, 29
Granat, Robert, 29
Grau, Shirley Ann, 14
Green, Galen, 40
Green, Hannah, 29
Greenberg, Alvin, 17
Greenberg, Joanne, 9
Griffin, Susan, 5
Griffith, Paul, 19
Gronowicz, Antoni, 29
Grosvenor, Vertamae, 29
Guerard, Albert J., 5
Gunn, James, 13

Guthrie, A. B., Jr., 30

Haggerty, Joan, 30
Haiblum, Isidore, 30
Hale, Janet Campbell, 5
Hale, Nancy, 44
Hall, Donald, 17
Hall, James B., 5
Hall, Lawrence Sargent, 14
Hallinan, Nancy, 30
Hand, Joan Carole, 22
Handke, Peter, 30
Hanley, William, 9
Hannah, Barry, 42
Hannibal, Edward, 22
Harnack, Curtis, 30
Harrington, Alan, 2
Harris, Mark, 5
Harrison, Jim, 17
Harrison, William, 2
Hawkes, John, 42
Hayden, Julie, 30
Hazzard, Shirley, 30
Hebald, Carol, 22
Heifetz, Hank, 15
Heinlein, Robert, 30
Heller, Joseph, 30
Hendrie, Don, Jr., 15
Henley, Charles, 45
Henry, DeWitt, 15
Hensley, Joe L., 12
Herlihy, James Leo, 30
Herman, Jan, 44
Hernton, Calvin, 40
Hersey, John, 30
Higgins, Dick, 44
Higgins, George V., 15
Hill, Carol, 30
Himes, Chester, 30
Hine, Daryl, 12
Hinojosa, Rolando, 43
Hitchcock, George, 5
Hoagland, Edward, 30
Hochman, Sandra, 30
Hoffman, Stanley, 30
Holland, Cecelia, 5
Holmes, John Clellon, 9
Holst, Spencer, 30
Honig, Donald, 9
Horgan, Paul, 9
Horovitz, Israel, 30
Houston, James D., 5
Houston, Robert W., 2
Huddle, David, 44
Humphrey, William, 31
Hunter, Evan, 31
Hunter, Kristin, 19
Hutchins, Maude, 9
Hutchinson, Robert, 31

Ignatow, Rose Graubart, 22
Ik, Kim Yong, 41
Iko, Momoko, 12
Inada, Lawson Fusao, 41
Irving, John, 13
Isherwood, Christopher, 5
Israel, Charles, 31

124

Israel, Peter, 31

Jacobsen, Josephine, 14
Janeway, Elizabeth, 31
Jeffers, Lance, 39
Jerome, Judson, 14
Johnson, Charles, 22
Johnson, Diane, 5
Johnson, Joe, 31
Johnson, Josephine, 40
Jones, Gayl, 13
Jones, James, 11
Jong, Erica, 31
Jordan, June M., 31
Joseph, Stephen M., 31
Jurkowski, John, 31
Just, Ward, 44

Kaplan, Bernard, 40
Kaplan, Johanna, 31
Karlen, Arno, 31
Karmel, Alex, 10
Karp, Lila, 31
Kashiwagi, Hiroshi, 6
Katz, Elia, 31
Katz, Steve, 31
Kaufman, Bel, 31
Kaufman, Sue, 31
Keeley, Edmund, 20
Keithley, George, 6
Kelley, William Melvin, 32
Kelly, Robert, 22
Kentfield, Calvin, 6
Kesey, Ken, 41
Kessler, Jascha, 6
Killens, John Oliver, 32
Kim, Richard E., 15
Kinnell, Galway, 32
Kirack, Alex, 6
Kirkpatrick, Smith, 11
Kittredge, William, 18
Klein, Norma, 32
Knight, Arthur Winfield, 41
Knight, Wallace E., 13
Knowles, John, 32
Koch, Kenneth, 23
Koning, Hans, (Koningsberger), 46
Kosinski, Jerzy, 32
Kostelanetz, Richard, 32
Kotker, (Mary) Zane, 32
Kotker, Norman, 32
Kotlowitz, Robert, 32
Koumjian, Vaughn, 32
Kovak, Teri, (Shapiro), 6
Kozer, Jose, 32
Kraf, Elaine, 32
Kranes, David, 32
Kuhns, William, 45
Kumin, Maxine, 15

Lahr, John, 32
Lamming, George, 46
Lamott, Kenneth, 32
Lardas, Konstantinos, 22
Lardner, Ring, Jr., 32
Larner, Jeremy, 6
Larsen, Carl, 41

Lee, Audrey, 42
Lee, Harper, 32
Leggett, John, 13
LeGuin, Ursula K., 41
Leiber, Fritz, 33
Lelchuk, Alan, 19
Lengyel, Cornel Adam, 6
Leonard, John, 33
Leong, Russell, (Wallace Lin), 6
Lessing, Doris, 33
Lewis, Clayton W., 22
L'Heureux, John, 6
Lieberman, Herbert, 22
Litwak, Leo, 6
Loeser, Katinka, 9
Logan, John, 11
Lopate, Phillip, 33
Lowery, Bruce, 33
Lowry, Robert, 40
Lukas, Susan, 6
Lunde, David, 22
Lurie, Alison, 22
Lyons, Richard, 41
Lytle, Andrew, 13

McAfee, Thomas, 18
McCall, Dan, 33
McCarthy, Cormac, 33
McCarthy, Mary, 14
McCauley, Carole Spearin, 10
McClure, James G., 6
McClure, Michael, 6
McConkey, James, 22
McCord, Howard, 40
McCormick, James, 12
McCullough, Ken, 19
McDonald, Julie, 13
McDonald, Walter R., 43
McElroy, Colleen, 45
McElroy, Joseph, 33
McGuane, Thomas, 33
McHale, Tom, 33
McKinley, Georgia, 33
McMurtry, Larry, 10
McNamara, Eugene, 45
McPherson, James A., 16

Macauley, Robie, 12
Macleod, Norman, 39
Madden, David, 14
Mailer, Norman, 33
Maiolo, Joseph, 44
Major, Clarence, 33
Malamud, Bernard, 44
Maloff, Saul, 10
Malone, John, 33
Mandel, Oscar, 6
Manfred, Frederick, 17
Mangione, Jerre, 42
Mannes, Marya, 33
Mano, D. Keith, 22
Markfield, Wallace, 33
Marquand, John P., Jr., 15
Marshall, Paule, 33
Mathews, Harry, 47
Mathis, Sharon Bell, 33
Matthews, Jack, 40

Matthiessen, Peter, 33
Maxwell, William, 34
Mazor, Julian, 34
Melford, Larry, 34
Meltzer, David, 6
Meriwether, Louise, 34
Merrill, James, 10
Merwin, W. S., 34
Michaels, Leonard, 6
Micheline, Jack, 6
Midwood, Barton, 34
Miller, Arthur, 34
Miller, Heather Ross, 39
Miller, Henry, 34
Mills, Alison, 34
Milton, John R., 42
Minot, Stephen, 10
Mirabelli, Eugene, 22
Mirsky, Mark, 34
Molinaro, Ursule, 34
Momaday, N. Scott, 7
Montgomery, Marion, 11
Moore, Brian, 7
Moose, Ruth, 39
Mori, Toshio, 7
Morressy, John, 19
Morris, Willie, 22
Morris, Wright, 19
Morrison, Toni, 34
Morton, Carlos, 43
Moss, Rose, 16
Mott, Michael, 11
Mountzoures, H. L., 10
Mphahlele, Ezekiel, 42
Murray, William, 7

Nabokov, Vladimir, 47
Neill, Peter, 10
Nemec, David, 41
Nemerov, Howard, 18
Neugeboren, Jay, 16
Newman, Leslie, 34
Nicholson, Joseph, 42
Nin, Anais, 7
Nissenson, Hugh, 34
Niven, Larry, 7
Norman, Marc, 7
Nova, Craig, 34
Noyes, Stanley, 20

Oates, Joyce Carol, 46
O'Connor, Philip F., 41
Offit, Sidney, 34
Ohle, David, 13
Olsen, Tillie, 7
O'Rourke, William, 34
Ortego, Philip D., 7
Ostroff, Anthony, 41
Ostrow, Joanna, 46
Otero, Manuel Ramos, 34
Owen, Guy, 39
Owens, Iris, 34
Ozick, Cynthia, 22

Padgett, Ron, 35
Painter, Charlotte, 7

Paley, Grace, 35
Papaleo, Joseph, 35
Party, Hugh, J., 46
Pauker, John, 10
Payack, Paul J. J., 16
Peck, Richard, 35
Peden, William, 18
Penaranda, Oscar Florentino, 7
Percy, Walker, 14
Pereira, Teresinha Alves, 12
Perera, Victor, 7
Perry, Richard, 35
Perutz, Kathrin, 23
Petesch, Natalie L. M., 42
Petrakis, Harry Mark, 12
Petroski, Catherine, 12 •
Phelps, Dean, 19
Phillips, Robert, 23
Piercy, Marge, 16
Plymell, Charles, 23
Pohl, Frederik, 20
Polite, Carlene Hatcher, 23
Pomerantz, Edward, 35
Popham, Melinda, 12
Porter, Bern, 14
Porter, Katherine Anne, 35
Portillo, Estela, 43
Potok, Chaim, 35
Pournelle, Jerry, 7
Powers, J. F., 35
Price, Nancy, 35
Price, Reynolds, 40
Price, Richard, 35
Prokosch, Frederic, 47
Puechner, Ray, 45
Puigdollers, Carmen, 35
Purdy, James, 35
Puzo, Mario, 35
Pynchon, Thomas, 35

Quist, Susan, 23

Rand, Peter, 35
Rane, Bill, 20
Raphael, Frederic Michael, 46
Raphael, Phyllis, 35
Ray, David, 18
Rechy, John, 7
Reed, Ishmael, 23
Reeve, F. D., 10
Reid, Randall, 19
Reinbold, James S., 42
Ribar, Joe, 23
Rindfleisch, Norval, 19
Rivera, Edward, 36
Rivera, Tomas, 43
Robin, Ralph, 10
Robinson, Leonard Wallace, 47
Rogers, Michael, 7
Rogin, Gilbert, 36
Roiphe, Anne, 36
Rooke, Leon, 46
Rosen, Leo, 36
Rosen, Norma, 23
Rossner, Judith, 36
Rosten, Norman, 36
Roth, Arthur J., 23

Roth, Henry H., 23
Roth, Philip, 36
Roueche, Berton, 23
Rovit, Earl, 36
Rumaker, Michael, 36
Rushmore, Robert, 16
Russell, Charles, 36

Sadoff, Ira, 41
Salamanca, J. R., 36
Salinger, J. D., 36
Salter, James, 9
Sanchez, Ricardo, 43
Sanchez, Thomas Robert, 7
Sanders, Ed, 23
Sargent, Pamela, 23
Saroyan, William, 36
Sarton, May, 14
Schaeffer, Susan Fromberg, 36
Schell, Jessie, 16
Schoonover, Shirley W., 18
Schorer, Mark, 7
Schulberg, Budd, 36
Schwartz, Howard, 18
Sebenthal, R. E., 45
Segal, Lore, 36
Selby, Hubert, Jr., 7
Sewell, Elizabeth, 40
Shapiro, Karl, 7
Shaw, Irwin, 47
Sheed, Wilfrid, 23
Sherwin, Judith Johnson, 36
Shetzline, David, 36
Shulman, Alix Kates, 36
Sigal, Clancy, 37
Silbert, Layle, 37
Silko, Leslie Marmon, 2
Simmons, Charles, 37
Simpson, Louis, 23
Singer, I. B., 37
Skillings, R. D., 16
Slavitt, David R., 16
Smith, Dave, 18
Smith, Lee, 40
Smith, Mark, 19
Soledad, Sabire, 37
Solomon, Barbara Probst, 37
Solotaroff, Theodore, 37
Sontag, Susan, 37
Sorrells, Robert T., 42
Sorrentino, Gilbert, 37
Sourian, Peter, 37
Southern, Terry, 37
Spacks, Barry, 16
Spanier, Muriel, 23
Spencer, Elizabeth, 46
Spencer, Sharon, 20
Spielberg, Peter, 37
Spike, Paul, 37
Spingarn, Lawrence P., 8
Spinrad, Norman, 37
Stafford, Jean, 23
Standiford, Les, 44
Stanfill, Dorothy, 42
Steele, Max, 40
Stegner, Page, 8
Stegner, Wallace, 37

Steiner, Robert, 16
Stephens, Michael Gregory, 37
Stephens, Rosemary, 43
Stern, Daniel, 37
Stern, Richard G., 12
Stevens, Shane, 37
Stewart, John, 12
Still, James, 13
Stone, Alma, 37
Stone, Robert, 16
Stout, Robert Joe, 8
Strong, Jonathan, 16
Sturgeon, Theodore, 37
Styron, William, 10
Sukenick, Ronald, 9
Summers, Hollis, 41
Sward, Robert, (Vasvdeva), 46

Tagatac, Samuel C., 8
Targan, Barry, 23
Tate, Allen, 43
Taylor, Eleanor Ross, 45
Taylor, Peter, 45
Theroux, Alexander Louis, 16
Theroux, Paul, 46
Thomas, Audrey, 46
Thomas, Piri, 38
Thompson, James W., 17
Thompson, John A., 38
Thompson, Robert S., 18
Tipton, James, 17
Topkins, Katharine, 8
Trevisian, Dalton, 38
Trillin, Calvin, 38
Tucci, Niccolo, 38
Tuten, Frederic, 38
Tyler, Anne, 14

Ullian, Robert, 16
Updike, John, 16
Urdang, Constance, 18

Van Dyke, Henry, 38
Vasquez, Richard, 8
Veitch, Tom, 8
Vidal, Gore, 38
Villasenor, Victor Edmundo, 8
Vincent, Peter, 8
Vivante, Arturo, 16
Vliet, R.G., 44
Vonnegut, Kurt, Jr., 38
Vreuls, Diane, 41

Wagoner, David, 45
Wakefield, Dan, 16
Walker, Alice, 38
Walker, Gerald, 38
Walker, Margaret, 18
Wallop, Douglass, 14
Walters, Anna Lee, 2
Wang, Karl, 38
Ward, Robert M., 23
Warren, David, 24
Warren, Robert Penn, 10
Waters, Frank, 20
Watson, Robert, 40
Weaver, Gordon, 18

Weidman, Jerome, 11
Welburn, Ron, 38
Welty, Eudora, 18
West, Jessamyn, 8
West, John Foster, 40
West, Paul, 42
Whalen, Philip, 8
White, James P., 44
White, Jon Manchip, 44
White, Robin, 8
Whitehead, James, 2
Wiesel, Elie, 38
Wilbur, Richard, 16
Wilkinson, Sylvia, 40
William, Edward G., 38
Williams, John, 9
Williams, John A., 20
Williams, Joy, 11
Williams, Tennessee, 38
Williams, Thomas, 19
Willingham, Calder, 38
Willis, Meredith Sue, 38
Wilner, Herbert, 8
Wilson, Robley, Jr., 13
Winters, Janet Lewis, 8
Woiwode, Larry, 12
Wolfe, Gene, 12
Wolff, Geoffrey, 44
Wolitzer, Hilma, 24
Wong, Shawn Hsu, 8
Woolf, Douglas, 45
Wright, Austin M., 41
Wright, Charles, 39
Wright, Sarah E., 39
Wurlitzer, Rudolph, 39

Yaffe, James, 9
Yamamoto, Hisaye, (DeSoto), 8
Yates, Richard, 39
Yellen, Samuel, 13
Young, Al, 8
Young, Marguerite, 39
Yount, John A., 19
Yurick, Sol, 39

Zahn, Curtis, 8
Zawacki, Franklin, 42
Zebrowski, George, 24
Zekowski, Arlene, 20
Zelazny, Roger, 39
Zukofsky, Louis, 39

DATE DUE

#47-0108 Peel Off Pressure Sensitive